Shakespeare, Machiavelli,
and Montaigne

Shakespeare, Machiavelli, and Montaigne

Power and Subjectivity
From *Richard II* to *Hamlet*

HUGH GRADY

OXFORD
UNIVERSITY PRESS

OXFORD
UNIVERSITY PRESS

Great Clarendon Street, Oxford ox2 6DP

Oxford University Press is a department of the University of Oxford.
It furthers the University's objective of excellence in research, scholarship,
and education by publishing worldwide in

Oxford New York

Auckland Bangkok Buenos Aires Cape Town Chennai
Dar es Salaam Delhi Hong Kong Istanbul Karachi Kolkata
Kuala Lumpur Madrid Melbourne Mexico City Mumbai Nairobi
São Paulo Shanghai Taipei Tokyo Toronto

Oxford is a registered trade mark of Oxford University Press
in the UK and in certain other countries

Published in the United States
by Oxford University Press Inc., New York

British Library Cataloguing in Publication Data
Data available

Library of Congress Cataloging in Publication Data
Data applied for

ISBN 0–19–925760–4

1 3 5 7 9 10 8 6 4 2

Typeset by Regent Typesetting, London
Printed in Great Britain
on acid-free paper by
Biddles Ltd,
Guildford and King's Lynn

For

LAURA ROSE GRADY

And from the soul itself must there be sent
A sweet and powerful voice, of its own birth,
    Of all sweet sounds the life and element!
Pure of heart! thou need'st not ask of me
What this strong music in the soul may be;
    What and wherein it doth subsist,
This light, this glory, this fair luminous mist,
    This beautiful and beauty-making power!
Joy, O beloved! joy, that ne'er was given
Save to the pure and in their purest hour,
Life of our life, the parent and the birth,
Which, wedding nature to us, gives in dower
    A new heaven and new earth. . . .

Acknowledgements

THIS BOOK HAS benefited from suggestions and comments on early drafts of specific portions by Susan Wells, Phyllis Rackin, Wayne Rebhorn, Charles Whitney, Stephen Cohen, and Michael Baylor. My thanks to each of them for their time and efforts. In addition the comments and reactions of colleagues to papers based on portions of the work in progress were also helpful—at the 1996 MLA Special Session on Shakespeare and Renaissance Skepticism; at presentations to the Arcadia University Faculty Forum in 1998 and to the University of Pennsylvania Medieval-Renaissance group in 2000; and in two seminars (chaired respectively by Edmund Taft and Shankar Raman) of the Shakespeare Association of America in 1998 and 2000. The final version responds to the comments and criticisms of the anonymous readers for Oxford University Press.

Portions of the present book have appeared in somewhat different and recontextualized form in two earlier articles: 'Shakespeare's Links to Machiavelli and Montaigne: Constructing Intellectual Modernity in Early Modern Europe', *Comparative Literature*, 52/2 (Spring 2000), 119–42; and 'Falstaff: Subjectivity between the Carnival and the Aesthetic', *Modern Language Review*, 96/3 (July 2001), 609–23, reproduced by permission of the Modern Humanities Research Association.

The early research and initial drafting of this work were greatly facilitated by a sabbatical study leave and several faculty development grants from Arcadia University.

My thanks as well to Gwen Taylor, secretary of the Arcadia University Department of English, for her assistance in word processing and formatting and to my assistant Francis Camardella for his help in compiling the bibliography.

Contents

X CONTENTS

Introduction: Historicism and the Cultural Present in Shakespeare Studies: Subjectivity in Early and Late Modernity

When I surveyed innovative forms of literary criticism in the late 1980s for the last chapter of my 1991 *The Modernist Shakespeare*, there seemed to be three separate if related newer critical paradigms which had come into existence to replace older methods: deconstruction, new historicism/ cultural materialism, and feminism. In only a few years more these three had essentially become only one, as 1980s textualist deconstruction and an older feminism largely disappeared from view, and newer forms of each appeared after having made accommodations with historicism. Thus today in early modern literary studies, historicism, new or old, interwoven with feminism and psychoanalysis or not, has become virtually an unrivalled paradigm for professional writing. The turn to historicism has become taken for granted, its connections to the cultural present often unexamined or suppressed.

The major exception to this generalization has been the growth of a new trend, especially in Shakespeare studies, of 'presentist'[1] studies of literary classics as cultural phenomena in later periods, particularly in the twentieth century.[2] In one sense these works are extensions of new

---

[1] I borrow and redefine this term from the field of history and the philosophy of history, where it is a pejorative designating a naive view of the past as homogeneous with the present. However, so dominant have historicist premises become in Shakespeare studies that we need a positive term for that necessary form of historical perception which understands that *any* view of the past is formed within discourses of the present. Because of its pejorative associations, 'presentism' is perhaps not ideal, but it serves here for want of a better. See Terence Hawkes, *Shakespeare in the Present* (London: Routledge, 2002), for a similar positive use of *presentism* to advocate a consciousness of the present's influence on our constructions of the past.

[2] See Terence Hawkes, *That Shakespeherian Rag: Essays on a Critical Process* (New York:

historicism, inasmuch as they perform the same kind of contextualizing of cultural production, using some of the same theorists (Marx and Foucault, for example) as have new historicists. But in another sense they constitute an important challenge to historicist premisses because they underline the salient point that all our knowledge of works from the past is conditioned by and dependent upon the culture, language, and ideologies of the present, and this means that historicism itself necessarily produces an implicit allegory of the present in its configuration of the past. Far from being a defect of our knowledge of the past, let me emphasize, this quality is inescapable and a key to understanding the necessary cultural labour of renewing the past as we create new art and new culture for a new century. To put it simply, the past takes on new contours and qualities for us as our own thinking shifts in the present. History changes as we evolve and develop, and so do historical figures and cultural icons like Shakespeare. I tried to demonstrate this dynamic in my last book, *Shakespeare's Universal Wolf*, by showing how familiar themes of 'good and evil' in four central Shakespearian plays could be reconceptualized in the light of recent cultural and social theory as representing emerging modernity and its logic of reification. Of course, part of this work of reinterpretation involved coming to understand how and why themes of late modernity might have been produced in the discourses of early modernity in forms close enough to our own to seem cognate to us. Thus, while the major thrust of that work was 'presentist', in the sense of using theory from our cultural present to help understand and reinterpret works from the past, it also involved a historicist dimension, an investigation into those qualities of the Jacobean *mentalité* analogous enough to suppositions of our own cultural present to allow for an interpretative 'translation' to a late twentieth-century idiom. Given the primary presentist thrust of that work, however, this historicist dimension was necessarily subordinate and sketchy. In the present work I am trying to reverse those priorities and bring the historicist moment of my Shakespearian critical project into greater prominence—without losing sight of its presentist dimensions. Thus while this book shares its theoretical frame and certain of its central concepts with my previous work, the emphasis of the two books is quite different: the present work is more self-consciously historicist—in the sense of concentrating on the Renaissance

Methuen, 1986) and *Meaning by Shakespeare* (London: Routledge, 1992); Graham Holderness (ed.), *The Shakespeare Myth* (Manchester: Manchester University Press, 1988); Hugh Grady, *The Modernist Shakespeare: Critical Texts in a Material World* (Oxford: Clarendon, 1991); Michael D. Bristol, *Big-Time Shakespeare* (New York: Routledge, 1996); and Richard Halpern, *Shakespeare among the Moderns* (Ithaca, NY: Cornell University Press, 1997).

sources for concepts which proved analogous to nineteenth- and twentieth-century ones, if not in attempting new historicist negotiations with the details of contemporaneous texts—a method I believe to be only one of a number of useful ways to study cultural history. Instead, I am sketching a broad historical overview to substantiate some of the theoretical notions developed in my earlier work and to provide context for discussion of the specific plays of concern here.

I am focusing on plays which borrow central themes and contradictions from the discussion of Machiavelli's *The Prince* which was pervasive in the 1580s and 1590s within the political class of London—a class which supplied an important audience and important patrons for Shakespeare and his company. Similarly, I am using Montaigne's *Essays* as another predecessor text which directly or indirectly impacted on the works of Shakespeare and other dramatists of his era. In *Shakespeare's Universal Wolf*, I had indicated in a general way the importance of Machiavelli and Montaigne in a broad process of desacralizing modernization[3] but deferred a more specific historicizing discussion until a later occasion—which has now arrived. This book is thus meant as at least a partial redemption of the claim made in the introduction to *Shakespeare's Universal Wolf* that 'the thesis I am arguing is historical, and it can be, in fact, supported in great historical detail'.[4]

Allegories of the Present in Historicism

By turning to the discourses of Machiavelli and Montaigne, however, I am also addressing central problems on the nature of subjectivity prominent in the literary and cultural studies of the late twentieth century. Every historicism, as I emphasized, necessarily has an allegorical dimension, encoding a story for the present as it attempts as rigorously as possible to reconstruct for us stories of the past.[5] In studying the configuration and reconfiguration of the themes of power and subjectivity in central Shakespearian plays, I have come to the conclusion that these plays, in effect, constitute interventions within our own theoretical discourses on these

[3] Hugh Grady, *Shakespeare's Universal Wolf: Studies in Early Modern Reification* (Oxford: Clarendon, 1996), 53–4, 140, and 218–19.

[4] Ibid. 24.

[5] This notion, central to both of my earlier books, goes back at least to Marx's remarks on the presentist dimensions of discourses on republican Rome in the French Revolution in his *The Civil Wars in France*; but it was an important idea as well for critics as different in their values and politics as Walter Benjamin and T. S. Eliot. For a bracing and provocative reassertion of these ideas within a Shakespeare studies now given over almost completely to a present-suppressing historicism, see Halpern, *Shakespeare among the Moderns.*

topics within late modernity. The Foucault- and Nietzsche-influenced theories of the subject which have dominated much of recent literary and cultural theory reproduce, inadvertently or not, the dynamics of Machiavellian approaches. The parallel is particularly relevant in the way all these discourses treat subjectivity as an effect of impersonal power. Of course, as I will discuss in Chapter 1, Machiavelli has notoriously suffered from oversimplifying accounts of his often complex arguments, and the notion of the self implied in *The Prince* is complicated in the further-ranging discussions of *The Discourses*. But it has been precisely the Machiavelli of *The Prince* who has been most consequential in cultural history. Nor is Machiavelli necessarily a direct 'source' of recent cultural materialist discussions of the subject. Cultural transmission is rarely that direct, and Machiavellian discourse conceptualizes central tenets of the cultural contradictions of modernity, contradictions which have been discussed, reconceptualized, and rediscovered many times since their Renaissance formulations. My focus here is less on Machiavelli as source than on Machiavelli as a figure for a discourse which he helped inaugurate and which has descended to us marked by any number of other interventions by theorists from Hobbes to Foucault. The discourse of power that circulated in the Renaissance and found its way into the Elizabethan theatre was coded 'Machiavellian' in its own day, and I will retain and investigate that helpful labelling. Four hundred years later, theories of power have proliferated and can no longer be considered 'Machiavellian' in the same way—they have many other 'authors', with complex relations to Machiavelli.[6] At times, however, it will be useful to designate the theories of power of our own day with the term Machiavellian in order to bring out the important analogies and parallels that can be discerned.

The connection of Shakespeare and his contemporaries with Renaissance power dynamics—conceptualized in the 1980s as informed by Foucauldian and Nietzschean, rather than Machiavellian, dynamics—has in recent years encountered its own critics, leading to a corrective counterdiscourse which questions the adequacy of these theories of power for understanding social life, human history in general, and Shakespeare's

---

[6] Foucault, for example, argued that modern political theory descends not from Machiavelli, but from the reaction against him typified in Gentillet's *Contre-Machiavel;* see Michel Foucault, 'Governmentality', in Graham Burchell, Colin Gordon, and Peter Miller (eds.), *The Foucault Effect: Studies in Governmentality* (Chicago: University of Chicago Press, 1991), 87–104; 88–90. Similarly, Althusser defined the relation between Machiavelli and Marxism as 'one of coincidence and repetition, rather than one of direct influence'; Louis Althusser, *Machiavelli and Us,* ed. François Matheron, trans. Gregory Elliott (London: Verso, 1999), 116.

plays in particular.[7] New themes of resistance to power have emerged as cultural theorists have addressed these criticisms.

What has occurred to me more recently in thinking about the parallels between these themes in early and late modernity is that, in this regard, the Renaissance theorist of resistance, parallel to new theorists of subjectivity of the 1990s, is Michel de Montaigne. Montaigne, of course, was a political pragmatist who made sure his own works never provoked the ire of the authorities of Church and State in France. Underneath that, however, is a potentially subversive scepticism and, interestingly in the modern context, an account of subjectivity which emphasizes its potential for resistance to power and ideology as these terms have come to be defined in the late twentieth century. In short, Montaigne, with all his sceptical contradictions and complexities, is a Renaissance proto-theorist who challenges the relatively one-dimensional theories of power I associate with Machiavelli, Nietzsche, and Foucault. And I began to see the potential for undertaking within Shakespeare's own treatment of power and subjectivity a fascinating investigation of the connections and contradictions of these two Renaissance intellectuals who have often figured previously in accounts of Shakespeare's intellectual sources and who seemed to me now highly relevant to late twentieth-century debates about power and subjectivity. We are dealing, it is worth repeating, with analogies rather than the 'source-and-influence' dynamics of traditional positivist historicism. In what follows Machiavelli and Montaigne are convenient labels for discursive formations associated with the writings of each, but not every work of these iconic Renaissance humanists is relevant to the discourses being discussed. With these provisos in mind, however, I believe the terms will prove useful and enabling.

In these terms, then, Shakespeare in the plays studied here complicated his Machiavellian thematics with Montaignean ones, and in so doing implicitly and presciently criticized the theories of power and the subject which dominated the insurgent Shakespeare criticism of the 1980s.

---

[7] There have been many critiques of the power-oriented theories from the standpoint of earlier established critical methods; see for example Edward Pechter, 'The New Historicism and its Discontents', *PMLA* 102 (May 1987), 292–303; Graham Bradshaw, *Misrepresentations: Shakespeare and the Materialists* (Ithaca, NY: Cornell University Press, 1993); Brian Vickers, *Appropriating Shakespeare: Contemporary Critical Quarrels* (New Haven: Yale University Press, 1993); Lynda Boos, 'The Family in Shakespeare Studies; or—Studies in the Family of Shakespearians; or—The Politics of Politics', *Renaissance Quarterly*, 40 (Winter 1987), 707–42; Howard Felperin, *The Uses of the Canon: Elizabethan Literature and Contemporary Theory* (Oxford: Clarendon, 1990). More recent critiques include Katharine Eisaman Maus, *Inwardness and Theater in the English Renaissance* (Chicago: University of Chicago Press, 1995), and John Lee, *Shakespeare's 'Hamlet' and the Controversies of Self* (Oxford: Clarendon, 2000).

For example, it seems to me, he depicts subjectivity as something of a dialectical negation of power, not a mere effect of its operations; as an orientation to multiple potential selves or identities, not merely the production of a unitary one; as a mental space critically distanced from, and not entirely defined by, the circulating ideologies and discourses of institutions of power. In short, then, to follow Shakespeare, we will have in turn to follow a dynamic of much cultural theory since the 1980s, from notions of subjectivity wholly determined by power to notions of subjectivity as potentially resistant to power—and this is particularly true within the plays of the *Henriad* and of the milestone tragedy which soon followed these, *Hamlet*.

Postmodernism within New Historicism

In what follows, I am pursuing a version of historicism, in the sense that I am trying to define probable meanings the Shakespearian texts had in their own social contexts. As I indicated, I am leaving the specific, 'localized' reading techniques which have been perfected by leading new historicists to others better situated and more inclined than I am to pursue them; instead I am following my own interest in what I take to be competing discourses or intellectual frameworks (connected, as we will see, to specific texts and specific material practices) in early modern Europe. I am arguing that in the Shakespearian works of roughly 1595–1600 we can discern the working out of a complicated set of concepts and themes—concepts of political power and of autonomous subjectivity—in a changing but interconnected development which is distinct from the constellation of these same themes in earlier and later Shakespearian plays.

In addition, I am investigating themes which have been central ones in the poststructuralist-influenced criticism of the last twenty years in Shakespeare studies: power and the subject.[8] These themes have been central for two broad reasons: first, they have been crucial terms in the unfolding array of critical theory for the present, as we try to understand our own embedded situation within late, globalized capitalism in a post-Cold War world. In our new cultural and intellectual context (which I

[8] For a useful thematizing review of treatments of the subject in recent years, see Margreta de Grazia, Maureen Quilligan, and Peter Stallybrass, 'Introduction', in de Grazia, Quilligan, and Stallybrass (eds.), *Subject and Object in Renaissance Culture* (Cambridge: Cambridge University Press, 1996), 1–13. As the argument demonstrates, subjects and objects need to be conceptualized as dialectically interconnected. However, as will become clear, I believe the further argument against the long tradition linking Shakespeare to modernity is mistaken.

think of as one dominated by a new Postmodernist aesthetic paradigm), older notions of autonomous, rational selves, which had been in any case under attack since the nineteenth century in discourses inaugurated by Marx, Freud, and Nietzsche, but which have nevertheless persisted as central categories of political and aesthetic discourse to the present, came under new critical scrutiny and aesthetic representation. Life in the rapidly modernizing late twentieth century became increasingly dominated by new technologies and economic arrangements productive of massification, globalization, and cultural homogenization.

Western art in Romanticism had been constituted as an enclave resistant to these processes, and even Modernism, while it coquetted with the aestheticizing of modernization itself in a few experiments, by and large continued Romanticism's search for enclaves in myths and traditions, condemning technology as soulless and inhuman. Shakespeare was a major icon for both aesthetic movements, the Poet of Nature and Character for the Romantics, then the Poet of Myth and Symbolic Meaning for Modernists, but in each case a repository of values and meanings seen as redemptive of life in a degraded modernity.

In the turn to aesthetic Postmodernism of recent decades, however, Shakespeare's meaning has shifted once again in a complex process still very much in progress, in both academic and popular culture. Aesthetic Postmodernism, as almost all of its major interpreters have agreed, has been involved in intensifying and thematizing a Modernist tendency to undermine prevalent notions of a unitary, rational 'bourgeois' subjectivity, championing images and representations of fragmented, decentred selves. And the Postmodernist decentred self, instead of being situated in a 'Primitivist' enclave, freed of the corruptions of capitalist commodification and modernizing technology (as in Romanticism and mainline Modernism), has been more often represented as fully enmeshed in the (ambivalently aestheticized) surfaces of a commodified and reified social reality.[9] The 1996 film version of *Romeo and Juliet* by Baz Luhrmann is an excellent example of this trend at a popular level. By being resituated in the highly commodified, media-saturated environs of the greater Los Angeles of today, the play became a study in the colonization of idealized sexuality by a reified commodity culture of random violence and alienated street gangs. Similarly Michael Almereyda's 2000 version of

---

[9] I am drawing here on an earlier treatment of Postmodernism and Shakespeare in Grady, *The Modernist Shakespeare*, 204–11, and from a more recent update of those themes, Hugh Grady, 'Modernity, Modernism, and Postmodernism in the Twentieth Century's Shakespeare', in Michael Bristol and Kathleen McLuskie (eds.), *The Performance of Modernity: Shakespeare and the Modern Theatre* (London: Routledge, 2001), 20–35.

Hamlet is set in a contemporary, globalized New York, in which com-
puters and video define a kind of hyperreality which is also the medium
through which the play's Ghost first appears. And while several other of
the recent spate of Shakespeare films are much less consistently Postmodernist in their approach—Branagh's *Much Ado About Nothing* and
Hamlet seem particularly to have been conceived within the aesthetic
idiom of an older 'classical' (not even consistently Modernist) theatrical
idiom—Postmodernist ideas have certainly penetrated massively into
contemporary avant-garde productions, particularly in non-English-
speaking countries[10]—and much recent academic Shakespeare criticism.

In academia, Postmodernist theories of subjectivity, perhaps surprisingly, have proven to have important relevance for 400-year-old
Shakespearian texts, revealing for us aspects of Shakespearian character
dynamics kept hidden as long as these plays were read through the
theoretical lenses formed by assumptions of unitary, static, or 'essentialist'
ideas of the self and of literary characters modelling the self. These 'essentialist' readings began as early as the eighteenth century, then entered a
Romantic phase from Schlegel to A. C. Bradley. They continued into the
twentieth century, but more sporadically than before, because the
'character' became a suspect literary category for Modernist Shakespearian criticism after T. S. Eliot and G. W. Knight.

Since the 1980s a number of pioneering works of contemporary Shakespearian criticism, influenced by recent cultural theory and aesthetic
Postmodernism, have demonstrated the fruitful results of dropping these
older 'essentialist' assumptions about Shakespeare's characters and conceptualizing them instead through the descendants of the decentring
discourses of Marx, Nietzsche, and Freud—most notably, of course, those
produced from the remarkable theoretical ferment of post-Second World
War structuralism and poststructuralism, first in France, then throughout
the Western academy.

Much of the early thrust of this collective labour was directed against
essentialist ideas of 'author' and 'text', as they had come to be constituted
in an interacting mid-century Anglo-American critical methodology
variously called New Criticism or 'liberal humanism'. Freed from narrow
assumptions that Shakespeare's plays, like other works of literature
proper, were timeless masterpieces whose most lasting values resided in

[10] This was particularly clear at the October 1997 conference on Shakespeare and
Theatrical Modernism held at McGill University in Montreal, which featured presentations
on a number of 20th-century Shakespearian productions influenced by Modernist and
Postmodernist aesthetics. See Bristol and McLuskie (eds.), *The Performance of Modernity*, for
selections from the presentations of this conference.

their formal artistic properties, the newer readings tended to resituate the works in politicized, social contexts that brought out their inter-connections with structures of power and domination, then and now. Shakespeare's plays thus became interconnected with vital social questions and debate again, reasserting something of the cultural centrality that had not been theirs since the heydays of Eliot, Empson, Leavis, and Brooks in the 1930s and 1940s, but of course in a completely new social context and invoking ideas and methods anathema to earlier generations of critics.

I have written elsewhere on the crucial role in this critical revolution played by Stephen Greenblatt in resituating the literary works of early modern England in a newly defined cultural context and in producing models of anti-dogmatic, socially conscious, and aesthetically supple literary/cultural criticism that were crucial as models for me and many others in imagining possibilities for new directions in Renaissance or (as it now came to be called) early modern studies.[11] On the other side of the Atlantic, in an analogous development influenced by an emerging British cultural studies, critics Terence Hawkes, John Drakakis, Catherine Belsey, Jonathan Dollimore, and Alan Sinfield among others developed a more theorized but equally political and historicizing critical method out of French structuralist and poststructuralist theories, especially in the 1980s those of Louis Althusser and Michel Foucault. British cultural materialism has been critical of Greenblatt on some issues, congruent with him on many more, but also provides both impetus and models for a new generation of critics. While Greenblatt and other related American new historicists were certainly interested in issues of selfhood, identity, and subjectivity (in the chapters that follow I return continually to points Greenblatt had earlier made about the plays discussed here), they tended, as a self-conscious practice of their own methodology, to avoid the kind of theory-construction that was a major feature of such cultural materialists as Catherine Belsey, Jonathan Dollimore and Alan Sinfield. Consequently, theories of the self are much easier to discern in the pro-ductions of British cultural materialism than in those of American new historicism, and in much of what follows immediately I take these as a starting point.

My own viewpoint develops out of a 'coming-to-theoretical-age' quite distinct from those of leading British cultural materialists, more cognate in its way to the development Greenblatt described in his personal

---

[11] Grady, *The Modernist Shakespeare*, 228–30; and 'Containment, Subversion—and Postmodernism', *Textual Practice*, 7/1 (Spring 1993), 31–49.

introduction to *Learning to Curse*.[12] In particular, like any number of others caught up in the United States' political turmoil of the 1960s and 1970s, my search for left-wing alternatives to the doctrinaire and oppressive ideologies constituted by Soviet and Chinese Communism led me, before the poststructuralist revolution, to versions of feminism and socialist-feminism and to a number of 'unorthodox' critical versions of Marxism in theorists like the young Lukács, Gramsci, Raymond Williams, and the Frankfurt School. In this context the writings of Louis Althusser, with their rhetoric of fidelity to Lenin and the dictatorship of the proletariat and their tightly controlled but evident psychodrama of submission to and rebellion against parental/ecclesiastical/Communist orthodoxy, seemed like a completely wrong-headed return to Marxist-Leninist dogmatism.

My early aversive reaction to Althusser was completely at odds with the creative ferment Althusser's works provoked at roughly the same time in analogous left-wing circles in the UK, where Althusser, instead of representing orthodoxy, was a crucial figure in the development of an avantgarde critical method responsible for transporting a good deal of the letter and the insurgent spirit of post-1968 French poststructuralism to the anglophone world. In that context structuralism-poststructuralism seemed the insurgent force challenging a reformist-tending, older-generation cultural Marxism, and Althusser—and the most Althusserian, anti-humanist moments of Foucault—played a central role in early cultural materialist interventions in Shakespeare studies, inciting me to a closer study of Althusser, a new appreciation for his challenges to Marxist orthodoxy, but an ultimate wish to move beyond him into other areas of French poststructuralism (notably Foucault and Lacan) which seem to me less theoretically problematic and much more compatible with some of the central Frankfurt School motifs which I have found indispensable to my own critical thinking. As I have worked more closely with early modern texts, I have come to believe that these Althusser- and Foucault-influenced theories of the subject were, in the analogous sense previously defined, Machiavellian in their approach. In fact, for the case of Althusser, the posthumous publication of his manuscript *Machiavelli and Us* has belatedly demonstrated that Machiavelli's influence on the French philosopher was direct and major.[13] One of his students defined the influence this way:

[12] Stephen J. Greenblatt, *Learning to Curse: Essays in Early Modern Culture* (New York: Routledge, 1990), 1–15.
[13] Althusser, *Machiavelli and Us*. See especially the introduction by Gregory Elliott for

The name of Machiavelli is rarely cited in Althusser's work. . . . I can only find two citations of any importance. . . . A more meticulous and detailed examination . . . would turn up a few supplementary references. But it would not change the general impression that Machiavelli is explicitly present in Althusser's published works only occasionally and in a scattered way. Yet all who were taught orally by Althusser know it: this impression is misleading. It does not at all reflect the extreme importance that Althusser accorded to the thought of the Florentine Secretary, the historical role he recognized in him. In the presence of such silences, I always remember this verse by St.-John Perse: 'And the sun is unmentioned but his power is amongst us'.[14]

But this confirmation of a connection between Machiavelli and Althusser only underlines the relevance of Renaissance literature and philosophy for our own times and reinforces for me the view that we, like Shakespeare, need to supplement Althusser and Machiavelli with more Montaignean theories, more appreciatory of the resistance of the subject to interpellation and cognizant of the instability of identity and the openness of subjectivity to new investments, identities, and relations to power.

In what follows I am attempting to approach contemporary theories of the subject, as it were, allegorically—by using Montaigne as a major source of concepts to think the subject and subjectivity, as a corrective to Machiavelli and the Machiavellianism of much contemporary theory. As we will see, Machiavelli and Montaigne turn out to have some very significant commonalties, and both seem to be in their own ways 'anti-essentialist'; at issue particularly is that 'Machiavellian' version of the self which impacted on Elizabethan and Jacobean dramatists as can be seen in their creation of stage-villains like Marlowe's Barabas and Shakespeare's Richard III.[15] This Machiavellian model of the self consists of an inner will-to-power and an outer deceptive façade drawing on the conventional pieties of received tradition to mask its anti-traditional intentions and actions. And this emphasis on a deceptive surface and an interior of power dynamics in turn mirrors the most problematic aspects of the theories of subjectivity of Foucault and Althusser that were so influential in the 1980s and persist in today's Shakespeare studies.

specific information on the composition of the work and its relation to Althusser's other writings.

[14] Emmanuel Terray, 'An Encounter: Althusser and Machiavelli', trans. Antonio Callari and David F. Ruccio, in Callari and Ruccio (eds.), *Postmodern Materialism and the Future of Marxist Theory: Essays in the Althusserian Tradition* (Hanover: University Press of New England, 1996), 257–77; 257–8; quoted in Althusser, *Machiavelli and Us*, p. xi.

[15] See Maus, *Inwardness and Theater in the English Renaissance*, 35–71, for a discussion of the Machiavellian self in the Elizabethan theatre and culture generally.

In the complex case of Foucault two concepts tended to be appropriated within literary criticism as part of theories of subjectivity. One of
these was the idea of the episteme, which seemed to provide a map of an
era's *mentalité* which could explain observed differences in historical or
cultural periods and account for what was thought to be a common shared
mentality in an era. Use of this large-scale determiner of *mentalité* as
a basis of subjectivity lies behind a number of the most problematic
generalizations in the theories of subjectivity of the 1980s, for example, in
Leonard Tennenhouse's *Power on Display* and Catherine Belsey's *The
Subject of Tragedy*. However, I would argue, this particular interpretation
of the idea of the episteme went against the literal grain of Foucault's own
definitions, in which he insisted he was defining a structure of *scientific
discourse*, somewhere between general culture and an individual's specific
ideology[16]—a definition which would seem to rule out the episteme as a
medium of subjectivity.

But Foucault also had recourse to a related but different concept to
explain modern subjectivity: that of *discourse*—a concept central to me
here and to which I will return in the opening of Chapter 1. Discourses
could be loosely defined as culturally generated sets of ideas working to
create and define power relations in institutions and, cumulatively, in
society generally. They were much more 'local' than epistemes and much
more closely associated with the institutions (prisons, hospitals, factories,
schools) of which they were essential, generative components. The notion
of discourses thus overcame many of the over-generalizing tendencies of
the episteme. In some of Foucault's most powerful passages, to be sure,
discourses were indeed the agents of a subjectivity falsely imagined to be
autonomous, against which resistance was futile. Foucauldian subjects
were locked in an ironclad process which seemed to make challenging it
impossible. A number of interviews given by Foucault in the years before
his untimely death, however, showed clearly that this outcome was
far from his intention. He spoke of counter-discourses and counter-
memories as providing alternatives to dominating discourses. But because
of the gap between his formal theory-building and his interviews, it was
necessary to appropriate the Foucault of resistance against the Foucault of
containment, and this was not always appreciated by his followers.

Althusser's related reformulation of the classical Marxian concept of
ideology led to similar problems. As I think is now widely appreciated,
what Althusser left out when he appropriated Lacan on the formation of

[16] Michel Foucault, *The Archaeology of Knowledge*, trans. A. M. Sheridan Smith (New
York: Pantheon, 1982), 191–2.

the subject in his own theory of 'interpellation by Ideology' turned out to be decisive and crippling of the new theory. In contrast to such a one-dimensional account, Lacan had described a complex, differentiated subject closely connected to both pre-linguistic and linguistic stages of development. The complex Lacanian self is both 'interpellated' by social discourses and resistant to such interpellations. It is resistant because one of the four centres of the Lacanian decentred self is formed outside language and hence outside ideology. Instead of Althusser's singular subject, in Lacan the subject is just one aspect of a more complicated schema . In Lacan's terms there is a division between the 'speaking self' or *je*, formed in language, and the 'bodily ego' or *moi*, formed outside language in the mirror stage.[17] Lacan identified reductive notions of the subject—which of course, had a basis, in his model, in the phenomenon of the *je*—with Descartes.[18] Interesting in the present context is that Lacan thought a much better understanding of the complexity of the whole self-system could also be found in another classic figure of French philosophy-literature: Michel de Montaigne, whom Lacan invoked as a precursor of his theory of a radically split subject, and a corrective of Descartes's subsequent construction of a singular subject:

I would show you that Montaigne is truly the one who has centered himself, not around scepticism but around the living moment of the *aphanisis* ['fading'] of the subject. And it is in this that he is fruitful, that he is an eternal guide, who goes beyond whatever may be represented of the moment to be defined as a historical turning point.[19]

In short, the discourse of the Lacanian speaking subject is influenced not only by the logic of the ideologies contained in the received wisdom of the culture (whose language of course conditions the speaker's discourse) but also by the unconscious and by the libido of the (mirror-stage) bodily ego or *moi*, in the domain Lacan calls the Imaginary, which is separate from the speaking subject. Or as one of Lacan's premier English-language interpreters has written, this mirror-stage ego or *moi* 'gives life and focus to the speaking subject. The latter would otherwise be a neutral automaton,

[17] Lacan himself summarized this complex, differentiated concept of the self in terms of a diagram with four corners he called 'Schema L' (in reference to the visual diagram's similarity in shape to the French cursive letter 'L'); see Jacques Lacan, *Écrits: A Selection*, trans. Alan Sheridan (New York: Norton, 1977), 193–7.

[18] Jacques Lacan, *The Four Fundamental Concepts of Psycho-analysis*, ed. Jacques Allain-Miller, trans. Alan Sheridan (New York: Norton, 1981), 44–5, 221–6.

[19] Lacan, *The Four Fundamental Concepts of Psycho-analysis*, 223–4; and see Ellie Ragland-Sullivan, *Jacques Lacan and the Philosophy of Psychoanalysis* (Urbana: University of Illinois Press, 1987), 7–10, for an elaboration of Montaigne's key place in the history of the concept of the subject in a Lacanian reading of the history of French literature.

mouthing the cliches and conventions of a given culture.'[20] Lacan can thus help us avoid those reductive tendencies of Foucault and Althusser, which too easily make of the subject the kind of 'neutral automaton' indicated above, and I return to Lacan more than once in the following chapters.

Althusser, however, omitted reference to an unconscious, to desire, or to a decentred self, and so turned the subject into a single, simple effect of the social power arrangements encoded by Ideology.[21] Ideology becomes in this schema a straitjacket which, for Althusser in his original texts, could only be removed by science—and that meant, in this context, the 'science' of Marxism-Leninism, as elaborated by himself and a few comrades. To the extent that social change meant critical distance from Ideology, then, it could only be effected by a 'scientific' vanguard party with the correct line.

As the scandalous, highly ideological nature of this claim became more and more of an embarrassment, post-Althusserianism developed, in which the notion of ideology-escaping science was jettisoned in favour of a view that all human mental life, including versions of science, is ideological—that is, textual in regard to a presumed and unreachable reality as well as serving the material interests of contending classes and other socio-economic agents. This post-Althusserianism is thus very close to Foucault on the self, and both these positions are essentially Nietzschean (and, in an analogous sense, Machiavellian), with ideology and power displaced but unmistakable versions of Nietzsche's will-to-power.

As Jürgen Habermas has tirelessly repeated throughout the age of post-structuralism, however, this position leaves us abandoned in a world without rationality and without alternatives to force and violence.[22] And it lands us squarely in that antinomy of Nietzschean thought which Peter Dews recently defined in one of the clearest and most consequential critiques of this aspect of French poststructuralism that I know.

Dews, a contemporary British critic of French poststructuralism from the point of view of German philosophy generally and Habermas and Adorno in particular, argues that Nietzsche, and those aspects of the poststructuralist theorizing based on him, never overcame a fundamental contradiction between two strands of Nietzsche's thought: on the one hand, all our knowledge of the world is an imposed, imperializing

[20] Ragland-Sullivan, *Jacques Lacan and the Philosophy of Psychoanalysis*, 59.

[21] See David Macey, 'Thinking with Borrowed Concepts: Althusser and Lacan', in Gregory Elliott (ed.), *Althusser: A Critical Reader* (Oxford: Blackwell, 1994), 142–58, for a detailed discussion of Althusser's misunderstandings of Lacan.

[22] Jürgen Habermas, *The Theory of Communicative Action*, 2 vols. (Boston: Beacon, 1984, 1987).

knowledge, the product of the desperate human need to cover the chaos of existence underneath a veneer of systematic but false rationality—or ideology in Althusser's terms. On the other hand, we can recognize the falsity of that rationality because we somehow 'know', in contradiction to the earlier idealist epistemology described above, a fluid, Dionysian reality underneath the false appearance of Apollonian rationality. In short, as Dews summarizes it, there both is and is not a knowable 'thing-in-itself' in Nietzsche. And his French poststructuralist followers Lyotard and Foucault reproduce this dilemma in several forms, while Althusser had recourse to a neo-positivist concept of science precisely to solve this problem. The jettisoning of Althusser's solution in post-Althusserianism, then, simply brings us back to the original problem, which we can see elsewhere: in, for example, Foucault's difficulties in attempting to present madness and sexuality solely in terms of the histories of the various discourses which have constituted them over several centuries, while time after time backing into acknowledgements of a madness beyond any of its specific discourses and of a body and its pleasures beyond any specific discourses of sexuality.[23]

However, late twentieth-century critics are far from the first to discuss these fundamental problems of knowledge and power. In the next chapter I will show in detail how Machiavellian discourse produced a conceptual crisis in the sixteenth century through a set of arguments with some crucial parallels to those of Nietzsche-influenced theories of the subject. This Machiavellian crisis was the context for Montaigne's complex response to be discussed below as well. Crucially, Montaigne creates a sphere of freedom—but at the considerable price of overtly withdrawing from the political world and by conducting an enquiry into the flux of subjectivity released by the withdrawal. The resulting subjectivity is in a sense 'subjectless', and thus the subjectivity I am discussing in the chapters that follow is a quite different one from that which earlier instances of new historicism and cultural materialism have defined in Shakespeare studies. In the 'presentist' allegory represented by these historicizing concepts, then, the idea of Montaignean subjectivity acts in our own time as a call to rethink the relation of subjectivity and power, and of course a number of contemporary critics and theorists have been doing exactly that.[24] In that

[23] Peter Dews, 'Adorno, Poststructuralism and the Critique of Identity', in Andrew Benjamin (ed.), *The Problems of Modernity: Adorno and Benjamin* (London: Routledge, 1989), 1–22.

[24] See Hugh Grady, 'Renewing Modernity: Changing Contexts and Contents of a Nearly Invisible Concept', *Shakespeare Quarterly*, 50/3 (Fall 1999), 268–84, for a selected survey of such theorists of the 1990s.

sense the cultural theory of the 1990s became less Machiavellian, more Montaignean over the years. In the 1990s, for example, the more complex view of Lacan as a theorist of a complexly constituted self began to form, to replace his image from the 1970s and 1980s as essentially a structuralist. Similarly, the 1990s saw the rediscovery of the Frankfurt School (especially Adorno, Benjamin, and Horkheimer)—a development which was from my point of view one of the most crucial developments of critical theory in recent decades.

Prematurely dismissed in the excitement of the encounter with French structuralism and poststructuralism in the 1970s and 1980s, Frankfurt theory has become in the last ten years an object of new appreciation precisely because it helped overcome some of the most serious blind spots of poststructuralism, deepening without overthrowing the latter's political, socially critical agenda. In what follows it will serve as a prime example of what I mean by calling certain cultural theories relatively 'Montaignean'. In this connection Adorno and Benjamin were incisive counter-critics of those would-be radical critics of the 1980s who surrounded the aesthetic and the subjective with steel walls of suspicion, reduction, and dismissal through their narrow reading of Foucault and their mistaken appraisal of Althusser as a major theorist. Adorno and Benjamin in particular showed how the aesthetic and the subjective were instead historically new categories generated in the processes of Enlightenment that created modernity and its economic engine, capitalism. Rather than being merely containers of disciplinary discourses and capitalist-imbued ideology, however—as they were in influential formulas of Foucault and Althusser much discussed in the earliest phases of the new historicism and cultural materialism—they were *in addition* repositories, or potential repositories, for psychic and social impulses resistant to the homogenizing, commodifying dynamics of both instrumental reason and capitalist economics. They contained archaic, premodern impulses of meaning-giving and value-creation, but they did so without an 'objective' structure like that of the Great Chain of Being to provide a ground for these impulses. Instead, Adorno argued (often elliptically and borrowing selectively from Kant, Hegel, Nietzsche, Marx, and Freud, among many others), the categories of the aesthetic and the subjective slowly came into cultural existence in variegated attempts across the cultures of modernity to conceptualize, understand, contain, and champion such impulses.[25]

[25] Theodor Adorno, *Aesthetic Theory*, ed. Gretel Adorno and Rolf Tiedemann, trans. and ed. Robert Hullot-Kentor (Minneapolis: University of Minnesota Press, 1997).

Recently, Slavoj Žižek has memorably thematized the return of the autonomous subject to critical respectability with a bravura exaggeration but to trenchant effect. With its strong grounding in Lacanian psychoanalytic theory, French structuralism-poststructuralism, and Frankfurt School critical theory (and its background in both Marxism and classical German philosophy), Žižek's work is an excellent example of the critical trends of the 1990s I am describing, and his *The Ticklish Subject* is a major contribution to its development. Žižek begins his argument with a tongue-in-cheek defence of 'the Cartesian subject' written in parallel with the famous opening of *The Communist Manifesto*:

A spectre is haunting Western Academia . . . the spectre of the Cartesian subject. All academic powers have entered into a holy alliance to exorcise this spectre. . . . Two things result from this:

1. Cartesian subjectivity continues to be acknowledged by all academic powers as a powerful and still active intellectual tradition.
2. It is high time that the partisans of Cartesian subjectivity should, in the face of the whole world, publish their views, their aims, their tendencies, and meet this nursery tale of Cartesian subjectivity with the philosophical manifesto of Cartesian subjectivity itself.[26]

The writer being Žižek, one should not take this defence completely literally, although the language signals a clear intent by Žižek to part company with the reductive tendencies of French poststructuralism, and he goes on to lead the reader on a provocative journey through Kant, Hegel, Heidegger, Althusser and four of his critics, Judith Butler, Freud, and Lacan in search of usable theories of the subject. Despite his opening gambit, he clearly ends up as a critic of the Cartesian subject, but not in any simple, completely negative way. It is not necessary to agree with each of his (often deliberately provocative) theses to welcome this rich discussion of what I am calling Montaignean subjectivity—a process and approach, perhaps, more than a set of doctrines.

Up to this point, however, the new appreciation of these themes of Frankfurt theory has been relatively neglected in Shakespeare studies.[27]

[26] Slavoj Žižek, *The Ticklish Subject: The Absent Centre of Political Ontology* (London: Verso, 2000), 1–2.

[27] An important exception is John J. Joughin, 'Shakespeare, Modernity and the Aesthetic: Art, Truth and Judgement in *The Winter's Tale*', in Hugh Grady (ed.), *Shakespeare and Modernity: From Early Modern to Millennium* (London: Routledge, 2000), 61–84. As I write Joughin is working on a book-length study of these issues informed by Adorno's aesthetic theory. In addition, the Frankfurt contribution to recent cultural studies is reflected in the work of a number of newer voices in Shakespeare studies influenced by cultural studies; see, for example, several of the contributions in the anthology Jean E. Howard and Scott Cutler Shershow (eds.), *Marxist Shakespeares* (London: Routledge, 2001).

One reason for this relative neglect of a potentially rich lode of cultural analysis is the uncanny way in which the major Frankfurt themes seem to echo the discredited Modernist theorizing of a pre-Enlightenment 'unified sensibility' from Eliot, Knight, Brooks, and Tillyard. Indeed, the parallel is not merely a mirage; Adorno, in his exile in the USA in the 1940s, encountered American New Critical father-figure John Crowe Ransom and found striking areas of convergence and agreement in their otherwise disparate critical theories. Clearly both men identified with those strains of international Modernism which championed art as a refuge from and potential challenge to a culture now overwhelmed by the new entertainment industries of twentieth-century mass media and commercialism.[28]

But one of the crucial differences between the Anglo-American Modernists and the Frankfurt theorists is precisely the resistance of the latter to the temptation of making of pre-modern societies and cultures a Paradise Lost of human meaning and plentitude. Their approach instead is always complex and dialectical, constantly reconceptualizing and re-evaluating the richness of cultural moments and cultural value itself, seeing modernity as full of the potential for both human liberation and human catastrophe, seeing non-modern societies as rich, variegated, and contradictory. It was the nostalgic collector of pre-industrial art Walter Benjamin, for example, who famously and trenchantly wrote that every history of civilization is a history of barbarism, and his classic essay 'The Work of Art in an Age of Mechanical Reproduction' is a corrective case in point for anyone trying to construct a unitary narrative of the production of modernity in Frankfurt School theory, as it in turn celebrates and deplores the end of the aura of the artwork in twentieth-century society.

Similarly, if Adorno's definition of 'negative dialectics' is a dazzling critique of positivist dreams of objective knowledge, it is also a corrective to the most extreme poststructuralist or Postmodernist denials (found in certain readings of Derrida, for example) of the referential quality of concepts. Scientific concepts, Adorno argued, have at least that adequacy to reality which allows technology to dominate nature.[29] And for related reasons cultural theory must acknowledge and make use of the relative adequacy of its many narratives and concepts for understanding the development, strengths and weaknesses, limits and potentials, of the world we live in. No concept, Adorno argues, is identical with its object; we must always assume a certain non-identity in any concept.[30] Concepts

[28] Grady, *The Modernist Shakespeare*, 154–6.
[29] Theodor Adorno, *Negative Dialectics*, trans. E. B. Ashton (New York: Continuum, 1983), 174–97.   [30] Ibid. 146–8 *et passim*.

are to facts as constellations are to stars, Benjamin famously wrote.[31] They always involve selection, exclusion, and construction. Without them, however, the world is blank to us; with them, we can grasp aspects of the world and live within it. In what follows I am making central use of constellations constructed under the rubrics 'modernity', 'subjectivity', 'instrumentality', 'Machiavellian', and 'Montaignean'. The simultaneous production of a new kind of objectivity in Machiavelli and Renaissance science and a new kind of subjectivity in Montaigne and Shakespeare is profoundly connected with the epochal differentiations between subject and object described in Frankfurt and related critical theory.[32] This ground was opened up by some of the early work of Max Horkheimer centrally preoccupied with issues of sixteenth-century history. Calvin, Luther, Machiavelli, and Montaigne are major figures for the development of modernity and modern subjectivity in several essays from this period,[33] and at times the Horkheimer of the 1930s reads like a prescient critic of poststructuralist Machiavellianism, with an acute sense of how subjectivity both embodies and resists ideology:

a person's deeper psychic layers are not determined by it [ideology] alone, but equally by the constant experience of contradictory reality. The manifest ideology is just one of the factors that give rise to the personalities typical of the society. The humanism that pervades the history of the new spirit shows a double face.[34]

In these essays, however, Horkheimer had yet to be influenced by the theories of negative dialectics and of aesthetics of his colleague and friend Theodor Adorno, and they are most relevant here for specific insights rather than their overall picture of the era. The best Frankfurt text on the epochal differentiations of modernity I am investigating here remains

---

[31] Walter Benjamin, *The Origins of German Tragic Drama* (1928), trans. John Osborne (London: New Left Books, 1977), 14.
[32] The fullest and most recent treatment of the Frankfurt School is Rolf Wiggershaus, *The Frankfurt School* (1986), trans. Michael Robertson (Oxford: Polity, 1994). For still useful (and more succinct) introductions to Frankfurt critical theory, see Martin Jay, *The Dialectical Imagination: A History of the Frankfurt School and the Institute of Social Research, 1923–1950* (Boston: Little, 1973), and David Held, *Introduction to Critical Theory: Horkheimer to Habermas* (Berkeley and Los Angeles: University of California Press, 1980); and for central Frankfurt theorists, see Fredric Jameson, *Marxism and Form: Twentieth-Century Dialectical Theories of Literature* (Princeton: Princeton University Press, 1971). A very helpful recent study, focused around the concept of modernity, is Douglas Kellner, *Critical Theory, Marxism, and Modernity* (Baltimore: Johns Hopkins University Press, 1989).
[33] The most interesting have been collected and newly translated in Max Horkheimer, *Between Philosophy and Social Science: Selected Early Writings*, trans. G. Frederick Hunter, Matthew S. Kramer, and John Torpey (Cambridge, Mass.: MIT Press, 1993).
[34] Horkheimer, *Between Philosophy and Social Science*, 98–9.

Horkheimer and Adorno's jointly written *The Dialectic of Enlightenment* (1944).

Rather than trying to work out the specific constellation of Frankfurt and contemporary theories of subjectivity and modernity relevant to the readings of Shakespearian texts below, however, I intend instead to pursue the readings in terms of their own contemporaneous discourses, primarily those of Machiavelli and Montaigne. Occasionally, references to twentieth-century theories can help clarify a point or enable a reading of Shakespeare, and when that is the case a note or comment will identify the borrowing. While the chapters below have a clear 'presentist' dimension related to contemporary debates in cultural theory about subjectivity and modernity, I am choosing in this work, as I indicated, to put the historicist dimension first, to complement the opposite procedure of my previous book *Shakespeare's Universal Wolf*. As I argued in that work, the case constituted by the works of William Shakespeare suggests that important aspects of the dialectic of enlightenment defined by Horkheimer and Adorno were in operation already in the sixteenth century—and earlier in Italy. Shakespeare's works depict a dialectic of enlightenment in all genres and 'periods' of his writing, with characteristic differences of emphasis and evaluation. The following study is dedicated to exploring one of the most interesting of these phases, the plays from 1595 to 1600 that form both a dialectic of enlightenment and a kind of 'Machiavellian moment' in Shakespeare's work. This moment is Machiavellian, not in the sense that Shakespeare necessarily read or took in the many facets of the complex body of work of this singular Renaissance humanist and harbinger of modernity, but in the sense that many of the plays written in this period take Machiavelli's most famous ideas on value-free realpolitik and use them as the starting point for multidimensional probings and conflicting interpretations of the cultural and political crises these ideas produce. Shakespeare was never 'a Machiavellian' in any straightforward sense—in fact, there is no direct evidence that he ever read a page of Machiavelli's works. Instead, *The Prince*'s problematic was the political problematic of the day, both in Elizabeth's Privy Council and on the stages of the London public theatres. In the terms I am developing here, Machiavelli was the conduit through which what Horkheimer and Adorno called 'instrumental reason' came to be thought about in Shakespeare's day. Of course this role as a provider of the concept of autonomous, instrumental reason by no means exhausts Machiavelli's impact on English political thought in the sixteenth and seventeenth centuries and beyond. J. G. A. Pocock famously argued, for example, that Machiavelli's republican concepts were the seeds from which eventually blossomed a whole new discourse of anti-monarchical, republican, and democratic ideas which infiltrated the Puritan discourse of the English Revolution of 1642 and eventually became incorporated in the founding documents of the democracy of the United States. There is a clear sense in which the whole tradition of Marxist critical theory, including that of the Frankfurt School, could be said to descend from the meditations on class struggle and the corruption of the people from Machiavelli's *The Discourses*. That creative Marxist Antonio Gramsci famously praised Machiavelli as the theorist of the possibility of autonomous political activity, of providing a way to think about shaping human society and history with some measure of intentionality and humanization, rather than consigning history to the blind operations of fortune and fate. And, as already mentioned, the late Althusser also found Machiavelli a seminal figure, albeit one who directly influenced not Marx and Engels, but Gramsci and himself. But while these aspects of Machiavelli's thought will occasionally come into view in what follows, for the most part I am asking readers to 'bracket' the richness of Machiavelli's legacy and to focus instead—as much of the world has always done—on some of his most controversial, even shocking ideas concerning the necessity of deception, immorality, and violence in politics in a world in which men are not good and he who would be good invites defeat. This is a doctrine which appears to have preoccupied a segment of the English political class in the Elizabethan era, and it is a set of ideas in particular which seems to animate the puzzling actions of the young Earl of Essex in this period, including and most importantly his failed attempt to overthrow Queen Elizabeth and set himself up as England's monarch. Most importantly here, they seem to be concepts which challenged the imagination and rationality of William Shakespeare.

It is no surprise that Shakespeare might be preoccupied with such issues. Since at least Hegel, he has been recognized as a figure who has achieved his ultimate cultural centrality precisely because he was one of the first and most original enunciators of modernity and its peculiar conception of the modern subject. Hegel's specific approach to the modernity of Shakespeare, however, is badly in need of an updating for which the development of contemporary cultural theory has now produced the elements.[35]

---

[35] For further development of this theme, see Grady, 'Renewing Modernity', and Hugh Grady, 'Introduction', in Grady (ed.), *Shakespeare and Modernity*, 1–19.

Toward a non-reductive theory of subjectivity

One of the crucial preconditions for 'modern' subjectivity for Frankfurt theory and its descendants is the fragmentation of belief systems and the desacralization (at least in principle) of hitherto sacred domains so that within modernity meaning and value are problematic, 'private', and uncertain. Modern subjectivity is paradoxically both a social and a private mythology, the atomized subject's more or less unique configuration of the bewildering array of socially produced beliefs, opinions, world views, tastes, values, feelings, prejudices, cognitive processes, and so on. These provide a framework for experiencing and understanding the world in a situation in which the 'normal' condition of pre-modern cultures—a shared mythology and belief system—has fragmented and been replaced by the various forms of modern, secular rationality. One of the central myths of received Western ideology about itself has been the notion that such subjectivity is autonomous, the basis of the sovereign individual, the 'bourgeois' or 'liberal' subject of much recent left-wing criticism. I want to be clear that in trying to improve Machiavellian theory with Montaignean understandings of subjectivity, it would be no improvement at all if in the process one ended up reproducing 'bourgeois' illusions of a sovereign self.

The ideological functions of subjectivity are potent and have been closely associated with capitalism since the age of Shakespeare at least. The cultivation of self-authored identity and interiority celebrated by Iago in his 'Virtue, a fig!' speech, for example, helps to justify a new social fetishism of commodities and profits. 'Put money in thy purse,' Iago repeats to Roderigo, underlining the connections between the egoistic celebration of self and the profit necessary for the functioning of capitalism. The innumerable celebrations of the individual, the subject, and the ego of subsequent capitalist modernity serve the unmistakable ideological function of justifying these ethically dubious values. Throughout modernity, ideologies of individualism have entered subjectivity through socialization, sometimes at a very deep, identity-connected level. We all attempt to 'fit in' to the world we are given in one way or the other. In short, going beyond what I am calling Machiavellian theories of subjectivity need not mean abandoning their critique of the myth of the autonomous subject. I am not attempting here to deny the ideological component of subjectivity—but to deny instead that subjectivity is always and only ideological. Just as people believe in the social status quo, they sometimes come to feel alienated from it, to question it, to criticize it, even to make revolution against it. They can do so, it seems to me, only because ideology is not as completely totalizing and enchaining as widely influential aspects of Althusser, Foucault, and Lyotard have argued that it is. Both belief and the conceptual system of language, in short, as many theorists of the 1990s have argued, are open to negotiation. People learn from, and criticize, their experiences with mental structures; they are not inevitably enchained by them.

One of the corollaries of these views of the subject is the need to abandon earlier attempts to identify a single, unitary ideology or discursive formation—'liberal humanism'—which constructs modern subjectivities out of whole cloth.[36] Instead, I want to follow a motif defined not only in the Frankfurt School and in Habermas, but emphasized as well in works of Pierre Bourdieu and Charles Taylor, on the *differentiations* which constitute modernity and modern subjects.[37] In probably the most influential theory of unitary 'liberal humanism', *The Subject of Tragedy*, Catherine Belsey had in fact defined three distinct components of liberal humanism which she argued were ultimately amalgamated by the mid-seventeenth century to produce a unified 'liberal humanist' ideology. The first was that associated with Hamlet, Milton's Satan, the Duchess of Malfi, and a number of others, and it is a liberal humanism defined by (an apparently new) 'interiority' seen as 'author and origin of meaning and choice'.[38] The second was constituted by the objectifying methods of Francis Bacon and, more importantly, the empirical philosophy of John Locke, whereby the liberal subject creates science and positive concepts generally through an instrumental language.[39] The culmination of these first two, in the late seventeenth century, was Locke's conception of an autonomous, natural self, endowed with certain inalienable rights—only, of course, Locke made the right to own property the central one of these and thus became one of the great ideologues of a rapidly maturing capitalism.

My own view is that, rather than constituting a single 'liberal humanism', these motifs are differentiated practices and discourses, with the first two of them dialectically related, agonistic socio-historical developments

---

[36] For a more detailed development of this thesis, see Hugh Grady, 'On the Need for a Differentiated Theory of the (Early) Modern Subject', in John J. Joughin (ed.), *Philosophical Shakespeares* (London: Routledge, 2000), 34–50.

[37] Pierre Bourdieu, *Language and Symbolic Power*, ed. John B. Thompson, trans. Gino Raymond and Matthew Adamson (Cambridge, Mass.: Harvard University Press, 1991) and Charles Taylor, *Sources of the Self: The Making of the Modern Identity* (Cambridge, Mass.: Harvard University Press, 1989).

[38] Catherine Belsey, *The Subject of Tragedy: Identity and Difference in Renaissance Drama*, (London: Methuen, 1985), 35.

[39] Ibid. 83.

key to understanding the structures and dynamics of early modernity. That is, in what follows, I want to argue that two of the three strands Belsey united as part of 'liberal humanism' ('interiority' and instrumental reason) can be more adequately conceptualized as forms of rationality which became differentiated from each other in a meaningful way in Renaissance intellectual developments that would be institutionalized and established as basic features of the social order later in the Enlightenment. In separating, however, they also constituted a dialectic; that is, their constitution as separate categories left within each concept traces of their logical links to each other. Belsey's third strand of Lockean social contract theory, in contrast, I believe to be a genuinely Enlightenment construct foreign to the thinking of the age of Shakespeare in England.

Thus I will be presupposing an alternative 'Montaignean' theory of early modern subjectivity, one based much more on themes of Adorno, Horkheimer, Lacan, and others to be identified below as the discussion develops, rather than the 'Machiavellian' French poststructuralism that has set the agenda for much previous cultural materialism. In the theory I am working with here, subjectivity cannot be reduced to the effect of static structures of domination like ideology and discourses. Instead, it participates in a relatively autonomous, socially constructed realm of meaning and communication, which rather than being static and reified is in principle open to negotiation, modification, and reconstitution through dialogue. This has been an emphasis of many different versions of the social theory of the 1990s, but it was of course as well an insight marvellously articulated more than 400 years earlier:

Les autres forment l'homme; je le recite et en represente un particulier bien mal formé, et lequel, si j'avoy à façonner de nouveau, je ferois vrayement bien autre qu'il n'est. Meshuy c'est fait. Or les traits de ma peinture ne forvoyent point, quoy qu'ils se changent et diversifient. Le monde n'est qu'une branloire perenene. Toutes choses y branlent sans cesse: la terre, les rochers du Caucase, les pyramides d'Ægypte, et du branle public et du leur. La constance mesme n'est autre chose qu'un branle plus languissant. Je ne puis asseurer mon object. Il va trouble et chancelant, d'une yvresse naturelle. Je le prens en ce point, comme il est, en l'instant que je m'amuse à luy. Je ne peints pas l'estre. Je peints le passage: non un passage d'aage en autre, ou, comme dict le peuple, de sept en sept ans, mais de jour en jour, de minute en minute.[40]

(Others form man; I tell of him, and portray a particular one, very ill-formed, whom I should really make very different from what he is if I had to fashion him over again. But now it is done.

[40] Michel de Montaigne, 'Du repentir', Les Essais, 3.2 ed. Pierre Villey (Quadrige: Presses Universitaires de France, 1988), 804–5.

Now the lines of my painting do not go astray, though they change and vary. The world is but a perennial movement. All things in it are in constant motion—the earth, the rocks of the Caucasus, the pyramids of Egypt—both with the common motion and their own. Stability itself is nothing but a more languid motion.

I cannot keep my subject still. It goes along befuddled and staggering, with a natural drunkenness. I take it in this condition, just as it is at the moment I give my attention to it. I do not portray being; I portray passing. Not the passing from one age to another, or, as the people say, from seven years to seven years, but from day to day, from minute to minute.[41])

---

[41] Michel de Montaigne, *The Complete Essays of Montaigne*, trans. Donald M. Frame (Stanford, Calif.: Stanford University Press, 1965), 610–11.

1
A Shakespearian 'Machiavellian Moment', 1595–1660: An Overview

The histories and tragedies written by Shakespeare between 1595 and 1600[1] form an interconnected set of dramatic works, five of which (the four plays of the *Henriad* and *Hamlet*) will be explored in this book. What differentiates these plays from the earlier histories and tragedies, and again from the Jacobean tragedies, is their relative positivity about political power. They all seem to take for granted a secular, realpolitik understanding of political power as a force for both good and evil, a view that is widely identified with the discourse of Machiavelli's 1513 *The Prince* and related writings. Because the plays centre on princes in two distinct but here fused senses—the prince as embodiment and agent of power, the prince as royal apprentice and heir—the linked thematics of these plays can be described as investigations into the complex process of the internalization by princes of discourses of power—Machiavelli's and related discursive material pre-eminently. But part of the process of internalization central to these plays is the resistance to an identity as a political prince by Richard II, Hal, and Hamlet. The discourse of princes produces a counter-discourse of subjectivity, of a distinctly modern valorization of a subjective flux which is not exhausted by interpellation into pre-established social roles. In the new conditions of the European

[1] According to Stanley Wells and Gary Taylor, *William Shakespeare: A Textual Companion* (New York: Norton, 1997), other plays composed in this period were: *Love's Labour's Lost* (1594–5), the missing *Love's Labour's Won* (1595–6), *Romeo and Juliet* (1595), *King John* (1596), *The Merchant of Venice* (1596–7), *The Merry Wives of Windsor* (1597–8), *Julius Caesar* (1599), and *As You Like It* (1599–1600). *King John* and *Julius Caesar* both have obvious relations to the theme of Machiavellian political power, and I argued in *Shakespeare's Universal Wolf* (Oxford: Clarendon, 1996) that *As You Like It* does as well. *Romeo and Juliet* investigates erotic subjectivity within a hostile, reified social milieu. The remaining comedies all have links to themes of power, but a large area of autonomous comedic matter as well, and deserve separate treatment.

Renaissance, these roles suddenly seemed escapable, malleable, or simply to be alternatives which one might defer successfully by the kinds of stratagems forced on Richard II, adopted by Prince Hal and Falstaff, and undertaken by Prince Hamlet in some undecidable combination of choice and necessity. The discourses of these princes, in short, begin in issues of power but generate discourses of subjectivity as well. This facet of these plays directly or indirectly mirrors the concepts of another celebrated Renaissance predecessor, Michel de Montaigne, so that in a meaningful sense Shakespeare's Machiavellian moment is also a Montaignean one— and thereby, of course, hangs much of the tale.

If, as I argued in the Introduction, literary and cultural theory from the 1980s and 1990s evolved from one-dimensional theories of power and subjection to a number of different but complementary attempts in the 1990s to theorize resistance to power and a critical dimension within subjectivity, something of the reverse happens in the plays of this period. The trajectory of intertwined power and subjectivity as we move chronologically through the four plays of the *Henriad* is one of growing pessimism. *Richard II*, a kind of prologue, leaves us poised between cold Machiavellianism and ineffectual but hopeful subjectivity. But the Prince Hal trilogy enacts a precise reversal of the trajectory from despair to hope of the Jacobean phase of Shakespeare's career. The plays take us from the carnival subjectivity of Hal and Falstaff in the tavern to a fully reified political realm (at the end of *Part 2* and throughout *Henry V*) in which subjectivity has become wholly subordinated to political expediency. This situation in turn provides the starting point of *Hamlet*, a famously complex drama which seems to affirm subjectivity, but without the utopian, socially oriented valences of *King Lear* and notably without any hope of social amelioration. But these complexities are best defined in the context of the readings of the plays below.

Shakespeare, that gifted synthesizer, was not the first to define these themes, but he may have been the first to tie them together in the exact configuration in which they are presented from 1595 to 1600. And the fact that these themes predominate in a compact five-year period in Shakespeare's career is of course attention-getting and suggestive that there might have been some 'external' influence on this pattern. What leaps out in any enquiry as to why Machiavellian and Montaignean themes might be of interest to the audiences of this period is that the years from 1595 to early 1601 encompass the spectacular climax of the career of the Earl of Essex— from hubristic heights, to peripeteia, to death—in a series of events that riveted the attention of town and court beyond anything between the

Armada of 1588 and the 1603 death of Elizabeth. Essex and his faction have been, for good reason, often associated with English Machiavellianism, and, as we will see, Machiavelli himself was a major cultural icon of the era, and a complex one. Attempts to establish connections between Shakespeare and the Essex faction have ebbed and flowed in Shakespeare scholarship for over a century. There are tantalizing, well-known clues of such a linkage, and I will review these in brief detail below. However, after more than 100 years of attempts, Shakespeare scholarship has never gone beyond informed speculation on this matter. We can establish connections between Shakespeare and the Essex faction, but we do not know how significant or consequential these were. And even though numerous historians affirm the importance of Machiavelli and his sources to several of Essex's advisers, all we can finally say on this issue is that like all the other members of the Elizabethan political class, but more openly than most of them, Essex employed advisers steeped in the political discourses of Machiavelli and related writers of the humanist tradition. In the theatrical world, with its complex connections with the political, on a separate but parallel track, we can observe Shakespeare developing political ideas which explore familiar Machiavellian themes, and taking them several degrees further in complexity and sophistication than did earlier dramatists of the Machiavellian like Kyd and Marlowe. But how does one undertake a parallel investigation of Machiavellian concepts in court and on stage with only the sketchiest of information as to the channels of communication between court and theatre? Should we simply remain silent in the absence of knowledge of concrete, material links between these central Elizabethan institutions?

The methodological answer to this, I believe, is provided by Michel Foucault's ideas concerning discursive formations.[2] The term 'discourses' in Foucault's writing is protean and complex, resisting simple definition, but it is extremely useful for thinking about the transmission of ideas in society. Most importantly, it 'brackets' issues of human agency and concentrates on the close connections of ideas with the institutions and social structures which both embody and animate them. To be sure, this 'bracketing' has consequences, producing some of Foucault's notorious blind spots, as I indicated in the Introduction. But the procedure is also a

---

[2] See Paul A. Bové, 'Discourse', in Frank Lentricchia and Thomas McLaughlin (eds.), *Critical Terms for Literary Studies*, 2nd edn. (Chicago: University of Chicago Press, 1995), 50–65. For one of Foucault's most accessible discussions of the term see Michel Foucault, 'What Is an Author?' (1969), in his *Language, Counter-Memory, Practice: Selected Essays and Interviews*, ed. Donald Bouchard, trans. Donald Bouchard and Sherry Simon (Ithaca, NY: Cornell University Press, 1977), 113–38.

powerful and productive one, used within its limits. Among other things, discourses are sets of interconnected assumptions and practices which provide small-scale mental frameworks for the creation of concepts. Foucault scandalously insisted that discourses are always formed in contexts defined by power relations and are therefore always implicated in domination and submission at one level or another—although he also spoke at times of counter-discourses, challenging of established power. The concept in fact has something of a Machiavellian aura, as I suggested in the Introduction, but Foucault would also insist that Machiavelli's writings themselves, like all others, are implicated in the dynamics of discourses and power. As such, the ideas embodied in the Machiavellian texts came to circulate independently of those texts, carried by the political and cultural institutions which absorbed, modified, and disseminated them. Without our being certain of quite how it happened, several sets of discourses of Machiavellian provenance somehow got transmitted into the remarkable theatre of late Tudor, early Stuart London. Recent historical research allows informed speculation about how this might have happened, and there is no real mystery involved—just a dearth of specific information. We do not know precisely how Machiavellian ideas were transmitted to the dramatists. For example, Shakespeare's knowledge of *The Prince*'s Machiavellian logic might simply have been derived from close attention to Marlowe's *Tamburlaine* and other plays. Marlowe, we can say, was at Cambridge at a time when Gabriel Harvey informs us many of his friends were reading *The Prince* and/or *The Discourses*.[3] But the circulation of discourses in society is normal and unremarkable, and the network of connections between court and theatre a rich, complex, and multidirectional one well defined in some of its contours in the extensive writings of cultural materialists, new historicists, feminists, and Marxists over the last twenty years.

In what follows I intend, contrary to the new historicism, to focus primarily on readings of the plays rather than on their social and political contexts. But I will take it for granted that when the plays put recognizable Machiavellian and Montaignean concepts in the mouths of their characters, or create chains of cause and effect which parallel those in contemporary political texts like Machiavelli's *The Prince* or *The Discourses*, it is reasonable to assume that discursive dynamics are at work even if we cannot be certain of what microcircuitry was responsible for each specific transmission. In the end, it matters little whether Shakespeare directly

---

[3] Victoria Kahn, *Machiavellian Rhetoric: From the Counter-Reformation to Milton* (Princeton: Princeton University Press, 1994), 94 and 275 n. 3.

read either Machiavelli or Montaigne. What matters is that we can observe the discursive parallels among them, parallels which help us to read the plays in new (and sometimes old) ways and which help us to see the extent to which Shakespeare participated in the creation of intellectual modernity as he entertained and challenged his audiences.

As we will see below, several works of contemporary scholarship have established that the topics and paradoxes of Machiavelli's *The Prince* and *Discourses* permeated the writings of Renaissance political thinkers, including many who denounced them. While Machiavelli had been condemned by both Protestants and Catholics and was officially banned in Elizabethan England, he was also much discussed and widely read within the Elizabethan political class. Machiavelli became in the sixteenth century what Foucault called a 'founder of discursivity'—someone who was not an author in the ordinary sense, an organizer of circulating discourses, but one who forges a new form of discourse which enters into a culture or cultures generally.[4] We can see the influence of Machiavellian discourse (in this case probably mediated by the theatre) in one of the official documents of the era, issued shortly after the putting down of the Essex rebellion in February 1601, when Elizabeth's Privy Council issued the following directive to the preachers of the realm as to how they should characterize the rebellious Earl. He was, in a word, a theatrical machiavel:

All this time he has carried himself after a very insolent and ambitious sort, especially for six or seven years past, wherein he has been contriving this most traitorous attempt, for the better effecting whereof, he has diligently trodden the steps of all arch-traitors, seeking by popular conversation to allure the hearts of the simple. In matters of religion, his dissimulation and hypocrisy are now disclosed. As he behaved, he was accounted in effect the only nobleman that cared for religion; his manner was to censure all men; some were cold professors, others neuters or Atheists, and lately, whilst he has been busy in plotting his treasons, two sermons in a day could scarce content him, such was his burning zeal for the Gospel.[5]

Interest in the flamboyant Robert Devereux, second Earl of Essex (1567–1601), has resurged in Shakespeare studies in recent years as a consequence

---

[4] Foucault, 'What Is an Author?', 113–38. The suggestion that Machiavelli should be seen as a discourse-author, however, is my own, not Foucault's. In his later essay 'Governmentality' (1978), in Graham Burchell, Colin Gordon, and Peter Miller (eds.), *The Foucault Effect: Studies in Governmentality* (Chicago: University of Chicago Press, 1991), 87–104, he asserts that modern political discourse descends only indirectly from Machiavelli, instead forming itself around the various responses to Machiavelli pioneered by Gentillet in his *Contre-Machiavel.*

[5] *Calendar of State Papers, Domestic*, ed. Mary Anne Everett Green (London: Stationers Office, 1869), 278, 63 (5: 566).

of the influence of the new historicism.[6] As with similar attempts to link Shakespeare with Montaigne and Machiavelli (to be discussed shortly), this interest represents a revival of what had been a more-or-less abandoned theme of the Shakespeare studies of the late nineteenth and early twentieth centuries.[7] In the era after the ascendancy of the New Criticism and Tillyard's historical criticism, attempts to establish definitive linkage between Shakespeare and Essex waned both because of a paucity of documentary evidence and because critical paradigms shifted toward the view that Shakespeare was a political traditionalist, with little in common with the historical personage in Renaissance England who most flagrantly violated decorum and respect for the office of the monarchy.

In today's changed critical environment, with its appreciation of Shakespeare's use of a Machiavellian analysis in a number of tragedies and histories, it seems much more plausible to suppose some kind of link between a Machiavellian theatre and the faction within Elizabethan politics with a reputation for the appreciation and use of Machiavelli's political philosophy, Essex's group, with its formidable ideologues, Anthony and Francis Bacon. As I have emphasized, the climax of Essex's career occurred during the very years when Shakespeare composed the plays of the *Henriad*. The unobtrusively assumed Machiavellian politics of the plays, their study of the vulnerability of the symbols of sovereignty to the realities of political power, their portrait of a half-rebellious, half-

---

[6] Of numerous available accounts of relations between Essex and Elizabeth, I have found the following most useful: Susan Bassnett, *Elizabeth I: A Feminist Perspective* (Oxford: Berg, 1988); Christopher Highley, *Shakespeare, Spenser, and the Crisis in Ireland* (Cambridge: Cambridge University Press, 1997); Lisa Jardine and Alan Stewart, *Hostage to Fortune: The Troubled Life of Francis Bacon* (New York: Hill & Wang, 1999); Joseph M. Levine, *Elizabeth I: Great Lives Observed* (Englewood Cliffs, NJ: Prentice-Hall, 1969); Wallace T. MacCaffrey, *Elizabeth I: War and Politics, 1588–1603* (Princeton: Princeton University Press, 1992); Lacey Baldwin Smith, *The Elizabethan World* (1967; repr. Boston: Houghton Mifflin, 1991), 207–33; and her *Treason in Tudor England: Politics and Paranoia* (London: Jonathan Cape, 1986); David Starkey (ed.), *Rivals in Power: Lives and Letters of the Great Tudor Dynasties* (New York: Grove Weidenfeld, 1990); and Perez Zagorin, *Francis Bacon* (Princeton: Princeton University Press, 1998).

[7] The earliest attempt to link Essex and Shakespeare was a paper given at the first meeting of London's New Shakspere Society, on 13 Mar. 1874, Richard Simpson, 'The Politics of Shakespeare's Historical Plays', *Transactions of the New Shakspere Society*, 1st ser. 2 (1874), 396–441. The theme was later developed by Evelyn May Albright, 'Shakespeare's *Richard II* and the Essex Conspiracy', *PMLA* 42 (1927), 686–720, and there was a later critique by Ray Heffner, 'Shakespeare, Hayward, and Essex', *PMLA* 45 (1930), 754–80, then a response by Albright, 'Shakespeare's *Richard II*, Hayward's *History of Henry IV*, and the Essex Conspiracy', *PMLA* 46 (1931): 694–719. The results of the debate are distilled and further developed in Lily B. Campbell, *Shakespeare's 'Histories': Mirrors of Elizabethan Policy* (San Marino, Calif.: Huntington Library, 1947).

chivalrous young prince, and their investigation of image and public exposure were issues for Essex as well as for the plays of the *Henriad*.

While these thematic parallels might in themselves be seen as what Walter Cohen has called, in reference to some of Greenblatt's breath-taking cultural 'negotiations', instances of 'arbitrary connectedness',[8] there are of course well-known, much more direct connections as well. In *Henry V*, just before the last act, the Chorus links Essex—then (1599) in Ireland—with the triumphant Henry V in these lines:

> But now behold,
> In the quick forge and working-house of thought,
> How London doth pour out her citizens.
> The Mayor, and all his brethren, in best sort,
> Like to the senators of th'antique Rome,
> With the plebeians swarming at their heels,
> Go forth, and fetch their conquering Caesar in—
> As, by a lower but high-loving likelihood,
> Were now the General of our gracious Empress—
> As in good time he may—from Ireland coming,
> Bringing rebellion broachèd on his sword,
> How many would the peaceful city quit
> To welcome him! Much more, and much more cause,
> Did they this Harry. (5.0.23–34)

Secondly, as is well known, Shakespeare's company was paid by Essex's men in the ill-fated uprising of 1601 to stage a play of Richard II apparently to encourage his followers in his move against Elizabeth.[9] This now much alluded-to command performance at the Globe by Shake-speare's troupe the Chamberlain's Men is known to us because it came up in the investigation following Essex's failed rebellion. In fact, the direc-tions for preachers of the Privy Council of 14 February 1601 which I cited previously already alluded to Richard II's fall: 'If he [Essex] had not been prevented, there had never been a rebellion in England since Richard II more desperate or dangerous.'[10]

---

[8] Walter Cohen, 'Political Criticism of Shakespeare', in Jean E. Howard and Marion F. O'Connor (eds.), *Shakespeare Reproduced: The Text in History and Ideology* (New York: Methuen, 1987), 34.

[9] One of several essentially similar accounts of the request for a performance goes: 'Sir Chas. Percy, Sir Josceline Percy, Lord Mounteagle, and several others spoke to some of the players to play the deposing and killing of King Richard II, and promised to give them 40s. more than their ordinary, to do so. Examinant and his fellows had determined to play some other play, holding that of King Richard as being so old and so long out of use that they should have a small company at it, but at this request they were content to play it' (*Calendar of State Papers, Domestic*, 278, 85 (5: 578).   [10] Ibid. 278, 63 (5: 567).

This mention of Richard demonstrates that the very earliest reactions to the event from within Elizabeth's court associated the rebellion with the story of Richard, and it is not impossible that they were in part stimulated by an awareness of the performance of a play of Richard II at the Globe the day before the rebellion, although it is clear that there were other sources for connecting Elizabeth and Richard. The comparison with Richard II comes up again and again in the interrogations before and during Essex's trial. For example, when the Earl of Southampton asked Attorney General Coke what he thought he and Essex would do to the Queen had they been successful, Coke replied, 'The same (said he) which *Henry* of *Lancaster* did against *Richard* the Second. He went to the King and fell on his Knee, pretending onely to beg the removing of his evil Counsellors: but having once gotten the King in his power, he deprived him both of Crown and Life.'[11] A contemporary letter describing some of the legal proceedings quoted Sir Robert Cecil accusing Essex once more in analogy to Richard II: 'He would have removed her Majesty's servants, perhaps let her continue a time, and then stepped into her chair and put her where Richard II was.'[12]

But the case for a Shakespearian connection is complicated because of another treatment of the story of Richard's deposition, by lawyer and civil servant John Hayward in his *The First Part of the Life and Raigne of King Henrie IIII*, published in February 1599 and dedicated (like numerous other works of the day) to the Earl of Essex. Hayward was committed to the Tower some months after his book's publication, but before Essex's rebellion, in the period of his house arrest, for having brought out this book. His crime, to which he pleaded innocent, was to have attempted to draw analogies between Richard, Elizabeth, and Essex.[13] In truth, his wrongdoing seems rather to have been dedicating his book to the wrong man at a breathtakingly wrong moment.

Queen Elizabeth's own famous comments in the matter came only some six months after the rebellion. Her much repeated short remark, 'I am Richard the Second, know ye not that?' was made when she was

[11] William Camden, *The History of the Most Renowned and Victorious Princess Elizabeth, Late Queen of England*, 4th edn. (1866; repr. New York: AMS Press, 1970), 616.

[12] Letter of Vincent Hussey, *Calendar of State Papers, Domestic*, 278, 94 (5: 584).

[13] The fullest account of Hayward's ordeal is John J. Manning, introduction to John Hayward, *The First and Second Parts of John Hayward's 'The Life and Raigne of King Henrie IIII'*, ed. John J. Manning, Camden Fourth Series 42 (London: Royal Historical Society, 1991), 1–57. See also Peter Ure, introduction to William Shakespeare, *King Richard II*, The Arden Shakespeare (London: Methuen, 1956), pp. lvii–lix; Annabel Patterson, *Censorship and Interpretation: The Conditions of Writing and Reading in Early Modern England* (Madison: University of Wisconsin Press, 1984), 46–8; and Leeds Barroll, 'A New History for Shakespeare and his Time', *Shakespeare Quarterly*, 39 (1988), 441–64.

examining a compendium of records kept at the Tower that she had had
made into a book by the antiquarian William Lambarde. The anecdote
goes:

so her Majestie fell upon the reign of King Richard II. saying, 'I am Richard II.
know ye not that?'
W.[illiam] L.[ambarde]: Such a wicked imagination was determined and
attempted by a most unkind Gent. the most adorned creature that ever your
Majestie made.
Her Majestie: He that will forget God, will also forget his benefactors; this tragedy
was played 40tie times in open streets and houses.[14]

Here, for Lambarde and Elizabeth, the author of the Richard–Elizabeth
parallel is clearly neither Hayward nor Shakespeare, but Essex himself—
he who was a most unkind gentleman, 'the most adorned creature that
ever your Majestie made' and he 'that will forget God . . . [and] his benefactors'. Certainly Elizabeth moves without a pause from records of
Richard II to Essex, to a 'tragedy . . . played 40tie times in open streets and
houses' as if they were one. There was a similar movement from Hayward
to a play of Richard II in another of the statements at Essex's trial, in which
Essex was accused of having been behind the printing of 'that treasonable
book of Henry IV'—this clearly a reference to Hayward's work—with the
additional damning detail of 'the Earl himself being so often at the playing
thereof, and with great applause giving countenance to it'.[15] No one can be
certain that 'the playing thereof' refers to Shakespeare's *Richard II*,
although it is possible that it does.[16] Hayward's account and Shakespeare's
play cover much of the same ground, although Hayward includes many
details and judgements not found in Shakespeare's play—and vice versa.
One important difference is the pro-Richard speech of the Bishop of

---

[14] Quoted in Ure, introduction, p. lix. Unlike the other pieces of evidence involved here,
this is not from the *Calendar of State Papers* but from a manuscript held by the Lambard
family. It was first printed in John Nichols, *The Progresses and Public Processions of Queen
Elizabeth*, 3 vols. (1783; repr. London: John Nichols & Son, 1823), iii. 552. An old-spelling
transcription is provided by E. K. Chambers, *William Shakespeare: A Study of Facts and
Problems*, 2 vols. (Oxford: Clarendon, 1930), ii: 326–7.

[15] *Calendar of State Documents, Domestic*, quoted in Ure, introduction, p. lix.

[16] An additional complication is that the play associated with the rebellion and Hayward's
book is sometimes identified as a play of Henry IV, in line with the title of Hayward's work.
For example, Essex's follower Sir Gelly Merrick testified on 17 Feb. that he and a group of
Essex's supporters 'went all together to the Globe over the water, where the Lord Chamberlain's men used to play, and were there somewhat before the play began, Sir Charles telling
them that the play would be of Henry the Fourth. . . . thinks it was Sir Chas. Percy who pro-
cured that play to be played at that time. The play was of King Henry the Fourth, and of the
killing of Richard the Second, and played by the Lord Chamberlain's players'; *Calendar of
State Papers, Domestic*, 278, 78 (5: 575).

Carlisle after the deposition. While in Shakespeare it is a sharp but brief moment of counter-discourse in the swift movement that crowns Bolingbroke,[17] it is soon superseded in the play by the unfolding of Richard's new subjectivity, blurring political issues. However, in Hayward's book, Carlisle is given a much longer, more elaborate speech which in many ways is the climax of the narrative, even though it is presented as one point of view among others. After it is reported, Hayward states, 'This speech was diverslie taken, as men were diverslie affected betweene, feare, hope, and shame.'[18] If anything, as John Manning, editor of a 1991 edition of Hayward's work (including a previously unpublished 'Second Part' of the story of Henry IV), argues, Hayward is more critical of Bolingbroke (supposedly a figure for Essex) than of Richard (the figure for Elizabeth), especially in the later portions.[19] Peter Ure, in what is still a valuable discussion of the question, had suggested that what Essex was accused of attending was not necessarily Shakespeare's play but perhaps a reading of Hayward's work or some performance derived from it,[20] and Manning thinks that it was possibly a different play altogether.[21] Leeds Barroll's recent article on the issue also makes an excellent case for the view that it was Hayward's book and not Shakespeare's play that was considered truly seditious and was probably behind most of the allusions to Richard II in the entire discussion of Essex.[22]

At least two critics have speculated that Essex may have used his own players to mount the mysterious play of Richard II, thus explaining Elizabeth's reference to a 'tragedy . . . played 4otie times in open streets and houses'. Following a family tradition, Essex was patron of a troupe of players (the Earl of Essex's Men) whose performances in provincial towns were occasionally recorded from 1581 to 1596.[23] There is no conclusive

[17] *King Richard II*, 4.1.105–40, The *Norton Shakespeare*, ed. Stephen Greenblatt et al. (New York: Norton, 1997); subsequent quotations from Shakespeare are from the same edn.
[18] Hayward, *The First and Second Parts of John Hayward's 'The Life and Raigne of King Henrie IIII'*, 149.
[19] Manning, introduction, 31–41.
[20] See also Ure, introduction, p. lxi.
[21] Manning, introduction, 21–2.
[22] Barroll, 'A New History for Shakespeare and his Time', 441–54. See also Louis Montrose, *The Purpose of Playing: Shakespeare and the Cultural Politics of the Elizabethan Theatre* (Chicago: University of Chicago Press, 1996), 92–3, for another argument that Hayward's work is implicitly Machiavellian (and Tacitean) and was more controversial than Shakespeare's play.
[23] See Paul Whitfield White, *Theatre and Reformation* (Cambridge: Cambridge University Press, 1993), and Scott McMillin and Sally-Beth MacLean, *The Queen's Men and their Plays* (Cambridge: Cambridge University Press, 1998). My thanks to Andrew Gurr for alerting me to these two works.

evidence either way, but such a theory also might explain why Shakespeare's troupe the Chamberlain's Men seems to have attracted little if any official displeasure for its role in mounting a production of a play of Richard II the night before the uprising.[24]

In any case it is clear that Hayward's work post-dates Shakespeare's, and Shakespeare's play is in no sense a straightforward dramatization of Hayward's. Under detailed questioning in the Tower, Hayward cited previous English historians as his sources—Hall, Vergil, and others—and steadfastly maintained his innocence of any contemporary political meaning beyond the most general. He never mentioned Shakespeare's play. Francis Bacon, whose own intellectual project of organizing knowledge for use-value is clearly compatible with Hayward's Tacitean aims, defended the book to Elizabeth, saying that its crime was not treason but theft—he alluded to a number of passages in the work that translated Tacitus without acknowledgement.[25] Elizabeth was apparently unpersuaded; the investigation went on, with questions focusing on why Hayward had chosen the deposition of Richard as his unique topic and whether someone else had put him up to it.[26] But an examination of his text tends to bear out Hayward rather than his interrogators. While his account is extremely pointed in its analysis of why Richard II lost his political base and then his title, and in that sense could be construed as critical of Richard/Elizabeth, it is, as Manning argued, even more critical of Bolingbroke's claim to the throne, treating it specifically as specious and pointing out that Bolingbroke changed the basis of his claim at his coronation. What we can say is that after the Essex rebellion, for Elizabeth and her supporters, these distinctions became meaningless, and perhaps that is the final word on a subject destined to be ever shrouded in lack of precise information.[27] In Elizabeth's remarks to William Lambarde, as in the proclamation cited previously, the story presented by Shakespeare six years previously in *Richard II* of a Machiavellian plotter overthrowing a

---

[24] In response to my query, Andrew Gurr expressed doubt that Essex's Men could have played such a role. The fact that they never performed at court, despite their patron's high standing and with the precedent of numerous performances there by Leicester's Men, suggests to him that they were more ephemeral than several of the other provincial groups.

[25] Manning, introduction, 2.

[26] Ibid. 31.

[27] Cf. Montrose, *The Purpose of Playing*, 72. After discussing the use of Hayward's book as evidence in the Essex trial and Elizabeth's cryptic references to multiple playings of a play of Richard II, Montrose writes: 'Nevertheless, the two anecdotes constitute evidence suggesting that *any* public representation in late Elizabethan London of the dethronement and murder of King Richard II would have been politically volatile and would have stirred strong topical interest.'

sitting monarch had become a trope for the Essex rebellion which she had survived. Unlike Richard, Elizabeth was a skilled enough Machiavellian herself to have in her service councillors who had kept an eye on Essex's preparations, acted decisively, forced Essex into blunders, and peremptorily ended his threat.

As will become clear below in Chapter 5, I believe that the claims made around *Richard II* as a political weapon of Essex's political faction are actually much more applicable to *Henry V*. However, *Richard II* itself, we will see, is a thoroughly Machiavellian document that is perhaps at least remotely connected with the Essex faction; it probably became so several years after its composition, however. It may have been among the stimuli which shaped the imagination of Essex to think he might succeed in over-throwing the Queen, but this is an idea impossible to verify.

Two of the most interesting recent discussions of possible links between Shakespeare's plays and Essex's career have focused on the sensational events of February 1601, when the Earl, having returned from his disappointing campaign in Ireland to confront the ageing Queen Elizabeth and having been placed under house arrest, organized his ill-conceived armed march through the streets of London toward Whitehall aimed at least at forcing the Queen to restore his liberty and condemn his enemies—and probably, as prosecutors believed, to depose the Queen and establish Essex as monarch. Eric Mallin (rightly in my view) found parallels between the Essex rebellion and the Shakespearian play written in the immediate aftermath of the rebellion, *Troilus and Cressida*. Mallin suggests that the dark, even nihilistic tenor of *Troilus and Cressida* is an outcome linked with the sudden defeat of a figure with whose fortunes Shakespeare was publicly linked (through the allusion to Essex in *Henry V* and his earlier dedications of poems to the Earl of Southampton, Essex's chief confederate).[28] In another article on Essex and Shakespeare, Karin S. Coddon found significant parallels between Essex's last years and Hamlet's complex flirtations with madness in a play pitting a young prince against a reigning monarch.[29] Coddon tries to avoid earlier positivist scholarship's hypothesis that the character Hamlet is 'modelled' on Essex (there are of course many uncertainties as to *Hamlet*'s date of

---

[28] Eric S. Mallin, 'Emulous Factions and the Collapse of Chivalry: *Troilus and Cressida*', *Representations*, 29 (Winter 1990), 145–79; later incorporated in revised form in Eric Mallin, *Inscribing the Time: Shakespeare and the End of Elizabethan England* (Berkeley and Los Angeles: University of California Press, 1996).

[29] Karin S. Coddon, ' "Suche Strange Desygns": Madness, Subjectivity, and Treason in *Hamlet* and Elizabethan Culture', *Renaissance Drama: New Series*, 20 (1989), 51–75; repr. in William Shakespeare, *Hamlet*, ed. Susanne L. Wofford (Boston: Bedford, 1994), 380–402.

composition, for one thing); she prefers instead to see the connection as 'a reciprocity more complex than a mere one-to-one correspondence between history and fictions' and positing a parallel drawing on common cultural materials around madness, identity, and treason instead.[30]

Like Mallin, Coddon, and any number of earlier scholars, I believe that the new tone and the new approach to the themes of power and subjectivity evidenced in *Hamlet* (to be discussed in the Conclusion) and in *Troilus and Cressida* and subsequent Jacobean tragedies (discussed in *Shakespeare's Universal Wolf*) resulted at least in part from the impact on Shakespeare's view of politics of Essex's downfall and execution. Like a somewhat smaller group, including recent critics such as Louis Montrose, Graham Holderness, and Annabel Patterson, I think that it is likely that the treatment of power and subjectivity in the plays of the *Henriad* is also connected to the fortunes of Essex in his heroic phase,[31] and in any case the parallels between the thematics of Shakespeare's *Henriad* and the rhetoric and practice of Machiavellian power in the Essex faction constitute a significant homology between court and theatre, regardless of how direct the connections were. Certainly, simply as a matter of chronology, the period I am terming a Shakespearian Machiavellian moment coincides with Essex's glory years, and the two, as I have indicated, are very probably linked.

However, while there is only sketchy, inconclusive evidence of a direct connection between Shakespeare and the Essex faction, the extraordinary new scholarship on the 'history of reading' pioneered by Lisa Jardine, Anthony Grafton, William Sherman, and Kevin Sharpe gives us a clear window into the Machiavellian world views of key political advisers in the late Elizabethan (and beyond), and this is a world with which the London theatres continually interacted. It is also one which has left a much richer set of archives allowing us access to its thinking. Francis Bacon, for example, is a key case in point.

At Essex's trial, Bacon became one of the sponsors of the apparent strategy of associating Essex with Machiavelli. Rising to speak immediately after an intervention by Robert Cecil, Bacon declared, according to a contemporaneous account, 'that he had never seen such favour, so many digressions, such delivering of evidence by fractions, and so silly a defence

[30] Codden, '"Such Strange Designs"', 381–2.

[31] J. Dover Wilson, *The Essential Shakespeare: A Bibliographical Adventure* (Cambridge: Cambridge University Press, 1932); Campbell, *Shakespeare's 'Histories'*; Graham Holderness, *Shakespeare's History* (New York: St Martin's Press, 1985), 131–44; Annabel Patterson, *Shakespeare and the Popular Voice* (Oxford: Basil Blackwell, 1989), 71–92; and Montrose, *The Purpose of Playing*, 76–98.

of such great and notorious treasons. Further, to prepare matter and give fire at once was one of Machiavel's precepts.'[32] Bacon was in an excellent if precarious position to make this assertion, since his own voluminous writings demonstrate that he was himself a careful student of Machiavelli. Machiavelli was one of a number of humanist and classical writers Bacon liked to cite to illustrate his points in both *The Advancement of Learning* and the *Essays*, and references show Bacon to have been well acquainted at least with *The Prince*, *The Discourses*, and *The Art of War*. He admires Machiavelli for his keen observations and his example in showing how to create useful knowledge from history by writing of concrete instances and problems. But Bacon is careful on more than one occasion to criticize Machiavelli for failure to make necessary moral distinctions and faults him for relying on the appearance rather than the reality of virtue. In perhaps the most telling of several short passages by Bacon touching on Machiavelli, he praised Machiavelli in *The Advancement of Learning* for providing us with a crucial form of knowledge, 'so that we are much beholden to Machiavel and others, that write what men do and not what they ought to do'.[33] Thus, he writes, as Milton would in *Areopagitica*, we can only combat evil by knowledge of it, and Machiavelli shows us evil. There is an interesting equivocation in this last claim, representative of Bacon's generally mixed attitude toward Machiavelli: we are never quite certain in Bacon's discussion whether Machiavelli is seen as evil's portrayer or its embodiment. Machiavelli can be for Bacon in one of the *Essays* 'one of the doctors of Italy, Nicolas Machiavel',[34] while in another he is chidden in an otherwise positive context for his 'evil-favoured instance'.[35]

Bacon's interest in Machiavelli was a seminal influence on one of the most explicitly Machiavellian thinkers of the next generation, whose works have recently been explored by historian Kevin Sharpe. The materials studied by Sharpe were first thought to have been prepared for Francis Bacon in the early Stuart period by his steward William Tothill, but in fact they are later and are essentially the commonplace books and papers of Sir William Drake (1607–69), grandson of Bacon's steward

---

[32] Quoted in G. B. Harrison, *The Elizabethan Journals: Being a Record of Those Things Most Talked of During the Years 1591–1603* (Ann Arbor: University of Michigan Press, 1955), iii. 159.

[33] Francis Bacon, *The Advancement of Learning*, bk. 2 in *Francis Bacon* ed. Vickers, (Oxford: Clarendon, 1996), 254.

[34] Francis Bacon, *Essays or Counsels, Civil and Moral* (1625), in *Francis Bacon*, ed. Vickers, 363.

[35] Bacon, *Essays*, in *Francis Bacon*, ed. Vickers, 418.

Tothill.[36] In Sharpe's studies this extensive set of writings is prime material toward furthering a history of reading in the early modern, building on the work of Antony Grafton and Lisa Jardine. Sharpe's conclusion is that Drake was an ardent admirer of the works of Niccolò Machiavelli, the Roman and Florentine historians he drew from, and Francis Bacon (whom his grandfather had served). He attempted repeatedly, even obsessively, to apply Machiavellian realpolitik both to his personal and political life: 'Consider exactly when plain dealing and when dissimulation is necessary, likewise when virtue when vice,' he wrote.[37] He repeatedly returned to several of Machiavelli's works as well as an extensive library of other classical and humanist sources, all, as Sharpe emphasizes, in the hopes of producing marketable advice for political practitioners, including himself.

Such familiarity with Machiavelli extended beyond Bacon's and Essex's extensive networks of 'intelligencers' and advisers. Victoria Kahn's recent reinvestigation of Machiavelli's influence in late Renaissance England shows how central works of Sir Walter Ralegh—one of Essex's rivals—as well as those of Bacon are permeated with Machiavellian approaches.[38] Kahn wrote that 'the Essex circle was a conduit of Machiavelli's ideas, as well as of Tacitism and Neostoicism, in the late sixteenth century'.[39] And the chief warrant for this is an essay by historian Blair Worden which defines the Machiavellianism of Essex's faction as consisting principally in an immersion in the thought and precepts of the great Roman historian Tacitus, one of Machiavelli's favourite sources, credited by many with having taught the Florentine much about power and its uses.[40] It was probably this reputation for favouring Tacitus, in fact, that led to John Hayward's ill-advised decision to dedicate his *Life and Raigne of King Henrie IIII* to Essex; Hayward's work, as Bacon recognized, was clearly a Tacitean history.

Worden's argument is an intricate one and perhaps less the 'smoking gun' in regard to the Essex faction's Machiavellianism than Kahn implies, but it certainly is suggestive. Worden believes that an important source for the 'classical republicanism' that Pocock and a number of other relatively

[36] Kevin Sharpe, *Reading Revolutions: The Politics of Reading in Early Modern England* (New Haven: Yale University Press, 2000), 71–3.

[37] Sir William Drake, Odgden MSS, University College London 7/7, fo. 89; quoted in Sharpe, *Reading Revolutions*, 95.

[38] Kahn, *Machiavellian Rhetoric*, 115.

[39] Ibid. 106.

[40] Blair Worden, 'Classical Republicanism and the Puritan Revolution', in Hugh Lloyd-Jones, Valerie Pearl, and Blair Worden (eds.), *History and Imagination: Essays in Honor of H. R. Trevor-Roper* (New York: Holmes & Meier, 1981), 182–200.

recent writers on the subject have familiarized us with in the Civil War era derived from family traditions of three central Puritan republicans, all of whom descended from Sidney or associated members of the Dudley faction whose leadership Essex assumed in the 1590s. The 'Machiavellian-ism' involved here is clearly that of Machiavelli the republican author of *The Discourses* rather than Machiavelli the pragmatic monarchist author of *The Prince*. But there seems in fact to be warrant for the idea that prominent members of the Essex faction, from its days under Dudley and Sidney, were admirers of Machiavellian precepts and that in recruiting the Bacon brothers to his service Essex reinforced such a philosophy. If we add to this Essex's employment of the extraordinary Antonio Perez, former Secretary of State to King Philip II of Spain, who fled arrest in Spain and arrived in England in 1593, where he worked at Essex House in Essex's *de facto* intelligence service, we see another strong connection with philo-sophical Machiavellianism and Tacitism in Essex's faction, since Perez was a well-known exponent of these related political philosophies.[41] As mentioned, Hayward had dedicated his work to Essex; Essex objected, but, as his accusers later noted, only after the work had sold several hundred copies. Louis Montrose argued that Essex probably encouraged the work and subscribed to its philosophy, citing connections between Essex's secretary Henry Cuffe and the English translator of Tacitus, Sir Henry Savile, Warden of Merton College, Oxford.[42] Cuffe was later singled out by Essex as an instigator of his rebellion, and Savile was restrained by the Privy Council in the repression that followed.

Essex thus employed central advisers who admired and made use of Machiavellian concepts and rhetoric, and he carried out what was arguably the most purely Machiavellian political act of the Elizabethan era in his failed coup attempt. In a heated letter written to Lord Keeper Egerton in the depressed months leading up to the rebellion, Essex had said, in justifying his reaction to an affront to him by the Queen (she had boxed his ears):

Nay more, when the vilest of all indignities are done unto me, doth religion enforce me to sue? or doth God require it? Is it impiety not to do it? What, cannot princes err? cannot subjects receive wrong? Is an earthly power or authority

---

[41] Gustav Ungerer, *A Spaniard in Elizabethan England: The Correspondence of Antonio Perez's Exile*, 2 vols. (London: Tamesis Books, 1974–6); Worden, 'Classical Republicanism', 186–8; Kahn, *Machiavellian Rhetoric*, 106; MacCaffrey, *Elizabeth I*, 480–2.

[42] Montrose, *The Purpose of Playing*, 68–70 and 89–93. Montrose's principal source on Hayward's Tacitean connections is David Womersley, 'Sir Henry Savile's Translation of Tacitus and the Political Interpretation of Elizabethan Texts', *Review of English Studies*, NS 42 (1991), 313–42.

infinite? Pardon me, pardon me, my good Lord, I can never subscribe to these principles.[43]

This last was a heated outburst that was possibly within the orthodoxy of the doctrine of the king's two bodies, but it could be read as suggesting a Machiavellian disdain for fictions of the divine sources of power, and this meaning was not lost on Bacon, who used the letter as evidence in his case against Essex.

As this excursus should indicate, the contradictory attitudes toward Machiavelli which still mark discussions of his philosophy in our own day were already evident in sixteenth-century England. On the one hand, he was a potent enough symbol of political cunning and violence that he served the young Shakespeare as a touchstone against which to test the depravity of Richard of Gloucester in *3 Henry VI*:

> I can add colours to the chameleon,
> Change shapes with Proteus for advantages,
> And set the murderous Machiavel to school. (3.2.191–3)

However, as we have seen, this condemnatory attitude to Machiavellian ideas was by no means universal in the period. And I believe the shifts in the depiction of power from the first historical tetralogy to that of the plays of 1595 to 1600 indicate that in the later period Shakespeare had absorbed something of a political insider's more positive attitude toward Machiavelli, at least in one 'layer' of his complex, often dialogic representations of issues of power and ideology.

Because the Machiavellian is itself a complex concept, open to opposing interpretations, a certain ambiguity necessarily exists in its meaning and connotations. The sixteenth-century stage image of Machiavelli as a proponent of political deception and power for power's sake persists today, and for most readers the term 'Machiavellian' still carries negative connotations associated with this conception of him. Against this reductive (but not simply dismissible) image, humanist readers in contemporary England and elsewhere, along with the scholarship of our own day, pose another, more complex Machiavelli: a figure who founded modern political discourse as such, and therefore one better seen as a definer of moral dilemmas than as an advocate of unabashed political evil. The work most crucial to this broader view of Machiavelli is not *The Prince*, but the longer, explicitly republican work *The Discourses on the First Ten Books of Titus Livius*. In *The Discourses* Machiavelli reveals himself to be a passionate proponent of republican liberty, though at the same time an

---

[43] Quoted in Smith, *Treason in Tudor England*, 222.

exceedingly hard-headed, pessimistic historian-philosopher. He often opines that the societies of his day have been corrupted by tyranny and historical Christianity and are unlikely candidates for any revival of ancient freedoms. *The Discourses* provides a larger, more value-laden political philosophy than *The Prince* by itself, but it shares with the more famous work that incisive, critical-minded approach to politics current and past which describes (as Bacon put it) 'what men do and not what they ought to do'. Machiavelli's new discursivity is one of relentless secularity, a removal of divine Providence from the historical stage in favour of all-too-human actors motivated by self-interest and the logic of power. Machiavellian politics are based in the workings of value-free, instru-mentalist rationality and a secular, but not completely value-free, humanistic attitude toward politics. Machiavelli, as I will describe in Chapter 2, is seldom simply or absolutely amoral or instrumentalist. His writings encompass actions and attitudes about which he often makes complex moral judgements, and for an active reader of Machiavelli, these judgements themselves are resistant to either blanket moral condemna-tions or blanket moral exonerations.

How Shakespeare Used Machiavelli

One of the most venerable but discontinuous traditions of Shakespeare studies has been the view that Machiavellian ideas were a prime ingredient in the Elizabethan theatre, particularly for Marlowe and Shakespeare,[44] and this is a point of view which has been revived in recent years.[45] Here, as

[44] Edward Meyer, *Machiavelli and the Elizabethan Drama* (Weimar: Literarhistorische Forschungen, 1897), is one of the earliest relevant discussions, arguing that *The Prince* was probably known by Shakespeare and other Elizabethan-Jacobean dramatists more through Gentillet's demonizing *Contre-Machiavel* than through direct acquaintance. However, Mario Praz, 'The Politic Brain: Machiavelli and the Elizabethans' (1928), in *The Flaming Heart: Essays on Crashaw, Machiavelli, and Other Studies in the Relations between Italian and English Literature from Chaucer to T. S. Eliot* (Garden City, NY: Doubleday, 1958), 90–145, found a widespread first-hand knowledge of Machiavelli in England although he thought that a Machiavellian element within Cinthio's Italian version of Senecan tragedy influenced the dramatists. In a later influential study Campbell, *Shakespeare's 'Histories'*, 321–6, also argued for a popular first-hand acquaintance with Machiavelli's *Prince* in Elizabethan England, and this view was supported in detail by Felix Raab, *The English Face of Machiavelli: A Changing Interpretation, 1500–1700* (London: Routledge, 1964), 30–76. More recent scholarship , as I indicate in the text, has tended to follow this view. See also Leslie Freeman, 'Shakespeare's Kings and Machiavelli's Prince', in Anne Paolucci (ed.), *Shakespeare Encomium* (New York: The City College, 1964), 25–43, and Barbara J. Baines, 'Kingship of the Silent King: A Study of Shakespeare's Bolingbroke', *English Studies*, 61 (Feb. 1980), 24–36.

[45] The long reign of the Providential interpretation of the histories put forward by E. M. W. Tillyard, *Shakespeare's History Plays* (1944; repr. New York: Macmillan, 1946),

indicated, I argue that Shakespeare's plays indeed display a multivalent complex influence of and reaction to Machiavellian themes—and that they go beyond the logic of *The Prince* to explore the cultural crisis of meaning which its logic creates. It is from such a Machiavellian crisis, portrayed in *Richard II*, that perhaps Shakespeare's first consistent representation of what I will call modern subjectivity is formed. And this connection is not of merely antiquarian interest. The new Renaissance emphasis on individual subjectivity has long been identified as one of the most crucial components of emerging modernity in the era, and these issues are key to understanding Shakespeare's complex relation to a modernity which continues into the twenty-first century.[46] Put succinctly, my argument here is that Shakespeare's first historical tetralogy, along with other plays written in the earlier 1590s, makes use of the 'evil' or lurid image of Machiavelli which had already been pioneered on the stage by Christopher Marlowe, in tandem with an implied Providential view of history that ultimately 'contains' the Machiavellian. But in the plays of 1595–1600, beginning with *Richard II*, Shakespeare's use of Machiavelli undergoes a sea-change, and the plays of the second historical tetralogy in particular seem to become intertextual with the more complex, secular

which dominated discussion from 1944 until about 1970, marginalized views of the histories as conceptually based in Machiavellian ideas. Instead, the Machiavellian strand of the plays tended to be read as offensive material which the plays were representing in order to condemn it. See particularly for this view Irving Ribner, 'Bolingbroke, a True Machiavellian', *Modern Language Quarterly*, 9/2 (June 1948), 177–84; Ribner sees the Machiavellian content of the play as embodied by Bolingbroke, and he assumes that the audience would understand his Machiavellian actions as reason to condemn him and his usurpation. As Tillyard's views have receded in influence, arguments for the centrality in the histories of Machiavellian concepts have grown. Jan Kott's much discussed *Shakespeare our Contemporary* (New York: Doubleday, 1966) sees the framework for virtually all of Shakespeare's histories and tragedies as (in effect) Machiavellian, although he does not use the term. Norman Rabkin, *Shakespeare and the Common Understanding* (New York: The Free Press, 1967), 80–149, to which I return below, also emphasized a Machiavellian strand in the histories. And Michael Manheim, *The Weak King Dilemma in the Shakespearian History Play* (Syracuse, NY: Syracuse University Press, 1973), argued that Machiavellianism is a strong current in the second historical tetralogy and that a positive version of it is mastered by Henry V. More recently the centrality of Machiavellian ideas in the histories has been demonstrated by Phyllis Rackin, *Stages of History: Shakespeare's English Chronicles* (Ithaca, NY: Cornell University Press, 1990), who charts a 'Renaissance transition from providential to machiavellian accounts of historical causation' which in turn anticipates 'the twentieth-century movement from providential to Machiavellian interpretations of Shakespeare's history plays' (p. x). For a helpful discussion of this critical controversy and a more complete bibliography on proponents of a Machiavellian framework in Shakespeare's histories, see Rackin, *Stages of History*, 40–6.

[46] See the essays collected in Hugh Grady (ed.), *Shakespeare and Modernity: From Early Modern to Millennium* (London: Routledge, 2000), for a multifaceted discussion of this issue and many of its ramifications.

Machiavelli known to readers, in Shakespeare's day and our own, willing to accept the terms of Machiavelli's new discursivity.

In these plays of 1595–1600, to be sure, Machiavellian ideas are not simply passively accepted; rather, they constitute a problematic for Shakespeare, a set of political suppositions which create problems of their own, a set of ideas probed, questioned, and searchingly critiqued, but never dismissed or simply condemned. In its complexity, then, if not in every other particular, the Shakespearian 'Machiavellian moment' of 1595–1600 is similar to the one classically described by J. G. A. Pocock:

'The Machiavellian moment' is a phrase to be interpreted in two ways. In the first place, it denotes the moment, and the manner, in which Machiavellian thought made its appearance. . . . In the second place, 'the Machiavellian moment' denotes the problem itself. It is a name for the moment in conceptualized time in which the republic was seen as confronting its own temporal finitude.[47]

Pocock goes on to chart the development of a republican discourse in the age of absolutism and sees its flowering in the English Civil War and the American federalist period. His Machiavelli is overwhelmingly that of the republican *Discourses* rather than the monarchical *The Prince*. Shakespeare's, at least in the plays examined here, is very much the opposite, and even in the plays set in republican Rome or Athens, there is little trace of Machiavelli's adulatory attitude toward republican institutions and liberties. Shakespeare in his republican plays *Julius Caesar, Coriolanus, Antony and Cleopatra*, and *Timon of Athens* seems more attracted to the problematics of one particular facet of Machiavelli's complex discussion of classical politics, that of the great man in a popular political context, so that even when he is exploring republican politics, he does so largely outside that republican discourse which for Pocock constituted the 'Machiavellian moment' ancestral to modern Western political theory. But of course Pocock's now classic work, impressive and eye-opening as it is, hardly exhausts the array of meanings of the Machiavellian. Shakespeare may or may not have known Machiavelli's *The Discourses*—I suspect he did not—but he could not have been a man of the theatre in his time without knowing other aspects of Machiavellian thought. Specifically, the problematic at the centre of *The Prince*, the problematic of the eruption of instrumental reason into political discourse, is central to the *Henriad* and *Hamlet*. I am concentrating for these plays, then, on the Machiavelli of *The Prince* rather than his complexly intertextual cousin, the Machiavelli of *The Discourses*. But even though this distinction between *The Discourses*

[47] J. G. A. Pocock, *The Machiavellian Moment: Florentine Political Thought and the Atlantic Republican Tradition* (Princeton: Princeton University Press, 1975), pp. vii–viii.

and *The Prince* is meaningful and useful, it can also be overstated, since, as I suggested, there is a large area of intertextuality between the two, and instrumental reason is continually on display in *The Discourses*, if never in so pure a form as in *The Prince*. Shakespeare's treatment of Machiavellian themes is itself complex and layered so that the resulting texts are resistant to succinct formulas as they register a continually shifting configuration of themes, attitudes, and discourses. At the same time, however, it is possible to trace a trajectory and a thematic development.

To summarize, then, we can identify several different kinds of Machiavellian influence in the various phases of Shakespeare's career. In the earliest work he is clearly working within a popular discourse of the Machiavellian which he inherited from Kyd and Marlowe. This is the kind of Machiavellianism defined in E. E. Stoll's analysis of the dramatic figure of the machiavel, a character who promulgates a false façade of virtue covering over an interiority of malevolent power-seeking.[48] Characters like La Pucelle and Richard of Gloucester/Richard III are clearly Machiavellian characters of the same mettle as, say, Kyd's Balthazar or Marlowe's Barabas. It is important to note that the sense in which these characters and their plays are Machiavellian is a sense which implies a condemnation of the doctrine with which the character is associated. Such plays are constructed to generate successive *frissons* of horror in an audience privileged to be aware of each machiavel's hypocritical exterior and diabolic interiority, and such a thematization of Machiavellianism ultimately works to discredit Machiavelli, a certain fascinating allure notwithstanding.

The second kind of Machiavellianism discernible in Shakespeare's plays—it will define the principal terrain explored in this book—emerges in the plays of the *Henriad* as a kind of implied intellectual framework or discourse. This kind is a much less lurid Machiavellianism, although it

[48] This character-type was defined early and influentially in Shakespeare studies—arguably as a central means of domesticating and regularizing what is potentially among the most scandalous qualities of Elizabethan/Jacobean drama: its invitation to the audience to revel vicariously in the transgressive pleasures of a Tamburlaine, Richard III, or Edmund. Perhaps the earliest such attempt was Meyer, *Machiavelli and the Elizabethan Drama* (1897). The idea of the machiavel was important to E. E. Stoll's influential project of defining a series of Elizabethan stage conventions to guide our interpretations of cruxes in Shakespeare—see his *Shakespeare Studies: Historical and Comparative in Method* (New York: Stechert, 1942), 345–6. More recently Katharine Eisaman Maus, *Inwardness and Theater in the English Renaissance* (Chicago: University of Chicago Press, 1995), 35–71, discussed stage machiavels as embodying a secret inwardness which is crucial to understanding Elizabethan attitudes toward interiority. However, I see the machiavel as basically anti-subjective (in the sense that the hidden inwardness is reducible to autotelic power) and thus take an almost opposite tack from Maus.

does not repress the 'hard' doctrines of *The Prince*. But it is one which the plays often explore as an attractive and explanatory philosophy of history and politics: Machiavellianism from the inside, as it were, a Machiavellianism at times encompassing a critical rationality pioneered in Machiavelli's incisive analyses in both *The Discourses* and of *The Prince* but pointedly aware of the use of deception, force, and violence in politics. In what follows, I will use the term 'Machiavellian' principally to characterize this set of ideas and this phase of Shakespeare's career. This Machiavellian moment of Shakespeare's seems to come to a halt in the three most famous Jacobean tragedies, and everything happens as if the Essex rebellion and its failure marked a turning point, registered dramatically in *Troilus and Cressida* and *Hamlet*. But in *King Lear*, *Othello*, and *Macbeth*, the instru- mental reason which seemed a neutral instrument for Prince Hal and Prince Hamlet becomes itself an agent of corruption and destruction, with the result that these plays are in an important sense centrally anti-Machiavellian (even if they could be seen also as magnifying the darkest passages of *The Discourses* about the corrupting properties of tyranny). However, Shakespeare does not leave the matter here but comes back to it again in two late Roman tragedies, *Coriolanus* and *Antony and Cleopatra*, and these two in turn can be linked with the late romances and *Timon of Athens* to constitute a final phase of Shakespearian involvement with the themes of Machiavelli. In these last, world-weary plays, political power is neither an invigorating positive force nor a completely evil destroyer of human society; rather it is amoral and merely human. In these plays power creates historical change through tragedy, but the changes are not neces-sarily the most central ones in human experience and value, their tragic consequences partially offset by the processes of nature and human generation. But this development constitutes a subject with complexities that cannot adequately be treated here. There are more than enough com-plexities within the plays I have chosen, as we will see.

The Machiavellian in the Henriad

The four plays of the *Henriad* themselves present multiple attitudes toward Machiavellianism. *Richard II* establishes Shakespeare's new atti-tude toward Machiavelli in its treatment of the skilled politician Boling-broke, which departs significantly from the valences established in the earlier treatment of those skilful manipulators Aaron of *Titus Andronicus* or Richard III. The latter two are explicit villains and agents of evil, with a subversive but contained allure; the former is much more ambiguous, more impersonal, and ultimately much more successful. Thus *Richard II* is Machiavellian in two ways that *Richard III* and *Titus Andronicus* are not: first, it implies a secular, realpolitik, non-Providential view of power and legitimacy, through its strategic silences and cool depiction of the triumph of political skill over ineptitude; but second, more subtly, the play never condemns Bolingbroke's manipulations in the way the earlier plays or *King Lear* and *Macbeth* later clearly do in regard to their own central machiavels. It instead presents power neutrally, almost technically. In *1 Henry IV*, however, the presentation of power seems to 'tilt' in the treatment of Bolingbroke/Henry IV towards a more critical direction: his court is emotionally cold, his status as king troubled, and the future of his dynasty clouded. In that way, the efficacy of his 'Machiavellianism' in the previous play is undercut. But young Harry, his son, is involved in a complex game of avoiding or postponing the putting on of the mantle of Machiavellian prince while at the same time plotting a Machiavellian ploy of *virtù* which culminates at the end of the *Henry IV* plays in his emerging as a prince in two senses of the word: the dynastic and the Machiavellian. *1 Henry IV*, I will argue, implies a relatively optimistic interpretation of Machiavellian politics, one compatible with a Montaignean cultivation of freedom, subjectivity, and pleasure. Instead of being repudiated, it seems, Machiavellianism is enlarged.

Another, more decisive tilt, however, occurs in the closely connected sequel to *1 Henry IV*. *Henry IV, Part 2* treats the story of the emergence of Prince Hal as a hero-king in considerably darker tones than had *Part 1*, and the effects of this shift are complex in terms of what is implied about Machiavelli. On the one hand the efficacy of Machiavellian politics is affirmed as strongly as it had been in *Richard II*: manoeuvre and deception work, and Hal's plan to emerge from the clouds of the tavern life succeeds stunningly—but of course at the cost of a heavy-handed repression of Doll Tearsheet, Pistol, and Falstaff. The balance that had been obtained at the end of *Part 1* is irrevocably lost, and the heroicizing rhetoric surrounding the newly crowned Henry V at the play's end is undercut by the banishment of the tavern-dwellers. Thus the Machiavellian politics affirmed at a pragmatic level seems to be negated at an emotional one, as one of the most familiar objections to Machiavelli's logic—that the end is achieved only by dubious means—surfaces for the audience strongly at the ambivalent end of this play. And this highly bifurcated split in attitudes is only intensified in *Henry V*'s strange combination of layers glorifying the hero-king with others condemning him.

Thus these last two plays are still part of this Shakespearian

Machiavellian moment because they both affirm the efficacy of Machiavellian politics in a way different from what came before and what would
come after in the Jacobean tragedies. But they both begin to construct a
discourse of anti-Machiavellianism as an implied if muted moral dissent
from what is seen as politically efficacious nevertheless. Finally, *Hamlet*
will move this trajectory one decisive step further and reveal Machiavellianism as self-destructive if, perhaps, an unavoidable outcome of
power politics.

Montaignean Resistances to Power in the Henriad

Thus far my argument, with its emphasis on power and discursivity,
might appear to be a variation on familiar themes of new historicism and
cultural materialism, and of course in some ways it is. The reorientation to
political issues which these new critical paradigms accomplished was a
productive one in my view. The main problem with the first wave of
Shakespearian political criticism, as my Introduction suggests, was not in
its pursuit of issues of power and oppression long neglected in previous
critical paradigms. Rather, the main problem was that in reacting against
the earlier paradigms, the new methods tended to abandon rather than to
critique such key concepts of the older paradigms as subjectivity and the
aesthetic. In the long run, this critical abdication constitutes a serious
weakness, but one which, as I indicated in the Introduction, is already
being redressed by a number of different critics. One important way into
the problems left unresolved in the first generation of political criticism of
Shakespeare is to trace how Shakespeare's 'Machiavellian' treatment of
power leads him into new concepts of subjectivity and identity which are
'Montaignean' in much the same way that the analysis of power is
'Machiavellian'. That is, these concepts display a number of significant
parallels which suggest discursive connections, direct or indirect, with
these two seminal Renaissance writers.

Shakespeare certainly had a direct acquaintance with Montaigne's
Essays by the time of his composition of one of his very last plays, *The
Tempest* (1611), for which he pastiched a passage from one of the most
startling of Montaigne's *Essays*, 'On Cannibals', in the speech on a perfect
commonwealth by Gonzalo.[49] And while no such detailed parallels have

---

[49] The passage can be found in *The Tempest*, 2.1.147–65. The language in the quoted
passage echoes in detail Florio's rendering of Montaigne; see Michel de Montaigne, *The
Essayes of Montaigne*, trans. John Florio (New York: Modern Library, 1933), 164, as is noted in
virtually all academic edns. of the play. The parallel was first noted in the 18th century by
Edward Capell in his *Notes and Various Readings to Shakespeare*, 2 vols. (London: Henry
Hughs, 1779–80), ii. 63.

ever been discovered for other plays, a number of critics over the years have argued for intellectual links between these two, and we at least have the assurance for works composed after 1603 that John Florio's great translation of the complete *Essays* was in print. Additionally, we know that there were some links between Florio and Shakespeare: Florio had been a tutor to Essex's boon companion the Earl of Southampton,[50] and a series of studies since the nineteenth century has argued for both verbal and thematic parallels between Montaigne's *Essays* and several of Shakespeare's plays, most commonly *Hamlet* (1600–1), *Measure for Measure* (1603), *Othello* (1603–4), *King Lear* (1605–6), and *Coriolanus* (1608).[51] As the case of *Hamlet* suggests, the date of publication for Florio's translation (1603) does not necessarily constitute an ironclad boundary for Shakespeare's possible acquaintance with Montaigne. The translation of a manuscript which in modern editions takes up over 1,000 pages was clearly a matter of several years' labour: Florio's biographer Frances Yates believes Florio began work on it in 1598, and there are existing allusions to parts of the manuscript circulating before publication, so that Shakespeare conceivably could have known Florio before publication. And in addition, it is a mistake to think that knowledge of Montaigne in England

[50] Frances A. Yates, *John Florio: The Life of an Italian in Shakespeare's England* (1934; repr. New York: Octagon, 1968), 215–24.

[51] John M. Robertson, *Montaigne and Shakespeare and Other Essays on Cognate Questions*, 2nd edn. (1909; repr. New York: Burt Franklin, 1969), cites two mid-19th-century articles developing a more general comparison of the thought of Montaigne with the character Hamlet (John Sterling, *London and Westminster Review* (July 1838), 321) and with the tragedies *Hamlet*, *Othello*, and *Coriolanus* (Philarète Chasles, *Journal des débats*, 7 Nov. 1846; repr. in *L'Angleterre au seizième siècle*, ed. 1879). Two German scholars took up the question of the relationship between Shakespeare and Montaigne later in the century: G. F. Stedefeld, *Hamlet: ein Tendenzdrama Shakespeares gegen die skeptische und kosmopolitische Weltanschauung des Michel de Montaigne* (Berlin: Gebrüder Paetel, 1871) and Jacob Feis, *Shakespeare and Montaigne* (1884; repr. Geneva: Slatkine, 1970), both of whom felt Shakespeare was critical of Montaignean scepticism. Robertson, who was a self-educated iconoclast now better known for his disintegrating approach to Shakespeare textual studies, wrote on the issue in a series of magazine articles (1896) which he later developed into two editions (1st edn. 1897) of the book cited above; Robertson argued for a profound, philosophical influence of Montaigne on Shakespeare, using both verbal and thematic parallels in support of his thesis. George Coffin Taylor, *Shakespeare's Debt to Montaigne* (Cambridge, Mass.: Harvard University Press, 1925), is perhaps the most systematic of studies arguing for a Montaignean influence on Shakespeare as evidenced by verbal parallels. But this general method was criticized by several scholars, as noted below in n. 57, and no consensus was ever reached. See Robert Ellrodt, 'Self-Consciousness in Montaigne and Shakespeare', *Shakespeare Survey*, 28 (1975), 37–50, for a scrupulous accounting of the evidence. At the 2001 World Shakespeare Conference in Valencia, Spain, Ellrodt updated his argument for a significant Montaignean influence on Shakespeare in a plenary presentation, and new interest in this topic was evidenced by a seminar on Montaigne and Shakespeare in which most participants assumed a significant parallel.

began only with Florio's work. Such knowledge can be dated back as early as 1591, when the elder brother of Francis Bacon, Sir Anthony Bacon—a key adviser to Essex in the period investigated here—returned from twelve years in France and a personal acquaintance with Montaigne.[52] The first version of Francis Bacon's *Essays*—modelled in many ways on Montaigne's—appeared in 1597. As it happens, we know that for some time before and after 1604 Shakespeare was lodging with the French Huguenot refugees the Mountjoys,[53] and Montaigne, despite his Catholicism, was a favourite of many Huguenots, who appreciated his relative religious toleration. And finally, as the French scenes in *Henry V* demonstrate, Shakespeare had acquired a passable knowledge of the French language and conceivably could have encountered Montaigne in the original.

Again there is much possibility, little certainty when it comes to how much, when, and in what language Shakespeare might have read Montaigne. For the plays under consideration in this book, the case for a direct influence of some sort is not precluded (for *Richard II* and *1 Henry IV* it would depend on Shakespeare's having discovered Montaigne before the probable date Florio began his translation, and for *2 Henry IV*, *Henry V*, and *Hamlet*, it would depend on either pre-Florio acquaintance with the *Essais* or access to Florio's work-in-progress). Accordingly the case is weaker than it is for the plays written after the publication of Florio in 1603, except, perhaps (as previously indicated), for *Hamlet*, for which there are complicating circumstances. If, as is generally thought today, *Hamlet* was performed in 1600–1, it was clearly composed before the publication of Folio's translation—but after 1598, when Florio is thought to have begun work on his manuscript. In addition, the second quarto of *Hamlet* was published in editions dated 1604 and 1605,[54] after the publication of the Florio translation, and one prominent proponent of the case for Montaigne's influence on *Hamlet*, J. M. Robertson, has claimed that verbal and thematic parallels between *Hamlet* and the *Essais* are almost all connected with passages found in the second quarto but not the first one.[55] If, as some scholars think, the second quarto is a revision of an earlier stage version represented by the first, then Robertson's case for claiming that

---

[52] On all this see Serena Jourdan, *The Sparrow and the Flea: The Sense of Providence in Shakespeare and Montaigne* (Salzburg: Institut für Anglistik und Amerikanistik Universität Salzburg, 1983), 3–5.

[53] Samuel Schoenbaum, *Shakespeare's Lives*, new edn. (Oxford: Oxford University Press, 1993), 18; Jourdan, *The Sparrow and the Flea*, 4; Ellrodt, 'Self-Consciousness', 38.

[54] Wells and Taylor, *William Shakespeare*, 396.

[55] Robertson, *Montaigne and Shakespeare*, 161–84.

the second quarto is a revision done under the strong intellectual impetus of Shakespeare's reading of Montaigne is at least plausible. However, the relation of the three received texts of *Hamlet* remains controversial—Wells and Taylor argued that the first quarto is essentially what Greg and Pollard called a 'bad' quarto, one memorially reconstructed and hence corrupted,[56] and Robertson's (and others') case for a direct influence is at best circumstantial and suggestive.[57] In what follows, then, I want to make no assumption concerning Shakespeare's direct acquaintance with Montaigne's texts until *The Tempest*. What I will argue is that the two can be seen to share a common mental framework or discourse which we could call Renaissance scepticism,[58] and, starting at least with *Richard II* (1595), some common ideas about the nature of subjectivity in a Machiavellian world. Here again I am following Foucault's notions that discourses circulate in societies in fluid ways not necessarily dependent on direct, author-to-author contact; or, as an older critical idiom had it, sometimes ideas are 'in the air'. I believe that Shakespeare and Montaigne are linked at least through such an indirect connection, and I want to draw attention to the fundamental ways in which both of these quintessential early modern writers employ shifting viewpoints, critical rationality, and suspicion of final conclusions and system-building.

Thus, I think it is fair to say that linking Shakespeare with Montaigne, as with Machiavelli, was common in earlier times, suppressed during the heyday of the Modernist Shakespeare, and is now being revived within our era's Postmodernist paradigms. However, as common as these

[56] Wells and Taylor, *William Shakespeare*, 396–402.

[57] There is a tradition debunking arguments for direct evidence of Shakespeare's use of Montaigne in his plays virtually as large as its opposite. See for example, Churton Collins, *Studies in Shakespeare* (New York: Dutton, 1904); Elizabeth Hooker, 'The Relation of Shakespeare to Montaigne', *PMLA* 17 (1902), 313–66; Pierre Villey, *Les Sources et l'évolution des Essais de Montaigne*, 2 vols. (Paris: Hachette, 1908); Sidney Lee, *The French Renaissance in England* (New York: Scribner, 1910); and later in two American articles: Alice Harmon, 'How Great was Shakespeare's Debt to Montaigne?', *PMLA* 57 (1942), 988–1008, and Margaret Hodgen, 'Montaigne and Shakespeare Again', *Huntington Library Quarterly*, 16 (1952), 23–42.

[58] I am using 'scepticism' in a very different sense from that of two books by Stanley Cavell, *The Claim of Reason: Wittgenstein, Scepticism, Morality, and Tragedy* (Oxford: Oxford University Press, 1980) and *Disowning Knowledge: In Six Plays of Shakespeare* (Cambridge: Cambridge University Press, 1987): Cavell is talking about Cartesian rather than Montaignean (or what he calls, alluding to the ancient developer of sceptic doctrines, Pyrrhonian) scepticism, and, in terms of values especially, the two are in many ways opposites. The scepticism I see at work in Shakespeare is closer perhaps to that defined by Graham Bradshaw, *Shakespeare's Scepticism* (Ithaca, NY: Cornell University Press, 1987), but Bradshaw also excludes Montaigne from his discussion. My own conception is nearer to that evoked by Lars Engle, '*Measure for Measure* and Modernity: The Problem of the Sceptic's Authority', in Grady (ed.), *Shakespeare and Modernity*, 85–104.

connections have been within Shakespearian criticism, they suggest a problem which has never, I believe, been adequately addressed: how can we conceive of simultaneous and pervasive influence from two such different writers as these within Shakespeare's drama? What is the relation between the instrumental rationality of Machiavelli's *The Prince* and the critical, sceptical rationality of Montaigne?

In *Shakespeare's Universal Wolf*, I identified a dynamic with which Shakespeare experimented over and over, one in which the logic of reified power was represented in contrast to a linked, emerging subjectivity. The concept of power in question, I am arguing here, was a thematic development from Machiavellian concepts. To take perhaps the most powerful example, in *King Lear* reified power was created by a Machiavellian severing of the symbols of political legitimization from the actual exercise of power,[59] an operation that in one stroke emptied the older political ideology of its meaning and created a new realm of nameless, reified power.

Similarly, versions of recognizably 'modern' subjectivity emerged as a kind of counterpoint to reification in characters like Troilus and Cressida, Rosalind, Othello, Desdemona, and Edgar, Cordelia, and the transformed Lear.[60] Such subjectivity was coded as unfettered, aimless, disconnected, and alienated—but also suffused with libido and creative of some of the most remarkable insights, poetry, and dramatic moments of these great plays. This cluster of concepts is remarkably similar to central themes of Montaigne's *Essais*, as we will see in Chapter 3.

As I return to these earlier themes as they appear in a different constellation in a different set of plays here, then, I am suggesting that a useful way to think about this pervasive interaction within Shakespeare's works is that of an encounter between the discourses of Machiavelli and Montaigne. These plays depict kingdoms in the grip of Machiavellian political dynamics, and they depict characters who react to this dynamic through an acute identity crisis and explorations of a newly unfettered subjectivity. The prototype for this aspect of subjectivity, I argue, is the Montaigne of the *Essais*, that retiree from the political-religious nightmare of Renaissance France, that cultivator of an endlessly playful, protean self who attempts a radical regrounding of values in the face of the

---

[59] I discussed this theme in my *Shakespeare's Universal Wolf*, 142–8. See also for a similar description Richard Halpern, *The Poetics of Primitive Accumulation: English Renaissance Culture and the Genealogy of Capital* (Ithaca, NY: Cornell University Press, 1991), 231–4.

[60] This pairing, I hope it is clear, is one of the reasons I insisted, in my discussion of Belsey's *Subject of Tragedy* in the Introduction, on the need to differentiate an interior, libidinized subjectivity from an impersonal, objectifying instrumental rationality, rather than attempt as Belsey did to see each of these as a component of a unitary liberal humanism.

evacuated signifying systems of political and religious legitimacy.[61] We see such a figure, in varying configurations and implied evaluations, in all the characters I named above, but perhaps most clearly in *Lear*'s Edgar. And to draw from the plays to be discussed here, we can define a similar dynamic for three Shakespearian princes, Richard II, Hal, and Hamlet. In the plays in which these three are featured, subjectivity is a crucial element of the dramas. It first emerges as a theme in *Richard II*, finds a new form and development in *1 Henry IV*, and then succumbs to a firm Machiavellian containment in *2 Henry IV* and *Henry V*—only to re-emerge with great intensity again in *Hamlet*. As we will see, subjectivity is dialectically related to power in all of these plays.[62] Shakespeare expresses the logic of an emerging modernity, characterized by fragmented belief systems and instrumentalizing views of the natural and social worlds, by valorizing subjectivity (as, for example, in the second half of *Richard II*). This is a moment which resonated powerfully with both aesthetic Victorians and mainstream Modernists of the mid-twentieth century, a seeming preference for aesthetic interiority over hollow Machiavellianism. Some configuration like this seems to me to be implied in another play from this era in the figure of Brutus in *Julius Caesar*. Brutus, like Richard II, is another politically ineffective man of subjectivity overcome by more cynical and efficacious politicians—but politicians who are not, like Richard III or like the later Iago, Cornwall, Goneril, and Regan, 'monsters of the deep' in any sense, but rather morally ambiguous men who have chosen a different and necessary vocation for which Richard II and Brutus were not really temperamentally fit.

But Prince Harry, Falstaff, and Hotspur in *1 King Henry IV* present us with a quite different configuration of subjectivity and power. They seem to be able, at least in the golden-age conviviality of the play's first half, to have it all—rejecting the cold Machiavellianism of the court of Bolingbroke in power, mobilizing the qualities of unfixed subjectivities for service in the political realm, and forging alliances with the subaltern worlds of female domesticity and plebeian counter-communities. After the Battle of Shrewsbury, Hotspur is dead and Falstaff emerges as an amoral survivor, but the Prince manages to keep all the previous aspects of his complex self in play, 'redeeming' himself (in the words of his much discussed opening soliloquy), but without ever repudiating Falstaff and

---

[61] Cf. Michael Neill, introduction to William Shakespeare, *Antony and Cleopatra*, ed. Michael Neill (Oxford: Oxford University Press, 1994), 82, 85.

[62] For a related point of view, see Camille Wells Slights, 'Slaves and Subjects in *Othello*', *Shakespeare Quarterly*, 48/4 (Winter 1997), 377–90. This article sees the rise of slavery and new forms of 'emerging understandings of selfhood' to be connected, especially in *Othello*.

company along the lines hinted at when he indicated the temporary nature of his sojourn in the tavern world in the lines 'I know you all, and will awhile uphold I The unyoked humour of your idleness.'[63] Thus this play seems to unite what *Richard II* had divided and coded as irreconcilable: the active realm of Machiavellian politics and the withdrawn world of Montaignean subjectivity. Prince Hal and Falstaff, in their role-playing and theatricality, demonstrate instead how the latter can be sent back out into the world in the service of constructive, positive Machiavellian politics. To be sure this play more than hints at both the fragility and problematic ethics of this combination. When Falstaff enters the world as a corrupt captain (rather than remaining a harmless bar-room *miles gloriosus* with an unaccountably important friend), we begin to see the susceptibility of unfixed subjectivity to the (reified) ways of the world. His role changes from that of a carnival Lord of Misrule in a communitarian tavern to an equally libidinal, but now self-serving and corrosive exemplar of the atomistic, Hobbesian logic of warfare and market economics. But Falstaff remains funny and convivial because he himself becomes his own strictest critic, condemning his own actions in a series of brilliant, metadramatic, Brechtian monologues which allow him to remain in solidarity with plebeian portions of the audience even while he demonstrates the anti-plebeian effects of early modern political and economic power.

In *Part 2*, this trajectory of reification, begun in the previous play but checked when Prince Hal manages to be both true prince and true friend in the play's balanced ending, picks up again. In *Part 2* Machiavellian power is no longer one of several elements in a jovial exploration of a rich world of possibilities. In this play subjectivity becomes reified and hence subordinated to power, and the dramatic and poetic themes begin to register regret, nostalgia, and bitterness at this loss. In *Henry V* the darkening is intensified, but, contrary to a long critical tradition, I believe this play revives the theme of subjectivity celebrated in *1 Henry IV* when we catch glimpses of the young King's interiority in the scenes before the battle, and it is an interiority recognizably continuous with that of Prince Hal before the accession. This interiority is, of course, firmly contained and has no effect on the unfolding of Machiavellian power in death and destruction in the play's second half, nor does it really undercut the continuing celebration of Machiavellian power at another level of the play. But of all Shakespeare's plays, this one seems to me the one offering the most obstacles to our understanding of an Elizabethan's audience's

---

[63] *1 Henry IV*, 1.2.173–4.

reactions, which I suppose was as divided and confused as subsequent Shakespearian criticism has been.

A similar confusion, of course, has characterized the critical reaction to the play that was apparently written under the shadow of Essex's disgrace, rebellion, and defeat, but which, like *Henry V*, manages to register simultaneously characteristics of the more Machiavelli-friendly plays which preceded it and the anti-Machiavellian ones that followed in the Jacobean tragic period. However, *Hamlet* shows a radically different orientation to questions of political power from either *2 Henry IV* or *Henry V*: its Montaignean hero, stranded in a realpolitik Machiavellian world, simultaneously explores Machiavellian cunning and a radically unfixed subjectivity in a role that recapitulates elements of Richard II, Brutus, Falstaff, Prince Henry/Henry V—although political success continually eludes this Prince, who is simultaneously too good and not nearly good enough for the world he is condemned to inhabit. *Hamlet* has famously been a play that opens up far more questions than it ever solves, but by avoiding any irrevocable 'fixing' of the Prince's identity (he achieves a kind of inner peace and stability not through fixed identity but by an identification with flux in the form of Providence), and by sparing him the burdens of kingship which eclipsed the protean Hal, Shakespeare's tragic ending of *Hamlet* draws a final circle around his unfixed identity, canonizing it as an icon of an early modern decentred self—and then extracts it from the networks of instrumental power which had entrapped Falstaff and Hal and which threatened to entrap Hamlet in their one-dimensionality. The play's tragic ending, then, while it affirms the inescapability of suffering and death and thereby earns its right to claim a Nietzschean Greek sanity, also idealizes a protean subjectivity which never could adapt to a constricting, Machiavellian world, enshrining Hamlet as literature's supreme hero of subjectivity and setting the precedent for the Jacobean tragic heroes and heroines (and villains and malcontents as well—there is a very fine line between them) who, like Hamlet, display libidinous subjectivities alienated from a reified world. *Hamlet* thus serves as a coda for this investigation of Shakespeare's Machiavellian moment, as the play which at once climaxes and surpasses the problematics of power and subjectivity which had preoccupied Shakespeare over an extraordinary five-year period of dramatic creativity.

The intellectual triad of Machiavelli, Montaigne, and Shakespeare I am examining here has been formed because of their common fascination with discourses of power and subjectivity within the new intellectual milieu of post-traditional modernity which they both inform and are informed by. The works of Niccolò Machiavelli, or their widely disseminated ideas, constituted an intellectual crisis for both Montaigne and Shakespeare that was one of the starting points of their meditations on modern subjectivity. In the confluence of these three celebrated Renaissance authors, then, we can witness a significant episode in the development of intellectual modernity. And in *Richard II*, the confluence of Machiavellian and Montaignean discourses in Shakespeare begins to take shape.

The Discourse of Princes in *Richard II*: From Machiavelli to Montaigne

Richard II was first brought to the stage in or near 1595, six years before Essex's supporters arranged a special production of a play on the deposing of Richard II—almost certainly Shakespeare's—in order to galvanize their spirits for their own ill-fated undertaking. As I indicated in the previous chapter, it is clear that the many allusions to the deposing of Richard II which occurred in the prosecution of Essex and his followers in 1601 were inspired by a widespread discursive connection between Elizabeth and Richard, inadvertently crystallized during the early stages of the Essex crisis by John Hayward's 1599 *The Life and Raigne of King Henrie IIII* rather than Shakespeare's play. To be sure, in 1595 there were already comparisons being made between Richard and Elizabeth, notably in a tract from members of the exiled English Catholic party, *Conference about the Next Succession to the Crowne of Ingland*, written under an alias by the priest Robert Persons. This two-part tract undertook a 'genealogy of all the kings and princes of England from the conquest unto this day, whereby each man's pretence is made more plain',[1] and although the work was most notorious for its conclusion that among the best claims to the throne of England was that of the Infanta of Spain, it also devoted twenty-five pages to arguing that the deposition of a sovereign might be licit under certain conditions, and it took the case of Richard II as a prime example of such a situation. A subtext advocating the overthrow of Elizabeth was not

[1] Quoted in Lily B. Campbell, *Shakespeare's 'Histories': Mirrors of Elizabethan Policy* (San Marino, Calif.: Huntington Library, 1947), 179.

hard to discern in this material, and, to thicken the plot, the tract was dedicated to Robert Devereux, the Earl of Essex, with a hopeful message that Essex might play a decisive role in settling the succession after Elizabeth. Not surprisingly at Elizabeth's court the work was considered treasonable,[2] and Essex reportedly entered into one of his numerous periods of the Queen's disfavour as a result of the dedication to him. But the cloud, like so many others, soon passed, and he resumed his favoured place at court.

Since at least Lily Campbell, however, critics attempting to establish topical connections between *Richard II* and the Essex–Elizabeth struggles have had to concede that while there are hints that the early reception of Shakespeare's play might have been coloured by a Richard–Elizabeth link,[3] no incontrovertible direct evidence for such linkage exists. It is more likely, as I suggested earlier, that *Richard II* influenced Essex than that Essex was in 1595 a 'source' for Shakespeare's play. Essex's insubordinate return from Ireland in 1599 and his subsequent attempt to gain power over Elizabeth without directly deposing her read like bad imitations of Bolingbroke's return from exile and his artful manoeuvring of Richard's abdication. Whatever the play of Richard II which Essex was said to have applauded so vigorously, he evinced a fatal attraction to the narrative of Bolingbroke's Machiavellian triumph.

Despite the absence of easily identifiable topical allusions in *Richard II*, however, it is a play fraught at a more removed level with the political discourses of its day and defines a dialectic of Machiavellian power and Montaignean subjectivity central to the Shakespearian works to follow. It is in its indirect connections to Machiavelli and Montaigne, rather than those to Essex, that this play is central to my argument here. The 'Machiavellian' strand of the play is its political one, and it dominates the action until the celebrated mirror scene, to which I will turn below. This Machiavellianism, as indicated in the previous chapter, is largely that of *The Prince* and includes most of the features of Machiavellian discourse which have seemed characteristically 'modern' to twentieth-century commentators.

---

[2] Ian Wilson, *Shakespeare: The Evidence : Unlocking the Mysteries of the Man and his Work* (New York: St Martin's Griffen, 1993), 198–203.

[3] Quarto editions of *Richard II* printed in 1597 and 1598 lack the scene of deposition, which was printed for the first time only after Elizabeth's death, in the edn. of 1608. Scholars have suspected that this omission resulted from fear that the scene would give offence. However, other explanations are possible as well.

Machiavelli and Modernity

No work has been more consequential for the classic post-Enlightenment practice of seeing in the Renaissance the beginnings of a modernity still in force than Niccolò Machiavelli's *The Prince*, and the literature on this topic is hundreds of years old, multidisciplinary, and extensive.[4] In the present context, despite the great interest of Machiavelli's writings on numerous political and cultural topics, Machiavelli is most relevant as perhaps the most significant conduit for the dissemination in Tudor England of those two constitutive forms of modern rationality, instrumental and critical reason.

One of the crucial observations on *The Prince* in this connection was made by Frankfurt School theorist Max Horkheimer early in his career, when he linked Machiavelli with Renaissance science, seeing both as embodying a new attitude of mastery and domination that would become crucial to the Western project of modernity.[5] In terms developed in later Frankfurt School work, most notably *Dialectic of Enlightenment*,

---

[4] A recent introduction with an up-to-date list of suggested further readings is provided in Niccolò Machiavelli, *Discourses on Livy*, trans. Harvey C. Mansfield and Nathan Tarcov (Chicago: University of Chicago Press, 1996). Niccolò Machiavelli, *The Prince: A Norton Critical Edition*, trans. and ed. Robert M. Adams (New York: Norton, 1977) is still a good overall introduction; see especially Adams's essays 'The Rise, Proliferation, and Degradation of Machiavellianism: An Outline' (pp. 227–38) and 'The Interior Prince, or Machiavelli Mythologized' (pp. 238–50); the work's sampling of philosophical commentaries, including longer excerpts from Nietzsche, Arendht, and Gramsci, and brief epigrams from a host of mostly 19th- and 20th-century figures, is a good orientation to the range of commentary on *The Prince*. J. G. A. Pocock, *The Machiavellian Moment: Florentine Political Thought and the Atlantic Republican Tradition* (Princeton: Princeton University Press, 1975), has been influential in many recent treatments of Machiavelli's strategic centrality to modern political theory, while an earlier work, with applications to English Renaissance literature discussed, is Felix Raab, *The English Face of Machiavelli: A Changing Interpretation, 1500–1700* (London: Routledge, 1964). Other important situatings of Machiavelli in modernity are Leo Strauss, *Thoughts on Machiavelli* (Glencoe, Ill.: Free Press, 1958), and Isaiah Berlin, 'The Originality of Machiavelli', in Berlin (ed.), *Against the Current* (New York: Viking, 1980), 25–79. Wayne A. Rebhorn, *Foxes and Lions: Machiavelli's Confidence Men* (Ithaca, NY: Cornell University Press, 1988), changes the context for the reading of Machiavelli from earlier treatments of him as a proto-social scientist to a more literary-theory influenced treatment of him as centrally involved in myth, narrative, and literary genres. Hanna Pitkin, *Fortune Is a Woman: Gender and Politics in the Thought of Niccolò Machiavelli* (Berkeley and Los Angeles: University of California Press, 1984), is a pioneering feminist analysis. As indicated in the Introduction, the posthumous work by Louis Althusser, *Machiavelli and Us*, ed. François Matheron, trans. Gregory Elliott (London: Verso, 1999), is also of interest. For my purposes the most crucial analysis is that of Victoria Kahn, *Machiavellian Rhetoric: From the Counter-Reformation to Milton* (Princeton: Princeton University Press, 1994).

[5] Max Horkheimer, 'Beginnings of the Bourgeois Philosophy of History' (1930), in his *Between Philosophy and Social Science: Selected Writings*, trans. G. Frederick Hunter, Matthew S. Kramer, and John Torpey (Cambridge, Mass.: MIT Press, 1993), 315–88.

Machiavelli is thus one of the first producers of Western value-free instrumental rationality since the end of the classical Graeco-Roman 'Enlightenment' centuries earlier—an Enlightenment which Machiavelli consciously attempted to revivify. Instrumental reason—the splitting off of 'values' from 'facts', the production of a technical mentality indifferent to ends, focused only on means—became for the Frankfurt School a key concept as it attempted to come to grips with the disasters of modernity epitomized by the Holocaust and the massive destruction of world wars and a world depression. It was a key concept not only because its effects had become catastrophic, but because they were also powerful and liberatory in many ways, producing vast increases in productivity and greatly enlarging the possibilities of human existence. Accordingly, instrumental reason deserved careful and dialectical study, and of course the Frankfurt theorists were not the first to identify and analyse this form of rationality and its problematics. William Shakespeare was, as Marx recognized in his somewhat different terms and emphases, an important predecessor in defining these and related themes.[6] My assertion here is that Shakespeare seems to have developed his first sustained engagement with the theme of instrumental reason in the form of the Machiavellian logic of power which he dramatized and probed.

The instrumentality of *The Prince* has been one of its most thematized features in the extensive literature discussing it subsequently. Machiavelli has been seen, for example, as 'the first modern analyst of power'[7] in that he made the crucial division between facts and values constitutive of instrumentalization in Weber-influenced Frankfurt School theory. Similarly, he has frequently been hailed as the father of true social science for the same reason, and it seems to me that no one contemplating some of the most crucial and notorious of the passages of this little handbook could completely disagree. What else are we to make, for example, of the following famous passage which opens Chapter 15?

But my intention being to write something of use to those who understand, it appears to me more proper to go to the real truth of the matter than to its imagination; and many have imagined republics and principalities which have never been seen or known to exist in reality; for how we live is so far removed from how we ought to live, that he who abandons what is done for what ought to be done, will

---

[6] See Hugh Grady, *Shakespeare's Universal Wolf: Studies in Early Modern Reification* (Oxford: Clarendon, 1996), 26–57.

[7] Max Lerner, introduction to Niccolò Machiavelli, *The Prince and The Discourses* (New York: Modern Library, 1950), p. xxvi. This edn. supplies the text used in subsequent citations of *The Prince* and *The Discourses*. I will indicate chapters as well as page numbers for readers' convenience.

rather learn to bring about his own ruin than his preservation. A man who wishes to make a profession of goodness in everything must necessarily come to grief among so many who are not good. Therefore it is necessary for a prince, who wishes to maintain himself, to learn how not to be good, and to use this knowledge and not use it, according to the necessity of the case.[8]

In recent years, revolutions in literary studies have opened up *The Prince*, among other similar documents, to the close readings of post-structuralist-influenced critical methods, with the result that the textual complexities of this classic have now been much more adequately defined than was the case when it was read primarily for its positivist intimations of modernity.[9] And in addition, as I previously indicated, the situation is further complicated if we extend the discussion to *The Discourses* and other works. Much of the recent writing has concentrated on the relation of Machiavelli's political works to the norms of an Italian Renaissance humanism which it exemplifies yet breaks decisively with. But here, too, the issue of instrumental reason in Machiavelli is a central one, in a different context.

Victoria Kahn's *Machiavellian Rhetoric* is an important example of this trend, although from my point of view it is incomplete in identifying the 'instrumentalizing' qualities of Machiavelli which differentiate him from other, more Ciceronian Renaissance humanists. One problem is that Kahn never uses the term 'instrumentalize' (nor the Frankfurt School theory of instrumental reason), instead choosing to characterize this quality as an aspect of the larger 'rhetorical' qualities of Machiavellian discourse. This terminological choice is understandable in that rhetoric, as Socrates famously asserted, is profoundly instrumental in its operations: rhetoric is a technology of persuasion capable of taking up any position whatever. But the very familiarity and normalcy of the term 'rhetoric' tends to conceal the specific qualities of Machiavellian instrumentality I am emphasizing here. So while Kahn clearly recognizes Machiavelli's use of instrumental reason, she does not thematize the instrumentality in itself, asserting instead that Machiavelli's main difference from the humanist tradition is his denial that what is efficacious and prudent is also necessarily good:

In rejecting the Ciceronian and humanist equation between *honestas* and *utilitas*, the faith that practical reason or prudence is inseparable from moral virtue,

---

[8] Machiavelli, *The Prince*, 56; ch. 15.

[9] See esp. Rebhorn, *Foxes and Lions*; Albert Russell Ascoli and Victoria Kahn (eds.), *Machiavelli and the Discourse of Literature* (Ithaca, NY: Cornell University Press, 1993); and Kahn, *Machiavellian Rhetoric*.

Machiavelli thus turns prudence into what the humanists (and their detractors) always feared it would become—the amoral skill of *versutia* or mere cleverness, which in turn implies the ethically unrestrained use of force—in short, *virtù*.[10]

As recent commentators have emphasized (and as I suggested earlier), however, the instrumentalization of reason in *The Prince* is never total or final, and the text of *The Prince*, instead of being absolutely value-free, is honeycombed with contradictory cultural attitudes based on passionately advocated values of one sort or the next.[11] In some passages, we can intuit a moral subtext which seems to condemn the world of political power for its corruption and vanity.[12] At others, Machiavelli's multidimensional celebration of a polysemic *virtù* emerges as a moment in which the pleasures of masculine self-dramatization as an end in itself are at least as important as political efficacy.[13] And there are Gramscian moments when the text seems to celebrate and crystallize the ability of instrumental reason to subordinate historical fatality and contingency to some measure of human will and control, creating a realm of (partial) freedom from what had hitherto been fortune and fatality.[14] This attitude exists as a subtext throughout *The Prince*, and it was central in the book's extra-ordinary reception by the readers I discussed briefly in Chapter 1. An earlier and equally significant Machiavellian reader was the Catholic Bishop of Winchester under Queen Mary, Stephen Gardiner, who is credited with producing an unpublished treatise incorporating large, unacknowledged tracts from Machiavelli's *Prince* and *Discourses* and

[10] Victoria Kahn, '*Virtù* and the Example of Agathocles in Machiavelli's *Prince*', in Ascoli and Kahn (eds.), *Machiavelli and the Discourse of Literature*, 195–217; 198. This article first appeared in *Representations*, 13 (1986), 63–85, and was an early version of ch. 1 of Kahn's later book *Machiavellian Rhetoric*. I cite from the article here because this passage, particularly pertinent to my concerns, does not appear in the book chapter.

[11] See Rebhorn, *Foxes and Lions*, 16–26, and Kahn, *Machiavellian Rhetoric*, 237–41.

[12] For example, 'a prince who wishes to maintain the state is often forced to do evil, for when that party, whether populace, soldiery, or nobles, whichever it be that you consider necessary to you for keeping your position, is corrupt, you must follow its humour and satisfy it, and in that case good works will be inimical to you'; Machiavelli, *The Prince*, 71–2; ch. 19.

[13] Such is the case, I would argue, for the famous 'For fortune is a woman' passage (Machiavelli, *The Prince*, 94; ch. 25), but the celebration of virility is almost always closely intertwined in *The Prince* with the praise of a politically beneficial *virtù*, so that it is a matter of difficult judgement to specify where virility leaves off and political acumen begins. See Pitkin, *Fortune Is a Woman*, 285–306 *et passim*, for a detailed investigation of the ways in which Machiavelli's cultural misogyny undercuts other aspects of his argument.

[14] The central passage is ch. 25, 'How Much Fortune Can Do in Human Affairs and How Much It May Be Opposed' (Machiavelli, *The Prince*, 91–4). Pitkin, *Fortune Is a Woman*, 138–69, provides an excellent discussion of the conflicting values and desires at work in this chapter. This is the 'moment' of Machiavelli which inspired Antonio Gramsci's celebrated prison essay 'The Modern Prince'.

other works deriving from it.[15] The work, which is in the form of a dialogue, features one speaker, Stephano, who consistently urges Philip II to make use of every Machiavellian stratagem in order to forward the great cause of restoring the true faith to England. Philip II is figured as a proto-typical Machiavellian great prince who is to win and hold the English state by following the familiar advice of the unnamed Machiavelli.

In short, one of the great appeals of *The Prince*, despite its aggressive secularity and ironic evocations of religion as a mere façade to occlude cruelty used well, was that its very instrumentality made its methods suit-able for adaptation to any cause whatsoever, Catholic, Protestant, or secular. Wherever values or interests were deemed to be so great or abso-lute as to justify any ends, the instrumental logic of power described by *The Prince* could (and often did) come into play.

If we extend the analysis to include the more value-laden, republican writings of Machiavelli's *The Discourses*, however, we run into complica-tions that, while interesting in themselves, turn out not to be as germane to Shakespeare's works as is *The Prince*. In *The Discourses* it is clear that at one level a kind of value-free rationality is an important part of that work's complex textuality. Let us look, for example, at Machiavelli's trenchant, Nietzschean passage on the subject of the deleterious effects of Christianity on Renaissance Europe:

Reflecting now as to whence it came that in ancient times the people were more devoted to liberty than in the present, I believe that it resulted from this, that men were stronger in those days, which I believe to be attributable to the difference of education, founded upon the difference of their religion and ours. For, as our religion teaches us the truth and the true way of life, it causes us to attach less value to the honors and possessions of this world; whilst the Pagans, esteeming those things as the highest good, were more energetic and ferocious in their actions. We may observe this also in most of their institutions, beginning with the magnifi-cence of their sacrifices as compared with the humility of ours, which are gentle solemnities rather than magnificent ones, and have nothing of energy or ferocity in them, whilst in theirs there was no lack of pomp and show. . . . Besides this, the Pagan religion deified only men who had achieved great glory, such as commanders of armies and chiefs of republics, whilst ours glorifies more the humble and contemplative men than the men of action. Our religion, moreover,

---

[15] Stephen Gardiner, *A Machiavellian Treatise*, ed. and trans. Peter Samuel Donaldson (Cambridge: Cambridge University Press, 1975). The text, whose authorship is disputed, sur-vives only in an Italian translation *Ragionamento dell'advenimento delli inglesi et normanni in Britanni* [Discourse on the coming of the English and Normans to Britain] prepared for presentation to Queen Mary's Spanish husband Philip II and has been translated into English in this modern scholarly edition, which includes both the Italian text and the modern translation. See Kahn, *Machiavellian Rhetoric*, 277–78 n. 12, for further information.

places the supreme happiness in humility, lowliness, and a contempt for worldly objects, whilst the other, on the contrary, places the supreme good in grandeur of soul, strength of body, and all such other qualities as render men formidable; and if our religion claims of us fortitude of soul, it is more to enable us to suffer than to achieve great deeds.[16]

Here, certainly, Machiavelli achieves through his transparent irony a distantiation from the values of his own society, an ability to pose one set of values against another, of the kind that both Montaigne and Shakespeare display as well. However, at another level, it is clear that issues of value are not bracketed but probed and tentatively resolved in the favour of the ancients against his contemporaries. In *The Prince*, precisely because Machiavelli evidently felt constrained to omit reference to his republican sympathies, his discussion is not only critically distantiated from the official religious world view of his time and space, but often much more narrowly instrumentalist and value-free. This peculiar quality of *The Prince* arguably resulted from a contingent rhetorical choice of Machiavelli's: he wished to make his particular case that a strong Prince might unify Italy and save it from the barbarians, and so he decided not to lose his focus by bringing in his views on the liberties of republics, which might distract crucial portions of his intended audience. But in making this contingent decision, Machiavelli created in *The Prince* one of the central templates of intellectual modernity and of instrumental reason. And that is why it has been *The Prince*, not the more complex and in many ways more intelligent and interesting *Discourses*, that has defined the contours of the Machiavellian for posterity.

What do I mean in claiming that the logic of power in *The Prince* is instrumental? One of the great paradoxes of instrumental reason like that of (one central strand of) *The Prince* is that while it works to magnify and enhance the power of its user, it also entraps that very user because its logic works independently of any purely subjective intentions. Macbeth intuited this in his famous remark that 'I am in blood I Stepp'd in so far that, should I wade no more, I Returning were as tedious as go o'er.'[17] That is, the logic of power is a reified logic to which the prince must, qua prince, ultimately submit even while appearing to be utilizing it as his instrument. Efficacy, as Horkheimer and Adorno argued trenchantly, ultimately becomes its own end, corrosive to any other values or intents.[18] Finally,

---

[16] Machiavelli, *The Discourses*, 284–5; 2.2.

[17] Shakespeare, *Macbeth*, 3.4.135–7.

[18] Max Horkheimer and Theodor W. Adorno, *Dialectic of Enlightenment*, trans. John Cumming (Boston: Seabury, 1972); trans. of *Dialektik der Aufklärung* (New York, 1944).

then, as not only Horkheimer and Adorno, but also Milton and Shakespeare came to see, the instrumentality of this form of rationality undermines its subordination to any end whatsoever and creates a reified logic
of power for its own sake. Underneath the apparent neutrality of instrumental reason is a will-to-power which results from its very status as
efficacious instrument. That is, the stance of instrumental reason to be a
means to any end creates, or amounts to, self-perpetuating power. And
despite all of Machiavelli's love of liberty and his use of critical rationality,
The Prince remains a classic instance of this process.

Because of their instrumental, all-serving qualities, the topics and paradoxes of *The Prince* infiltrated the writings of numerous Renaissance
political thinkers, including many who denounced them. Not only was
Machiavelli condemned and caricatured in print as well as on the stage
through the much studied figure of the Elizabethan villainous machiavel;
he was also studied and recommended, as we have seen, by policy-makers
like Ralegh and Bacon for his wise political insights and by rhetoricians for
his humanist method of studying politics through his numerous examples
from ancient and modern history. By the time of the seventeenth-century
Civil War period, Machiavellian topics and methodology permeated the
political discourse on both sides of the struggle. In this, however, the
Puritans and Cavaliers were following Shakespeare's example. Instrumental reason and its relation to political power is a theme central to
Shakespeare's tragedies, histories, and several of the comedies.[19] Moreover, these themes from Machiavelli play also into that other crucial
rewriter of Renaissance humanism, Michel de Montaigne, and a common
interest in and reaction to Machiavellian themes of power is, I believe,
something Montaigne and Shakespeare share, as I will discuss in the next
chapter. Taken together, Machiavelli and Montaigne form an intertextuality which opens up in turn into central issues of power, identity,
and subjectivity in Shakespeare, issues which form the thematic matter of
this book. *Richard II* discloses a world ruled by this Machiavellian reduction, and it projects an alternative which is completely inefficacious within the reality of the play, but which has been more potent within the
imaginations of its viewers and readers: the flux of subjectivity. In two
princes to come, in Prince Hal and Prince Hamlet, we will see an examination of a similar dialectic given even fuller and richer development.

---

[19]   Grady, *Shakespeare's Universal Wolf,* 55–6.

The Machiavellian World of Richard II

From its very opening the world depicted in *Richard II* is already a fully fallen, Machiavellian—and to that extent 'modern'—world. In this play we are engaged in one of the crucial dynamics of early modern politics, a struggle between aristocrats and a centralizing state.[20] In fact, the value-free logic of power at work in the play's politics will turn out in hindsight to be central to the dynamics of long-period modernity in the West and world. But the essential 'modernity' of the dynamics involved has been occluded in the critical reception of the play, because the initiating struggle of the play may appear at first as 'feudal':[21] two powerful members of the nobility, Harry Bolingbroke, Duke of Hereford (the future Henry

[20] Perry Anderson, *Lineages of the Absolutist State* (1974; repr. London: Verso, 1979), has defined this dynamic as in fact the essence of the mode of production which obtained in the early modern period, and he sees that mode of production as still feudal—a feudalism, however, which has invented absolutism to save it from the systemic crisis which nearly destroyed it in the 14th century. However, paradoxically, perhaps, Anderson has defined this society as the locus of a powerful mode of modernization: 'The royal States of the Renaissance were first and foremost modernized instruments for the maintenance of noble domination over rural masses' (p. 20), and he identifies a developing mercantile capitalism in urban areas politically free of aristocratic domination as an overdetermining but secondary factor in absolutist societies (pp. 20–4). I am suspicious of the attempt to distinguish 'secondary' and 'primary' factors as Anderson does here, as well as of his certainty that the absolutist state was an instrument of the nobility: the resulting social formation to me is no longer really feudal but not yet fully capitalist. Following *Annales* school usage, I simply call it 'early modern' society, with its own unique characteristics. For a variety of Marxist-influenced approaches to the relation of the age of Shakespeare to modernity, see the essays collected in Rodney Hilton (ed.), *The Transition from Feudalism to Capitalism* (London: Verso, 1976).
[21] Most influential in this regard was undoubtedly E. M. W. Tillyard, *Shakespeare's History Plays* (1944; repr. New York: Macmillan, 1946), 234–303; he was echoed and further developed in this argument by Alvin Kernan, '*The Henriad*: Shakespeare's Major History Plays', *Yale Review*, 59 (Oct. 1969), 3–32; and repr. in Kernan (ed.), *Modern Shakespearian Criticism: Essays on Style, Dramaturgy, and the Major Plays* (New York: Harcourt, 1970). In the next decade T. McAlindon, *Shakespeare and Decorum* (London: Macmillan, 1973), 19–43, also claimed the play is steeped in 'medievalism' but that Richard violates it as seriously as does Bolingbroke. The recent work of Perry Anderson discussed in the previous note has led many Marxist-influenced writers to understand feudalism as persisting well into what has conventionally been called the 'modern' period. A view much like Anderson's informs the argument of Graham Holderness, *Shakespeare's History* (New York: St Martin's Press, 1985), 40–65 (see his 'Shakespeare's History: "Richard II"', *Literature and History*, 7/1 (Spring 1981), 2–24, for an earlier version), which undertakes a milestone anti-Tillyard reading of the play but sees a strong medievalism in it nevertheless—in Bolingbroke and his allied barons (as champions of aristocratic prerogatives against a centralizing state) rather than in Richard. However, Phyllis Rackin, *Stages of History: Shakespeare's English Chronicles* (Ithaca, NY: Cornell University Press, 1990), 118–35, sees both medievalism and modernization anachronistically mixed in the text of the play in three different time perspectives: in the opening the play is feudal; after Richard stops the trial by combat, feudalism ends; and after the deposition, events are in effect allegorical of the Elizabethan present.

IV), and Thomas Mowbray, Duke of Norfolk, are locked in a high-stakes struggle in which each accuses the other of treason and offers a fight to the death to settle the question. However, one of them has to be lying, and it is of the essence of the epistemology of this understated play that the audience can never be certain which one is.[22] Certainly one of the most extraordinary qualities of this play—especially compared with its predecessor *Richard III*—is its complete and strategic silence concerning Bolingbroke's interiority—and hence his intentionality and possible hypocrisy. In contrast, as we will see, Richard himself, after his defeat, becomes a paragon of interiority, especially in his extraordinary soliloquy in Act 5. But in respect to the actions of princes as princes, *Richard II* follows an ironclad and Machiavellian rule: appearances are the very essence of politics; and they constitute all we ever learn about Bolingbroke in this play.

The feudal trappings of the opening scenes are an essential aspect of that appearance. The two political foes present their accusations in a feudal ritual of challenge and counter-challenge before their liege-lord, the young Richard II, in language redolent of respect for chivalry and aristo-cratic tradition, allegiance to the crown, and aristocratic self-assertion and belligerence:

BOLINGBROKE. Pale trembling coward, there I throw my gage,
 Disclaiming here the kindred of the King,
 And lay aside my high blood's royalty,
 Which fear, not reverence, makes thee to except.
 If guilty dread have left thee so much strength
 As to take up mine honour's pawn, then stoop.
 By that, and all the rites of knighthood else,
 Will I make good against thee, arm to arm,
 What I have spoke, or thou canst worse devise.
MOWBRAY. I take it up, and by that sword I swear
 Which gently laid my knighthood on my shoulder,
 I'll answer thee in any fair degree
 Of chivalrous design of knightly trial;
 And when I mount, alive may I not light,
 If I be traitor or unjustly fight![23]

[22] Cf. Katharine Eisaman Maus, *Inwardness and Theater in the English Renaissance* (Chicago: University of Chicago Press, 1995), 57. Maus sees such mutual accusations as mirroring the religious polemics of both anti-Catholics and anti-Protestants and as one of the basic stances of stage Machiavellianism.

[23] William Shakespeare, *Richard II*, 1.1.69–83, *The Norton Shakespeare*, ed. Stephen Greenblatt et al. (New York: Norton, 1997). All subsequent quotations are given parentheti-cally and are from this edn.

The play proceeds to build toward a climactic fight between these two, with the opening of scene 1.3 a full-blown demonstration of feudal ritual as high theatre, complete with formulaic questioning, the sounding of trumpets, more accusations and taunts, preparations for death, and a father's blessing.

Only, of course, the audience is deprived of its catharsis when Richard steps forward at the last possible moment to order the end of the combat and announce a politic settlement, based on the exiling of the two would-be duellists. And the exile is characterized by Mowbray in peculiar terms that have captured the attention of many critics, past and present:

> The language I have learnt these forty years,
> My native English, now I must forgo,
> And now my tongue's use is to me no more
> Than an unstringèd viol or a harp,
> Or like a cunning instrument cased up,
> Or, being open, put into his hands
> That knows no touch to tune the harmony.
> Within my mouth you have enjailed my tongue,
> Doubly portcullised with my teeth and lips,
> And dull unfeeling barren ignorance
> Is made my jailer to attend on me.
> I am too old to fawn upon a nurse,
> Too far in years to be a pupil now.
> What is thy sentence then but speechless death,
> Which robs my tongue from breathing native breath. (1.3.153–67)

Mowbray's understanding of language as creating the social network in which one lives life and finds purpose and meaning might seem too casual to be interpreted as involving more than a 'local' metaphoric meaning, were it not so pervasive across Shakespeare's oeuvre in general[24]— and, as we shall see, over the plays of the *Henriad* in particular. Here as elsewhere in Shakespeare's work, language works as a metaphoric model of what the twentieth century has disparately called anthropological culture, ideology, or discourse: those symbolic systems through which we structure our understanding of the world, mark out our values within it, and define our own sense of self and personhood. Self-consciousness of these symbolic systems in the Renaissance was never defined in the theoretical-analytic language which the Enlightenment has taught us to

---

[24] Terry Eagleton, *William Shakespeare* (Oxford: Basil Blackwell, 1986) was among the first to define this centrality in the brief career of textualist deconstruction in Shakespeare studies.

demand for such abstract and theoretical concepts.[25] However, a number of Renaissance authors, writing from the peculiar open window between the theocentrism of the late medieval and the new absolutisms of the seventeenth century and Enlightenment, clearly work with such concepts. Montaigne is perhaps the most explicit of them, and Shakespeare, it seems clear from passages such as the one I am discussing, is another. At this point in *Richard II*, such a concept begins to move us out of the appearances of a feudal, chivalrous world whose rhetoric we have been immersed in, and into a world where chivalry and all such ideologies are seen to be languages to be learned (or unlearned) rather than all-encompassing, unquestioned belief systems known only as the fish knows the sea. And as the ensuing dialogue picks up and develops this theme, the audience's attention is directed to the status of the symbols as symbols; it is in the nature of symbolic systems, like languages, to be efficacious only when their code is shared by a community; outside this context, they are meaningless. Furthermore, it is not only a question of communication, but, as Mowbray emphasizes, one of identity itself. Outside the world of English-speakers, he has to look forward to only a kind of death since the symbolic order in which he has spent his life and through which he has built his identity will henceforth be a nullity.

Machiavelli's approach to these questions is, of course, much more pragmatic, but no less relevant to the investigation of themes of ideology and the self in this and other Shakespearian plays. As indicated earlier, Katharine Eisaman Maus rightly suggested that Machiavelli also has a sort of theory of the self,[26] one predicated on a simple but extremely consequential bifurcation between the inner and the outward person. It was Machiavelli's celebrated insight that successful politics depend greatly on image and appearance and that a complete correspondence between the inner and outer man is in fact dangerous and undesirable: the successful prince must appear virtuous and religious, but if he truly is, Machiavelli's infamous argument goes, he will be at a grave disadvantage vis-à-vis those

---

[25] But see the appendix 'Elizabethan Naming' in James L. Calderwood, *Metadrama in Shakespeare's Henriad: 'Richard II' to 'Henry V'* (Berkeley and Los Angeles: University of California Press, 1979), 183–220, which discusses Bacon's ideas on language and the 16th-century currency of Jacob Boehme's doctrine of an Adamic language in which words were perfectly adequate to things, a perfection which was lost after the Tower of Babel. However, Calderwood's argument that the plays of the *Henriad* metatheatrically move from Richard II's quasi-Adamic language to a fallen linguistic world in *1 and 2 Henry IV*, to a partially redeemed linguistic world in *Henry V*, seems to me to be profoundly mistaken, albeit the book is often quite interesting when individual passages within it argue against the grain of this overall thesis.

[26] Maus, *Inwardness and Theater in the English Renaissance*, 35–71.

numerous evil men who understand this simple truth.[27] Thus the prince
must have a deep understanding of the belief systems or ideology of those
whom he is attempting to rule or otherwise influence, but he himself
must be distantiated from that ideology in order fully to make use of the
political possibilities opened up to him by the beliefs of his subjects.

In *Richard II* the first two acts induct us into a world in which at least
one of the participants—the unknown liar—is operating according to
this Machiavellian model of the self, projecting a deceptive outer belief
in chivalry and truth in order to effect a ploy of power and political
manoeuvre. And one self-conscious manipulator of ideology is quite
enough to cause the audience to reconsider the status of the ceremonious
feudalism we have been witnessing and of whose deadly climax we have
been so suddenly deprived. The rituals of chivalry, we can say, prove
empty; or rather, Machiavellian logic has evacuated chivalry of inner
meaning, leaving it as a set of signifiers whose signified has now been
transferred to a completely different register, open only to those 'in the
know' and able to decode the meaning. But the play provides no way to
resolve the questions of truth raised by the mutual accusations, and that is
one index of the Machiavellian structure of this play. At best, there is an
equivocal hint: if we pay close attention to the end of the scene of aborted
combat, and think ahead to the unfolding of the rest of the play's logic and
action, we can discern suggestions as to who the Machiavellian operative
is in Mowbray's final comments to Bolingbroke:

> No, Bolingbroke, if ever I were traitor,
> My name be blotted from the book of life,
> And I from heaven banished as from hence.
> But what thou art, God, thou, and I do know,
> And all too soon, I fear, the King shall rue.
> Farewell, my liege. Now no way can I stray
> Save back to England, all the world's my way. *Exit.* (1.3.194–200)

Such is the logic of this aspect of Machiavellian rhetoric, however, that we
cannot be certain of Mowbray's veracity: we can as easily say of a speech
like this that it creates excellent deception as that it rings true and has
choric suggestiveness. Of course, to the extent that dramatic functionality
creates contexts and restricts the play of possible meanings (such as this
Machiavellian interpretation), the context here supports premonitions
about Bolingbroke as a politically ruthless, destructive character and thus
helps sweep us along into the play's narrative, suggesting an epiphany of

---

[27] Machiavelli, *The Prince*, 65; ch. 18.

Bolingbroke as a Machiavellian. Whether such a categorization is necessarily bad in the context of this drama is another subject and one to which
I will turn below. In order to get to that discussion, however, I want to try
to trace the way the design of the next few scenes begins to modify the
audience's perceptions of both Richard and Bolingbroke.

One of the effects created by the precepts of Machiavellian rhetoric, we
learn in the opening dialogue of the next scene (1.4), is a devaluation of
words themselves,[28] and Richard's supporter Aumerle is pointed in his
report on his 'hollow parting' (1.4.9) from the exiled Bolingbroke in insist-
ing that neither he nor Bolingbroke wastes any words with each other.
With equal point, however, he reports Bolingbroke's careful courting of
'the common people, | How he did seem to dive into their hearts | With
humble and familiar courtesy' (1.4.24–6). Bolingbroke is thus presented,
from the point of view of Richard's supporters, as a political rival to be
watched, rather than what he might have seemed previously, a ceremonious if hot-headed aristocrat.

Just as we take in this new view of Bolingbroke, however, we also have
to rethink our initial impressions of Richard as, abruptly, the audience is
shown a hitherto hidden side of Richard's own policy as he introduces the
terminology which will subsequently be used by his enemies to condemn
him:

> And for our coffers, with too great a court
> And liberal largess are grown somewhat light,
> We are enforced to farm our royal realm,
> The revenue whereof shall furnish us
> For our affairs at hand. (1.4.42–6)

And immediately after this follow two more pointed details: the giving of
'blank charters' to his ministers to appropriate money from the wealthy
(1.4.47–51) and, even more egregious, Richard's callous reaction to the
grave illness of that saint of feudal rectitude in this play, his uncle John of
Gaunt:

> Now put it, God, in the physician's mind
> To help him to his grave immediately.
> The lining of his coffers shall make coats
> To deck our soldiers for these Irish wars.
> Come, gentlemen, let's all go visit him.
> Pray God we may make haste and come too late! (1.4.58–63)

---

[28] Cf. Calderwood, *Metadrama in Shakespeare's Henriad*, 13–32. However, Calderwood
does not see this devaluation as a consequence of Machiavellian politics.

The characterizations of both Bolingbroke and Richard in this scene, then, are both de-heroicizing; each of them undertakes actions that could easily be assimilated to those of that Elizabethan stage favourite, the machiavel, in that each appears to be motivated largely by power-seeking and each seems to display that Machiavellian combination of inner contempt for all but the self and its aggrandizement. However, the comparison is limited, precisely because Richard, while (in these brief scenes, at least) he is a machiavel, is a poor Machiavellian who needs to study the details of his *Prince* much more closely. When he seizes the estate of the dead John of Gaunt and prevents the passing on of the hereditary rights of the Duke of Lancaster to their legal heir Bolingbroke, he violates one of that book's essential tenets: 'but above all he [the prince] must abstain from taking the property of others, for men forget more easily the death of their father than the loss of their patrimony.'[29] And when he returns from Ireland and finds himself outmanoeuvred at every juncture by Bolingbroke and his allies, he becomes the very opposite of Machiavelli's prince: rather than the realities of power, he seems to believe in symbols of the divine power of the cosmic order to protect him against the impetuous, opportunistic, and consummately skilful Bolingbroke.

It is of course the latter who undertakes a series of highly efficacious political stratagems that could have been taken directly from *The Prince*. 'Nothing', Machiavelli writes, 'causes a prince to be so much esteemed as great enterprises and giving proof of prowess.'[30] Bolingbroke proves the truth of this observation with his bold, decree-breaking return to England in Richard's absence, his skilful organization of military support of his cause, his neutralization of the Lord Regent York, and his peremptory arrest and execution of Richard's advisers Bushy and Green. In contrast, Richard does almost everything wrong—most particularly in his unwise choice of his critic and Bolingbroke sympathizer, the Duke of York, as regent in his absence. And in scenes which come as close to choric commentary as anything in this beautifully understated, clear-eyed drama, Richard's tax policies and alienation of both the commons and the nobility are thematically underscored.

The first of these near-choric moments is that of the deathbed accusations of John of Gaunt against Richard:

> Why, cousin, wert thou regent of the world
> It were a shame to let this land by lease.
> But, for thy world, enjoying but this land,

---

[29] Machiavelli, *The Prince*, 62; ch. 17.   [30] Ibid. ch. 21.

> Is it not more than shame to shame it so?
> Landlord of England art thou now, not king.
> Thy state of law is bondslave to the law. (2.1.109–14)

John of Gaunt serves in this play almost exactly like one of Corneille's embodiments of feudal piety in the French seventeenth-century classical theatre, in plays like *Le Cid* and *Horace*. In the context of the failure of the Fronde (1648), that last French aristocratic revolt against the centralizing monarchy, Corneille depicts fathers who represent the vanishing class of the aristocracy-of-the-sword as stern embodiments of virtue who serve as both models for and foils against their equally heroic but no longer completely feudalistic sons. In *Richard II*, John of Gaunt, poet of an idealized golden-age England and staunch exponent of the glory, rights, and duties of aristocratic blood, serves an almost exactly analogous role. His passing from the scene signals the complete end of that golden age of which he had been a last remnant and furnishes the occasion for the Machiavellian contest for power between Richard and Bolingbroke to begin in earnest. With his departure, we have completely left behind the chivalrous world which had served as a kind of concealing façade for the amoral power struggles of the play's opening acts. In a move clearly desecrating of the rhetoric of nobility just enunciated by John of Gaunt, Richard immediately acts to alienate his legacy in a display of cultural stripping and reification which we 400 years later can recognize as of the very essence of a modernity we still inhabit:

> The lining of his coffers shall make coats
> To deck our soldiers for these Irish wars. (1.4.60–1)

The abstraction of values and logic of equivalency evoked here is of a piece with the levelling practices of the mercantile world which Shakespeare put to such searching criticism in later plays like *Troilus and Cressida* and *Timon of Athens*; here, instead of the market's common price on radically disparate commodities, however, an aristocratic patrimony is equated to the coats of common soldiers, all to the purpose of Richard's self-perpetuating power.[31]

The references here and elsewhere in the play to farming, weeds, and caterpillars, however, suggest a connection to another form of reification investigated by Shakespeare in other plays: the social context for this language, as a number of recent works have understood, is the enclosure

---

[31] See Rackin, *Stages of History*, 100–3, for a similar analysis of these references, seen in the context of Rackin's study as anachronisms which serve the dramatic purpose of discrediting the character (here Richard) with whom they are associated.

movement which was proceeding apace as Shakespeare wrote in the 1590s, a slow economic process in which once customarily held lands which had existed largely outside a money economy were alienated by their legal possessors and turned over from farming to sheep-raising for the woollen trade—all in the interest of the money to be made from such transactions.[32] Richard has turned England, as he said in his own words earlier in the play (1.4.44), and as John of Gaunt reiterated, into a farm, with himself as landlord. Rather than a pre-modern, customary society of mutual obligations and ties, the cold logic of the cash nexus is substituted as the bond between people.

The desecration of tradition and custom enacted by Richard here does not go unchallenged by the one surviving member of John of Gaunt's aristocratic generation, the Duke of York—and he recognizes this profaning logic to be one which will redound against Richard himself:

> Take Hereford's rights away, and take from Time
> His charters and his customary rights.
> Let not tomorrow then ensue today;
> Be not thyself; for how art thou a king
> But by fair sequence and succession? (2.1.196–200)

Once more, then, we see Richard not as a representative of an idealized feudal realm in which virtue and bravery justified and preserved a natural hierarchy of feudal bonds, but rather as a desecrator of those bonds, a Machiavellian manqué who ignores to his peril Machiavelli's requirement that the prince's real, power-serving behaviour must be hidden from men's eyes by a façade of pretended virtue.

This is a mistake which Bolingbroke emphatically does not make, and the play's dialogue will not let us miss this point as we witness, one after the other, the approving witnesses to Bolingbroke's courtesy, kindness, and adherence to the political status quo and the rights of inheritance and legal succession. As I noted, the play thus gives us two machiavels, or egregious violators of customary right and morality, but only one real Machiavellian—Bolingbroke—who truly understands the political necessity of appearances of virtue.

The second of the two nearly choric moments of which I spoke is the remarkable garden scene (3.4), which puts into the mouths of royal gardeners the terminology of farming and caterpillars which had passed from Richard's sudden introduction of these terms, to John of Gaunt's

[32] See Richard Wilson, *Will Power: Essays on Shakespearian Authority* (New York: Harvester, 1993), 63–82, for an informative discussion of enclosures and the impact this movement had on several of Shakespeare's plays.

deathbed accusations against the young King, now to representatives of the commons. Here, however, gardeners evoke rather than evacuate the golden-age vision of a feudal-pastoral England which had been enunciated in those much quoted, patriotic words of John of Gaunt:

> This royal throne of kings, this sceptred isle,
> This earth of majesty, this seat of Mars,
> This other Eden, demi-paradise,
> This fortress built by nature for herself
> Against infection and the hand of war,
> This happy breed of men, this little world,
> This precious stone set in the silver sea,
> Which serves it in the office of a wall,
> Or as a moat defensive to a house,
> Against the envy of less happier lands;
> This blessèd plot, this earth, this realm, this England,
> This nurse, this teeming womb of royal kings,
>
> .   .   .   .
>
> Is now leas'd out—I die pronouncing it—
> Like to a tenement or pelting farm. (2.1.40–60)

The refunctioning of this vision from the defunct aristocratic realm of John of Gaunt to the musings of commoners is an interesting and suggestive one, which picks up imagery that had been bandied about, as we have seen, from several previous points of view, but introduces a new modality for it. In the first place, the gardeners present a vision not of aristocratic rights, but of the kingdom as a whole. While at some moments they respect hierarchy—

> Go, bind thou up young dangling apricots,
> Which, like unruly children, make their sire
> Stoop with oppression of their prodigal weight.
> Give some supportance to the bending twigs. (3.4.30–3)

—at others these fellows seem to be Levellers of a kind:

> Go thou, and like an executioner,
> Cut off the heads of too fast-growing sprays
> That look too lofty in our commonwealth.
> All must be even in our government. (ll. 34–7)

Thus, as a counterpoint to the monarchical and aristocratic rhetoric and logic which has dominated almost every scene in the play up to this point (and in a sense, as we shall see, even in this scene), we are given an image of a golden-age organic community modelled on that blend of artifice and nature exemplified here by gardening, but which takes other forms as well in such consummately Shakespearian utopian evocations as the sheep-shearing scene of *The Winter's Tale*, the Forest of Arden, or Prospero's island:

> our sea-wallèd garden, the whole land,
> Is full of weeds, her fairest flowers choked up,
> Her fruit trees all unpruned, her hedges ruined,
> Her knots disordered, and her wholesome herbs
> Swarming with caterpillars? (ll. 44–8)

The logic of this description is, as I indicated, quite different from that of John of Gaunt's more feudal vision. Here we have no rhetoric connecting nature itself with royalty and kings, nor the gods and warfare of Gaunt's aristocratic vision. Rather, we are in a garden tended by—gardeners. And one aspect of the simile remains at first undeveloped: what equivalents from the realm of gardens might be posited in the mirroring, metaphoric realm of the kingdom? This latent aspect of the simile is addressed, how-ever, when the King finally appears, not exactly as a gardener, but as one who 'suffered this disordered spring'—that is, he is a relatively passive agent who neglected his garden.

Most interesting of all, the political defeat of Richard by Bolingbroke—a clear violation of the ethos of chivalry and feudalism championed by John of Gaunt and the Duke of York—is presented by the gardeners as a process of nature:

> He that hath suffered this disordered spring
> Hath now himself met with the fall of leaf.
> The weeds which his broad spreading leaves did shelter,
> That seemed in eating him to hold him up,
> Are plucked up, root and all, by Bolingbroke—
> I mean the Earl of Wiltshire, Bushy, Green. (ll. 49–54)

Thus this vision of the commoners embodies a complex mixture of value-free and value-laden discourse. On the one hand, the pastoral traditions evoked by the close connections between the natural organic processes of gardening with the political affairs of the kingdom are value-laden, at once ideological and utopian—certainly evocative of values of cooperation, mutual interdependency, and relative social equality. As noted, they are a class-based, ideological counterpoint to that more famous aristocratic pastoral of England declaimed earlier by the dying John of Gaunt, presenting a much more plebeian view of English politics. On the other hand, they perform an important function in the play's implied political analysis of the power struggle between Richard and Bolingbroke: they illustrate how Richard had lost his political base, first that of the nobility, and now that of the commons. And in the commons' vision of pastoral politics is embodied a paradoxical Machiavellian vision: by figuring Richard's (imminent) fall as a process of nature, like the changing of the seasons, they dissolve that feudal, aristocratic legality of succession which, as York had pointed out to Richard, was the crucial linchpin of legitimized power in this still formally feudal society and which was held by him and the other aristocrats (at least publicly) as inherent in the structure of the cosmos and of God's delegation of power to king and nobility. In that way, these simple gardeners are worthy ancestors indeed to the king-deposing Levellers who would rise to prominence about fifty years after the composition of this play. The effect within the conceptual architecture of the play is subtle but decisive: the political mythologies which underlie monarchical and aristocratic legitimacy in Tudor and Stuart England are here revealed as part of that pious appearance, that hollow but imperative façade of legitimizing values, which Machiavellian philosophy holds is crucial to maintaining the power of the prince.[33] By refiguring this naturalistic philosophy as part of a pastoral, even organic political utopia associated with the commons, Shakespeare effectuates a vertiginous alternative mythology in which the cold power struggles of princes momentarily appear as subordinated instruments of a warm organic community of balanced, interdependent social bonds. And perhaps most important for this controversial play's contemporary audiences, there is enough of a commonality in the two garden-visions of John of Gaunt and the common gardeners to allow audiences to assimilate both to a utopian nationalism which could be countenanced by all parties and classes.

After this scene, however, the utopian seems to dissolve, and the play returns us in Scene 4.1 almost literally back to the world of the play's opening scenes, as two other politicians (Bagot and Aumerle) engage in a deadly Machiavellian game of mutual accusations of treachery and treason, only this time with Bolingbroke playing the role of king and with the deck utterly stacked against his adversary Aumerle. This pointed repetition, and the accompanying prophecies by Carlisle of strife and bloodshed to come (4.1.134–49) when the deadly game is interrupted by the news of Richard's abdication, suggest what every English viewer of this play knew, that Bolingbroke's personal triumph of Machiavellian political

---

[33] For a distinctly different reading of this scene, which sees what it calls its 'stylized unreality' as forbidding the audience from relating the scene to the Elizabethan present, see Rackin, *Stages of History*, 126.

skill would prove a prelude to a destructive cycle of further political intrigue, bloodshed, and civil war. Whatever pastoral potential might be inherent for England in the deposing of a king, it would not be actualized in the already written histories of Henry VI and Richard III.

Thus *Richard II* discloses a multi-perspected view of Machiavellian power that leaves us finally in a fallen but not devastated world. Power in this play is far from what it would become in such later ones as *King Lear* and *Macbeth*—a downward spiral to a dissolution of all values, a process thus worthy of linkage to ancient symbols of evil. Certainly the play presents no refutation of Machiavelli's observations that in a world of bad men, it is folly to be good. However, in this play, Richard's problems have little to do with any goodness we might care to impute to him. Instead, his downfall unfolds in large measure due to his own political incompetence, and the dramatic dynamic around which the play is built—the confrontation between skilled and unskilled Machiavellians—implies an understanding of the Machiavellian arts similar to the one Machiavelli himself promulgated throughout *The Prince*. And as we will see below, the same can be said of the other three plays within the second tetralogy.

How could such a 'subversive' portrayal of what was in many ways the ideological linchpin of England's ensconced political system at the time of this play's composition and first performances get by the court-appointed censors? Part of the answer has already been given: the subversiveness probably *was* recognized, at least by Essex and his Machiavellian faction, if, as seems likely, it was this play that Essex had performed as an accompaniment to his unsuccessful rebellion. And a similar uneasiness about the implications of the play is suggested, as noted above, by the fact that the deposition scene was struck from the quarto version of the play, restored only in the reign of King James. But even though here as elsewhere the empirical reactions of contemporary audiences remain a blank for us, we have four centuries of subsequent reactions to work with, and they show that the perception of the political message of this play, as elsewhere in Shakespeare, depends greatly on the politics of the beholder.[34] We are working with texts in which a clash of disparate discourses and ideologies can be interpreted in disparate ways. But I want to concentrate here on readings of the play that seem most interesting and consequential for us now, and those involve a focus on how the clash of discourses works to produce scepticism about Elizabethan ruling ideologies.

[34] For illustration, see Hugh Grady, *The Modernist Shakespeare: Critical Texts in a Material World* (Oxford: Clarendon, 1991); Terence Hawkes, *That Shakespeherian Rag: Essays on a Critical Process* (New York: Methuen, 1986); and Holderness, *Shakespeare's History*.

In this context, Richard's part in the slow-motion process of his own deposition deserves close attention. While much of the interest in his character has been based on his actions and mentality after the abdication (when, as we will see shortly, he becomes a figure of a kind of unfixed modern subjectivity), the stance he takes before that point is of great interest as well. Left to his own devices after his return from Ireland, Richard first turns to the ideology of the king as God's deputy which he himself had undermined when he seized John of Gaunt's property. In fact, this short sequence of scenes comes as close as any in the London Renaissance theatres do to an outright demonstration of the inadequacy of divine-right theory. In a piece of theatrical irony perhaps refunctioned from Christopher Marlowe's *Tamburlaine* plays (where it was of course distanced as taking place in a heathen culture), Richard ostentatiously invokes the power of God and his angels as protectors of the king's lawful power:

> Not all the water in the rough rude sea
> Can wash the balm off from an anointed king.
> The breath of worldly men cannot depose
> The deputy elected by the Lord.
> For every man that Bolingbroke hath pressed
> To lift shrewd steel against our golden crown,
> God for his Richard hath in heavenly pay
> A glorious angel. Then if angels fight,
> Weak men must fall; for heaven still guards the right. (3.2.50–8)

As the play develops further, these lines reverberate in a more and more hollowed context within a political world from which God has apparently withdrawn. And in this Machiavellian context, Richard's own political folly comes more sharply into focus. To take perhaps the most crucial example, just when the audience is puzzling over how Bolingbroke can possibly solve the problem he created for himself by his repeated insistence that he sought only his inheritance as new Duke of Lancaster and had no desires for the crown, it is Richard himself who solves Bolingbroke's dilemma by offering the crown to his adversary unbidden. It is thus no exaggeration, but actually something of an understatement, when the mourning Richard later accuses himself:

> Nay, if I turn mine eyes upon myself
> I find myself a traitor with the rest,
> For I have given here my soul's consent
> T'undeck the pompous body of a king,

> Made glory base, and sovereignty a slave,
> Proud majesty a subject, state a peasant. (4.1.237–42)

Shakespeare and company thus walk a very tight line in this play. As mentioned, they provide material that could be interpreted by many separate interested parties, in the interest of the pro-Tudor claims classically defined by Tillyard, but also and simultaneously by any surviving adherents of either Yorkist or Lancastrian provenance.[35] There is even fleetingly, in the allegorical language of the gardeners, a plebeian-commoners' viewpoint enunciated. However, all of these interpretations—Tudor, plebeian, 'Yorkist', and 'Lancastrian'—seem to be compatible with the play's implied proposition that Richard was a king who brought on much of his own (and his country's later) suffering by his own political incompetence and that Bolingbroke was clearly the superior, more politically skilled 'prince'. This, then, constitutes another clear sense in which this play affirms the value of Machiavellian political skill: Richard is a disaster for England because he lacks it, and he crumbles before an opponent skilled in the Machiavellian arts. The logic of Machiavellian power is thus never condemned wholeheartedly as evil, in the way that cognate themes of the Jacobean tragedies (the 'Machiavellianism' of Macbeth and the *Lear* villains, for example) implicitly but unmistakably are. Again, *Richard II* comes close to one of the major attitudes toward power of *The Prince* itself: it is an instrument, a tool, neglected to one's peril, but neither good nor bad in itself. It is certainly corrosive, however, to central tenets of the ruling political ideology of Tudor England, the idea of the king as God's deputy. To go immediately to the most central issue, the sum total of such thematized deconstruction—or scepticism—is, as Sigurd Burckhardt suggested years ago,[36] corrosive to all specific claims to the English or any other throne for those in the audience willing to make the generalizations and deductions inherent in the play's depiction of realpolitik power struggles. This complex play is nothing if not an affirmation of the accuracy of Machiavellian theory as a model for the dynamics of the great dynastic struggles of English history, an implied but powerful

[35] That is, dramatizing Richard's self-destructive actions helped buttress the Yorkist narrative (contained in this play side by side with the Lancastrian one) by blaming Richard's usurpation not on any problems of legitimacy in his claim, but on his weakness as a man—a weakness exploited by the unscrupulous usurper Bolingbroke, as this interpretation had it. And simultaneously it gave credence to a Lancastrian narrative in which Richard voluntarily relinquishes the throne and Bolingbroke becomes Henry IV legally and legitimately. On all these perspectives and their sources, see H. A. Kelly, *Divine Providence in the England of Shakespeare's Histories* (Cambridge, Mass.: Harvard University Press, 1970).

[36] Sigurd Burckhardt, *Shakespearian Meanings* (Princeton: Princeton University Press, 1968), 83–6.

rebuttal of the culture's official divine-right theory qua theory; certainly, however, *Richard II*, like *The Prince*, affirms the necessity of such theories as ideological justification to win favour from the populace at large. And like *The Prince* as well, but more directly, its cynicism shades over at moments into a critique of and utopian longings for alternatives to the power of manipulated consensus.

The acceptance of instrumentality has more in common in some ways with Marlowe than with the Shakespeare of the Jacobean tragedies. Unlike *King Lear* and *Macbeth*, *Richard II* presents a vision of a world in the grip of necessary reifications which must be acknowledged and utilized. But it is more characteristically 'Shakespearian' in its focus at the end on Richard rather than on the Machiavellian triumph of Bolingbroke. And this focus is implicated with a new theme that functions as a 'surplus' of the Machiavellian—that is, as a residuum of Richard's being-in-the-world not destroyed by his deposition and not functional within Machiavellian power dynamics. One way to describe this development would be to say that the play makes something of a Montaignean turn in its second half, becoming one of the first of Shakespeare's explorations of an unlikely coupling of these two Renaissance humanists/post-humanists and one of his first explorations of a theme that will become central to many of his most celebrated plays: modern subjectivity as at once the outcome and the antithesis of Machiavellian dynamics.

2. MODERN SUBJECTIVITY IN *RICHARD II*

I hope to have established the thoroughly 'modern', Machiavellian assumptions underlying the political narrative of *Richard II*, contrary to a pronounced strand of twentieth-century interpretations which has seen the play as providing a medieval 'base' against which to measure the production of modernity begun in this play by Bolingbroke and culminating in the remaining three plays of the *Henriad*. Instead, I have argued, Richard himself is a Machiavellian, though an unskilled one, but one who is clearly associated with such modernizing activities as the eroding of the customary rights of the nobility and the developing capitalization of agriculture through the enclosure movement. Feudalism (in the sense of a world view of personal bonds, prerogatives, and obligations) exists in this play almost exclusively as a panoply of emptied rituals and symbols which provides the appearance of that virtue which Machiavelli argued was essential to mask the necessary evil of power politics. Some twenty to thirty years after the first performances of *Richard II*, the Machiavellian ideologue Sir William Drake exemplified this Machiavellian attitude toward political symbolism, writing in one of his commonplace books that princes need to pay particular attention to the use of ceremony because 'ceremony suffices to breed opinion and opinion draws on substance'.[37] *Richard II* shows us how ceremony may be efficaciously used in the hands of a skilful manipulator like Bolingbroke and how it may be disastrously misused when its merely instrumental qualities are forgotten, as they are near the end of his reign by Richard.

In defining these qualities of the play, however, I have neglected themes which have been central to many of its commentators, especially a line of classical Modernist critics who are in this instance developing three nineteenth-century Romantic encomia to Richard's tragic dilemma and character by S. T. Coleridge, Walter Pater, and W. B. Yeats. While eighteenth-century commentators on this play were puzzled and largely negative, Coleridge, other Romantics, and Victorians generally made *Richard II* one of the more popular plays in the Shakespearian canon— only not in the terms I have been arguing for, as a drama undermining Elizabethan ideologies of legitimization and coming close to endorsing the terms of Machiavellian realpolitik. Rather, much of its popularity in the history of Shakespearian criticism since 1800 is clearly connected with the figure of the deposed Richard.

I want to look at this strand as a way into the question of Richard's subjectivity and as a prelude to my own argument concerning early modern subjectivity and its early expression by Montaigne. I indicated in the Introduction that much new-paradigm work on subjectivity had involved a kind of Machiavellian reduction of the subject to power; however, these recent treatments were themselves reacting against mid-century Modernist (and covertly Romantic) sacralizations of subjectivity which emphasized its autonomy from power at the expense of under-standing its connections to it. Lest I be understood as advocating a return to such Modernist mystification, I want to discuss some typical examples of Modernist analysis in order to delineate both their moments of truth and falsity (from our present cultural vantage point). This is a perilous enterprise in that I will be trying to separate out in these readings that portion of the interpretation which can be safely labelled paradigmatic— that is, meaning produced primarily from the critical paradigm, the set of critical assumptions and pre-structurings built in, as it were, into the act of

[37] Quoted in Kevin Sharpe, *Reading Revolutions: The Politics of Reading in Early Modern England* (New Haven: Yale University Press, 2000), 105.

reading at any particular point of cultural history[38]—and what we can take as the text's own 'contribution', if I may put it that way, to our reading of it. Such a distinction is by no means unproblematic—how can we finally isolate a meaning completely independent of our interpretation of it? But if we cannot isolate a transcendent meaning above all interpretations, we must on the other hand posit the text's contribution to all possible interpretations of itself, as Wolfgang Iser, for example, has argued on a number of occasions. We can never encounter this 'contribution' of the text in any direct, unmediated form, but we can posit its existence in its disturbances, displacements, and resistances to the various paradigms and by observing the continuities of meaning that get passed on from one paradigm to the next. And I am undertaking this delicate operation here precisely because I believe that the Romantic-Modernist strand of *Richard II* criticism which slighted the play's political themes in favour of a focus on Richard as a type of the artist or actor has isolated a motif of the play which deserves to be refunctioned within the newer critical paradigms of today, rather than ignored or treated as merely an illusion of liberal humanism.

This strand of commentary begins, fittingly enough, with Coleridge. Like other commentators before him, he was uneasy with Richard as a king; unlike them, however, he was fascinated by Richard as a character:

He scatters himself into a multitude of images, and in conclusion endeavours to shelter himself from that which is around him by a cloud of his own thoughts. . . . The whole is joined with the utmost richness and copiousness of thought, and were there an actor capable of representing Richard, the part would delight us more than any other of Shakespeare's master-pieces,—with, perhaps the single exception of King Lear. I know of no character drawn by our great poet with such unequalled skill as that of Richard II.[39]

Behind this unprecedented high evaluation of the play and its central character is the new, Romantic way of conceiving the subject matter of the play which Coleridge played such a strategic role in disseminating: the exhibition of a unified conception of a character is itself the main content of Shakespearian drama. In the case of Richard we are presented with the portrait of a man of emotional extremes unsuited to be king yet admirable as a man. On the one hand, this choice allowed Coleridge to defend the unity of Richard as a character (unity being a privileged aesthetic category for him). On the other hand, the idea depoliticized the play by subordinating issues of power to those of personality; and it covertly

[38] Grady, *The Modernist Shakespeare*, 22–4 and 89–92.
[39] Samuel Taylor Coleridge, *Shakespearian Criticism*, ed. Thomas Raysor, 2nd edn. (London: Dent, 1960), ii. 146–7.

introduced an aesthetic dimension into Richard's personality in its praise of his creative poet-like powers—an idea to be further developed in the subsequent criticism, as we will see.

Coleridge's reading is a rich one, with possible contributions to contemporary, Postmodernist understandings of the play. We might, for example, compare its description of Richard's self with a recent remark of Christopher Pye, who wrote that the Elizabethan subject seems 'less bound, more dispersed, as if inwardness had yet to assume the ideological weight it would take on in the bourgeois era'.[40] For the moment, however, I am more interested in how Coleridge's remark set the stage for later Victorian and Modernist readings, which will be more aestheticist, less concerned with Richard's failings as a king, and more taken with what is revealed of him when he steps down.

Several decades after Coleridge, Walter Pater reproduced Coleridge's idea but (unsurprisingly) pushed it further in an aestheticist direction. Pater saw Richard explicitly as a poet:

an exquisite poet if he is nothing else, from first to last, in light and gloom alike, able to see all things poetically, to give a poetic turn to his conduct of them, and refreshing with his golden language the tritest aspects of that ironic contrast between the pretensions of a king and the actual necessities of his destiny. What a garden of words![41]

And at the end of the era Coleridge helped inaugurate, a *fin-de-siècle* Yeats made of him an artist—a category which, strictly speaking, did not exist in Shakespeare's day but which for Yeats captured something crucial about Richard. Less concerned with Richard's political shortcomings and complaining that critics of Richard's political acumen were like schoolboys delighting in 'persecuting some boy of fine temperament, who has weak muscles and a distaste for school games', Yeats assumed that politics were as relatively unimportant for Shakespeare as for himself:

I cannot believe that Shakespeare looked on his Richard II with any but sympathetic eyes, understanding indeed how ill-fitted he was to be king.... He saw indeed, as I think, in Richard II the defeat that awaits all, whether they be artist or saint, who find themselves where men ask of them a rough energy and have nothing to give but some contemplative virtue, whether lyrical fantasy, or sweetness of temper, or dreamy dignity, or love of God, or love of His creatures.[42]

[40] Christopher Pye, *The Regal Phantasm: Shakespeare and the Politics of Spectacle* (London: Routledge, 1990), 106.
[41] Walter Pater, 'Shakespeare's English Kings', in *Appreciations: With an Essay on Style* (1889; repr. London: Macmillan, 1910), 185–204; 194.
[42] William Butler Yeats, 'At Stratford-on-Avon' (1901), in *Essays and Introductions* (London: Macmillan, 1961), 96–110; 105–6.

All three of these critics perceive something about Richard which lifts him out of the political dynamics which entrap him within the narrative of the play; all three see him as miscast in his role as king and much better suited for an aesthetic rather than a political function. And all three conceptions situate Richard in roles based in the cancellation of real social existence in favour of imaginary, even utopian aesthetic reconstructions of the real. Poet, artist, or saint—Richard for these critics is a man suited for the same destination imagined by Baudelaire as a title (in English) to one of his prose poems: 'Any where out of the world'.[43] For quasi-Symbolist creators like the three English critics under discussion, Richard himself seems a Symbolist who has unaccountably wandered into a Machiavellian political drama.

After two world wars had made some of the virtues questioned by Pater seem less dispensable, it became difficult to find pure defenders of Richard such as they.[44] But a number of critics took on the daunting challenge in effect left by Pater and Yeats, that of deciding whether the audience of this play is really meant to take Richard's side. In the mid-twentieth century, critics of this play influenced by American or British versions of New Criticism in fact made less use of New Critical notions of ambiguity, ambivalence, or balance than might be supposed. Rather, irony was the topic of choice, so that the question was nearly always one of whom we are to be *against* in what most readings of the play from the era saw as an ironic structure disclosing the shortcomings of the various dramatic agents depicted in the play, particularly the principals, Richard and Bolingbroke. Disagreement tended to focus around how much to blame Richard, how much to excuse him—no one finding Bolingbroke anything but reprehensible. And in finding a moral resting point from which to establish the judgements implied in ironic effects, these critics had recourse to a closely related set of assumptions and values, mostly implied but not defined in classical New Critical texts. One essential component of the set of ideas mobilized in both Romantic and Modernist discussions of Richard's subjectivity seems to me to have a Rousseauistic provenance, but this connection would have to have been covert in mid-century precisely because T. S. Eliot and company had made Rousseau anathema to two or three generations of Anglo-American Modernists—while

[43] Charles Baudelaire, *Le Spleen de Paris*, XLVIII, *Œuvres complètes de Baudelaire*, ed. Y.-G. Le Dantec and Claude Pichois (Paris: Pléiade, 1961), 303–4.

[44] An exception is G. Wilson Knight, *The Imperial Theme: Further Interpretations of Shakespeare's Tragedies* (London: Oxford University Press, 1931), 351–67, in a note at the end of the book which discusses Richard's prison soliloquy as a 'Shakespearian aesthetic psychology' (p. 351) akin to Keats's and further developed by Shakespeare in later tragedies.

covertly using several of his essential concepts. The central one of these was that of an interior self alienated from and resistant to the superficial, artificial socializations of post-Enlightenment 'civilization'. One of the problems with calling this notion a 'bourgeois subject', to digress briefly, is that it was so often opposed to the everyday lifestyle of the historical bourgeoisie, although it was certainly a prominent ideology within those societies dominated by the bourgeois class and within many members of that class.[45] Nor is it necessarily 'liberal' either in the nineteenth- or twentieth-century senses of that word, forming a decisive part of the sensibilities of numerous reactionaries, royalists, Fascists, and even Communists.[46] 'Humanist' is better, but not specific enough, and its current pejorative associations for many are injurious to understanding what I see as a quite two-edged, not always reactionary function in the twentieth century for these ideas. For these reasons, then, I will refer to Rousseauistic ideas of an authentic, pre-social self to label the concepts in question and go on to show how they became part of more specifically Modernist paradigms. After this, I hope to be in a better position to try to specify how the self gets conceptualized in *Richard II*.

While the reception of *Richard II*, then, certainly provides material for a cultural materialist thesis that the Shakespearian classics have been most highly valued as reinforcements of what Dollimore calls 'essentialist humanism'[47]—or, as I have it here, Rousseauistic notions of an eternal, unchanging human nature at the core of each of us—this interpretation

---

[45] In one of the most acute passages of Raymond Williams's classic *Culture and Society, 1780–1950* (1958; repr. New York: Columbia University Press, 1983), he uses the *Autobiography* of John Stuart Mill to show the construction of a Victorian mentality of divided sensibilities in which a mental 'department' is created, in Arnold's phrase, for 'the very culture of the feelings', a 'department' first revealed to him in a reading of Wordsworth's poetry. As Williams emphasized, this amounted to a strategy to isolate and contain whatever challenge to conventional wisdom and positivist methodology Romanticism posed and thus describes perhaps the major way in which a potentially transgressive subjectivity was contained in Victorian and 20th-century bourgeois cultures; see pp. 66–70.

[46] For example, Gorky tells the following story about Lenin's relation to Beethoven, beginning with Lenin's reported words: ' "I know nothing which is greater than [Beethoven's] Appassionata; I would like to listen to it every day. It is marvelous superhuman music. I always think with pride—perhaps it is naive of me—what marvelous things human beings can do!" Then screwing up his eyes and smiling, he added, rather sadly: "But I can't listen to music too often. It affects your nerves, makes you want to say stupid, nice things, and stroke the heads of people who could create such beauty while living in this vile hell. And now you mustn't stroke any one's head—you might get your hand bitten off" '; see Maynard Solomon (ed.), *Marxism and Art: Essays Classic and Contemporary* (New York: Vintage, 1974), 164.

[47] Jonathan Dollimore, *Radical Tragedy: Religion, Ideology, and Power in the Drama of Shakespeare and his Contemporaries* (1984; 2nd edn. London: Harvester, 1989), 189–203 and 249–71.

was far from universal at mid-century: another reason to see these concepts not as epistemic, but as part of specific paradigms which compete with other paradigms in a highly differentiated and contested modern culture. Clearly not every mid-century critic celebrated Richard's subjectivity. Tillyard's influential intervention in the discussion of the histories deflected much of the debate away from this topic; instead, for Tillyard the play was supposed to be the enactment of the great usurpation which brought about all the disorders of the Wars of the Roses, and Richard was described, as we have seen, in historicizing terms as the last of the purely medieval kings.[48] Thus the specificity of his characterization, which had fascinated key cultural figures of the nineteenth century, was again subordinated to interest in the play's supposed political attitudes. Many subsequent critics were thus brought back into contact with eighteenth-century concerns about the play's implied politics—only Tillyard found them to be much more 'orthodox'[49] than had many in the post-Restoration period, who apparently suspected the play's attitudes towards monarchy.[50]

Even critics immune from Tillyard's influence and who were following up on the Coleridge–Pater–Yeats line were not always enthusiastic about Richard and his subjectivity. Mark van Doren found him distasteful:

The play is organized about a hero who, more indeed then contenting himself with the role of minor poet, luxuriates in it. His theme is himself. He dramatizes his grief. He spends himself in poetry—which is something he loves more than power and more than any other person.[51]

And two prominent Shakespearian critics associated with Leavis's *Scrutiny*, D. A. Traversi and L. C. Knights—who can usually be counted on to champion within the Shakespearian play 'human' subjectivity over the inherently inauthentic political (as they do, we will see, in connection with the ending of 2 *Henry IV*)—found Richard's self-indulgence a bit too

[48] Tillyard, *Shakespeare's History Plays*, 252–63.

[49] As did J. Dover Wilson, 'The Political Background of Shakespeare's "Richard II" and "Henry IV"', *Shakespeare-Jahrbuch*, 75 (1939), 36–51; Ribner, 'Bolingbroke, a True Machiavellian'; and Brent Stirling, 'Bolingbroke's "Decision"', *Shakespeare Quarterly*, 2/1 (Jan. 1951), 27–34.

[50] This, at least, was the impression given by Nahum Tate in justifying the publication of his adaptation of *Richard II*, which had failed on the stage, in such marked contrast to the success of his *King Lear*. 'They that have not seen it Acted, by its being silenc't, must suspect me to have Compil'd a Disloyal or Reflecting *Play*', he wrote; see his preface, *The History of King Richard the Second* (London: Richard Tonson & Jacob Tonson, 1681); excerpted and repr. in Mark W. Scott (ed.), *Shakespearian Criticism: Excerpts from the Criticism of William Shakespeare's Plays and Poetry, from the First Published Appraisals to Current Evaluations*, vol. vi (Detroit: Gale, 1987), 251.

[51] Mark van Doren, *Shakespeare* (New York: Holt, 1939), 92.

much to take.[52] In this vein, too, Michael Quinn, writing in 1959, while valuing the inner man in true Rousseauistic fashion, dissented from the praise of Richard's subjectivity with an argument that he is as inauthentic in his prison-cell soliloquy as he had been earlier in his role as king; in both cases he failed to be a true man matching his inner self with outer appearances.[53] And the more influential critic A. P. Rossiter followed up on Tillyard's focus on political themes and condemned the whole play as more or less incoherent without the aid given to the reader by the historical interpretation of the anonymous chronicle-play *Woodstock*.[54]

Thus, it is clear, the Rousseauistic valorization of subjectivity in *Richard II*, initiated in the Romantic period by Coleridge and given its classic incarnation in the *fin-de-siècle* aestheticisms of Pater and Yeats, was by no means the hegemonic approach to understanding the play in the heyday of Modernism in the mid-twentieth century.[55] This line was under attack, I would argue, from two different cultural developments: on the one hand, the positivist methodologies of professional academics in the United States held out in the Academy against the much more 'aesthetic' and 'humanist' versions of New Criticism until about 1955[56] (they have survived as a minority position up to the present), and these were inherently hostile to the celebration of subjectivity, founded as they were on an attempt to efface subjectivity in favour of scientific objectivity. Second, the massive political upheavals and wars of the first half of the century had made aestheticism culturally suspect among many sympathetic to its values, but who found its withdrawal from the world irresponsible. Both of these developments are in evidence, it seems to me, in different ways among the critics discussed above. Nevertheless, the counter-Enlightenment celebration of culture, spirit, subjectivity, and aesthetics, channelled

[52] Derek Traversi, *Shakespeare: From 'Richard II' to 'Henry V'* (Stanford, Calif.: Stanford University Press, 1957), 12–48, does find Richard more 'human' than Bolingbroke (p. 30), but his account of the play is highly influenced by Tillyardian architecture, so that Richard's role in his own disastrous deposition is necessarily highlighted by Traversi, and his 'subjectivity', according to Traversi, is always a mixture of artificiality, self-dramatization, and 'true feeling' (pp. 40–3). L. C. Knights, *William Shakespeare: The Histories* (London: Longmans, 1962), 31–9, endorses Traversi's definition of Richard's mixed subjectivity (p. 37) and sees Richard as a failure both as a king and as a man.

[53] Michael Quinn, ' "The King Is Not Himself": The Personal Tragedy of *Richard II*', *Studies in Philology*, 56 (1959), 169–86.

[54] A. P. Rossiter, 'Richard II', in *Angel with Horns and Other Shakespeare Lectures*, ed. Graham Storey (New York: Theatre Arts Books, 1961), 23–39.

[55] Reportedly, however, productions of *Richard II* starring John Gielgud in an interpretation of Richard inspired by the Coleridge–Pater–Yeats line reinforced this interpretation during an era when it was much less prominent in the written criticism.

[56] Grady, *The Modernist Shakespeare*, 123.

as it became in Britain into the 'culturalist' current of Coleridge, Matthew Arnold, T. S. Eliot, and so on (classically described by Raymond Williams)—and which had its analogues and effects within the American literary tradition—was too strong a feature of post-Enlightenment culture and society not to reassert itself against even these formidable opponents. We can trace something of its counter-presence in several important mid-century commentaries on *Richard II*, which return to a focus on Richard's subjectivity.

In all these readings we can find very similar assertions of the absolute value of an inner self whose authenticity also discloses the inherent inauthenticity of the political: the qualities that make for a successful king, according to this view, are the qualities that detract from the values of humanity, and thus, while Bolingbroke wins the political game, he unquestionably loses morally. Perhaps Norman Rabkin's 1967 study of the play can serve as a *locus classicus* for this approach, common to a number of critics:

> From Aeschylus to Ibsen and Camus, great dramatists have found in politics the kind of problem which enables them to examine the human condition as only art can examine it, but always when their art is great it is so because it uses politics not to tell us about the polity what the historian and the political scientist can tell us with greater precision and knowledge, but to make us understand man in politics and therefore in the world. A historian might rest content with the knowledge that Henry IV saved England and managed to pass on his crown to his more successful son. Shakespeare recognizes all this and would not have us underestimate its importance, but he is more concerned with the human loss involved.[57]

Rabkin goes on to argue that Richard is a bad king, but a much better man than his nemesis and much more in touch with 'issues fundamental to the growth and understanding of man'. And what Bolingbroke lacks above all, 'and the lack accounts in good part for his success, is inwardness, the capacities to suffer and to dream'.[58] While Rabkin argues for a basic 'ambivalence upon which the play is constructed' (p. 88), in passages such as the above it is clear that the 'inner man' is of fundamentally greater moral importance than the mere external man of action.

We hear a variation on these themes, and a fascinating quest to pin down the ineffable, in an earlier essay on the play by Travis Bogard, who developed the often repeated notion that *Richard II* was a way station toward the great tragedies in which Shakespeare experimented with

[57] Norman Rabkin, *Shakespeare and the Common Understanding* (New York: The Free Press, 1967), 92.
[58] Ibid.

characterization and themes which he would perfect in *Hamlet* and *King Lear*. Bogard creates a speculative scenario in which a series of contingencies in the sources led Shakespeare to his great technical/ visionary discoveries. For example, the fact that Richard is described in Holinshed as gentle must have led Shakespeare to tone down the rhetoric of *Richard III*, which in turn led him to a depth of characterization he had not before attempted. As Bogard puts it, 'There must be something at the character's core which can be seen; a spiritual reality must be projected at all costs.'[59] And how is spiritual reality to be 'projected'? Bogard insists that the 'idea' of suffering is not enough; only the 'reality' of suffering, which in fact, he says, Shakespeare manages to deliver in black and white through—what else?—metaphor and poetic style. For the secret Shakespeare discovers is that 'true grief can only be imaged as it is, in silence and unseen'—that is, in a series of short lines in the staccato dialogue between Richard and Bolingbroke quoted as the locus of the 'substance' of suffering.

In this 1955 *PMLA* article we are recognizably within the classic New Critical paradigm of Cleanth Brooks's *Well-Wrought Urn*, that paean to strategic silences and ironies which, properly and mysteriously intuited, says Brooks, re-create the spiritual splendour of the past, the fruit of an extinct organic society, which the evacuated modern world is in such need of. In Bogard's particular version of the familiar ideas, however, the importance of an 'inner subject' is much more clearly articulated than it tended to be in Brooks's own writings, concerned as they were to locate all such values as much as possible within 'the texts themselves'. But Bogard is articulating a tendency which is inherent but covert in the New Critical celebration of the subjective, the poetic, and the mature over and against the sterile objectivity of instrumental discourse. Both Bogard and Brooks criticize one of the characteristic cultural malaises of twentieth-century capitalist societies, their spiritual vacuity and consequent openness to the manipulations of circulating commodities, images, desires, and ideologies. The problem here, as I have argued previously, is not with this implied diagnosis—which is more relevant than ever and which in fact dropped out of New Criticism as it became more and more professionally ensconced[60]—but with the implied solution, allegorized in these readings of Richard: that atomistic subjects could through an act of aesthetic will, by acting out a mirage-like 'true self', solve what is at its heart a societal, not an individual problem. Here a hypostatized stream of consciousness is

---

[59] Travis Bogard, 'Shakespeare's Second Richard', *PMLA* 70/1 (Mar. 1955), 192–209.
[60] Grady, *The Modernist Shakespeare*, 113–26 and 153–7.

absolutized in a desperate attempt to solve the crisis of meaning inherent in modernity. And this attempt became ubiquitous in the criticism of *Richard II* for a season as the influence of Tillyard began to fade in the 1970s.

In 1972, for example, Sidney Homan wrote: 'the price Bolingbroke pays, however, for being a man of the present world is the loss of his soul . . . his victory is charged with moral defeat';[61] and, later in the same article: 'As much as Shakespeare is concerned in *Richard II* with reordering the kingdom, he is also concerned with a man's finding of his true self, however incompatible that true self be with the affairs of the public world.'[62] The next year Harold F. Folland returned to the idea that Richard achieves a moral victory over Bolingbroke and discloses the latter's manipulative use of naked power.[63] In this vein too, T. McAlindon, while ostensibly developing Tillyard's theme of the play's medievalism, defined medieval feudalism in effect as that state where men are true to their inner selves and in their words to each other, thus inserting this tradition within Tillyardism.[64] And James Calderwood in 1979, in a deeply flawed but provocative book which explores terrain (issues of the relation of 'words and things') already occupied outside Shakespeare studies by Derrida and Foucault, and ignores these last two to the detriment of the argument, produces a new, language-oriented version of these themes in a thesis claiming that *Richard II* depicts the erosion of a pre-modern, quasi-Adamic language in which words and things were perfectly attuned.[65]

In 1983, with paradigm shifts in full progress in Shakespeare studies,[66] James P. Driscoll ramified these themes yet again in his Jung-influenced psychoanalytic reading of a Richard caught between his 'social identity' and a 'real identity' which can create 'a more comprehensive and coherent philosophy of life' for him.[67]

---

[61] Sidney Homan, ' "Richard II": The Aesthetics of Judgment', *Studies in the Literary Imagination*, 5/1 (Apr. 1972), 65–71.   [62] Ibid.

[63] Harold F. Folland, 'King Richard's Pallid Victory', *Shakespeare Quarterly*, 24/4 (Autumn 1973), 390–9.

[64] McAlindon, *Shakespeare and Decorum*, 19–43.

[65] Calderwood, *Metadrama in Shakespeare's Henriad*, 13–32.

[66] See Grady, *The Modernist Shakespeare*, 201–11. For the case of *Richard II*, the moment of the paradigm shift seems to me to be represented in John W. Blandpied, *Time and the Artist in Shakespeare's English Histories* (Newark: University of Delaware Press, 1983), which defines within the play an 'overt ambiguity' which 'makes it finally impossible to say whether Richard reveals an inner emptiness or the play itself can simply go no further in its self-consuming momentum' (p. 139). That is, these formulas express ideas of Postmodernist paradigms in the terms of Modernist ones.

[67] James P. Driscoll, *Identity in Shakespearian Drama* (Lewisburg, Pa.: Bucknell University Press, 1983), 31.

Thus, we can trace a single concept—that Richard, because of the nature of his true inner self, is unfit for his royal vocation—crystallizing as a crucial ingredient within related yet distinct critical paradigms (Coleridge's Romanticism, Pater's and the early Yeats's aestheticism), then disappearing for a (positivist) season before reappearing within New Critical paradigms in the mid-twentieth century—not coincidentally, within that generation of Shakespeare critics who were the teachers (and who are now the critical Others) of many of the active, new-paradigm Shakespeare scholars of the present. And we can posit a connection of this conception with that fascination with subjectivity which is one of the observable reactions against the instrumentalizing modes of perception which, beginning with the Machiavellianism of the Renaissance, began to dominate the construction of reality within modernity, but which seemed to leave out of their purview the apparently purposeless flux of subjectivity—which comes to be conceptualized in metaphysical and aesthetic terms in the Enlightenment and its aftermath.

In short we can say that what all of these readings have in common is their conflation of the theme of subjectivity in *Richard II* with Rousseau-istic notions of an authentic inner self which acts as a locus of absolute values through which Machiavellian politics is condemned. *Richard II* is thus deprived of much of its intellectual interest and put in service of ideologies of political quiescence and withdrawal. To be sure, these Romantic-Modernist readings all maintain a crucial and critical notion of the importance of values in politics and of the insufficiency of pure instru-mental reason in that regard. But they do so through a kind of abdication of their own, a refusal of the political *tout court* that in fact hands the political over to pure instrumentality. And they evoke Romantic myths of an authentic inner self that have long since been surpassed through a number of the discourses of contemporary criticism. Subsequently, how-ever, in our own era, as I have suggested, the kind of subjectivity evoked by the character Richard has become almost impossible to conceptualize in a set of contemporary critical discourses so keen on distancing themselves from Modernist thematics that they have very nearly capitulated to pure instrumental reason.

In what follows, I want to address this latter problem by taking up the motif of Richard's subjectivity, but connecting it to what seems to me the play's palpable Machiavellianism—rather than, as have so many previous critics, seeing these two themes as the irreconcilable opposites of an eternal human nature against a contingent season of Machiavellian power. In the process the play emerges as centrally involved in the production and analysis of important terms of a continuing modernity. Richard's subjectivity, I will argue, is closely connected to the Machiavellian framework of the play; it is in an important sense an outcome of that framework, but one which goes in a very different direction from that of the specific logic of *The Prince*.

Richard's Subjective Phase

Despite the claims of many—most notably Coleridge—that the character of Richard is consistent throughout the play, Richard's speech takes on its highly valued dimensions of poeticized subjectivity, I argue with a number of twentieth-century critics, only when he has been severed from the powers of kingship,[68] and it takes its most characteristic forms in the brief period between his abdication and death. Perhaps the most crucial speech occurs immediately after the abdication, shortly after Richard has blamed himself for his political folly in the lines quoted above. In this new context of self-consciousness, Richard declaims:

> I have no name, no title,
> No, not that name was given me at the font,
> But 'tis usurped. Alack the heavy day,
> That I have worn so many winters out
> And know not now what name to call myself!
> O, that I were a mockery king of snow,
> Standing before the sun of Bolingbroke,
> To melt myself away in water-drops! (4.1.245–52)

We can and should insert this reference to a name within the context created by Mowbray's earlier definition of the identity-conferring and social world-constituting powers of language in Act 1. Richard, too, laments his loss of identity in the transformed world. Disconnected from the symbolic system of titles, functions, and conventions of kingship which structure the power relations of this world and confer on him hitherto unquestioned privileges, Richard seems to himself to have lost not only his title but his very name. His identification of self and his lost title is so great that he imagines his body transformed into a melting

---

[68] Thus I am following a line of 'disunifiers' of Richard, a line which arose in the 20th century; see Bogard, 'Shakespeare's Second Richard'; Rossiter, 'Richard II'; and, of course, E. H. Kantorowicz, *The King's Two Bodies* (Princeton: Princeton University Press, 1957), 24–41. More recently Pye, *The Regal Phantasm* (which discusses Kantorowicz at length), sees the play as at one level exploring the complexities of a split self. As indicated earlier, 18th-century critics thought that the play was somewhat incoherent and were often puzzled about the significance of Richard.

snowman losing its substance through the agency of his deposer's brilliance.[69]

In the new context created by Richard's abdication, Mowbray becomes a kind of figure for Richard's new condition. Mowbray had disappeared, the report of his death in the Holy Land constituting perhaps his own discovery of how it might be possible to 'speak' within the signifying systems and values of his society even in exile. And Richard as well discovers that there persists something within nothing. What Richard discovers within 'nothing' is his own interiority, here presented as a core of emotion which Richard begins to value as a kind of rock of stable meaning in a world of lying external symbols (most pointedly, of course, those of his own royalty). This theme had been introduced much earlier in the play, in the interlude-like scene between the Queen, Bushy, and Bagot, in which the Queen was troubled by an apparently irrational sense of foreboding:

> Yet I know no cause
> Why I should welcome such a guest as grief,
> Save bidding farewell to so sweet a guest
> As my sweet Richard. Yet again, methinks
> Some unborn sorrow, ripe in fortune's womb,
> Is coming towards me; and my inward soul
> At nothing trembles. With something it grieves
> More than with parting from my lord the King. (2.2.6–13)

Just as Richard would later, the Queen here turns to her 'inward soul' (the phrase is used twice) while the instrumentalists Bagot and Bushy counsel that her feeling is 'nothing but conceit'—that is, of artificial conception, merely intellectual and unsubstantiated. But the Queen is not satisfied:

> 'Tis nothing less: conceit is still derived
> From some forefather grief; mine is not so;
> For nothing hath begot my something grief—
> Or something hath the nothing that I grieve—
> 'Tis in reversion that I do possess—

[69] Richard's loss of identity and suspicion of mere words were defined as early as 1957 in M. M. Mahood, *Shakespeare's Wordplay* (London: Methuen, 1957), 73–88, and the idea became more common under the influence of emerging literary theory in the late 1960s and 1970s, as in Terence Hawkes, *Shakespeare's Talking Animals: Language and Drama in Society* (London: Edward Arnold, 1973), 73–104; an earlier version was Hawkes, 'The Word against the Word: The Role of Language in "Richard II" ', *Language and Style*, 2/1 (Spring 1969), 296–322. See also James Winny, *The Player King* (New York: Barnes & Noble, 1968); Calderwood, *Metadrama in Shakespeare's Henriad*, 13–19; and A. D. Nuttal, 'Ovid's Narcissus and Shakespeare's Richard II: The Reflected Self', in Charles Martindale (ed.), *Ovid Renewed: Ovidian Influences on Literature and Art from the Middle Ages to the Twentieth Century* (Cambridge: Cambridge University Press, 1988).

> But what it is that is not yet known what,
> I cannot name; 'tis nameless woe, I wot. (2.2.35–40)

This dialogue is 'dramatic foreshadowing' in more ways than one. While serving the familiar function of alerting the audience to the mood of events to come in the play, the Queen is also calling attention to the very quality which Richard will turn to when he is confronted with his own version of 'nothing'—the nothing in which he is plunged after his abdication. At that point he discovers, as his Queen has done, that subjectivity persists in its inner life of feeling and judgement even in adversity—and that it can represent its own version of truth contradicting one's own intellectualizing rationalizations.

While, as we have seen, numerous Modernist critics described this theme as Richard and the Queen's discovery of their 'true selves', I want to emphasize that this rhetoric is not to be found in the play. The Queen, as we have seen, speaks of an 'inner soul'; the King, in the extraordinary mirror scene after his deposition, speaks of having found the 'substance' of his feeling. The concept of the self presented in this play, it seems to me, is a richer one than that of the familiar Rousseauistic terms of inner authenticity and outer deception (and, as we shall see, it becomes more complex yet in the two *Henry IV* plays and *Hamlet*).

Richard, immediately after naming himself as 'a traitor with the rest' (4.1.247), and after he has declaimed on the loss of his name and identity (in the passage quoted above), calls for a mirror to be brought

> That it may show me what a face I have,
> Since it is bankrupt of his majesty. (4.1.256–7)

Richard shatters the glass to prove that his 'face' is as 'brittle' as was his glory (4.1.277–8), and Bolingbroke, ever the deprecator of mere symbols, replies:

> The shadow of your sorrow hath destroyed
> The shadow of your face. (4.1.282–3)

Behind this positing and questioning of the efficacy of the king's image, as a number of critics have noted, lies the late medieval and Renaissance legal doctrine of the 'king's two bodies', classically defined by Ernst H. Kantorowicz forty years ago in a still relevant, much cited study of this play.[70] The doctrine, which drew on theological conceptions of the two natures of Christ, distinguished the king's natural, physical body from his

---

[70] '*The Tragedy of King Richard II* is the tragedy of the King's Two Bodies', wrote Kantorowicz, *The King's Two Bodies*, 26; see also pp. 24–41.

'body politic', a mystical fiction which embodied the king's divinely constituted authority. Here, the shattering of the glass alludes to the destruction of Richard's body politic through his abdication, and in that context
Bolingbroke's reply is a Machiavellian allusion to the unreality of this
concept, which is but 'a shadow' like the visible image in the glass.

But this powerful stage image of breaking glass is overdetermined with
other significations. Richard also breaks the glass because he is distraught
that his body natural has shown no change since his abdication—his
ruling illusion, as it were, in the early stages of the struggle with Bolingbroke was of course that his being was exhausted in his function as king—
that there was no distinction, as it were, between his two 'bodies'. But in
breaking the mirror he also accuses it of betrayal and falsity in not
adequately capturing his own inner experience of change—that shock
to his inner sense of self, which is different from the legal authority
symbolized in the concept of the body politic:

> No deeper wrinkles yet? Hath sorrow struck
> So many blows upon this face of mine
> And made no deeper wounds? O flatt'ring glass,
> Like to my followers in prosperity,
> Thou dost beguile me! (4.1.267–71)

And he apparently interprets Bolingbroke's cynical remarks on the twin
insubstantialities (shadows) of Richard's emotion and his image in his
own way:

> 'Tis very true: my grief lies all within,
> And these external manners of laments
> Are merely shadows to the unseen grief
> That swells with silence in the tortured soul.
> There lies the substance. (4.1.285–9)

This remarkable bit of stage business can as easily, and with a better 'fit',
be assimilated to Lacanian theories of the self as to Rousseauistic ones. The
distinction implied by the survival within Richard of one sense of selfhood
after the destruction of another through his abdication evokes the
Lacanian theme of a divided self which forms one unifying self-image
in the non-verbal, imagistic Imaginary register, a second (after the
acquisition of language) in the cultural codes and rules of language of
the Symbolic order. Here it is as if Richard discovers something of
what Lacan called his *moi* (bodily ego)—originally formed when the pre-
verbal child conceptualizes a mirror image of herself as the missing unity
of her experiences—after the destruction of Richard's linguistic, social

self.[71] Or, we could read the scene in a less complex frame by saying that what is left of Richard after the destruction of his identity is *emotions*, those pre-linguistic, semi-autonomous registers of perceptions and values which, as we saw in the case of the Queen's grief, are notoriously less open to the manipulations of rationalization than are our linguistically coded representations or analogues of them.[72] The inner self arrived at here bears the same relation to Richard's gestures and words as does his natural face to its image in a mirror: he values it as a 'substance' over those words and gestures which are mere 'shadows'. Deprived of his social being and identity through his deposition, Richard clings desperately to what he feels is all that remains to him, the flux of his own emotional experience.[73] This stream of consciousness, 'unfixed' from the Symbolic order of social life and self-identity, with its paradoxical properties of continuing to evaluate, feel, and reproduce a sense of the real even when his entire identity and conceptual framework have been shattered, constitutes the Shakespearian conception of unfixed, modern subjectivity central to the ending of *Richard II*, to a number of subsequent tragedies and comedies, and to this study. And this moment of the cultivation of the flux of the inner life is, as I shall discuss in the next chapter, very near to the experiments with his self which Montaigne described throughout his essays. This is a moment, *contra* Althusser, which we might describe as 'disinterpellation'. If, in Althusser's influential formula (discussed in the Introduction), a sense of a fixed, ideology-centred self is created when the self comes into existence through an affirmation of a socially produced identity-ideology, here we see something very like the opposite of this process depicted in Shakespeare: a self is severed from its ideology-identity and set adrift to

[71] Pye, *The Regal Phantasm*, within a stimulating general argument that links Lacanian themes with a Greenblatt-inspired study of the theatricality of royal power in Shakespeare's and other similar absolutist political systems, also discusses parallels between themes of Lacan and the Queen's and the mirror scenes in an analysis different from mine; see pp. 84–95.

[72] See Robert Solomon, *The Passions: The Myth and Nature of Human Emotion* (Garden City, NY: Doubleday, 1976), for a development of this idea of the 'rational' content of emotions.

[73] Wolfgang Iser, *Staging Politics: The Lasting Impact of Shakespeare's Histories*, trans. David Henry Wilson (New York: Columbia University Press, 1993), 102–14, discusses many of the same passages from this play in this bracing study, stimulating precisely because of its distance from (and occasional surprising convergences with) contemporary Anglo-American Shakespeare studies, but concludes that Richard's private self is empty and his search to reach it chimerical. Richard in the prison scene becomes 'aware of the degree to which his life had been a masquerade, even though this awareness still does not release him from role-playing. Evidently there is nothing beyond whatever Richard has been trying to embody in his roles, and the "unseen grief" he calls his "substance" is ultimately only a way of glossing over something that seems impossible to grasp' (p. 106).

construct a new one in a world now (consequently) seen as alien and unmeaningful.

This moment reaches a new level of conceptualization in the celebrated soliloquy performed by Richard in prison. Here Richard, instead of despairing, decides to investigate the interior world which is the remainder of his subjectivity after his disinterpellation. As nothing new is ever invented *ex nihilo*, Richard's unfixed subjectivity follows the procedures of rhetoric enshrined in the Ciceronian stage of *inventio*, and characteristically of English Renaissance rhetoric, with emphasis on dialectics:[74]

> I have been studying how I may compare
> This prison where I live unto the world;
> And for because the world is populous,
> And here is not a creature but myself,
> I cannot do it. Yet I'll hammer it out.
> My brain I'll prove the female to my soul,
> My soul the father, and these two beget
> A generation of still-breeding thoughts. (5.5.1–8)

Rhetoric is apposite here because one strand of the received rhetorical tradition, as Kahn pointed out in her discussion of the intersections of Machiavelli and rhetoric, conceptualized rhetoric as a technology, a means of persuasion adaptable to any topic and any audience.[75] And while Renaissance humanists generally endorsed the Ciceronian rejoinder to this instrumentalistic self-description—the truly useful, Cicero insisted, cannot finally be in contradiction to the good[76]—the Machiavellian ethos delineated in Kahn's work as highly pervasive in England (and, as I have tried to demonstrate, pervasive as well within this play) tended to reinforce rhetoric's instrumental dimensions to the detriment of its practical or ethical ones.

Richard's rhetoric here, then, is the mirror within the sphere of subjectivity to Machiavellian rhetoric within the sphere of politics: both of them display the dynamics of purposeless purposefulness, but within radically different arenas, productive of radically disparate discourses. In the intersubjective network of power a relationship among men and women is constituted through which society is organized to accomplish social tasks of every sort, although by its nature power is in itself as indifferent to the concrete tasks undertaken as it is to the human costs of

---

[74] See Kahn, *Machiavellian Rhetoric*, 114–15.
[75] Ibid. 5–10.
[76] Ibid. 9.

its implementation. It is a technology, a means to any end whatever, and as such its ultimate goal can only be to sustain and augment itself.[77]

Within the radically diminished realm constituted by Richard's isolated mental life, however, the same dynamic produces a quite different result. The play of free thought in unfixed subjectivity displays the dynamics of Lacanian desire: an endless deferral of satisfaction as the mind flits from one desired (mental) object[78] to another:

> And these same thoughts people this little world
> In humours like the people of this world.
> For no thought is contented. (ll. 9–11)

Taken a few steps, further, we will see below, such 'purposeless purposiveness' within the mental sphere produces the basis not only of what I am calling subjectivity, but of what Adorno would term modern art, now no longer integrated into the relatively more holistic cosmologies and religious mythologies of pre-modern cultures, but autonomous,[79] ungrounded in larger myths, and capable of critical reflection on the society which produces it. Within the cleared space of this new kind of subjectivity, desire continues to conceptualize a 'real' and work within it as well:

> Thoughts tending to ambition, they do plot
> Unlikely wonders: how these vain weak nails

[77] The characterizations of power are from Foucault; see esp. *The History of Sexuality*, i: *An Introduction* (1976), trans. Robert Hurley (New York: Vintage, 1990), 92–8. The analysis of technical or instrumental reason as self-perpetuating and dominating is from Horkheimer and Adorno, *Dialectic of Enlightenment*, 3–42 *et passim*. I discuss the connections between these two approaches in Grady, *Shakespeare's Universal Wolf*, 47–55.

[78] This is a reference to the Lacanian concept of the *objet petit a*, the process through which desire is constituted in an endless series of alienated objects; see Jacques Lacan, *The Four Fundamental Concepts of Psycho-analysis*, ed. Jacques Allain-Miller, trans. Alan Sheridan (New York: Norton, 1981), 67–104; for a helpful exposition of the concept see Ellie Ragland-Sullivan, *Jacques Lacan and the Philosophy of Psychoanalysis* (Urbana: University of Illinois Press, 1987), 78–82; and for a different use of the concept, as it relates to Lacan's notions of the gaze and the scopic field in a reading of *Richard II*, see Pye, *The Regal Phantasm*, 82–105.

[79] This Frankfurt School term can cause confusion if it is assumed that the formula means that art has no connection with the social realm of which it is a product; for Adorno and related Frankfurt theory, art bears within itself the birthmarks of its production within a class-based and reified society. The term 'autonomous' is meant rather to denote what Adorno saw as the post-Enlightenment production of a historically new, specialized, secular category—art—linked historically to but functionally distinct from more totalizing cultural productions such as, say, Greek epic or Dante's *Divine Comedy*, which were seen as much more integrated with, and less critical of, the surrounding cultures which produced them. As I have suggested, the Renaissance seems to me to begin in many ways processes which Adorno assigned to the Enlightenment, and I am arguing that Shakespeare's plays (among others) are very early examples of modern art in Adorno's sense.

> May tear a passage thorough the flinty ribs
> Of this hard world, my ragged prison walls. (ll. 18–21)

The subjective is not a simple solipsism. While it has the potentiality to become purely 'aesthetic', it is also oriented to the ordinary world, the 'lifeworld' of recent Habermassian theory. Such an orientation to sociality helps explain why Richard would, in his profound isolation, still strive to 'people this little world, I In humours like the people of this world'. Within the flux of his unfixed subjectivity, deprived of any anchoring identity in the lifeworld, he still constitutes a world of social relations. At the same time, the site of this scene of the discovery of modern subjectivity is a prison; and this association is appropriate to the extent that such subjectivity is now alienated from a world in which it had previously been dispersed, within the collective constructions of the ideology of divinely constituted monarchy as a link in a universe understood as simultaneously symbolic and empirical. Now (and henceforth) meaning will be confined to a subject seeking fruitlessly to find itself among the instrumentalized objects of a disenchanted nature and society.

One crucial difference, however, between Richard's 'unfixed' and alienated subjectivity and that of an 'anchored', identity-bound relation to the lifeworld is that the unfixed subjectivity has easier access to resources of imaginary compensation when desire runs up against its limits, and fantasies of escape 'die in their own pride' (l. 22). In such cases, Richard argues, it is possible to identify imaginatively with a host of fellow sufferers and in that reflection 'find a kind of ease' (l. 28). And this last thought leads him to a remarkable (and Montaignean) view of the possibilities of multiple identities within subjectivity:

> Thus play I in one person many people,
> And none contented. Sometimes am I king;
> Then treason makes me wish myself a beggar,
> And so I am. Then crushing penury
> Persuades me I was better when a king.
> Then am I kinged again, and by and by
> Think that I am unkinged by Bolingbroke,
> And straight am nothing. But whate'er I be,
> Nor I, nor any man that but man is,
> With nothing shall be pleased till he be eased
> With being nothing. (5.5.31–41)

After this comes the sound of music, and a closing disquisition in which Richard leaves the imaginary and brings his thoughts back to time,

Bolingbroke, and 'this all-hating world' (l. 66). His murder follows hard upon this.

Thus, in the privileged moments before his death, Richard has conceptualized and exemplified one of the characteristic outcomes of the desacralized world of modernity. He has untied his social identity—or more accurately, had his social identity untied—from what Lacan called the Symbolic order into which he was born, that chain of significations representing the world into which he was thrust—and in which he had been one of the master signifiers as the king holding through his office divine authority.

That chain being broken through his abdication or deposing—and the Machiavellian reductions which preceded it—he is thrown into a virtual abyss, and he employs a rhetoric of nothingness to describe it: he is, as we saw above, 'straight . . . nothing' (l. 38); and he longs for a time of ease when he grows 'eased | With being nothing' (ll. 40–1).

This rhetoric will of course be repeated to even greater effect and dramatic intensity in a play which shares many of the themes and concerns of this one, *King Lear*. Both plays enact the disastrous abdication of a king, who then becomes separated from his social identity and the Symbolic order generally while his kingdom falls under the sway of subjects of Machiavellian power. And both explore the experience of nothingness— of separation from the Symbolic order and imaginative explorations of alternative identities and values—through Richard's soliloquy in *Richard II* and through the metamorphoses of Edgar, Lear, and the other exiles in *King Lear*.[80] And in both of these treatments 'nothing' turns out to have suggestive positive coloration, once the initial disorientation of the identity crises in question is overcome—briefly, at the very end of Richard's soliloquy in *Richard II*, much more extensively in the 'redemptions' of Lear and Edgar in *King Lear*.

Machiavellian rhetoric, we have seen in the first part of this chapter, had reconceptualized the human world as a realm of naturalistic power struggles in which men only appeared to be battling for values and visions: through the cool analytics of Machiavellian theory, these values and visions in turn were reduced to so many versions of mere appearance, empty counters which the prince knew were essential in order to influence the actions of the many, but which he himself could not afford to absolutize or surrender himself to.

This is one version—certainly among the most important in theRenais-

[80] This connection was first suggested to me by passages in Eagleton, *William Shakespeare*, 77, and developed in my chapter on *Lear* in *Shakespeare's Universal Wolf*, 137–80.

sance—of that larger movement of the massive cultural *disenchantment of nature*, that undermining of the received, meaning-giving mythologies of religion and custom, which the Western world undertook in the long production of Enlightenment and the post-Enlightenment world which we now inhabit.[81] Contrary to a central strand of Horkheimer and Adorno's indispensable *Dialectic of Enlightenment*,[82] enlightenment as a process of disenchantment meaningfully commences in the Renaissance, with the intertwined productions of mutually anathematizing Christian polemics between Catholics and Protestants, the rise of secular modes of thinking through 'rediscovery' of the classics, the beginnings of the scientific method, the development of mercantile capitalist economies with their corrosive processes of the commodification of daily life,[83] and, as I have emphasized here, the unfolding of consciousness of Machiavellian power as an unmistakable dynamic of international and civil politics and war. One of the cultural corollaries of this process was the much discussed crisis of meaning which pervades the literature and philosophy of Renaissance England and which is arguably the precondition for Shakespeare's dramatic art and the secret of its continuing relevance within a world still experiencing this quintessential property of a still unfolding modernity.

Subjectivity and its Critics

Before returning to the play, however, I need briefly to distinguish these themes from related ones of two seminal contemporary critics of early modern power and subjectivity, Jonathan Dollimore and Stephen Greenblatt.[84] Jonathan Dollimore usefully conceptualized something like

[81] See Charles Taylor, *Sources of the Self: The Making of the Modern Identity* (Cambridge, Mass.: Harvard University Press, 1989), for a treatment of modernity and the modern self as centrally implicated in an instrumental reason which becomes pervasive in the 16th and 17th centuries.

[82] See Grady, *Shakespeare's Universal Wolf*, 15–25 and 219–23.

[83] I am drawing on a more developed discussion of these themes in Grady, *Shakespeare's Universal Wolf*, 26–57 *et passim*. For further discussion of the role of commodification in Shakespeare's day, see Douglas Bruster, *Drama and the Market in the Age of Shakespeare* (Cambridge: Cambridge University Press, 1992).

[84] My critique of Dollimore and Greenblatt (like the earlier one of Belsey), however, has only incidentals in common with the sweeping polemics of two recent self-consciously 'reactionary' works of Shakespearian criticism, Brian Vickers, *Appropriating Shakespeare: Contemporary Critical Quarrels* (New Haven: Yale University Press, 1993), and Graham Bradshaw, *Misrepresentations: Shakespeare and the Materialists* (Ithaca, NY: Cornell University Press, 1993), which in my view are classic instances of works which throw out the baby (of the broad enterprise of cultural criticism) with the bathwater (constituted by specific local insights and criticisms each work contains).

the conceptions of power and subjectivity I am working with in his ideological reinterpretation of the Heideggerian and Lacanian concept of the 'decentred self'. He concentrates on the Jacobean malcontents, like the Edmund of *King Lear*, who, he said, were able, like actors involved in the famous 'alienation-effect' of Brechtian dramaturgy, to distance themselves from confining ideologies and make known to the audience the power-serving ideological nature of the discourses which constitute them and others in the play. Dollimore, as subsequent writings clearly indicated, thought that ideology could be 'subverted' by representations of it that identified its logical instabilities and power-serving social functions. He did so, however, while generally endorsing previous critical accounts of the 'liberal humanist subject' like Catherine Belsey's, but arguing that the age of the Elizabethan, Jacobean, and Caroline London theatres was a brief cultural window between the much more 'centred' eras of medieval synthesis and Enlightenment.[85]

My own version of this theme parallels these key elements of Dollimore's, but I think it is necessary to underline here what I see as its principal blind spot. As his argument develops, Dollimore gets caught up, I would argue, in the systemic inability of the contemporary Machiavellian theories of Foucault and Althusser to account for the values implicit within their concepts of ideology or power/knowledge. Thus Dollimore is forced to make of *ideological distantiation* itself the only possible source of value within *King Lear* and the other tragedies, and this turns out to be empty in the extreme because distantiation by itself can only create an empty space—on which something else needs to be written. But virtually every attempt to think about sources of values in *Radical Tragedy* calls up the spectre 'essentialist humanism'—so that Dollimore's Nietzschean idea that all ideals are ultimately based on violence and repression has here the effect which Nietzsche himself managed to evade through his aestheticism, of making it more or less impossible to think about value as such. Consequently, his idea of a pervasive essentialist humanism is finally disabling of our ability to think the crucial categories of what can lie conceptually beyond exposed ideologies.

Stephen Greenblatt, like Dollimore, also delineated a number of forms of ideological 'evacuations' of traditional religious world views, evacuations creative of a cultural crisis requiring new strategies of self-fashioning and new kinds of cultural texts negotiating meaning in a complex cultural configuration. And Greenblatt, reportedly influenced by Foucault's theories of subjection as he worked over the materials of *Renaissance*

---

[85] Dollimore, *Radical Tragedy*, 155–6.

Self-Fashioning and *Shakespearian Negotiations,* ended up emphasizing Foucault-like processes of the 'containment' of the potentially subversive outcomes of the mental productions of culturally evacuated spaces, so that new forms of subjection arise simultaneously with the overthrow of the older ones in the texts of figures like More, Tindall, Wyatt, Spenser, Marlowe, and Shakespeare. Thus, while a number of his essay-chapters define moments of meaning and values which are not simply ideological (as they are, for example, in Dollimore's discussion of *King Lear*), these were subordinated rhetorically to delineations of containment, so that for Greenblatt as well, new forms of subjectivity in the Renaissance were given a largely repressive functionality.[86]

In short, writing in the power-obsessed late 1970s and 1980s,[87] both of these pioneering critics of new historicism qualified their treatments of subjectivity so strongly (echoing the highly influential themes of Foucault and Althusser) that subjectivity emerged in their treatments essentially as an effect of power, while positive evaluations of subjectivity, especially in Dollimore, were placed under grave suspicion. They had, as I put it in the Introduction, reinvented a narrow Machiavellian world view.

In developing this critique of Dollimore and Greenblatt, then, I want to emphasize the positive dimensions of the Renaissance 'invention' of modern subjectivity. 'Invention' is here a relative term; similar forms of consciousness have clearly developed in other eras of Western history and in many of the other innumerable cultures of our planet.[88] But this form of subjectivity has taken on an unprecedented cultural centrality in modern Western societies, forming the basis for the (endlessly changing) production of solutions to the crisis of meaning which has constituted modern Western culture, most particularly its art, literature, and philosophy, since the Renaissance.[89]

[86] See Michael Bristol, *Carnival and Theater: Plebeian Culture and the Structure of Authority in Renaissance England* (New York: Methuen, 1985), 14–16, for similar critiques of Greenblatt and Dollimore from a Bakhtinian perspective.

[87] Don E. Wayne, 'Power, Politics, and the Shakespearian Text: Recent Criticism in England and the United States', in Jean E. Howard and Marion F. O'Connor (eds.), *Shakespeare Reproduced: The Text in History and Ideology* (New York: Methuen, 1987), 47–67, insightfully defines the connections between the new critical emphasis on power in Shakespeare studies and the ages of Reagan and Thatcher.

[88] That is, I am presuming that the kind of purposeless purposiveness characteristic of this mode of subjectivity might be possible in any number of cultural contexts in given times and places—for example (to draw only from the pre-modern literatures I am most familiar with): in the tragedies of Euripides in the Greek 'Enlightenment'; in any number of the urbane lyrics and stories of Roman literature; in the secular courtly love literature of the European high Middle Ages; or in the classical, sophisticated court poetry of the Arab world, China, and Japan.

[89] These are large claims, but in asserting them I am building on aspects of the crucial work

As with others of the constituting forms of modernity, Shakespeare (consciously or unconsciously) represented this post-disenchantment, differentiated form of privatized myth-making in its many facets. In the *Henriad* and *Hamlet* this theme works as a crucial dramatic counterweight to that sombre exposition of Machiavellian, disenchanting politics which, as we have seen, is also its conceptual precondition in *Richard II*. It will be further defined, probed, and enriched in the remainder of the *Henriad*; *Hamlet* is, so to speak, its epic poem.

Let me return briefly, then, in this new context, to the case of Richard II's subjectivity. Richard's deposition and imprisonment have brought him to that privileged mental space—at once terrifying and exhilarating—called 'nothing' in this play and in *King Lear*. It is a space in which his former sense of social identity and thus his place in the social world have been abandoned, and he is confronted by a now estranged world and a severed stream of consciousness and imagination, along with a vast residuum of shards from a shattered, formerly unified sense of culture and language which Richard had already undermined through the Machiavellian consciousness which understood such belief systems as necessary fictions rather than as inherent in reality.

In Richard's case—and in all the examples from Shakespearian drama discussed here—this form of subjectivity resulted from that kind of shock to one's sense of self that psychoanalyst Eric Erickson in the twentieth century has called an identity crisis. By identity I mean here something very close to what Althusser called 'interpellation' and to what the Hegelian tradition has called 'being-for-others'; in Lacanian terminology it refers to that identification within the Symbolic order formed in cultural and ideological terms, and not the pre-linguistic identity of the mirror stage. This identity is one's sense of how (idealized, imagined) others fit one into a social world of family, community, and the other institutions and networks of human interaction.

of Raymond Williams and the Frankfurt School critics, most particularly Adorno, Hork-heimer, and Benjamin, as indicated in the Introduction. All these figures used different terminology and employed somewhat different foci from those I am involved with here, but all of them have mapped out for different areas of modern Western culture the crucial role of subjectivity, and its dialectical relations to the cultural crisis caused by disenchantment or desacralization which I am discussing. In addition to the texts discussed in the Introduction, central works in this connection would be: Williams, *Culture and Society*; Theodor Adorno, *Aesthetic Theory*, ed. Gretel Adorno and Rolf Tiedemann, trans. C. Lenhardt (London: Routledge, 1984); Herbert Marcuse, 'The Affirmative Character of Culture', in *Negations: Essays in Critical Theory* (Boston: Beacon, 1968), 88–133; Walter Benjamin, 'The Storyteller' and 'The Work of Art in the Age of Mechanical Reproduction', in *Illuminations*, ed. Hannah Arendt, trans. Harry Zohn (New York: Harcourt, 1968).

As Shakespeare represents and dramatizes this crisis of identity, the crisis acts as a kind of shock therapy initially devastating to the character undergoing it, but eventually liberating in that it allows for an alienation from given social structures, values, assumptions, and ideologies, and it presents the possibility of forging new, self-fashioned identities constitutive of new relations to the lifeworld:

> Thus play I in one person many people,
> And none contented. Sometimes am I king;
> Then treasons make me wish myself a beggar,
> And so I am. Then crushing penury
> Persuades me I was better when a king.
> Then am I kinged again, and by and by
> Think that I am unkinged by Bolingbroke,
> And straight am nothing. But whate'er I be,
> Nor I, nor any man that but man is,
> With nothing shall be pleased till he be eased
> With being nothing. (5.5.31–41)

As Greenblatt in particular has been at pains to show, such self-fashionings are never quite the *ex nihilo* creations of a sovereign subjectivity mythologized in post-Enlightenment Western culture. In the above quotation, for example, Richard is clearly imagining himself in terms of the ideological givens of king and subject, simply varying his location within a stable social order. In the last two lines of the speech, perhaps, there are hints of a possible overcoming of that mental framework in the hitherto unthinkable idea that nothingness (the possibilities of a self freed from its original insertion into a social order) could become easeful, no longer a crisis of non-being but a precondition for personal and societal change. But these remain symbolic suggestions of a particularly indeterminate text open to other interpretative possibilities.

Through these thematics *Richard II* enacts a process which we will see repeated, developed, and ramified in numerous Shakespearian plays to come. It is a process that unfolds simultaneously at social and psychological levels, and it demonstrates the inescapable connections and interpenetrations of society and individuality that later ideologies of a sovereign self in the post-Enlightenment West would obscure. From *The Comedy of Errors* to *The Tempest*, Shakespeare presented moments like this repeatedly, with all kinds of affects: elation, terror, delight, and angst, as a long series of characters confront the possibilities conferred by emerging modernity for creating new selves: an unfixing of identity and the construction of alternative but unfixed subjectivity. Rosalind, Falstaff,

Prince Hal, Hamlet, Iago, Lear, and others in addition effect a self-severing—or disinterpellation—from a previously taken-for-granted world of legitimized values and ideologies, and each improvises her or his way from one alienated, socially and self-created role to another in a Montaignean play of subjectivity made deeper and more consequential by its being embedded in a Machiavellian political process which Montaigne had fled, but in which the world of Shakespeare (and ourselves) was (and is) very much entangled.

Shakespearian drama is one crucial and culturally central site for the construction within conditions of modernity both of a (relatively) new idea of subjectivity and of the new category of an autonomous aesthetic in Western culture. This is a project which it shares with the *Essais* of Michel Montaigne, and it is to Montaigne's version of these themes that I now turn.

3

Montaigne, Shakespeare, and the Construction of Modern Subjectivity

Montaigne and the Machiavellian

Machiavelli defines for Renaissance political culture forms of instrumentality which are central to modernity and crucial to understanding many of the social and political dislocations of the era. As if in answer to this new situation, the essays of Michel de Montaigne propose a strategy of resistance to the instrumentalization of politics defined by Machiavelli. This appears to be a form of resistance peculiarly attractive to Shakespeare and a series of successors who saw in the protean possibilities of new forms of subjectivity a dissenting force—with possibilities of harmless escapism, to be sure, but also of a critical rationality which makes social and political subversions thinkable. For most readers the idea of a Montaigne–Shakespeare connection, discussed off and on for the last 100 years or more without consensus, is probably less questionable than a Montaigne–Machiavelli connection. But if we examine the themes and terms of the very earliest versions of Montaigne's essays,[1] it is clear that he did not immediately arrive at his famous determination to retreat from the world and contemplate the workings of his own subjectivity.[2] Instead, a few of

[1] Montaigne's essays were composed in a complex, layered process. The earliest edn. of the *Essais* was published in 2 vols. in 1580. This was in turn the basis for an augmented edition, with substantial additions to many of the original essays, and a third volume of brand-new essays, in 1588. All modern editions are based on the so-called Bordeaux copy of the 1588 edn., with new passages in Montaigne's handwriting. Thus there were three chief 'strata' in the composition of the *Essais*, and these are distinguished with superscript letters A B C in scholarly French editions and in the well-known English translation by Donald Frame, *The Complete Essays of Montaigne* (Stanford, Calif.: Stanford University Press, 1957), used for all subsequent quotes here.

[2] The shifting, changing nature of Montaigne's project in the *Essais* has been a major topic of 20th-century commentary on him at least since the classic scholarship of Pierre Villey, *Les Sources et l'évolution des Essais de Montaigne*, 2 vols. (Paris: Hachette, 1908). A standard

the earliest essays show a preoccupation with diplomacy and suggest that he may have been honing his credentials as a humanist adviser to princes, perhaps with a view to securing a post somewhere in France. And of course, despite the fame of his eighteen years or more of retired life—the occasion for the composition of his famous work—he had a substantial public life, serving before retiring as a magistrate in one of the chief courts of France, the Parlement de Bordeaux, for sixteen years (1554–70) and interrupting his retirement (at the king's request) for a term as Mayor of Bordeaux (1581–5) for another four. In addition, he served from time to time on missions for kings and other leaders, particularly for Henry of Navarre, the quintessential French Renaissance man of power who became Henry IV in 1589.

In the early essays especially, there is a marked similarity in method and subject matter to Machiavelli,[3] most particularly the more humanist Machiavelli of the *Discourses*; but in subject matter, method of composition, and even tone we are at times reminded of *The Prince*.

In the two most 'Machiavellian' essays, 'Whether the Governor of a Besieged Place Should Go Out to Parley' and 'Parley Time is Dangerous' (chapters 5 and 6 of book 1), Montaigne shares Machiavelli's fascination with the autonomy of power and political success from morality, and he explores his theme, like his Florentine predecessor, with one anecdote after the other, drawn (again as in Machiavelli) from both his reading of the classics and his own experience of contemporary politics and warfare.[4] In the first of these short pieces, Montaigne surveys the conflicting opinions of the ancients over whether trickery in warfare is laudable or censorable, and then shifts to contemporary times:

As for us, who, less superstitious, hold that the man who has the profit of war has the honor of it, and who say, after Lysander, that where the lion's skin will not suffice we must sew on a bit of the fox's, the most usual chances for surprise are derived from this practice of trickery. And there is no time, we say, when a leader must be more on the watch than that of parley and peace treaties. And

English-language account is given in Donald M. Frame, *Montaigne: A Biography* (New York: Harcourt, 1965).

[3] Cf. Frame, *Montaigne*, 144. Frame also mentions Erasmus, Plutarch, and a number of lesser-known writers from the ancient and early modern worlds as possible models for the early essays.

[4] For a quite different reading of these two neglected early essays, see Thomas M. Greene, 'Dangerous Parleys—*Essais* I:5 and 6', *Yale French Studies*, 64 (1983), 3–23. Greene reads the theme of a besieged town or fortress as a metaphor for interiority besieged by the distractions of the world, concluding that 'these apprentice essays seem to condone indirectly their author's choice to withdraw from a parliament into his tower bastion' (p. 12).

for that reason there is a rule in the mouth of all military men of our time, that the governor of a besieged place must never go out himself to parley.[5]

Since Machiavelli is mentioned explicitly elsewhere in the *Essais*,[6] the reference to the lion and the fox may be meant to recall his previous use of this ancient figure. In any case Montaigne shares with Machiavelli something of his acceptance of the way of the world, to the extent of coolly observing in several examples the success of treachery in politics in both ancient and modern times. Characteristically, however, Montaigne soon enough, even in these early pieces, establishes his own quite value-laden judgements concerning the value-free dynamics of power and treachery. After quoting two Machiavellian lines from Ariosto ('To conquer always was a glorious thing, | Whether achieved by fortune or by skill'), Montaigne adds:

But the philosopher Chrysippus would not have been of that opinion, and I just as little. For he used to say that those who run a race should indeed employ their whole strength for speed but that, nevertheless, it was not in the least permissible for them to lay a hand on their adversary to stop him, or to stick out a leg to make him fall.[7]

That is, Montaigne reverts to the Ciceronian-humanist practice of subjecting the useful to the criteria of the honest, even while paying his respects to the Machiavellian observation that the two may not, in fact, coincide.

In book 2, chapter 17 ('Of Presumption') he returns to the Machiavellian challenge to values. At first he seems to take something of the Ciceronian position, arguing that deception may work at first, but not in the long run:

The gain that lures them to the first breach of faith—and almost always there is gain in it, as in all other wicked deeds; sacrilege, murder, rebellion, treachery are always undertaken for some sort of profit—this first gain brings after it endless losses, casting this prince out of all relations and means of negotiations in consequence of this breach of faith.[8]

---

[5] Montaigne, *Essays*, 17 (1.5). I quote Frame's translation throughout in the belief that it makes Montaigne most easily accessible to the majority of readers of this work, while neither the French text nor the admirable Renaissance English translation apparently used by Shakespeare (John Florio's) is directly relevant to my purposes. I cite volume and chapter number following the page number in Frame's edn. for the convenience of readers with other edns.

[6] Ibid. 497 (2.17) and 556 (2.34).

[7] Ibid. 19 (1.6).

[8] Ibid. 494 (2.17).

Later in the chapter, however, he is less certain that this kind of argument really represents the last word on the issue:

Machiavelli's arguments, for example, were solid enough for the subject, yet it was very easy to combat them; and those who did so left it no less easy to combat theirs. In such an argument there would always be matter for answers, rejoinders, replications, triplications, quadruplications, and that infinite web of disputes that our pettifoggers have spun out as far as they could in favor of lawsuits.[9]

And this consideration leads him directly into that advocacy of political stability which I will discuss below, in connection with Montaigne's scepticism. For the moment, it is clear that for Montaigne, it is not so much that Machiavelli is wrong; it is rather that 'the diversity of human events offers us infinite examples in all sorts of forms';[10] his truth takes its place in a larger, swirling, and finally incoherent truth which also contains its opposite.

In the first chapter of book 3—the last volume of essays which Montaigne composed for the 1588 edition and which for many commentators represents the culmination of the art and philosophy of the *Essais*—Montaigne returns once more to the challenge to Ciceronian humanism represented by *The Prince*. The essay is given the Ciceronian title 'De l'utile et de l'honneste' [Of the useful and the honourable]. Its solution, however, is neither Ciceronian nor Machiavellian.

Here Montaigne grants more to Machiavellian logic than he had previously conceded. He argues that in nature, in the individual, and in society, the apparently imperfect vices such as envy, jealousy, or cruelty serve a useful purpose and that 'Whoever should remove the seeds of these qualities from man would destroy the fundamental conditions of our life.'[11] The same is true, crucially, at a social level:

Likewise in every government there are necessary offices which are not only abject but also vicious. Vices find their place in it and are employed for sewing our society together, as are poisons for the preservation of our health. If they become excusable, inasmuch as we need them and the common necessity effaces their true quality, we still must let this part be played by the more vigorous and less fearful citizens, who sacrifice their honor and their conscience, as those ancients sacrificed their life, for the good of their country. We who are weaker, let us take parts that are both easier and less hazardous. The public welfare requires that a man betray and lie and massacre; let us resign this commission to more obedient and suppler people.[12]

---

⁹ Montaigne, *Essays*, 497 (2.17).   ¹⁰ Ibid.
¹¹ Montaigne, *Essays*, 600 (3.1).   ¹² Ibid.

Where sarcasm and irony leave off and world-weary resignation begins in this passage we are at hazard to define precisely. But that there is some mixture of both of these attitudes in this complex passage seems clear. The logic of this argument is no longer Ciceronian, inasmuch as it concedes the Machiavellian proposition that 'it is necessary for a prince, who wishes to maintain himself, to learn how not to be good, and to use this knowledge and not use it, according to the necessity of the case'.[13] But neither is it fully Machiavellian, for the language pins on to these necessary acts the negative moral judgements of the words 'vices', 'honor', and 'conscience', creating an effect much more discordant than Machiavelli's own moral oxymorons at similar junctures in The Prince. And of course these words are counterpoised by the equally strong judgements implied in the language of sacrifice and patriotism—unless we interpret these as hopelessly undermined by the context, and truly, this crux is undecidable. But a later passage helps us to see that he is not simply trying to demolish Machiavellian logic through indirect irony: 'I do not want to deprive deceit of its proper place; that would be misunderstanding the world. I know that it has often served profitably and that it maintains and feeds most of men's occupations. There are lawful vices, as there are many either good or excusable actions that are unlawful.'[14] But he is scrupulous to stipulate that ends can justify illicit means only for reasons of state: 'No private utility is worthy of our doing this violence to our conscience; the public utility, yes, when it is very apparent and very important.'[15]

As Montaigne's argument develops, however, this third attempt to take a position on Machiavellian logic in the Essais takes a new direction—not new for the Essais themselves, for it is one of their central leitmotifs—but new in this context. Montaigne opts for a policy of individual abstentionism, even if the end involved in a dubious action is public: 'If there should be a prince with so tender a conscience that no cure seemed to him worth so onerous a remedy, I would not esteem him the less. He could not ruin himself more excusably or becomingly.'[16] And the chapter ends with an analogy that would perhaps be strange for one so wedded as has been Montaigne throughout the Essais to a notion of the naturalness and desirability of sexual pleasure, except that it apparently contains just the logical structure he needed: marriage, he writes, is clearly 'the most necessary and useful action of human society'. However, he continues, 'Yet the

[13] Niccolò Machiavelli, The Prince, in The Prince and The Discourses (New York: Modern Library, 1950), 56; ch. 15.
[14] Montaigne, Essays, 604 (3.1).
[15] Ibid. 607 (3.1).
[16] Ibid.

council of saints finds the contrary way more honorable, and excludes from marriage the most venerable vocation of men, as we assign to stud those horses which are of least value.'[17]

This argument neither answers the disturbing questions raised by Machiavellian logic nor acquiesces to them either. It rather grants their cogency, then dissents from them as a matter of private, and higher, principle. The solution to the sad necessities of the world, in short, is privacy. If the public is irremediably implicated in the paradox of private vices for public good, one can try at least to abstain personally from such dilemmas. Montaigne has produced the public–private split endemic to the societies of modernity—a split that is ideological, to the extent that it justifies the cruel necessities of power; utopian and critical in that it posits and attempts to live out an ideal which the all-too-real world will not fully allow. In doing so, he has plunged us mid-stream into central thematics of *Richard II, 1 and 2 Henry IV* and *Hamlet*. Montaigne produces within his essays a dynamic between a Machiavellian value-free space and a compensating subjectivity of value-judgements; it is in fact a very historically consequential version of themes that will become basic to a developing modernity and to Shakespeare's plays, whether Shakespeare appropriated it from a reading of Montaigne or developed it separately.

In trying to contextualize Montaigne's momentous withdrawal to privacy and his milestone focus on his own self as subject for his work, it is hard to avoid suspecting after reading passages like these that his radical withdrawal to private life involved a kind of 'Give unto Caesar the things that are Caesar's' relinquishment of a public sphere deemed by him irremediably compromised by the exigencies of power.[18] Certainly the France of the second half of the sixteenth century, with its incessant religious civil wars, replete with massacres, atrocities, political assassinations, and betrayals, presents a particularly vivid canvas of human depravity in the realm of the political. It is true that Montaigne's retirement in 1571 had no more obvious external stimulus than a series of life-events—the death of his great friend La Boétie (1563), his marriage (1565), the death of his father and consequent coming into his patrimony (1568), and possibly, as Frame speculates, a near brush with death in 1569 or 1570 in a horse-riding accident.[19] And it is clear from his later comments that

---

[17] Montaigne, *Essays*, 610 (3.1).

[18] Cf. Richard L. Regosin, *The Matter of my Book: Montaigne's 'Essais' as the Book of the Self* (Berkeley and Los Angeles: University of California Press, 1977), who describes what is in effect Montaigne's great refusal of the world. Montaigne, Regosin writes, 'seeks to define himself against the world, in opposition to public ideology' (p. 36).

[19] Frame, *Montaigne*, 113–15.

the legal work he was involved in in his duties with the Parlement de Bordeaux left him cold and dissatisfied—albeit, as Frame says, also supplying him with innumerable further examples of human foibles.

The most infamous of all the atrocities of religious civil war in France, the St Bartholomew's Day Massacre, which involved the treacherous slaying of thousands of leading Huguenots in Paris and elsewhere throughout France, including Montaigne's Bordeaux, occurred in August 1572, a year and a half after Montaigne's withdrawal to his namesake estate. But such events could only deepen Montaigne's desire for private life and the extraordinary intellectual project which began to fill it up, and they seem to colour the additions to the essays of later years. In one of the quotes I reproduced above, for example—'The public welfare requires that a man betray and lie and massacre'[20]—the word *massacre* was added only in the last additions before Montaigne's death. But Montaigne's withdrawal was never complete or unequivocal; he continued a desultory public service, as mentioned previously, as Mayor of Bordeaux and as a kind of diplomat among the warring religious-dynastic factions. What is certain is that the intellectual project of the *Essais* never returned again to the kind of political prudence and fascination with realpolitik (except, as in passages we have seen, as part of larger meditations) that is evidenced in the brief 'Machiavellian' essays I discussed. Instead, Montaigne turns to the same realm as did Richard II in his prison-cell, the flux of subjectivity and its potential for 're-peopling' a world apparently bereft of human values through the evacuations of Machiavellian politics and rhetoric.

Montaigne Constructs the Subjective

In the famous 'Au lecteur' of the first and all subsequent editions of the *Essais*, Montaigne specifies:

This book was written in good faith, reader. It warns you from the outset that in it I have set myself no goal but a domestic and private one . . . Thus, reader, I am myself the matter of my book; you would be unreasonable to spend your leisure on so frivolous and vain a subject.[21]

That this warning cannot be taken at face value is soon apparent, although it took perhaps two or three more centuries before its audacity and constitutional relation to one of the central projects and characteristics of modernity was appreciated. Montaigne was praised by many of his contemporaries, but it was largely as a 'French Seneca', a wise philosopher of

---

[20] Montaigne, *Essays*, 600 (3.1).   [21] Ibid. 2.

Stoic sensibility, that he was celebrated.[22] His Whitmanesque treatment of self was generally seen as an eccentric weakness by his contemporaries.[23] To the classical absolutists of the immediately following generations this quality was often troubling, and it and the methodology of scepticism with which it is intertwined have remained scandalous to many readers and commentators since, even while it has been repeatedly celebrated by many others on the opposite side of the post-Enlightenment cultural divide between the subjective and objective.

The present climate of anglophone early modern studies, with its numerous theoretical attempts to overcome this divide, seems to me particularly propitious for an appreciation of the very qualities of Montaigne that seemed scandalous to his own age, and even more to absolutists and positivists of every persuasion subsequently, and I am surprised that he has not been more central in the rewriting of the Renaissance that has been so vigorously undertaken since about 1980 in an English studies now more open than ever to the contributions of comparative literature. In this brief section I want to contribute to a project of redefining Montaigne's place in the reconfigured disciplinary map of early modern culture produced by new historicists, cultural materialists, and feminists.[24] Montaigne is central to many of the themes of recent critical production. But like Richard II in his deposed state, and other Shakespearian characters to be discussed, he does not fit easily into the best-known paradigms of subjectivity of recent critical theory within English Renaissance studies.

[22] Frame, *Montaigne*, 310–23.

[23] Ibid. 311–12.

[24] Within French studies see especially the special issue of *Yale French Studies, Montaigne: Essays in Reading*, 64 (1983); Jean Starobinski, *Montaigne in Motion* (1982), trans. Arthur Goldhammer (Chicago: University of Chicago Press, 1985), a Geneva School 'phenomenological' study which shades into deconstruction; and Richard L. Regosin, *Montaigne's Unruly Brood: Textual Engendering and the Challenge to Paternal Authority* (Berkeley and Los Angeles: University of California Press, 1996), which explores the theme of children and offspring as a figure for the writing and textuality of the *Essais*. In English studies see particularly Timothy J. Reiss, 'Montaigne and the Subject of Polity', in P. Parker and D. Quint (eds.), *Literary Theory/Renaissance Texts* (Baltimore: Johns Hopkins University Press, 1986), 115–49; this article undertakes a significant rereading of Montaigne, showing the difficulties with the traditional position that Montaigne had produced an early version of the Cartesian self, arguing instead that there are two different 'subjects' in Montaigne with a complex interrelation; because of its relevance to my own argument I return to this below on specific points. David Quint, *Montaigne and the Quality of Mercy: Ethical and Political Themes in the Essais* (Princeton: Princeton University Press, 1998), also sees a protean, sceptical Montaigne, in this case one who is arguing for a new ethics of toleration and social peace. And see Susan Wells, *Sweet Reason: Intersubjective Rhetoric and the Discourses of Modernity* (Chicago: University of Chicago Press, 1996), 221–60, for an analysis of the *Essais* as defining *avant la lettre* the limits of the disciplinary projects produced by the differentiated rationalities of modernity.

One problem is undoubtedly his equivocal relationship to power, that characteristic double-edged position which could be called 'urbane accommodation'. On the one hand for Montaigne, every idea, every scrap of ideology and human belief, is open to doubt and scepticism:

each man calls barbarism whatever is not his own practice; for indeed it seems we have no other test of truth and reason than the example and pattern of the opinions and customs of the country we live in. There is always the perfect religion, the perfect government, the perfect and accomplished manners in all things.[25]

On the other hand, the very uncertainty of human knowledge and the unreliability of reason are themselves warrants for extreme caution in undertaking social change of any sort, especially, as Montaigne famously argued in the longest of the essays, 'The Apology for Raymond Sebond', in matters of religion, since the antiquity of the authority of the Catholic Church more than counterweights whatever rationality can be found in Protestant arguments against it. Thus at times, Montaigne sounds extraordinarily conservative:

And therefore, to my mind, in public affairs there is no course so bad, provided it is old and stable, that it is not better than change and commotion. Our morals are extremely corrupt, and lean with a remarkable inclination toward the worse; of our laws and customs, many are barbarous and monstrous; however, because of the difficulty of improving our condition and the danger of everything crumbling into bits, if I could put a spoke in our wheel and stop it at this point, I would do so with all my heart. . . . The worst thing I find in our state is instability, and the fact that our laws cannot, any more than our clothes, take any settled form. It is very easy to accuse a government of imperfection, for all mortal things are full of it. It is very easy to engender in a people contempt for their ancient observances; never did a man undertake that without succeeding. But as for establishing a better state in place of the one they have ruined, many of those who have attempted it have achieved nothing for their pains.[26]

In this equivocation, from our post-Enlightenment vantage point, there seems almost dissimulation, or at least a wasted intellectual effort: all things are criticized, only to be affirmed, we might say. In an important article, Timothy J. Reiss sees this contradiction as the key to a necessarily new reading of the relation of power and the self in Montaigne. It is only in the domain of private reason and a private self—which, Reiss argues, is a flux, an inconstancy, not really a subject at all because it cannot fix itself—that Montaigne's scepticism obtains. The 'public' self is on the contrary a conventional 'subject' in the double sense of intentional agent and of

[25] Montaigne, *Essays*, 152 (1.31).   [26] Ibid. 497–8 (2.17).

dutiful follower of a monarch. Only through the fixed system of a divinely enfranchised public state is the self permitted to act in the public world—otherwise, anarchy results, argues Reiss.

This thesis gets at the important way in which Montaigne was able to act in the world as an undisputed Catholic and supporter of normal royal succession. But it seems to me not to take into account enough the important theme in Montaigne of dialogue with Machiavelli. If Reiss is right that Montaigne is participating fully in the ideology of moderate Catholic politics, then Montaigne is a very naive reader of Machiavelli—and there is textual evidence that this is not the case. That is to say, Reiss's is a reading based squarely in a 'hermeneutics of belief' that does not for a moment question the way these ideas work as an ideology. Or rather, we should say Reiss assumes that they are of course ideological but that Montaigne could not have been conscious of this, or that the text cannot signal its own ideological status. But if we read instead through a 'hermeneutics of suspicion', a different picture of the relation of public and private reason emerges. I would rather put it in something like the terms Dollimore defined for the transgressive tendencies of the English Jacobean theatre: in a culture where a frontal assault on the intellectual pillars of its power arrangements is impossible, due to the repressive functions of Church and State, it is still possible to plant doubts, raise questions, and encourage critical rationality.[27] And this is Montaigne's accomplishment in the *Essais*.

Many works of twentieth-century Montaignean criticism—preeminently Donald Frame's—have been at pains, in response to earlier attempts to make of this sixteenth-century Frenchman a child of the Enlightenment *avant la lettre*, to underline the numerous protestations, in the *Essais* and in contemporaneous reports, of Montaigne's orthodox Catholic beliefs.[28] But the nature of belief is a vexed question, and all the evidence can as easily be assimilated to a view that Montaigne had concluded that Catholicism represented the best chance for peace and stability in his time and place and that it behoved him to take a public stance as a moderate Catholic, keeping any religious scepticism to himself.[29] He certainly stands out in his time as a proponent of broad-

---

[27] Jonathan Dollimore, *Radical Tragedy: Religion, Ideology, and Power in the Drama of Shakespeare and his Contemporaries* (1984; 2nd edn. London: Harvester, 1989), 15–22, discusses Montaigne, but he finds his scepticism counterbalanced by that affirmation of the laws and customs under which one is born that Montaigne states repeatedly.

[28] See Richard H. Popkin, *The History of Skepticism from Erasmus to Spinoza* (Berkeley and Los Angeles: University of California Press, 1979), 54–5, for an account of the debate, with a fittingly sceptical position on it.

[29] Cf. ibid. 55; and Pierre Leschemelle, *Montaigne: The Fool of the Farce*, trans. William J. Beck (New York: Peter Lang, 1995), who wrote (alluding to Henry IV's famous observation

mindedness in relation to other cultures and beliefs, particularly, as Frame pointed out in his biography, in the case of Jews—an attitude reflecting, perhaps, the Jewish ancestry of his mother (her family were *marranos*, or converted Spanish Jews[30]). And in any case, as all commentators agree, his acceptance (at whatever level) of Catholicism underwrites his scepticism; by publicly asserting a higher, supra-rational truth, he is enabled to investigate the mutability, uncertainty, and protean nature of human rationality without fear of censorship or persecution.[31] '[A]ll wisdom is foolish that does not adapt itself to the common folly,'[32] he remarked in a late addition of the essay 'Three Kinds of Association', and that remark may have application in this context as well as its original one.

It is of course his scepticism, not his Catholicism, that makes Montaigne such an interesting figure to study in our own time. His work is one of the major cultural outcomes of that brief window between a theo-centric late medieval absolutism and the later theo- and logocentrisms of the seventeenth century.[33] Reiss, in the article I discussed above, has his own version of the idea that Montaigne is involved in a major epistemo-logical rupture in which he plays a transitional role by producing two related concepts of the subject. One of these, as we saw, is the 'public' subject, constituted as such in submission to an absolutist social order and the figure of the king who personifies it.[34] The second—one much nearer

on his reasons for converting to Catholicism in order to become king): 'if Paris was worth a Mass, the *Essays* are really worth a few genuflections and "greetings". Besides, these pro-tective devices were so thinly disguised' (p. 192).

[30] Frame, *Montaigne*, 16–28.

[31] Montaigne had an unsolicited encounter with Vatican censors when his books were confiscated and examined (apparently a standard procedure for all visitors) during his five-month stay in Rome in 1580–1, and a copy of the *Essais* returned to him with some 'correc-tions'. However, he was told to make only those changes he wished and was asked to help the Church with his eloquence, according to Frame, *Montaigne*, 217–18.

[32] Montaigne, *Essays*, 622 (3.3).

[33] This way of conceiving the history of early modern *mentalités*, with its much greater emphasis on 'open-ended' or sceptical philosophy than in more conventional accounts, was forcefully argued by Popkin, *The History of Skepticism from Erasmus to Spinoza*. More recently a similar chronology was put forth by Stephen Toulmin, *Cosmopolis: The Hidden Agenda of Modernity* (New York: Free Press, 1990), which I discussed in *Shakespeare's Uni-versal Wolf* (Oxford: Clarendon Press, 1996), 15–20. Lars Engle, *Shakespearian Pragmatism: Market of his Time* (Chicago: University of Chicago Press, 1993), 8–9, and his '*Measure for Measure* and Modernity: The Problem of the Sceptic's Authority', in Hugh Grady (ed.), *Shakespeare and Modernity: From Early Modern to Millennium* (London: Routledge, 2000), 85–6, also sees Toulmin as having defined the kind of cultural opening exploited by Shakespeare and Montaigne.

[34] My objection here is not that there are not notions of submission to authority in Montaigne—they are a major theme of the *Essais*. However, I think it is just as plausible to see these themes as a politic submission which grants legitimacy to the more sceptical side of Montaigne's writings.

to my own idea of Montaigne's notion of subjectivity—is of a private, even withdrawn mental flux which is unfixed and undefined—barely a subject in some of the key traditional senses of the word at all, since it is not an agent in the world.[35] Here, I want to investigate Montaigne's production and analysis of early modern subjectivity as one of the defining moments of early modern reactions to a profound Renaissance-Reformation crisis of value.[36]

All parties to the dispute would acknowledge that Montaigne's ideas on subjectivity are complex, multivalent, and, as he cheerfully and proudly acknowledges, contradictory. We can get at some of this contradictoriness through one of his many remarks on sexual attraction:

It is madness to fasten all our thoughts upon it and to become involved in a furious and reckless passion. But on the other hand, to go into it without love and without binding our will, like actors, to play the standard role of our age and customs and put into it nothing of our own but the words, that is indeed providing for our safety, but in cowardly fashion, like a man who would abandon his honor, his profit, or his pleasure for fear of danger. For it is certain that from such a relationship those who form it can hope for no fruit that will please or satisfy a noble soul. We must have really desired what we expect to get real pleasure from enjoying.[37]

Here, as in the mock addresses to a penis in 'Of the Power of the Imagination' (1.21), Montaigne posits a complex, layered interiority.[38] There is a dynamic of sexual attraction which is largely autonomous from other aspects of the self, but which can be modified, magnified, or lessened

[35] Stephen Greenblatt, *Renaissance Self-Fashioning: From More to Shakespeare* (Chicago: University of Chicago Press, 1980), 252–3, briefly gave a description similar to Reiss's, emphasizing Montaigne's idea of subjectivity as a process rather than a substance and comparing these notions (rightly, I believe) to Shakespeare's. Dollimore, *Radical Tragedy*, 15–19, on the other hand, characteristically argued that Montaignean scepticism amounts to an early form of ideology-critique, thus avoiding any direct comment on subjectivity.

[36] Popkin, *The History of Skepticism from Erasmus to Spinoza*, 42–65, argues a similar view of Montaigne's intellectual centrality in the intellectual ferment of the 16th and 17th centuries.

[37] Montaigne, *Essays*, 626 (3.3).

[38] Wells, *Sweet Reason*, shows parallels between the conception of the self in 'Of the Power of the Imagination' (Montaigne, *Essays*,1.21) and Lacanian psychoanalytic themes: 'The uncertain boundaries of the self, its subjection to an uncontrollable desire, the blurred division between mind and body, and the uncontainable replication and splitting of the self'. (p. 228)—linking these qualities in turn to Montaigne's self-enacting scepticism through which his texts refuse to guarantee their own truth. As mentioned in the Introduction, Lacan in fact invoked Montaigne as a precursor of his theory of a radically split subject; see Jacques Lacan, *The Four Fundamental Concepts of Psycho-analysis*, ed. Jacques Allain-Miller, trans. Alan Sheridan (New York: Norton, 1981), 223–4; and see Ellie Ragland-Sullivan, *Jacques Lacan and the Philosophy of Psychoanalysis* (Urbana: University of Illinois Press, 1987), 7–10, for an elaboration of Montaigne's key place in the history of the concept of the subject in a Lacanian reading of the history of French literature.

through acts of will—and these acts of the will imply an intentional subject or agent, separate from desire. There is also an external self, an image for others, potentially a mere actor playing 'the standard role of our age and customs' but which can be created or produced 'with nothing of our own but the words'. And there is an ethical (perhaps here epicurean) ideal of harmony among these aspects of the self: the subject of (autonomous) desire and the subject of prudent reasoning in actions in the world should agree on their object in order to obtain both pleasure and nobility of soul.

It is worth recalling the Machiavellian self referred to earlier in order to compare that idea of the self with this one. In Machiavellian dynamics, there is a being-for-others, an outward appearance, which is theatrical, manipulated by the subject in order to manipulate others; and there is an inner self, occluded, but reducible to the desire for power and/or pleasure which generates the outer appearance. All the complicated middle elements in Montaigne's descriptions are eliminated through a kind of brutal Occam's razor. Now Montaigne is not blind to the desires for power and pleasure, nor to the possibilities of an outward appearance which can mask the inner reality; these functions exist, but so also do ethical rationality, degrees and depths of desires, and ideals of harmony between the outer and inner man or woman. Here the self is something that is observed and experienced, something that acts and performs, and something that feels and judges. It is both in the world and withdrawn from the world.[39] In short, Montaigne presents in his essays an approach to subjectivity far more complex and adequate than Machiavelli's, and he is thus of paradigmatic importance for us now, in an era when many are in search of alternatives to the Machiavellian theories of the self of French poststructuralism and the criticism within English studies it has spawned. With its emphasis on the self as not only immersed in ideology but capable of distantiating itself from it through complex, decentred interactions, Montaigne's views of subjectivity, as I argued in the Introduction, are much closer to those of critics like Adorno, Horkheimer, Habermas, Lacan, and Žižek than they are to Althusser's or Foucault's simpler models of the self.[40]

[39] Robert Ellrodt, 'Self-Consciousness in Montaigne and Shakespeare', *Shakespeare Survey*, 28 (1975), 37–50; 45–9, pursues a similar distinction which he defines as a contrast between 'Machiavellian characters' in Marlowe and early Shakespeare involved in 'self-assertion' and later characters of 'self-consciousness', fully achieved in Hamlet but partially by Richard II and Brutus, involving a character's reflection on himself or herself as an agent with more than one possible identity, if I might put it in terms different from Ellrodt's.
[40] See the Introduction above for my argument that this relation between a Montaignean

In addition, and famously, Montaigne's self is in constant flux:

I cannot keep my subject still. It goes along befuddled and staggering, with a natural drunkenness. I take it in this condition, just as it is at the moment I give my attention to it. I do not portray being; I portray passing. Not the passing from one age to another, or, as the people say, from seven years to seven years, but from day to day, from minute to minute. I may presently change, not only by chance, but also by intention.[41]

This passage from the beginning of 'Of Repentance' (to which I had recourse at the end of the Introduction) is perhaps the most important one in all the *Essais* for Postmodernist- and poststructuralist-inspired readings which tend to find in the Renaissance examples of pre-Enlightenment decentred selves which parallel contemporary, post-Enlightenment decentred selves. Here certainly Montaigne encapsulates a fluidity and flux which is constantly enacted at the level of writing practice in the celebrated free-form, chaotic order of his essays and which testifies to a sense of subjectivity impossible to contain or fix. To me, it is a passage which comes as close as any in the *Essais* to defining that unfixed subjectivity which is the crucial 'invention', as it were, of Montaigne's oeuvre—and one close to one of Shakespeare's.[42]

In the same essay, however, Montaigne speaks of a certain stability in the self, a certain habitual structure:

There is no one who, if he listens to himself, does not discover in himself a pattern all his own, a ruling pattern [*forme maitresse*], which struggles against education and against the tempest of the passions that oppose it. For my part, I do not feel much sudden agitation; I am nearly always in place, like heavy and inert bodies.[43]

In this passage, at least, he appears much less assimilable to Postmodernist claims for a consistent early modern anti-essentialism.[44] However, a

and a Machiavellian approach to subjectivity replicates that late 20th-century contrast between the one-dimensional theory of subjectivity through interpellation in Althusser and the much more complex one in Lacan and the Frankfurt School.

[41] Montaigne, *Essays*, 610–11 (3.2).

[42] Cf. Greenblatt, *Renaissance Self-Fashioning*, 252–3 (who quotes from the above passage and compares its ideas to Shakespeare's), and Reiss, 'Montaigne and the Subject of Polity', 132–43, who alludes to this passage among several others on similar themes as part of his important argument that the Montaignean private subject is distinct from the Cartesian subject as well as from the subject of possessive individualism of the bourgeois era in that it is unstable, unfixed, and unable to act in the world.

[43] Montaigne, *Essays*, 615 (3.2).

[44] Reiss, 'Montaigne and the Subject of Polity', 133–4, discussed this passage and argued that it was followed by contradictory references which revert to the idea of a decentred self, rather than to a Cartesian intentional self. For Reiss the idea of a centred self in Montaigne exists only as a desire and absence. In a more debunking vein, Tzvetan Todorov, 'L'Être et

crucial problem in trying to define concepts for Montaigne arises whenever we look for post-Cartesian consistency, as is made clear in an earlier observation in the same essay, an idea which followed, for Montaigne, from the mutability of the self: 'This [these essays] is a record of various and changeable occurrences, and of irresolute and, when it so befalls, contradictory ideas: whether I am different myself, or whether I take hold of my subjects in different circumstances and aspects.'[45] In a sense the very contradictoriness of these passages returns us to the theme of flux which they had seemed to deny.

Thus, while Montaigne seems at least at moments to have held the age's commonplace ideas on a fixed individual human nature or virtue, at times sounding more like the essentialist Roderigo of *Othello* ('It is not in my virtue to amend it') than the anti-essentialist machiavel Iago ('Virtue? a fig! 'tis in ourselves that we are thus or thus. Our bodies are our gardens, to the which our wills are gardeners'[46]), he is clear in the chapter that follows 'Of Repentance' that the apparent limits of our individual humours and tendencies can be overcome by application:

We must not nail ourselves down so firmly to our humors and dispositions. Our principal talent is the ability to apply ourselves to various practices. It is existing, but not living, to keep ourselves bound and obliged by necessity to a single course. The fairest souls are those that have the most variety and adaptability.... If it were up to me to train myself in my own fashion, there is no way so good that I should want to be fixed in it and unable to break loose. Life is uneven, irregular, and multiform movement. We are not friends to ourselves, and still less masters, we are slaves, if we follow ourselves incessantly and are so caught in our inclinations that we cannot depart from them or twist them about.[47]

Montaigne's approach to Machiavellian logic, to the complex mixtures of critique and accommodation which a prudent man should take to his age's ideology, to the nature of the self, and to the utopian qualities of critical rationality seems to me, as it has to a number of previous critics (see above at the end of Chapter 1), remarkably intertextual with many Shakespearian thematics. In particular, Montaigne's fascination with his

l'autre: Montaigne', *Yale French Studies*, 64 (1983), 113–44, discusses this and related passages in the third section of this essay (which is devoted to three aspects of the self in Montaigne) and finds the idea of a ruling pattern and its apparent opposite (the theme of a subject in constant flux) to recapitulate what he thinks is a recurring, monotonous pattern of opposing, absolutized oppositions throughout the *Essais* which ultimately serve ideological ends.

[45] Montaigne, *Essays*, 611 (3.2).
[46] Shakespeare, *Othello*, 1.3.316–27. I discussed Iago's 'anti-essentialism' at length in *Shakespeare's Universal Wolf*, 98–109.   [47] Montaigne, *Essays*, 621 (3.3).

own subjectivity and his valorization of that subjectivity as a response to the dilemmas of early modern decentring, desacralization, and instrumentalization involved in the Machiavellian closely resemble the characteristic dialectic in Shakespeare between desacralization and subjectivity in the histories and tragedies. There is no question, of course, of identity. Montaigne never undergoes—at least according to the account of the *Essais*—the kind of radical identity crisis that overtakes Richard II, Prince Hal, Hamlet, Othello, Lear and company, Macbeth, Antony, Timon, and so on. Montaigne never dramatizes the cultural crisis of meaning in the Renaissance as Shakespeare does, as a kind of descent into nothing, madness, and absurdity. But his sceptical practice produces a similar desacralization, a radical differentiation between an imperfect, always agnostic human rationality and a transcendent, non-human religious certainty—a certainty which, to judge by the myriad examples of the *Essais*, has a very limited relevance to everyday life in the human world. Of much greater import to that world are the imperfect judgements of subjectivity, predicated on a fallible but inevitably value-laden construction of the real. Montaigne thus can be construed as among the first modern champions of a purely secular ethical or practical rationality, grounded in an ungrounded subjective flux.[48] The elimination of intrinsic values through instrumental, value-free rationality, à la Machiavelli, does not mean, as Montaigne insists in his own terms, that we should do without values; it reveals rather that the source of value is other than a unified, mythopoeic, God-saturated universe (which for Montaigne is beyond our merely human capacities); it defines the sphere of subjectivity as their locus; but it is never able to stabilize subjectivity as a completely secure locus of values because by its nature it is impermanent, in flux, and open to all the myriad possibilities of human nature already revealed in the sobering texts that make up human history. Montaigne, like Shakespeare, delivers us into a world in a kind of permanent moral crisis, but one in

---

[48] Cf. Hugo Friedrich, *Montaigne* (1949, 1967), ed. Philippe Desan, trans. Dawn Eng (Berkeley and Los Angeles: University of California Press, 1991), who wrote: 'In the recognition that the self is a continuous process the visible aspects of which tell only part of the tale while the whole retreats or can be traced only by lining up its randomly comprehensible movements—in this recognition Montaigne is superior to all studies of man from antiquity and post-antiquity' (p. 211). Friedrich's chapter on the self in Montaigne (pp. 207–57) defines both his relation to precedents and the uniqueness of his treatment of the self in comparisons with Augustine and two contemporary autobiographies, Girolamo Cardano, *De vita propria* (written c.1575, published in France 1643), and the better-known autobiography (written between 1538 and 1562) by the Florentine sculptor and goldsmith Benvenuto Cellini (1500–71). A similar view is argued by Ellrodt, 'Self-Consciousness', 42–7, in a thumbnail sketch of the phases of selfhood from antiquity to the Renaissance in which Montaigne and Shakespeare are major figures in a radical late Renaissance break with earlier phases.

which life, perception, and evaluation (in an unfixed subjectivity) continue nevertheless[49]—a condition the cultures of modernity continue to express and explore.

The fascination with the flux of subjectivity that Montaigne and Shakespeare display is an index of the dilemma in which early modernity finds itself entrapped and defined. Subjectivity continues to represent and interpret the world in all the complex colorations of prudence and judgements of value and beauty which obtained in pre-modern societies. Only it does so in the absence of the certainties and beliefs in nature and the intrinsic through which the various forms of pre-modern mythology and cosmology had constituted the world.[50] Shakespeare and Montaigne, I argue, give a common answer to the Machiavellian reduction which had robbed the world of value and enchantment. Yet they cannot return the certainties, the vanished floor under the mythopoeic rug which modernity had so unceremoniously removed. Yes, there are values, there is beauty, there are ethics. But they cannot be grounded within the general nature of things or the will of a mysterious and absent God. Instead, Montaigne and Shakespeare can only display them and contrast them with the world that obtains without them—and perhaps posit a utopian hope for an intersubjectively constructed world more receptive to them.

[49] Cf. Starobinski, *Montaigne in Motion* : 'Montaigne reconciles himself to the fact that this world is inevitably a world of appearances, and that aesthetic form, and hence artifice and disguise, cannot be avoided in the pursuit of personal identity' (p. 86).

[50] Dollimore, *Radical Tragedy*, 19–21, makes a similar argument, but he, like Reiss, sees Montaigne's scepticism as leading 'perilously close to nihilism', so that not subjectivity, but religious fideism, as in 'An Apology of Raymond Sebond', is the antidote to the Machiavellian reduction.

4

The Resistance to Power in
1 Henry IV:
Subjectivity in the World

The unfixed, Montaignean subjectivity of the deposed Richard II
reappears in several new guises in the Prince Hal trilogy, which continues
the historical narrative begun in *Richard II*. The new plays relocate subjectivity from the enclosed privacy of Richard's prison to the communal and
public spaces of political and counter-political worlds. This development
is in a sense a return to the 'Machiavellian' subjectivity of *Richard III*,
because every private action in these plays is at least potentially political.
But the versions of the self represented in the *Henry IV* plays go well
beyond *Richard III*'s relatively simple structure of an inner drive for power
disguised by the various masks of apparent piety—even though, as a host
of contemporary critics have argued, such Machiavellian theatricality is an
important feature of what is represented in *1 and 2 Henry IV*. The problem
with this recent view is not its accurate recognition of the importance of
Machiavellian politics in these plays; the problem is one of incomplete-
ness. Here, as elsewhere in Shakespeare, Machiavelli is supplemented with
Montaigne. *Henry IV, Part 1* dramatizes for us a political world of king and
rebels, Machiavellian plotting, and political rhetoric close in many ways to
the Machiavellian atmosphere of *Richard II*—only to parody that world
unmercifully and to develop what was only an implication in *Richard II*,
the notion that the high seriousness of politics is grounded in nothing
more substantial than the wit combats and plays on words of a dis-
reputable tavern.

The two *Henry IV* plays are among Shakespeare's richest productions,
and a good deal of this richness is achieved through kaleidoscopic effects

which are among the clearest markers of the Montaignean, 'sceptical' qualities of Shakespeare's most characteristic works, resisting univocal interpretation. There is a dizzying set of possible connections among the various components of the two *Henry IV* plays—between the two constituent plays, between the interwoven plots considered separately or jointly, between the two plays' 'camps' or groupings of characters, and between these two plays and those that precede and follow them in the tetralogy, for example—and all of these possible parallels and contrasts suggest a variety of possible interpretations. I will present a truncated critical history of debate on some of these possible constructions of the plays below. Most critics agree, however, that the centre of the plays is filled by the complexly interacting pair Prince Hal and Falstaff, and they constitute the centre of my enquiry here into the plays' probings of Machiavellian power and Montaignean subjectivity. Connected as they are, however, Falstaff and Prince Hal each develop a distinct approach to subjectivity and the Machiavellian, and they are best treated separately, at least in that regard.

Falstaff resides in a Cervantesque metafictional realm in which he continually manufactures comic but efficacious counterfactual identities. In contrast, Prince Hal is a juggler of identities within the social real, able to move from one social context to the other, changing his sense of self almost as casually as he changes his clothes. Instead of a radical absence of identity of the sort suffered by Richard in prison or Lear on the heath, the Prince, like Hamlet after him, is faced with a surplus of them. A separate feminine-domestic sphere also appears prominently in *1 Henry IV*, and it provides additional resources for mobile identity, as we will see below.

It is not my position, however, that the counter-Machiavellian tavern and domestic realms of these plays directly challenge Machiavellian politics; rather, they interrogate and undermine it—only in turn to be interrogated and undermined themselves in an open-ended dialogic interplay. Of course the moments of counter-Machiavellianism prove, in *2 Henry IV*, as we will see in the following chapter, quite fragile and transitory, since in that play subjectivity begins to become reified, that is, co-opted by the abstract exchange systems of power and commodities which I discussed in *Shakespeare's Universal Wolf*. Finally, we watch in *Henry V* as reified power manufactures itself as such. Granting these qualifications, however, *1 Henry IV* is still a high point in the Elizabethan Shakespeare of the celebration of unfixed subjectivity; it is in that sense an instance of a smaller Montaignean supplement within the larger Machiavellian moment informing Shakespeare's works from 1595 to 1600.

But while a tradition of seeing 2 *Henry IV* as a play in its own right is now well established,[1] the same cannot be said for *Part 1*. The banishment of Falstaff at the end of *Part 2* and the habit of treating the two plays as one are each so powerful that it has become extremely difficult to read *Part 1* except with that sober moment as a kind of foreordained *telos*, and consequently critics and readers often fail to notice that *Part 1* has a quite different ending, with different implications, from that of *Part 2*. In what follows I want to read 1 *Henry IV* as a completely autonomous play, treating the banishment of Falstaff as what it remains throughout this play, a much imagined potentiality which, however, does not in fact occur. Because I believe both 2 *Henry IV* and *Henry V* present very different configurations of the themes of power and subjectivity, despite a good deal of continuity with this play, I break with long-standing critical precedent and treat them below in a separate chapter. *Part 2* decisively reconfigures the relation between unfixed subjectivity and reified power established in 1 *Henry IV*, in the direction of 'fixing' subjectivity and in heroicizing power; and this trajectory is continued and amplified in *Henry V*.

In 1 *Henry IV*, in contrast, a theme of resistance to the reduction of the self to an instrumentalized Machiavellian actor is, as it were, centre-stage. In *Richard II* subjectivity emerged after Richard's loss of identity as a kind of surplus with no apparent outlet in the world of activity; it existed as a purely imaginary potentiality. But 1 *Henry IV* shows us subjectivity in the social world and suggests that the domain of Machiavellian politics is only one of a number of possible locales for its energies.

The True, the False, and the Counterfeit

These marked differences between the worlds of 1 *Henry IV* and *Richard II* among other things constitute a new 'turn' in the development of a thematic motif we saw in *Richard II* and which is prominent in all four plays of the *Henriad*: that of language as a signifier of a prolix, protean realm of unstable signifiers—a theme invoked early in 1 *Henry IV* by Falstaff's wit battles around the notions of true lion and true prince, and then by the play's extraordinary playing with the term 'counterfeit'. This verbal dexterity is basic to both the Machiavellian and the Montaignean qualities of the play and helps to establish one of the strongest thematic continuities among the plays of the *Henriad*. Falstaff introduces it offhandedly:

[1] See the next chapter for documentation. The trend began in the 1920s and was debated in the 1940s, after which 2 *Henry IV* has slowly and unevenly climbed from out of the shadow of its great dramatic predecessor.

Why, hear you, my masters. Was it for me to kill the heir-apparent? Should I turn upon the true prince? Why, thou knowest I am as valiant as Hercules; but beware instinct. The lion will not touch the true prince—instinct is a great matter. I was a coward on instinct. I shall think the better of myself and thee during my life—I for a valiant lion, and thou for a true prince.[2]

As with so much of Falstaff's discourse, the lines are overdetermined. In the context of the Machiavellian-Montaignean view of monarchical succession established in *Richard II*, it is clear that all of Hal's tavern companions, and Falstaff a fortiori, share an interest in accepting the claim for Hal's essential royalty. 'Never call a true piece of gold a counterfeit—thou art essentially made, without seeming so' (2.5.449–50), Falstaff exclaims in a much disputed comment which may be partially explained in this context as a cheerful assertion of a necessary fiction which it is in all the parties' interests to share. Earlier, however, Falstaff had playfully put Hal's royalty in question as part of his persuasion of the Prince to take part in the planned robbery: 'There's neither honesty, manhood, nor good fellowship in thee, nor thou camest not of the blood royal, if thou darest not stand for ten shillings' (1.2.124–6). And these needling assertions-accusations were in turn answers to Hal's own double-edged rhetorical question (does he wink, or not?): 'Who, I rob? I a thief? Not I, by my faith' (1.2.123). If we want to take Falstaff's argument at its simplest face value, we could say that in thus cajoling Hal as to the genuineness of his manhood, honesty, and fellowship—trying, in effect, to interpellate Hal into Falstaff's conception of him—he is defining the inverted values of a male-centred carnival world over which he presides, a world which produces its own communal solidarity by its armed appropriation of some of the largesse of a non-carnival reality. And these lines contribute to such an idealized social inversion. But the intrusion of the question of the blood royal into this list resituates the whole assertion out of the realm of a (counterfactual, wish-fulfilling) carnival back to the all-too-real kingdom of which Hal is heir-apparent. And in that context, the lines can easily be read as an assertion that a true prince must be willing to be a thief, to boldly take as his own what is claimed (possibly quite appropriately) by others as their own. And this assertion can then be interpreted in two ways: as a Machiavellian statement of the way things are or as a critical protest against the royal robbery of the Lancasters in particular and/or of kings and aristocrats in general. This ambivalence is not only a local

---

[2] William Shakespeare, *1 Henry IV*, 2.5.247–53, *The Norton Shakespeare*, ed. Stephen Greenblatt (New York: Norton, 1997). All subsequent quotations from Shakespeare plays in this chapter are from the same edn.

quality of these lines, but a structural ambivalence underlying the entire second historical tetralogy. To be sure, the *Henriad* is by no means simply an uncritical endorsement of instrumental power politics; it is full of dramatic ironies, points and counterpoints, and other material critical of the subordination of all other values to those of the perpetuation of power. However, in ways that we had not seen earlier and will not see again, these plays represent for us the step-by-step processes of Machiavellian power politics as a reality of life working at times for good as well as evil—and as a reality whose good is never easily separated from its evil. This moral ambivalence is a quality of power politics which Machiavelli himself seemed to accept as a *sine qua non* of political activity in general, and at times these plays project a similar acquiescence to reality.

Also notable in these plays, however—it is concentrated in the first half of *1 Henry IV* but persists powerfully as a memory in *2 Henry IV*, and it extends into *Henry V* as well—is an additional dimension, linked in some ways to Machiavellian politics, but distinct from, even antithetical to, the political realm in others: the depiction of counter-political realms of tavern and domesticity, and a fascination with the potentiality of multiple identities and multiple social roles as a corollary of unfixed subjectivity. These themes can properly be called Montaignean because of their resonances with major themes of Montaigne's epochal explorations of modern subjectivity in the *Essais*. But these motifs—and the Gad's Hill high jinks accompanying them—not only echo and complicate the theme of legitimate succession crucial to the political plot; they also highlight a related, equally crucial theme of role-playing, disguise, and the elusiveness of the 'true self' that plays throughout all four plays of the *Henriad* as well—and, of course, all through some of Shakespeare's most memorable comedies and tragedies. These motifs suggest a (post-medieval, Machia-vellian-Montaignean) world in which everything is potentially counter-feit and in which what is true and what is false will shift as we move from one social and political context to another. Rebels and thieves are true to themselves, false to the ruling court culture, and what counts as a genuine coin is only its acceptance as such, not its essence, which is beyond all appearances.[3]

The word *counterfeit* is a strategic one in the development of this theme. It is used in two crucial scenes of *1 Henry IV*: once in the passage I just

---

[3] Cf. Patricia Parker, *Shakespeare from the Margins: Language, Culture, Context* (Chicago: University of Chicago Press, 1996), 157: 'For all of the talk of faith and honesty in both tavern world and political world, the first play of *Henry IV* is thus filled with counterfeiting, trans-lating and cozening.'

quoted from the long tavern scene, when Falstaff remarks to Hal, 'Never call a true piece of gold a counterfeit' (2.5.449–50), and again, several more times, in the climactic battle scene at the end of the play. The idea of counterfeiting usually implies a valorization of the genuine over the inauthentic, an idea that Falstaff evokes in his claim. However, if we contemplate Falstaff's ambiguous position as mentor to the Prince and as we consider the word's uses in the battle scenes, we begin to suspect that the very idea of counterfeiting is in itself Machiavellian, inasmuch as it asserts the efficacy of appearances over interior substance in the human world: counterfeit coins (to take the example used by Falstaff in the word's first appearance in the play) appear to be made of precious metal but are not, so that in passing them the counterfeiter profits by the power of appearances and reveals the social conventions that bestow value on circulating money and goods—just as a prince who follows Machiavellian dicta receives the advantages of appearing religious without the disadvantages of actually acting religiously.

When the word reappears in this play after Sir John's initial usage of it, it is in the mouth of Douglas upon seeing Henry IV at Shrewsbury:

> What art thou
> That counterfeit'st the person of a king? (5.4.26–7)

The reference is to a detail found in Holinshed, who tells us that the King had 'semblables' dressed like himself on the battlefield, but in the context of this play it takes on additional meaning: the rebels have questioned Henry's royal legitimacy, and the lines remind us of the charge; and Henry's tactic of having a number of fighters dressed like him gives credence to this charge at least symbolically.[4] Even though Henry claims to be 'the king himself', Douglas affirms the power of appearances in replying, 'I fear thou art another counterfeit' (l. 34). Finally, we have to say, what settles the question is the outcome of the battle: Henry wins and becomes the true king in the only way that matters in this play: he is accepted as such through his political and military prowess. But Falstaff—

---

[4] David Scott Kastan, ' "The King Hath Many Marching in his Coats", or, What Did You Do in the War, Daddy?', in Ivo Kamps (ed.), *Shakespeare Left and Right* (London: Routledge, 1991), 241–58. See also Kastan's earlier 'Proud Majesty Made a Subject: Shakespeare and the Spectacle of Rule', *Shakespeare Quarterly*, 37/4 (Winter 1986), 459–75, which argues that representation itself could undermine sovereignty by demystifying hierarchical ideology and revealing the theatricality of power, as in the case of the counterfeits at Shrewsbury (p. 465). A similar argument, showing that Henry IV's tactic of deploying many dressed like a king at Shrewsbury tends to undermine his legitimacy, is made by Jean E. Howard, *The Stage and Social Struggle in Early Modern England* (New York: Routledge, 1994), 145–53.

here as elsewhere in the last scenes, in a choric role—helps us see the dynamics at work:

'Sblood, 'twas time to counterfeit, or that hot termagant Scot had paid me, scot and lot too. Counterfeit? I lie, I am no counterfeit. To die is to be a counterfeit, for he is but the counterfeit of a man who hath not the life of a man. But to counterfeit dying when a man thereby liveth is to be no counterfeit, but the true and perfect image of life indeed. The better part of valour is discretion, in the which better part I have saved my life. Zounds, I am afraid of this gunpowder Percy, though he be dead. How if he should counterfeit too, and rise? By my faith, I am afraid he would prove the better counterfeit. Therefore I'll make him sure; yea, and I'll swear I killed him. Why may not he rise as well as I? (5.4.111–23)

In Sir John's repetitive usage of the term, we can see that what counts as counterfeit depends on context and is never absolute: sometimes a kind of counterfeiting is even the way to truth, when the world is topsy-turvy and what passes for truth is already counterfeit. But a more Machiavellian 'translation' of the theme of counterfeit in this play, I believe, would be to say that the distinction between the true and the counterfeit only comes into play if it is believed in, that since appearances are the only things that count, everything is always already counterfeit because open to enquiry. If discretion is the better part of valour, the feigned can be as efficacious as what it imitates, and Sir John, with Hal's collusion, makes this so in his feigned defeat of Percy. And, as we will see below, the whole of 2 Henry IV is a testimony to the power of such 'counterfeiting' to create social reality, and in that sense establishing the primacy of appearance over substance in the political world. The two Henry IV plays consistently enact this idea, ratifying, but in a different form, the theme carried in Richard II through the metaphors of 'language' discussed previously. In fact, as a number of critics have pointed out, each of the Henry IV plays (and Henry V as well) refers to language in contexts that suggest it is serving as a figure for the human world of appearances[5] which the twentieth century has conceptualized in such categories as culture, intersubjectivity, ideology, or discursive formations.

   The numerous plays on the shifting conceptual meaning of true and false, as in Falstaff's complaint at Gad's Hill, 'a plague upon't when

---

[5] In 1 Henry IV Hal refers to being able to 'drink with any tinker in his own language' (2.5.17) to describe his empathy with the lifeworld of the young apprentices in the tavern in an interchange to be discussed below; in 2 Henry IV Warwick excuses Hal's 'truancy' from the court in similar terms: 'The Prince but studies his companions, | Like a strange tongue, wherein, to gain the language' (4.3.68–9)—not to mention Rumour's mention of language as a vehicle for deception in the Prologue; and in Henry V, Hal famously gives English lessons to fair Catherine.

thieves cannot be true one to another!' (2.2.25–6), work in a similar way and reinforce these associations of counterfeiting. The play assumes a commonsensical understanding that everyone knows the difference between the true and the false, the genuine and the counterfeit, and then shows us how easy it is to call these commonsensical distinctions in question.

Machiavellian Power in 1 Henry IV

This linguistic motif, then, continues a theme that had already been established in *Richard II* and here as well connects with a dramatic depiction of Machiavellian power dynamics, which throughout the *Henriad* are taken for granted and morally ambivalent. These plays register the problems of Machiavellian politics, but with a different evaluative effect than Shakespeare surrounded them with either before or after the Machiavellian moment constituted by these plays.

The problem of how to justify a prince's power when the claim to his title is dubious takes up more than a little of Machiavelli's little book, but it is a problem for Henry IV mainly with the aristocracy. Clearly, his own undermining of the laws of succession worked to weaken the force of the older laws and traditions which he now desires to mobilize in support of his power and his son's succession. There is thus a political logic behind the odd dramatic focus of these dramas, remarked on by so many critics, that the centre of the plays named after King Henry IV is his son the future Henry V. In the logic of monarchical power, the question of the legitimacy of Henry IV's power comes down to a question of its transfer to his heir. Plays devoted to power in the unquiet reign of Henry IV can focus on Hal and his succession problems without being untrue to their ostensible subject, and in that sense Hal's madcap tavern days constitute a central political problem within the Machiavellian dynamics of the play. And of course the legitimacy of Henry's claim to the throne—and therefore that of his heir Prince Hal as well—is one of the themes raised by the rebels in seeking popular support, as we learn in the parley just before the Battle of Shrewsbury.

But if the rebels raise the issue of Henry IV's legitimacy, they do so with an odd emphasis. The issue lives a kind of half-life within their discourse, between a legalistic challenge and a simple disdain at being used and outwitted by Henry in his political manoeuvrings. It was only after the dispute about prisoners had incited Hotspur's anger that he (or anyone else in the play) raised questions about the justice of Henry's claim to the throne:

> Shall it for shame be spoken in these days,
> Or fill up chronicles in time to come,
> That men of your nobility and power
> Did gage them both in an unjust behalf,
> As both of you, God pardon it, have done:
> To put down Richard, that sweet lovely rose,
> And plant this thorn, this canker, Bolingbroke? (1.3.168–74)

But even here the language merely touches on terms of right and wrong ('unjust'), and lingers longer on themes of beauty—it even glances, in the reference to chronicles, at issues of historiography which a number of critics have recently discussed.[6] And Hotspur quickly leaves behind this brief moral and legal argument, turning instead to an appeal to an aristocratic code of honour and self-aggrandizement:

> And shall it in more shame be further spoken
> That you are fooled, discarded, and shook off
> By him for whom these shames ye underwent?
> No; yet time serves wherein you may redeem
> Your banished honours, and restore yourselves
> Into the good thoughts of the world again,
> Revenge the jeering and disdained contempt
> Of this proud King, who studies day and night
> To answer all the debt he owes to you
> Even with the bloody payment of your deaths. (1.3.175–84)

And this code of aristocratic self-assertion and the cult of honour (which a long critical tradition has seen Hotspur as epitomizing in its narrowness) is underlined once more in his celebrated speech:

> By heaven, methinks it were an easy leap
> To pluck bright honour from the pale-faced moon,
> Or dive into the bottom of the deep,
> Where fathom-line could never touch the ground,
> And pluck up drownèd honour by the locks,
> So he that doth redeem her thence might wear,
> Without corrival, all her dignities.
> But out upon this half-faced fellowship! (1.3.199–206)

[6] Graham Holderness, *Shakespeare's History* (New York: St Martin's Press, 1985); Matthew H. Wikander, *The Play of Truth and State: Historical Drama from Shakespeare to Brecht* (Baltimore: Johns Hopkins University Press, 1985), 13–49; Phyllis Rackin, *Stages of History: Shakespeare's English Chronicles* (Ithaca, NY: Cornell University Press, 1990); and Wolfgang Iser, *Staging Politics: The Lasting Impact of Shakespeare's Histories*, trans. David Henry Wilson (New York: Columbia University Press, 1993).

Here the audience's attention is deflected from the Machiavellian theme to the spectacle of Hotspur's poetic, absolutizing rhetoric, so that among the rebels, as elsewhere, the value-free play of power seems to become a background to the play of subjective proclamations and evaluations emanating from it. The effect of Hotspur's shifting rhetoric (is Henry's illegitimacy or his manipulations of the rebels the crucial problem?) is to make the issue seem simply instrumental to the larger power struggle in play between rebels and King—that is, to reinforce a Machiavellian analysis of the dynamics. Thus the audience is predisposed in favour of this kind of diagnosis as regards the rebels' motives when it is articulated by Henry:

> These things indeed you have articulate,
> Proclaimed at market-crosses, read in churches,
> To face the garment of rebellion
> With some fine colour that may please the eye
> Of fickle changelings and poor discontents,
> Which gape and rub the elbow at the news
> Of hurlyburly innovation;
> And never yet did insurrection want
> Such water-colours to impaint his cause,
> Nor moody beggars starving for a time
> Of pell-mell havoc and confusion. (5.1.72–82)

No one, of course, is better qualified in this play to understand the Machiavellian logic of such rhetoric than Henry. In his own private discourse with his son, Henry IV makes some very interesting disclosures, for example, in his analysis of his and Hal's political situation in the scene of reconciliation between them:

> For all the world,
> As thou art to this hour was Richard then,
> When I from France set foot at Ravenspurgh,
> And even as I was then is Percy now.
> Now by my sceptre, and my soul to boot,
> He hath more worthy interest to the state
> Than thou, the shadow of succession;
> For, of no right, nor colour like to right,
> He doth fill fields with harness in the realm,
> Turns head against the lion's armèd jaws,
> And, being no more in debt to years than thou,
> Leads ancient lords and reverend bishops on
> To bloody battles, and to bruising arms. (3.2.93–105)

Here Henry comes closer than anywhere within the three plays in which he is featured to owning up to the Machiavellian philosophy of praxis which has consistently guided his actions throughout. Henry's analogy compares Prince Hal (and himself by implication) to a King Richard in danger of deposition, but more tellingly he compares himself before the deposition to Percy now—a Percy, he says, who has 'no right, nor colour like to right' to the throne. The description functions within a Machiavellian logic of manipulated appearances and realpolitik, and, under the peculiar rules of Machiavellian rhetoric (defined retrospectively by Voltaire), they are underpinnings which should never be made explicit. They constitute a system of political thinking in which questions of succession are merely problems to be solved through a number of possible strategies—an assumption shared by both court and rebels, and by the members of the tavern world as well, though in somewhat disguised, displaced form, as we will see below.

If, then, like a number of critics in the past, we ask what attitude or attitudes this play projects concerning the question of the legitimacy of Henry IV's claim to the throne, or if we raise the ante and ask what attitude the play projects about the doctrine of a divinely ordained royal succession in general, we have to answer that *1 Henry IV* both assumes and demonstrates that Henry's claim and all such claims are instruments of autotelic power with only that weight which Machiavelli gave to traditions in which the populace continued to believe.[7] In this play Machiavellian politics are never put in moral question because they are the rules on which all parties seem to agree in the political intrigue.

Here as in *Richard II*, the question of how such a 'subversive' play could get by the censors arises, and in addition to the factors previously discussed, there are some specific qualities of this play to consider. Even more than *Richard II*, *1 Henry IV*'s potentially subversive meditation on legitimacy is indirect and, we could say, doubly 'protected' against any possible objections to its probing of the idea of legitimate succession: its scepticism exists as a potential within the play, like one of Donne's sly conceits, depending on the ingenuity of readers and listeners to constitute it in an act of interpretation; in the absence of such active constructing of the

[7] Cf. Sigurd Burckhardt, *Shakespearian Meanings* (Princeton: Princeton University Press, 1968), 179–205, and Kastan, 'The King Hath Many Marching in his Coats', 249–52. I am here arguing for Burckhardt's and Kastan's position—it is also that of H. A. Kelly, *Divine Providence in the England of Shakespeare's Histories* (Cambridge, Mass.: Harvard University Press, 1970)—and opposing Rackin's view in *Stages of History*, 67–8 *et passim*, that Henry IV's succession to the throne is clearly condemned (at least at one level) within the value system of the texts.

play's implied critique, we will see below, its emotional vectors all clearly support the royal party's case against the rebels. In addition, much of the critical commentary exists within a context of joking and humour which affords a further protection from too prying a scrutiny of this material. And finally, Falstaff steals the show in this respect as in so many others. The quite concrete issue of the satirical treatment of the ancestor of the powerful Cobhams apparently overshadowed any other concerns of a more general or philosophical nature as to an imputed meaning of a play which was otherwise quite a crowd-pleaser at court as well as among the commons.[8]

At another level, as I indicated, *1 Henry IV* moves beyond the Machiavellian world of *Richard II* without overturning it by expanding the range of represented social reality significantly beyond that of the political class. Here and in the sequel we are provided with such homely domestic details of daily life as the peach colour of Poins's leggings, Hotspur's pet name for his wife, Falstaff's tavern bill, the details of Francis the vintner's apprentice-arrangement, the drinking preferences of major characters, and so on. The rich 'realist' detail of the world of commodities in this play gives density to the non-political realm the presentation of which is one of its great innovations. This shift provides a kernel of truth to the much repeated critical observation that sees in both *Henry IV* plays an evolutionary leap from a feudal world in *Richard II* to a modern world in the rest of the trilogy. As I argued in Chapter 2, the political world of *Richard II* is fully Machiavellian and in that sense modern, its much noted feudal symbolics the empty counters of power politics. What changes from *Richard II* to *1 Henry IV* in that regard is only a lesser prominence given to the continuing Machiavellian dynamics. However, as Charles Taylor argued, one of the crucial transformations from the medieval to the early modern mentality is a new valorization of daily life, provided in important part by Protestant ideas of domesticity, the family, and the role of women.[9] Such a shift of focus is clearly in evidence here, especially in comparison to the portrayal of private life in the other histories. An important part of this shift, too, is the relative prominence of women, particularly within the rebel camp, but also in a tavern world in which Mistress Quickly and Doll Tearsheet are prominent citizens and in which Falstaff has a number of psychoanalytically significant links with the feminine as well as to the subaltern carnival tradition. The result is a dramatic structure of

    [8] Gary Taylor, 'The Fortunes of Oldcastle', *Shakespeare Survey*, 38 (1985), 85–100.
    [9] Charles Taylor, *Sources of the Self: The Making of the Modern Identity* (Cambridge, Mass.: Harvard University Press, 1989), 211–302.

unprecedented complexity—but also, to judge from a number of contemporaneous allusions—of unprecedented popularity.

The extension of social range is accomplished by the use of two interlinked plots with, as I discussed above, a rich potentiality for profligate
paralleling, parodying, and contrasting events, characters, and discourses.
Unlike the similarly double-plotted *Troilus and Cressida*, however, we are
in neither of the *Henry IV* plays consistently supplied with a chorus-like
Thersites to guide us in interpreting the parallels—unless it be Falstaff, the
'double man' who continually subverts and undermines the strong heroic
elements of the play around the development of Prince Hal. But whatever
choric function he plays, as we will see, is destabilizing of determinate
meaning rather than establishing or clarifying of it.

Over the years, critics have created what amount to quite different
plays out of the material provided by the ambiguously interrelated plots.
The two main divisions are between those like J. Dover Wilson and
Tillyard, who see Prince Hal as the positive figure of the plays and Falstaff
as an alluring but negative influence whom the young King Harry is right
to banish, and those, like Morgann, Hazlitt, Bradley, Bloom, and a
number of figures in the first half of the twentieth century, who see in
Falstaff a positive figure of vitality and/or anti-militarism against the
cold, calculating Machiavellianism that Prince Hal finally adopts—or, as
many of these critics have it, finally displays to those from whom he had
hypocritically kept it hidden during his wild-oats days. More recently,
we can distinguish a somewhat similar division between Foucault-
influenced readings of the plays as a modelling of an inevitable enactment
of power's production of subversion in order to contain it, and Bakhtin-
influenced celebrations of a carnival world in symbolic combat with
power.[10]

In what follows I want to argue a variation on this history of bipolar
readings. In *1 Henry IV* the Falstaffian and feminine counter-cultures
succeed in subverting the Machiavellian political realm, if only in the sense
that they win over the audience's imaginations and make Machiavellian
politics seem boring and lifeless. At the same time, however, politics
seems, to use a word highly favoured by King Henry IV in *Part 2*, 'necessary'. Machiavellian politics is the only game in town, and it has to be
managed skilfully to avoid continual war and upheaval. A highly selective

---

[10] As indicated in the Introduction, the influence of Foucault on Shakespeare studies since
about 1980 has been pervasive, especially in aspects of the work of Stephen Greenblatt to be
discussed below. For recent Bakhtin-influenced criticism see Ronald Knowles (ed.),
Shakespeare and Carnival: After Bakhtin (Basingstoke: Macmillan, 1998).

review of criticism can perhaps clarify some of the problems of interpretation bequeathed us by these plays' complex structure, show the choices we must make as construers of the text, and prepare the ground for the readings that follow. In addition, I want to show the extent to which, in both classical and contemporary commentary on *1 Henry IV*, it is construed in the context of the ending of *Part 2*.

Critical Constructions

In much of the early criticism of the *Henry IV* plays, the main issue is the relation among the plays' three 'camps' (court, tavern, rebel base) or two 'worlds' (upper-class political and plebeian-domestic). In the nineteenth century the German Hegelian critic Hermann Ulrici thought the comic scenes parodied the political scenes by exposing the element of theft and disorder caused by Machiavellian politicians. In this reading Sir John was a kind of comic Vice, clearly immoral and mirroring immoral rebels and a usurping monarch: 'the Pursuit of external power, influence, and authority', Ulrici wrote, 'is essentially no less immoral and material than the carnal and sensual pleasures of Falstaff.'[11] But when more sophisticated reading techniques were developed in the next century, L. C. Knights also saw the comic material of the two *Henry IV* plays as satirical of the historical ones, but he was less certain than Ulrici as to what 'positive' attitudes could be inferred from the negations of the satire:

Now satire implies a standard, and in *Henry IV* the validity of the standard itself is questioned; hence the peculiar coherence and universality of the play. 'Honour' and 'state-craft' are set in opposition to the natural life of the body, but the chief body of the play is, explicitly, 'a bolting-hutch of beastliness',—'A pox on this gout! or a gout on this pox, I should say'. Other speeches reinforce the age and disease theme which, it has not been observed is a significant part of the Falstaff theme.[12]

Knights's problem is clarified, however, if we separate *2 Henry IV*—the locus, as Knights points out elsewhere, of the disease motif in question—from *1 Henry IV*, which is much less corrosive in its depiction of carnival and flesh.

William Empson further complicated the discussion by claiming that the comic and political plots relate to each other not only as parody to its

[11] Hermann Ulrici, *Shakespeare's Dramatic Art: And his Relation to Calderon and Goethe*, trans. A. J. W. Morrison (London: Chapman, 1846), 375.
[12] L. C. Knights, 'Notes on Comedy', in F. R. Leavis (ed.), *Determinations: Critical Essays* (London: Chatto, 1934), 109–31; 128–9.

object, as Ulrici and Knights had theorized, but also as an exemplification of a complex pastoral effect, in which the lower classes stand for, dignify, and universalize sophisticated upper-class mores—so that 'the comic characters are in a sense figures of pastoral myth so far as they make profound remarks and do things with unexpectedly great effects', and he went on to complicate matters even further in a discussion of Shakespeare's Sonnet 94 ('They that have power to hurt'), in which the *Henry IV* plays are assimilated to yet another complex ironic structure analogous to that sonnet's in which, in the words of the chapter's subtitle, there is a 'Twist of Heroic-Pastoral Ideas into an Ironical Acceptance of Aristocracy'.[13] Few subsequent critics have been content to leave the matter in the finally impossible paradoxes of Empson's attempt to conceptualize opposing meanings as aspects of one overriding Complex Unity, however.

A new attempt to define the enigmatic relations between these two subplots (at this level, the court and rebels are conflated as forming a single 'political plot') was in the classic study by C. L. Barber, *Shakespeare's Festive Comedy. Henry IV, Parts 1 and 2* constitute one of Barber's chief cases in point, and he reversed the valences of Ulrici's pioneering exploration by defining what he called a 'saturnalian' rather than satirical relationship between the two. He claims 'that the misrule works, through the whole dramatic rhythm, to consolidate rule' through a 'nonlogical' pattern of ritual in which Falstaff 'carries off' unwanted passions and emotion as a scapegoat figure.[14] But the scapegoating of Falstaff is of course a motif of *Part 2*, not of *Part 1*, and *Part 1*, I would argue against Barber's classic reading, is virtually devoid of the theme of consolidating rule that he finds as a characteristic of the plays by conflating them.

Stephen Greenblatt took up the issue in what is recognizably a version of Barber's argument in one of the most reprinted works of contemporary Shakespearian criticism, 'Invisible Bullets'.[15] Barber's thesis is transformed through the influence of Foucault and his Nietzschean theory of

[13] William Empson, *Some Versions of Pastoral* (New York: New Directions, 1968), 27–45.

[14] C. L. Barber, *Shakespeare's Festive Comedy: A Study of Dramatic Form and its Relation to Social Custom* (1959; repr. Cleveland: Meridian, 1963), 205–7.

[15] Stephen Greenblatt, 'Invisible Bullets', in *Shakespearian Negotiations: The Circulation of Social Energy in Renaissance England* (Berkeley and Los Angeles: University of California Press, 1988). I cite this book chapter as an article because earlier versions of it were published in article form three times before it appeared (expanded) as ch. 2 in the above work. The earlier versions, all entitled 'Invisible Bullets', appeared in: *Glyph*, 8 (1981), 40–61; Jonathan Dollimore and Alan Sinfield (eds.), *Political Shakespeare: New Essays in Cultural Materialism* (Ithaca, NY: Cornell University Press, 1985), 18–47; and Peter Erickson and Coppélia Kahn (eds.), *Shakespeare's 'Rough Magic': Renaissance Essays in Honor of C. L. Barber* (Newark: University of Delaware Press, 1985), 30–52. The many reprints attest to the article's important influence.

power discussed in the Introduction:[16] the *Henry IV* plays, like others of Shakespeare's, 'are centrally, repeatedly concerned with the production and containment of subversion and disorder':[17] especially those plays like *1 and 2 Henry IV* which 'meditate on the consolidation of state power'.[18] In different ways, the three plays concerned with Henry V show how the subversion of the social order represented by Falstaff and company can be understood as produced by the very order it would seem to subvert, the better for order to consolidate itself. The comic subplot, then, as in Barber's saturnalian concept of the relation of the two plots, cannot be considered satirical in any sense at all. It neither criticizes nor undermines the main plot: it supports it. If Prince Harry is ultimately an ideal king, we need to observe that 'such an ideal image involves as its positive condition the constant production of its own radical subversions and the powerful containment of that subversion'.[19] Here, I would argue (and I will return to this point below, in the discussion of *2 Henry IV*), Greenblatt has faced up to the hard choices and unpleasant political realities given us by *Part 2*—and continued and heightened in *Henry V*. But this reading greatly underestimates the subversive qualities of *1 Henry IV*. And even if we accept the strong conclusion Greenblatt arrives at in the essay as applying only to *Part 2* and to *Henry V*, there are other problems to deal with:

The Henry plays confirm the Machiavellian hypothesis that princely power originates in force and fraud even as they draw their audience toward an acceptance of that power. And we are free to locate and pay homage to the plays' doubts only because they no longer threaten us. There is subversion, no end of subversion, only not for us.[20]

With all its insights, this passage is a prime example of the kind of power-obsessed 1980s criticism which I discussed in the Introduction as having put Postmodernist Shakespearian criticism on a path in which it has become almost impossible to conceptualize, let alone valorize, the theme of subjectivity which I believe is one of the singularly most valuable aspects of Shakespeare's oeuvre, but one which, we have seen, needs to be reclaimed from mystifying mid-century treatments of it against which new historicism and cultural materialism have been reacting. Greenblatt indicates these two alternatives briefly in 'Invisible Bullets', in a remark on

---

[16] See Michael Bristol, *Carnival and Theater: Plebeian Culture and the Structure of Authority in Renaissance England* (New York: Methuen, 1985), 14–16 and 30–2, for a similar, more detailed critique of Barber and Greenblatt on these issues.

[17] Greenblatt, 'Invisible Bullets', 40.

[18] Ibid.

[19] Ibid. 41.

[20] Ibid. 65.

Hal's promise to his father to 'Be more myself' (a phrase to which I will return below):

> 'To be oneself' here means to perform one's part in the scheme of power rather than to manifest one's natural disposition, or what we would normally designate as the very core of the self. Indeed it is by no means certain that such a thing as a natural disposition exists in the play except as a theatrical fiction.[21]

Here are the two false alternatives of Foucauldian anti-humanism: belief in an essentialist 'core' of the self, belief that 'theatrical fiction' is an empty, nihilistic category. But these alternatives are not the only terms through which one might understand the treatment of self and subjectivity in *1 Henry IV*, and in what follows I try to work out such an alternative reading. Such an approach can help depolarize a critical tradition which has, at least since Hazlitt's sardonic comments on Prince Hal as a traitor to his friends,[22] divided between two views—one seeing Hal as heroic and rightly rejecting a Falstaff who is an allegorical representation of Vice, the second seeing Hal as a type of an opportunistic politician with no real 'core beliefs' and Sir John as an exuberant symbol of life and vitality cruelly treated by his boon companion. I think the 'either-or' quality of this polarization is invidious, asking readers of the play to repress strong emotional vectors in favour of both the Prince and Falstaff. Instead, I want to depolarize these interpretations and give an account of changing perspectives on these themes from *Part 1* to *Part 2*. Then we might say that the first of these views rightly grasps the strong heroicizing vector of the development of Prince Hal in *1 Henry IV*, but projects it into the changed circumstances of *2 Henry IV*, underestimates Sir John's positivity in both plays but especially in *Part 1*, and ignores or subordinates the Machiavellian elements of the political world which Hal has joined. The second rightly grasps much of Sir John's positivity but imposes a moralizing, Rousseauistic conception of a core inner self on Hal, ignores or subordinates Hal's heroism and Falstaff's vices, and projects the banishment of Sir John from the end of *Part 2* retrospectively onto *Part 1*.

As indicated, then, my attempt here is to read the plays as autonomous

---

[21] Greenblatt, 'Invisible Bullets', 46.

[22] Hazlitt wrote of Hal: 'He was fond of war and low company:—we know little else of him. He was careless, dissolute, and ambitious;—idle, or doing mischief. In private, he seemed to have no idea of the common decencies of life, which he subjected to a kind of regal license; in public affairs, he seemed to have no idea of any rule of right or wrong, but brute force, glossed over with a little religious hypocrisy and archiepiscopal advice. His principles did not change with his situation and professions. His adventure on Gadshill was a prelude to the affair of Agincourt, only a bloodless one.' William Hazlitt, *Characters of Shakespeare's Plays* (London: Dent, 1906), 156.

and without demonizing either Hal or Falstaff, but relating both of them to the connected themes of modernization, power, and subjectivity discussed in the previous chapters. In a complicated perspective that shifts decisively from *Part 1* to *Part 2*, both Hal and Falstaff can be seen as produced, nurtured, and finally victimized by a process of modernization depicted in the plays in terms of modern subjectivity and Machiavellian power. Thus, Hal is simultaneously a Machiavellian and a hero of subjectivity, the great exception, along with Hamlet, to Shakespeare's more habitual practice of embodying these themes in antagonistic characters. However, the nuances of this evaluation shift as we move from *Part 1* to *Part 2* to *Henry V*, and they shift again, we will see in the Conclusion, in *Hamlet*, arriving finally at the dark view of Machiavellian power that informs the Jacobean tragedies.

This shifting, unstable evaluation of the Machiavellian also impacts decisively on Falstaff, who has long been seen as the composite Shakespearian character *par excellence*. He is involved in his own unstable attempt to combine the pleasures of subjectivity, the pastoral values of fellowship, playfulness, wit, and pleasure, and an ethic of self-serving, unscrupulous private Machiavellianism which Shakespeare pushes to the limit on more than one occasion in his depiction of Sir John in two history plays and a comedy. A crucial key to this long-discussed paradox, I believe, is that Falstaff is perhaps the most Brechtian, most meta-theatrical of all characters in Shakespearian drama, and those meta-theatrical qualities add to the complexity of understanding his dramatic role, particularly in terms of ethical questions. A second key to the paradox, I will argue, is the transitional nature of the historical moment of these plays' composition: Falstaff is poised, as it were, between a communal past and an atomistic future, and his 'character traits' produce radically opposed meanings in these two opposed contexts, both of which, however, he evokes.

2. SUBJECTIVITY, CARNIVAL, AND THE AESTHETIC: FALSTAFF IN *1 HENRY IV*

Falstaff is an experiment in a kind of imagined autonomous, autotelic subjectivity ('My lord, I was born about three of the clock in the afternoon, with a white head and something a round belly'[23]) specifically designed as a refuge from (and possibly alternative to) the Machiavellian logic of

[23] *2 Henry IV*, 1.2.170–1.

power which is slowly unfolding between the high jinks of the tavern scenes. Falstaff has a tremendously long and varied critical history, but the new historicism has not been kind to him. As we have seen for the case of Greenblatt's 'Invisible Bullets', the influence of Foucault led new historicists to define all-encompassing systems of power, with little if any room for resistance, and therefore little room for those qualities that have made this remarkable figure repeatedly hailed over three centuries as the best of all comic characters. The power-dominated world of new historical analyses is simply not very funny. I believe, however, that it is precisely Falstaff's role in 1 Henry IV to invert and resist the ideologies of power into which Hal is being interpellated, and his weapons are wit, pleasure, irreverence, and a remarkable ability to create and live within counterfactual fictions.

This kind of resistance to interpellation, while it has its heroic potentialities, is by no means automatically to be applauded, rife as it is with possibilities of the denial of reality, escapism, self-indulgence and self-centredness, egotism, and other kinds of self-destructive behaviour. Falstaff is indeed an excellent example of many of these potentialities. However, in a series of plays which will feature the transformation of the playful and harmless Prince of Wales into a formidable Machiavellian politician responsible for the deaths of thousands, Falstaff's resistance to the ways of the world is not to be dismissed lightly. William Hazlitt got it exactly right: Falstaff is the better man of the two, and he is a better man because he understands that ideology need not be the be-all and end-all of human social reality. Instead, one can play with it, and against it, as Hal does for a while and as Falstaff attempts until his end. This playfulness, this ability to subvert ideological interpellation through theatricality, is Falstaff's crucial characteristic, both as foil to Prince Hal and as thematic embodiment of resistance to power in all the plays of the Prince Hal trilogy.

But there is a kind of polarity in Falstaff's role connected to the plays' complex, layered, and contradictory evaluations of the role-playing demanded and forbidden by monarchy. At first Hal's tutor in role-playing and the unfixing of identity, Falstaff becomes at the end a victim of the logic of power which 'fixes' Hal's mobile sense of self. In addition, however, to complicate things further, Falstaff is also an embodiment of the destructive egoism which is one of modern subjectivity's most prominent potential outcomes. His dramatic functions, then, are as contradictory and many-layered as the rich and contradictory critical discourse on him over three centuries suggests. But while his is a multi-layered dramatic function, we should not let some parts of his complex dramatic role obscure others. Thus, while Falstaff is designed to be the very opposite of a Puritan saint (I will come back to this below), there are clear moments in *1 and 2 Henry IV* when his very theatricality—his ability to perform different selves and roles and escape the various tight spots that continually threaten him—is highlighted as a means of resistance to early modern power, and in such moments he emerges as a kind of anti-saint in the same inverted category twentieth-century wits have formed in the designations Saint Genet and Saint Foucault. I want to call attention to these precisely because they have been overlooked due to the preoccupation of recent criticism with power *tout court*.

At these moments, refusing to be limited by his actual material and social circumstances, Saint Falstaff creates a fictional world and acts out (as far as he is able within his material constraints) a fictional counter-reality. Thus, his cultivation of subjectivity is more like that of Richard II in prison than it is like Prince Hal's, as we will see below. Falstaff *imaginatively* subverts the reality principle in favour of the pleasure principle and thereby renders irrelevant objections from the real. The fuel of Falstaff's subjectivity is desire. The play of his wit and the motivation of his actions each manifests that Lacanian 'logic' of desiring which notoriously leads modern subjects from one coveted object to the next in an endless chain. This association of Falstaff (and modern subjectivity) with desire itself helps account for the marked critical polarization of opinion about him in the long tradition of Falstaff criticism from Dryden to the present. For desire is the ultimate double-edged sword. Without it, there is no human motivation, the world is colourless and empty, and life has no joy. On the other hand desire is that blind striving which enthrals humans to addictions and irrational cravings destructive of dignity and accomplishment. Falstaff evokes both of these sides of desire.

1 Henry IV: *From Carnival to Metatheatre*

Falstaff has been best appreciated by those versions of contemporary criticism based in assumptions that power systems are open to challenge, subversion, or inversion, for Falstaff is, among other things, a clear instance of Bakhtinian heteroglossia and carnival, as we will see below.

One of Falstaff's central paradoxes, however, is the extent to which this secular simulacrum of post-Reformation subjectivity is a manifestly artificial synthesis of pre-existing theatrical, folk, and literary types. It has been one of the most popular pastimes of twentieth-century academic criticism to define and analyse them. There are, for example, the direct theatrical forebears: the *miles gloriosus* and the Plautine parasite from Latin comedy;[24] the comic Vice of the late medieval moralities;[25] the tradition of fools and folly from the Middle Ages[26] and the related carnival tradition delineated by Barber, Bakhtin, Weimann, Bristol, and Laroque, to be discussed below; the *pícaro* tradition and the related discourse on the Elizabethan underground or rogue literature in sixteenth-century tracts and pamphlets;[27] the Renaissance celebration of the body in Cervantes and Rabelais;[28] and early and recently again, Falstaff has been connected to a series of satirical pamphlets against the aggressive and irreverent Puritan wit of the pseudonymous Martin Marprelate of the so-called anti-Marprelate tracts, including lampooning plays whose texts have not survived but which, according to the allusions to them in surviving pamphlets and tracts, were designed to satirize Puritanism as a grotesque, hypocritical carnival.[29] Many of these traditions, we can presume, were directly 'embodied' in the comic style of the celebrated performer who created the role of Falstaff, William Kempe, himself an apprentice to the famous Dick Tarlton and through him to an older popular comic tradition.[30]

[24]   E. E. Stoll, 'Falstaff', *Modern Philology*, 12/4 (Oct. 1914), 65–108.

[25]   Alfred Ainger, 'Sir John Falstaff', in *Lectures and Essays* (London: Macmillan, 1905), i. 119–55; John W. Spargo, 'An Interpretation of Falstaff', *Washington University Studies*. 9/2 (Apr. 1922), 119–33; T. A. Jackson, 'Letters and Documents: Marx and Shakespeare', *International Literature*, 2 (Feb. 1936), 75–97; J. Dover Wilson, *The Fortunes of Falstaff* (Cambridge: Cambridge University Press, 1943); and Robert Weimann, *Shakespeare and the Popular Tradition in the Theater: Studies in the Social Dimension of Dramatic Form and Function*, ed. Robert Schwartz (Baltimore: Johns Hopkins University Press, 1978), 128–31.

[26]   Enid Welsford, *The Fool: His Social and Literary History* (New York: Farrar & Rinehart, 1935); Willard Farnham, 'The Mediaeval Comic Spirit in the English Renaissance', in James G. McManaway, Giles E. Dawson, and Wedwin E. Willoughby (eds.), *Joseph Quincy Adams: Memorial Studies* (Washington, DC: Folger, 1948), 429–37; and Walter Kaiser, *Praisers of Folly: Erasmus, Rabelais, Shakespeare* (Cambridge, Mass.: Harvard University Press, 1963).

[27]   Herbert B. Rothschild, Jr., 'Falstaff and the Picaresque Tradition', *Modern Language Review*, 68/1 (Jan. 1973), 14–21.

[28]   Algernon Charles Swinburne, *A Study of Shakespeare* (London: Worthington, 1880), 105–8; and Wyndham Lewis, *The Lion and the Fox: The Role of the Hero in the Plays of Shakespeare* (London: G. Richards, 1927), 201–27.

[29]   Ainger, 'Sir John Falstaff'; Barrett Wendell, *William Shakespeare: A Study in Elizabethan Literature* (New York: Scribner's, 1895); and Kristen Poole, 'Saints Alive! Falstaff, Martin Marprelate, and the Staging of Puritanism', *Shakespeare Quarterly*, 46/1 (Spring 1995), 47–75, according to whom, 'The person of Falstaff is in and of himself a parody of the sixteenth-century puritan' (p. 54). A revised and abridged version of this essay appeared as Kristen Poole, 'Facing Puritanism: Falstaff, Martin Marprelate and the Grotesque Puritan', in Knowles (ed.), *Shakespeare and Carnival*, 97–122.

[30]   See Weimann, *Shakespeare and the Popular Tradition*, 185–92, and E. W. Talbert, *Elizabethan Drama and Shakespeare's Early Plays: An Essay in Historical Criticism* (Chapel Hill: University of North Carolina Press, 1963), 7–60 *et passim*.

Complex and contradictory as all these different attempts to conceptualize Falstaff are, they also overlap and suggest some themes in the present context and should not be simply relegated to the status of what Stephen Greenblatt called 'the traditional pieties' of that most dreary precinct of Shakespeare studies, source studies. Falstaff's rapid referencing of numerous stage, literary, and cultural types is the paradoxical key to what Harold Bloom has recently called, in his inflated way, 'the invention of the human'.[31] A less inflated approach to the function of Falstaff's protean theatricality takes us instead squarely within some of the key topics of the 'French Shakespeare' which Harold Bloom has dismissed, the poststructuralist-influenced attempts to define the impact of modernity on subjectivity. While, as I indicated above, there are significant problems with these attempts, they by no means deserve Bloom's cavalier dismissal. Jonathan Dollimore's *Radical Tragedy*, whose weaknesses I briefly discussed in Chapter 2, is valuable in defining a disjuncture between the brave new world of available social identities of early modern London and the older inflexible ideologies of social station. Dollimore delineated this growing gap between received ideologies and the new practices of developing modernity, and he thought that the ubiquitous 'malcontent' figure—epitomized by Marston's play *The Malcontent* but instanced in several other plays by Shakespeare and his contemporaries—was a crucial dramatic representation of the new dynamics.[32] However, the impact on the theatre of new modes of subjectivity goes far beyond the malcontent type. Falstaff exemplifies the same socio-historical development which Dollimore described for the malcontents, but in a very different mode. Like numerous other Shakespearian characters, he resists being tied down to any single identity and instead continually reinvents himself through a lengthy series of dramatic improvisations. In that way the theatre itself, in that fruitful *topos* that Shakespeare exploited over and over from his earliest to his latest work, becomes the model for life in a world newly open to the unfettered subjectivity created through shifting ideologies, religions, social stations, changing gender roles, and malleable sexuality.

Thus, if, as I argued in the Introduction, individuality in large measure is the unique sum of multiple choices from the differentiated discourses of modernity, Falstaff is a simulacrum of such a figure, a notably complex, paradoxical, and unique construct who displays the complexity of this

[31] Harold Bloom, *Shakespeare: The Invention of the Human* (New York: Riverhead, 1998).
[32] Jonathan Dollimore, *Radical Tragedy: Religion, Ideology, and Power in the Drama of Shakespeare and his Contemporaries* (1984; 2nd edn. London: Harvester, 1989).

kind of subjectivity, but in a completely different mode from Hal's. Unlike the Prince of Wales, he is certainly 'fixed' in his social role and position, as superannuated knight and tavern parasite, and his dreams of wealth and security when his 'sweet wag' becomes king simply amplify and consecrate this role: Falstaff is unable to imagine himself at court, as he indicates by deprecating the court in his response to Hal's jest to him that he will make him a hangman. That reviled profession, Falstaff tells us, 'jumps with my humour as well as waiting in the court' (1.2.60).

His frequent bouts of melancholy and short-lived resolutions to repent notwithstanding, he is content with life as a parasite, desiring only better provision. And in that regard, he clearly believes that in Prince Hal he has found his ultimate provider. He is not, as Hal is, poised between conflicting social roles and identities. And yet his subjectivity is not 'cabined, cribbed, confined' like that of Macbeth—or of Hal's insomniac father and troubled ruler either. Rather, Sir John, to the extent to which he can be abstracted from the theatrical and literary sources out which he has been constructed and taken as a character in a (meta)fictional space, is a self-author. Refusing to be limited by his actual material and social circumstances, he creates a fictional world and acts out as far as he is able a fictional counter-reality. Much less oriented to success in the world than his companion the Prince, he instead cultivates imagination—even specifically Lacan's Imaginary order, that locus of a lost unity and access to the (m)Other—and creates for himself and his companions a fictional, utopian projection of self not unlike that of his thin counterpart in *Don Quixote*, the knight-errant—with, of course, important similarities to Sancho Panza, for Falstaff's utopian self is a pampered, self-indulgent recipient of bodily pleasures more like Quixote's squire in that regard than like the thin Spanish knight.[33] Falstaff attempts to live out a carnival ideal suffused with a libido that is among the most successfully communicated of the multiple associations swirling around the remarkable prose[34] which Shakespeare has written for him, and this libidinally charged speech is perhaps the key feature behind the centuries-old legion of followers and champions of Falstaff who have responded to the multivalent and subversive richness of passages like the following, in which his powers of self-fictionalization are fully operative:

[33] Cf. Lewis, *The Lion and the Fox*, 201–27, on the parallel with Don Quixote; and Bloom, *Shakespeare: The Invention of the Human*, 281–2, on the parallel with Sancho Panza.

[34] See Rackin, *Stages of History*, 235–6, for an argument that the use of prose for Falstaff's speech is an emblem of his freedom and a marker for the subversion his lines enact against the dignified blank verse of the 'official' historical material.

Marry then, sweet wag, when thou art king let not us that are squires of the night's body be called thieves of the day's beauty. Let us be 'Diana's foresters', 'gentlemen of the shade', 'minions of the moon', and let men say we be men of good government, being governed, as the sea is, by our noble and chaste mistress the moon, under whose countenance we steal. (1.2.20–6)

Unlike Quixote's mad vision, however, Falstaff's seems to contain within itself some tacit knowledge of its own fictionality,[35] some unspoken acknowledgement with his fellows in fantasy that this is, after all, a grand joke, based actually on an inversion of the situation which everyone, including Falstaff, knows to be the case. Consider the following reply to Hal:

O, thou hast damnable iteration, and art indeed able to corrupt a saint. Thou hast done much harm upon me, Hal, God forgive thee for it. Before I knew thee, Hal, I knew nothing; and now am I, if a man should speak truly, little better than one of the wicked. I must give over this life, and I will give it over. By the Lord, an I do not, I am a villain. I'll be damn'd for never a king's son in Christendom. (1.2.80–6)

With their allusions to saints, the wicked, and damnation, these lines form part of a subtext within *1 Henry IV* connecting Sir John to that Elizabethan satirical view of Puritanism which, as mentioned previously, has been unearthed by Shakespeare scholarship. However, these allusions lost a good deal of their point when the character's name was changed to Falstaff from Oldcastle, since Oldcastle had clear Puritan connections, his namesake having been made into a proto-Protestant martyr in John Foxe's widely distributed *Actes and Monuments of Martyrs*. With the new name of Falstaff, this subtext becomes a set of veiled allusions, yet another layer of contextual complexity in Falstaff's character,[36] so that in the text as we have received it, the implied anti-Puritan satire merges unobtrusively into Falstaff's general self-fictionalizing project of creating inverted and inflated carnivalesque images of himself as a consummately good man in a grossly unfair, wicked world:

You rogue, here's lime in this sack too. There is nothing but roguery to be found in villainous man. . . . Go thy ways, old Jack, die when thou wilt. If manhood, good manhood, be not forgot upon the face of the earth, then am I a shotten herring. There lives not three good men unhanged in England, and one of them is fat and grows old, God help the while. A bad world, I say. (2.5.112–19)

---

[35] Of course the text of *Don Quixote* itself is replete with such signals of fictionality, for which it has been rightly and repeatedly celebrated. But Quixote himself as character is sublimely indifferent to virtually all of these signals, and thereby depends a good measure of what Lukács once called that novel's cosmic irony.

[36] Poole, 'Saints Alive!'; on the significance of the earlier name Oldcastle, see Taylor, 'The Fortunes of Oldcastle'.

This profound project of inverted fictionalizing is behind his strange assertions of youth. 'They hate us youth. Down with them, fleece them' (2.2.76–7), Falstaff cries out during the robbery; and 'ye knaves! Young men must live' (l. 81), and when this particular fiction is so profoundly punctured near the end of *Part 2*, in the 'chimes of midnight' dialogue with Master Shallow, it is perhaps the most important of the many signs that Falstaff's carnival is coming to an end, his self-fictionalizations having reached their material limits.

The fact that the many lies of this white-bearded old Satan form the very structure of the counterfactual carnival which he attempts to inhabit is crucial to our understanding the paradoxical irrelevance, insisted upon in their different ways by Morgann, Hazlitt, Bradley, and Bloom, of Falstaff's manifest vices and self-serving proclivities. If he were a murderer like Richard III, the same effect could not prevail.[37] But his failings generally involve victims, like Mistress Quickly, Master Shallow, the Prince and associates, even the hapless but careless robbed 'pilgrims' at Gad's Hill and the improvident inductees of the wars, who are at least partially complicit with or tolerant of their own fleecing. And Falstaff makes little secret of his self-serving and weakness: 'Dost thou hear, Hal? thou knowest in the state of innocency Adam fell, and what should poor Jack Falstaff do in the days of villainy? Thou seest I have more flesh than another man, and therefore more frailty' (3.3.151–4).

But beyond the misdemeanour-like quality of most of Falstaff's failings is the ritualistic, non-rational, wish-fulfilling, and symbolic nature of the carnival discourse which forms such an important part of Falstaff's dramatic function. In this connection, Falstaff's gargantuan body—a comedy in itself, Dryden said[38]—as well as his love of the pleasures of the 'lower bodily stratum' and his attempt to create a timeless realm of

---

[37] This formula echoes a similar one from Samuel Johnson, 'Notes on Shakespeare's Plays: "I Henry IV"', in *The Yale Edition of the Works of Samuel Johnson: Johnson on Shakespeare*, ed. Arthur Sherbo (New Haven: Yale University Press, 1968), vii. 453–89, and it has been repeated—and heatedly contested—many times over the centuries. Charles Whitney, 'Festivity and Topicality in the Coventry Scene of *1 Henry IV*', *English Literary Renaissance*, 24/2 (Spring 1994), 438–9, attacks this viewpoint as insensitive to the plebeian response to Falstaff's recruiting abuses, but then goes on to define a kind of festive vision in which Falstaff is seen as a plebeian symbol, his exploitations notwithstanding (pp. 439–44). In what follows I pursue a somewhat different reading of the implied audience responses to Falstaff's abuses of the king's press but a similar one of the symbolic, carnivalesque aspects of Falstaff which undercut his apparent realism, and I see these taken together as thus finally endorsing Johnson's point; see below.

[38] John Dryden, quoted in John Munro (ed.), *The Shakespeare-Allusion Book: A Collection of Allusions to Shakespeare from 1591–1700*, 2 vols. (London: Oxford University Press, 1932), ii. 146.

perpetual holiday all link him with that plebeian, subaltern tradition, inherited from the ancient and medieval worlds, described by Mikhail Bakhtin in one of the great critical works of the twentieth century, *Rabelais and his World*.[39] Bakhtin linked the grotesque aspects of the carnival tradition—its emphasis on swollen bodies, beatings, even dismemberments and bodily mutilations—to a half-conscious, ancient, and peasant-based vision of life as a communal, earth-oriented, materialistic, but meaning-imbued process encompassing death as a condition for life's renewal and vigour. The carnival is thus a locus for an inarticulate but powerful subaltern tradition of resistance to that series of 'official' ideologies, from ancient Platonism and its allied philosophies to spiritualist Christianity to Stalinism, which have exalted the spirit over the body, the upper classes over the lower, and the state over society. C. L. Barber of course defined the relevance of the carnival tradition to Shakespearian comedy independently of Bakhtin, and his work remains a valuable source of ideas in this area. However, Barber, specifically in the case of the *Henry IV* plays, as I noted above, interpreted saturnalian comedy essentially as a social pressure-valve, an instance of licensed merriment which in fact reinforced rather than challenged authority. As Michael Bristol has previously argued, Bakhtin's analysis goes deeper, taking a much longer-range view of things, one which while not blind to carnival's escapist functions, emphasizes instead its transgressive potential, its function as a continuing locus for embodying and preserving centuries of counter-memories and challenges to authority.[40] And while both Barber and Bakhtin are highly relevant to the case of Falstaff, I am relying on Bakhtin here for what I find to be his profounder sense of the long-term meaning of the carnival tradition, a meaning crucial to an understanding of how these plays embody within their complex layers challenges to, as well as celebrations of, royal authority.[41]

[39] Mikhail Bakhtin, *Rabelais and his World*, trans. Helene Iswolsky (Cambridge, Mass.: MIT Press, 1968); trans. of *Tvorchestvo Fransua Rable* (Moscow: Khudozhestvennia literatura, 1965).

[40] Bristol, *Carnival and Theater*, 26–39 *et passim*.

[41] Bakhtin does, in a single sentence, link Falstaff to Rabelais's treatment of the carnival (*Rabelais and his World*, 143), but his focus remains on Rabelais and the traditions which he drew on. The most comprehensive application of Bakhtin to Shakespeare studies is Bristol, *Carnival and Theater*; Bakhtin's relevance to Falstaff is pointed out as well by Holderness, *Shakespeare's History*, 83–95. See also Peter Stallybrass and Allon White, *The Politics and Poetics of Transgression* (Ithaca, NY: Cornell University Press, 1986); Leah Marcus, *The Politics of Mirth: Jonson, Herrick, Milton, Marvell, and the Defense of Old Holiday Pastimes* (Chicago: University of Chicago Press, 1986); and François Laroque, *Shakespeare's Festive World: Elizabethan Seasonal Entertainment and the Professional Stage*, trans. Janet Lloyd (Cambridge: Cambridge University Press, 1991). Here, I want to emphasize the crucial

Another area of Falstaff's dense overdetermination, identified only recently, but very persuasively, in the long history of Falstaff criticism is his hidden, unconscious connections with the feminine, even the specifically maternal.[42] In the most developed of several psychoanalytic investigations of these connections, Valerie Traub links the grotesque corporeality of Falstaff's stage presence, his own language, and the language of those about him with a pregnant female body, and argues that Hal ultimately forms his kingly identity by rejecting this representation of the maternal. Indeed, Traub argues that Bakhtin's grotesque body should be gendered as female in the first place, in recognition of its orientation to traditional female attributes of physicality, fecundity, and immanence. And taking Traub's argument a step further, we can see in Falstaff's hidden femininity an additional resource of opposition to instrumentalized Machiavellian politics, since in the sexual division of labour of modernity, women have been constructed as outside the political order and often, as is the case with Lady Percy in her memorable scene with Hotspur on the way to the wars, oppositional to its values, as, indeed, Falstaff reveals himself to be in his famous catechism on honour.[43]

To be sure, this opposition to a Machiavellian patriarchy coexists with a whole series of subtly inflected alternative viewpoints on the action of these plays. With Sir John as with everything else in Shakespearian desacralized space, there are no anchors to counter the shifting conceptual seas in which and through which we see and evaluate the variegated life

relevance of Falstaff's connections to the carnival tradition with the issues of power which have dominated recent new historicism and cultural materialism, an issue also discussed from a point of view close to my own by Whitney, 'Festivity and Topicality in the Coventry Scene of 1 *Henry IV*'.

[42] W. H. Auden, 'The Prince's Dog', in *The Dyer's Hand and Other Essays* (London: Random House, 1962), 195–6, made perhaps the earliest association of Falstaff with the feminine; Gayle Whittier, 'Falstaff as a Welshwoman: Uncomic Androgyny', *Ball State University Forum*, 20/3 (Summer 1979), 23–35, identified Falstaff as a 'submerged androgyn' or 'false woman'; Coppélia Kahn, *Man's Estate: Masculine Identity in Shakespeare* (Berkeley and Los Angeles: University of California Press, 1981), 72–3, defined a similar connection in psychoanalytic terms; Patricia Parker, *Literary Fat Ladies* (London: Methuen, 1987), 20–2, discussed the rhetorical and figural connections of this demonstration. Valerie Traub, 'Prince Hal's Falstaff: Positioning Psychoanalysis and the Female Reproductive Body', *Shakespeare Quarterly*, 40/4 (Winter 1989), 456–74, which develops the same theme, is discussed below.

[43] See R. A. Martin, 'Metatheater, Gender, and Subjectivity in *Richard II* and *Henry IV, Part I*', *Comparative Drama*, 23 (1989), 255–64, for a quite cogent demonstration of the oppositional role of women in 1 *Henry IV* and Falstaff's connections to them; and Rackin, *Stages of History*, 146–200, for a detailed account of how women are treated as subversive to patriarchal historiography throughout Shakespeare's history plays; and 203–4 for remarks linking Falstaff as a subversive representative of the common people to the transgressive role of women.

put before us. Many readers, for example (classically, Tillyard and Dover Wilson), have restored the morality-framework which the modernizing impulses of Shakespearian drama (if my reading is correct) had stripped from Falstaff and his play(s). But even in a secular space, we as spectators are not blind to the ways in which Sir John acts out for us as well the egotistical and destructive potentialities of a pleasure principle ungoverned by other values. In fact, one of Hal's roles in the play (assisted by a number of able seconds as well) is to puncture Sir John's amiable self-justifications and to note for us his exploitations of others:[44]

Charge an honest woman with picking thy pocket? Why, thou whoreson impudent embossed rascal, if there were anything in thy pocket but tavern reckonings, memorandums of bawdy-houses, and one poor pennyworth of sugar-candy to make thee long-winded—if thy pocket were enriched with any other injuries but these, I am a villain. And yet you will stand to it, you will not pocket-up wrong. Art thou not ashamed? (3.3.144–50)

Any attentive reader or viewer of *1 Henry IV* can work up a long list of ethically dubious actions by Falstaff: he lies, he robs, he takes advantage of the weak, and he sacrifices his friends' interest to his own on many occasion.[45] How, then, does he come away with readers' and viewers' good feelings? This question dates from the eighteenth century, but our answers must necessarily differ from those of the past. I have already given part of my own response to this perennial question: in this play there are no saints, Hal least of all. With every puncturing speech, such as the one I have quoted above, he risks sounding self-righteous and bullying. Has not he condoned many of Sir John's actions (as the robbery at Gad's Hill), and/or enjoyed the fruit of them in his pleasure in Sir John's company? The desacralized world depicted in this play (and a fortiori in *Part 2* and in *Henry V*) is a prescient, Machiavelli-tinged version of Hobbes's war of each against all, and in that context Sir John is one self-serving combatant among many others—and certainly the most entertaining. Thus the play's criticisms of Falstaff from Prince Hal and others are at least partially

---

[44] Cf. Brian Vickers, *The Artistry of Shakespeare's Prose*, rev. edn. (London: Methuen, 1968), 89–170.

[45] Does he, however, as Whitney, 'Festivity and Topicality in the Coventry Scene of *1 Henry IV*', 421, 427–4 (like a few earlier critics), asserts, deliberately lead his ragged troops to the death, in order to pocket their pay cheques, as unscrupulous Elizabethan officers sometimes did? The evidence, Falstaff's line, 'I have led my ragamuffins where they are peppered' (5.3.35–6), seems to me very equivocal as to Falstaff's intentions and role; in fact Morgann used these lines to argue for Falstaff's bravery in battle. Despite Falstaff's undoubted corruption, there is nothing in the text to affirm or deny the possibility of Falstaff's taking the dead's pay.

deflected because the play's world is one in which Falstaff is by no means an egregiously wicked man.

Metatheatrical Falstaff

But there is an additional and more important reason as well. In the second half of the play, as the action builds up to the climactic battle scenes and we have left behind the carnival world *per se*, Sir John takes on yet another dimension. He becomes the most metadramatic[46] and Brechtian[47] of Shakespeare's characters; or to put it perhaps more precisely, he provides a dramatic precedent, itself based on older festival traditions, which Brecht learned to exploit to the hilt. Like one of Brecht's characters exhibiting the 'alienation-effect', by stepping out of character and commenting, chorus-like, on his character's actions or situations, Sir John in the absence of a chiding Hal becomes his own accuser, and he wins sympathy because he is the character closest to the heavily plebeian popular audience of the play, pointedly exposing the corrupt manipulations of the wars, which he himself has acted out for us. In this way, too, his role is reminiscent not only of the Brechtian alienation-effect, but also of that of the medieval fool or Lord of Misrule who frequently acted as a kind of master of ceremonies at village processions or festivals. Similarly, as we have seen above, he recalls the dramatic descendant of the Lord of Misrule in the medieval moralities, the Vice character, who stands 'on the threshold between the play and the community occasion' and who, as an 'ambidexter', is 'both object of and spokesman for the attack' on vice.[48]

To see these effects at work, it is worth quoting at length from a

---

[46] D. A. Traversi, *Shakespeare: From 'Richard II' to 'Henry V'* (Stanford, Calif.: Stanford University Press, 1957), 102, defined a role for Falstaff very close to the idea of the metadramatical (without using the term): 'The essence of Falstaff lies in his standing, alone in this play and . . . outside the categories by which those round him are respectively defined and limited. . . . Falstaff is, let us say, a coward who can contemplate his own cowardice with detachment.' In the late 1970s James L. Calderwood, *Metadrama in Shakespeare's Henriad: 'Richard II' to 'Henry V'* (Berkeley and Los Angeles: University of California Press, 1979), 71–5, provides an excellent discussion of these qualities for the Falstaff of *Part 1*, although, unlike Calderwood, I believe Falstaff's metadramatic function extends into and is even intensified in *Part 2*; see Ch. 5. Most recently Robert Weimann has very fruitfully extended his discussion of the metatheatrical (here under the rubrics of 'performance' and 'playing') in his *Author's Pen and Actor's Voice: Playing and Writing in Shakespeare's Theatre*, ed. Helen Higbee and William West (Cambridge: Cambridge University Press, 2000).

[47] Falstaff's Brechtian dimensions in the battle scenes were first pointed out by Jan Kott, *Shakespeare our Contemporary*, trans. Boleslaw Taborski (New York: Doubleday, 1966), 43, and more recently discussed, in a somewhat different analysis from my own, by Whitney, 'Festivity and Topicality in the Coventry Scene of *1 Henry IV*', 416.

[48] Weimann, *Shakespeare and the Popular Tradition*, 43, 154, 224–46.

remarkable soliloquy, in which Sir John is clearly speaking directly to the audience:

I have misused the King's press damnably. I have got in exchange of a hundred and fifty soldiers three hundred and odd pounds. I press me none but good house-holders, yeomen's sons, enquire me out contracted bachelors, such as had been asked twice on the banns, such a commodity of warm slaves as had as lief hear the devil as a drum. . . . and they have bought out their services; and now my whole charge consists of ensigns, corporals, lieutenants, gentlemen of companies—slaves as ragged as Lazarus in the painted cloth, where the glutton's dogs licked his sores—and such as, indeed, were never soldiers, but discarded unjust servingmen, younger sons to younger brothers, revolted tapsters, and ostlers trade-fallen, the cankers of a calm world and a long peace. . . . A mad fellow met me on the way and told me I had unloaded all the gibbets and pressed the dead bodies. No eye hath seen such scarecrows. . . . Nay, and the villains march wide betwixt the legs, as if they had gyves on, for indeed, I had the most of them out of prison. There's not a shirt and a half in all my company; and the half-shirt is two napkins tacked together and thrown over the shoulders like a herald's coat without sleeves; and the shirt, to say the truth, stolen from my host at Saint Albans, or the red-nose inn-keeper of Daventry. But that's all one; they'll find linen enough on every hedge. (4.2.12–42)

Sir John the interlocutor has stepped out of the role of Sir John the corrupt recruiter; the former in fact denounces the latter. His voice, as Robert Weimann puts it in a passage on a group of Shakespearian characters, including Falstaff, helps to embody a 'sense of freedom from the burden of the ruling ideologies and concepts of honor, love, ambition, and revenge. . . . The power of negation is [thus] turned against the representatives of the *vicious world* itself: the negation of negation dialectically gives them a structural function.'[49] The effect is one of a simultaneous condemnation of exploitation and a dark, worldly-wise acknowledgement of the world's ways—only, we begin to realize (and this is a theme amplified in the plays to come), it is a way of the world and of 'commodity' (that subject of a similar puncturing soliloquy in *King John*) showing no signs of withering, an all-too ancient outcome of warfare as an instrumentalizing incursion into the lifeworlds of communities that destroys normal inhibitions and customs and opens them up to new forms of exploitation. Thus the exposure of the abuses of early modern recruiting is also a kind of proleptic demonstration of the logic of modernization more generally. And here Sir John is both the instrument and critic of such an incursion.

[49] Weimann, *Shakespeare and the Popular Tradition*, 159.

Falstaff between the Carnival and the Aesthetic

In the passage I quoted above, Robert Weimann emphasized Falstaff's role as an ideological 'negation' in the Hegelian-Marxian sense, a character who illustrates the shortcomings and untruths of an era's received ideology. In the case of his famous catechism on honour, Falstaff is negating concepts which in a sense were already critical negations, since honour, courage, and so on represented ideals against which the empirical world could be measured and found wanting. Falstaff's catechism in turn suggests how these ideals themselves are imbued with assumptions of the world which they pretend to critique. But this leads to a further question. If, as Weimann suggests, Falstaff is a negation of a negation, can we approximate this double negativity in terms of some positivity? What do Falstaff's negations add up to?

On the one hand, it is clear (and Weimann himself suggests as much) that Falstaff is allied to the ancient carnival traditions whose function over several centuries was to serve as a continuing negation of ruling ideologies repressive of the peasantry and other labouring classes, their vision and their values. The character of Falstaff is clearly constructed in large part from carnival and related traditions, as we have seen, and he exemplifies in many ways the world of holiday and festival.

However, C. L. Barber (and a host of followers) long ago pointed out in connection with this play that carnival unfolds through Falstaff within a modernizing society, in an urban commercial enterprise in which the ancient communal pastimes are now the stuff of nostalgic remembrance. In the absence of those communal structures, Sir John's plebeian cunning and self-preservation easily become the egoistic self-maximization that is the socio-psychological linchpin of emergent systems of power and capitalism of the early modern period. A Falstaff at liberty in a land where all the laws are at his commandment is dangerous in a way in which the charming rogue at the Boar's Head decidedly is not—the complaints of his creditors notwithstanding. In short, there is an important social as well as a psychological component to Sir John's emotional and ethical complexity, productive of disparate audience responses to him. Contained within the proto-communal structures of the tavern (themselves emblematic of the rural communities from which many members of the audience came, and partially re-created in new urban settings), Sir John's comic championing of the bodily self and its pleasures functions as a communal, class-conscious discourse of a plebeian social element oppressed by the idealisms of Church and State. Understood, however, in terms of a new Renaissance individualism, as an atomistic ego contending in the war of each against all, he is an emblem of the community-destroying dynamics of an embryonic capitalist society just visible at the turn of the sixteenth to the seventeenth centuries. Everything depends on the social context.

Thus the exploitative side of Falstaff can be seen as enacting one of the 'dangerous' aspects of unfixed subjectivity in the service of unchecked appetite. Here, as in several other Shakespearian plays, the limits of subjectivity and pleasure as 'solutions' to the crisis of emerging modernity are worked out in its very earliest stages. Whereas *joie de vivre* and pleasure are crucial values to assert in an instrumentalized world, they, too, in the evacuated cultural space of modernity, can be reified and established as a system of pointless circulation and exchange capable of enthralling individuals and entire societies, as Troy illustrated in Shakespeare's jaundiced *Troilus and Cressida*[50] and as modern consumer society demonstrates afresh in our own day. When Hal remarks early in the play that 'If all the year were playing holidays, | To sport would be as tedious as to work' (1.2.183–4), he is not only rationalizing his own sowing of wild oats, but he is enunciating the problem that Sir John lives: what are the limits of a carnival wrenched out of its setting in the cycle of the year's months and seasons and set up as an end in itself in a society of constant moral and cultural disintegration and reconfiguration, such as is constituted by modernity?

Drawing on ancient associations and traditions to provide a good measure of its content, then, Shakespeare constructs for Sir John a version of libidinal subjectivity particularly suited to act as a foil for the cold, value-free instrumental rationality at work in the Machiavellian dynamics of the political world. The foil, of course, as in any dialectic, will create its own problems in its turn. Nevertheless, Falstaff embodies a good deal of what is repressed in the construction of a world of value-free objects by a modernizing instrumental rationality. This libido-infused, pleasure-oriented subjectivity, represented verbally and symbolically in a popular genre, but destined to become a classic successively of high bourgeois, Modernist, and Postmodernist cultures, might even be said to evoke the sublime, unrepresentable 'subjectivity itself' that has been the elusive quarry of so much nineteenth- and twentieth-century literary criticism.[51]

---

[50] I discussed this theme in *Troilus and Cressida* and *Othello* in Hugh Grady, *Shakespeare's Universal Wolf: Studies in Early Modern Reification* (Oxford: Clarendon, 1996), 88–9 and 135–6. Other Shakespearian plays with a similar theme include *Twelfth Night*, *Much Ado About Nothing*, *Measure for Measure*, and *The Winter's Tale*.

[51] See the discussion of the Romantic, aestheticist, and Modernist attempts to evoke Richard II's subjectivity above in Ch. 2.

If Frankfurt School aesthetic theory is correct in diagnosing subjectivity and the aesthetic as related post-Enlightenment categories which preserve, refunction, and mystify the sense of (eroticized) feeling and rich meaning of which the world is bereft in the visions of instrumental reason, then subsequent critical fascination with Falstaff (and, as with Harold Bloom, with Hamlet) are explicable as attempts to produce within modernity the lost aura of pre-modern perception. In that way the peculiar pleasure-oriented subjectivity of Falstaff becomes subjectivity *tout court* through a kind of metonymy that is symptomatic of the instrumentalized rationality of Western modernity. Falstaff becomes a representation of what is always already missing in our world.

In their depiction of modernity and its construction of an instrumental rationality which disembodies objects of their sensual qualities the better to dominate them, Horkheimer and Adorno turned to and allegorized the episode in book 12 of *The Odyssey* when Odysseus and his crew have to sail past the Sirens. Odysseus, availing himself of the privileges of his rank, allows himself to hear the proverbial beauty of the Sirens' song, while forbidding his men to do the same by having them stop up their ears with wax. Of course, he has himself tied to the ship's mast so as to be unable to give way to the desires which the Sirens' song produces in him. And this story, Horkheimer and Adorno tell us, is a prescient representation of the dialectic of enlightenment which strips the world of all values except those of immediate utility, making its practitioners deaf to the world's beauty— except for those few modern Odysseuses who allow themselves to hear so long as they are unable to swerve from the paths of utility in which they are set. And what they hear are works of modern art, which represent something of the world's beauty but in a form separating it off from all other social reality.[52]

In Falstaff, particularly in his relation to Prince Hal, Shakespeare has given us his own version of this myth, in which the tavern world is a kind of Siren song potentially seducing the Prince from the instrumental path of Machiavellian politics. In the new context of modernity, carnivalesque Falstaff and his world embody the potential for pleasure and beauty within the emerging subjectivities of modernity. No longer anchored in communal celebrations, they have become individual and subjective— freed in the process from communal forms and open to all the new possibilities—and dangers—of the individual imagination.

Falstaff thus manifests a version of the carnivalesque that has been

<hr/>

[52] Max Horkheimer and Theodor W. Adorno, *Dialectic of Enlightenment*, trans. John Cumming (Boston: Seabury, 1972), 30–80.

recontextualized and given new meaning by the modernizing impulses of Puritanism/capitalism. Henceforth, what had been ritual and sanctioned disorder for pre-modern Europe would have to be transformed into an emerging, historically new category of autonomous, subjective art, and the London commercial theatres of Shakespeare's day were early proto-types for this development.[53]

In classical Frankfurt School theory, the aesthetic, like the other fragmentary components of modernity, entered the world in the Enlightenment, and this chronology is supported empirically by the fact that the idea of the aesthetic as we understand the term came into being in the eighteenth century. Here as elsewhere, however, the status of the Renaissance as a precursor of Enlightenment complicates the issue, and the fact that we are dealing with works of Shakespeare complicates it even further. The plays of Shakespeare were crucial documents in many of the seminal discussions of the aesthetic, particularly those of late eighteenth-century Germany, where Shakespeare had emerged as a major figure, both a vehicle for and a major instance of the new aesthetic thinking. For example, he was a key case in point in the paradigm-changing work of G. E. Lessing.[54] For Lessing and the German Enlightenment and Romantic periods generally, *Hamlet* was the key document, and much of the fasci-nation of it centred in the elusive subjectivity of the Prince, seen as an alienated artist or near-artist whose restless subjectivity rebelled against confinement to the role of revenge-tragedy hero. Harold Bloom, as I mentioned above, is palpably arguing a version of this moment of cultural history some 200 years after its original construction, with Bloom adding Falstaff to Hamlet as a figure for his putative 'creation of the human'. But what Bloom is describing could be more accurately termed the construc-tion of the aesthetic and the subjective. And I would add that although there is no question of identity between Shakespearian practice and Romantic aesthetic theory, they are at least sufficiently analogous to each other to have supported 200 years dominated by the idea that reading Shakespeare is essentially an aesthetic experience. I would posit that in the case of the emerging concepts and practices of the aesthetic and subjec-tivity, Shakespeare broke ground which post-Enlightenment art and

---

[53] Cf. the interesting argument in Richard Helgerson, *Forms of Nationhood: The Elizabethan Writing of England* (Chicago: University of Chicago Press, 1992), 195–245, that Shakespeare and company undertook a more-or-less conscious strategy of making their theatre less popular and carnivalesque over the years, mirroring a larger process creative of a new national culture.

[54] See, for example, Gotthold Ephraim Lessing, *Hamburg Dramaturgy*, trans. Helen Zimmern (New York: Dover, 1962).

theory cultivated centuries later to produce much of the conceptual world
we still inhabit. In short the great impact of the characters Hamlet
and Falstaff, in their own time and subsequently, is connected to their
embodiment of characteristics of the subjective and the aesthetic destined
to be central to the reified world of emerging modernity. However, not
Harold Bloom, but the Frankfurt School, can best guide us in understanding these developments.[55] In that theoretical context, it is not hard to see
why Falstaff became a representation of what is always already missing in
the disenchanted world of modernity: the modern concepts of subjectivity
and the aesthetic are related categories which preserve, refunction, and
mystify the sense of meaning obliterated in instrumental reason. Falstaff is
entangled in these emerging forms.

This is not the occasion to try to tease out answers to the elusive
question of just where to place Shakespeare's Falstaff in the cultural continuum between the carnivalesque and the aesthetic which was developing
apace in Renaissance London. What we can say is that Falstaff, in all his
contradictoriness, is a beautifully constructed instance of the process
whereby the carnivalesque metamorphoses into the aesthetic. This is a
process above all of refunctioning and recontextualization. Because the
social and intellectual contexts which had defined the carnival were
crumbling, the contents of the plays' medieval materials, including the
carnivalesque, took on new meanings in the new situation.

Let us look, for example, at the oft-repeated claim that Falstaff is a
reincarnation of the Vice figure of late medieval moralities, as suggested
within the text by his offhand reference to 'a dagger of lath' (1 Henry IV,
2.5.124), the traditional stage prop of the Vice. What has been far less often
discussed in this connection is what it could mean to refunction such a
figure in the secular space of the public theatres. For this particular Vice is
functioning quite autonomously from any clearly fixed moral categories,
in a comic grey area in which his own peccadilloes seem small change in a
larger Machiavellian world of power politics, with its wars and betrayals.

What Falstaff retains from the Vice of the moralities is his libidinal
energy, his wit, and zest for transgression. In the kind of cultural 'negotiation' theorized by Greenblatt, but with an outcome quite different from
those he discussed,[56] the commercial theatre has demythologized and
secularized a figure from a religious tradition, replacing the certainties of

---

[55] See John J. Joughin, 'Shakespeare, Modernity and the Aesthetic: Art, Truth and Judge-
ment in *The Winter's Tale*', in Hugh Grady (ed.), *Shakespeare and Modernity: From Early
Modern to Millennium* (London: Routledge, 2000), 61–84, for a pioneering application of the
Frankfurt category of the aesthetic to Shakespeare studies.

[56] Greenblatt, *Shakespearian Negotiations*, 1–20.

the one with the prolix, shifting, and uncertain moral frames which we see in play here in aesthetic space. The morally imbued cosmology of the moralities has been replaced, in short, by emerging modern subjectivity which erects an aesthetic sphere to refunction within an otherwise bleak space of autonomous Machiavellian power the possibilities of counter-values of pleasure, community, and solidarity drawn from a declining medieval tradition.[57] Falstaff stands within this inverted secular morality play as a kind of figure from a Blakean hell, representing a libidinal counterweight (of gargantuan proportions) to the Machiavellian power dynamics which *Richard II* (and a plethora of other plays of the era) had established as the most evident of the Renaissance outcomes of an emerging modernity.

Thus, as Weimann's history of popular stage traditions perhaps makes clearest, in Falstaff's contradictory amoral, self-serving, but community-associated virtue, we are in touch with central paradoxes associated with the centuries-old traditions of clown, carnival, and plebeian mirth. And as Frankfurt School aesthetic theory implies, these are also the very qualities refunctioned and uneasily contained in the modern category of the aesthetic. Because Falstaff is located precisely between these two 'moments', we can construct two quite different conceptual contexts for him—one, however, for which he is too late (the carnival), the other for which he is too early (the aesthetic). What we have to say is that he is transitional between the two and thus embodies a central moment in the development of Western modernity.

Falstaff thus steps out of the boundaries of the plays in which he is featured and becomes for a subsequent modernity a figure of an almost vanished subaltern world uneasily afoot in an emerging modern one—and he becomes thereby simultaneously a dream or wish-fulfilment, within an aesthetic register. That is why this comical figure, so often bested in his wit-duels with Hal in the two plays, so often submitted to devastating deflations and humiliations in the course of three plays, and so often sullied by his own misdemeanours, finally triumphs in a cultural collective memory as a comic colossus which indeed Hal is unable to bestride.

---

[57] If this is correct then Weimann's eloquent assertion of the crucialness of the carnivalesque popular theatrical traditions to Shakespeare's 'myriad-minded' critical rationality and richness (*Shakespeare and the Popular Tradition*, 174–7) should be supplemented with the recognition that this amounted to a refunctioning of those traditions within an emerging modern category of the aesthetic.

3. THE PRINCE'S SELF: BETWEEN MACHIAVELLI AND MONTAIGNE

As the one character with a foot in all three of the 'worlds' of this play (court, tavern, rebel camp), Prince Hal is given a privileged structural position, and in his case the unfixed subjectivity achieved by Richard II becomes an orientation not to an imagined theatre of limitless possibilities, but to a delimited but still rich ensemble of possible social roles. In one sense this new context limits subjectivity, but in another way it makes it much more of an active force in the world, displaying a transgressive potentiality. In *Part 1* the unfolding Machiavellian drama of national power and consolidation runs into resistance at almost every conceivable level—but nowhere more pointedly than in the resistance of the kingdom's heir-apparent to the supposedly coveted role of Machiavellian prince. He is more enamoured, at least in the short run, with his potentiality than with his title.

Prince Hal displays a protean self implicated for a time, as we have seen, in a plebeian carnival subversive of royal power. However, *1 Henry IV* explores additional possibilities for self-definition under conditions of modernity, demonstrating that the cleared field created by the waning of older, medieval ideologies and the myriad possibilities created by the shifting values and thought systems of modernity can be exploited not only in the service of power, but also in resistance to it. Thus the play demonstrates that Machiavellian politics are made possible by the theatrical potentialities of modern subjectivity—but can also be challenged by them.

As I noted above, for a number of critics since Hazlitt, Prince Hal has been the object of a good deal of vituperation for an apparent falseness to self. But here as well, everything depends on context, and we will need to review these classic critical questions in the context of treatment within *1 Henry IV* of a theme first defined in *Richard II*: the nature of modern subjectivity.

From the first mention of him by his father the King, it is clear that Prince Hal is in rebellion against that social role which, as Stephen Greenblatt pointed out, is referred to consistently in this play as a 'self'. We hear this usage early in the play, in King Henry's confrontation with the future rebels:

> You tread upon my patience; but be sure
> I will from henceforth rather be myself,

> Mighty and to be feared, than my condition,
> Which hath been smooth as oil, soft as young down,
> And therefore lost that title of respect
> Which the proud soul ne'er pays but to the proud. (1.3.4–9)

And Prince Hal employs the same usage in his reconciliation speech to his father:

> I shall hereafter, my thrice-gracious lord,
> Be more myself. (3.2.92–3)

—referring, as the context shows (his father has just lectured him on his absence from court and unseemly public self-display), to his duties as Prince of Wales.[58] Given this repeated usage, we should consider another deployment of this same locution—this one less clear-cut in meaning— from Prince Hal's much discussed soliloquy at the end of scene 1.2:

> Yet herein will I imitate the sun,
> Who doth permit the base contagious clouds
> To smother up his beauty from the world,
> That when he please again to be himself,
> Being wanted he may be more wondered at. (1.2.175–9)

The metaphor may make the usage here seem 'essentialist' at first: that is, since the sun is an unchanging heavenly body above the fickle sublunary world, its appearance is only obscured by clouds, its essence unchanged. And if we apply these properties of the sun back to the Prince, we seem to have an exception to the above uses of 'self' in that here, the self of the sun-prince can easily be understood as referring to (what King Henry called) the 'condition' of the Prince, what many critics have called his 'inner self', obscured by the clouds of the plebeian world in which he is sojourning. However, further consideration, I believe, will demonstrate that a reading even of this 'self' fits the pattern established above: what is obscured is not so much an inner self as the offices and duties of that station to which he is called. It is precisely the Prince's self-as-prince that is obscured and will shine forth later, as he promises his father in Scene 3.2. Here too, the 'self' is a social role, not an inner essence.

This repeated idea of the self as a social station which one can choose to serve or not inaugurates one of the most important themes of the two *Henry IV* plays: the complicated relation between this self of duty, clearly located in a socio-linguistic Symbolic order, and the more complex aspects of subjectivity which take up a relation to that station and which

---

[58] Cf. Greenblatt, 'Invisible Bullets', 46.

are far from exhausted in identifying with that station. In short, these plays make use of concepts analogous to current Poststructuralist ideas of a self formed by power such as I discussed in the Introduction, but only to show their limited application. In the second quote given above, Hal is clearly 'hailed' or 'interpellated' in a quite Althusserian sense into his role as prince. And yet it is clear from the entire play that there are important aspects of Hal's self that resist this interpellation; indeed much of the play is 'about' this resistance.[59] Furthermore, in *1 and 2 Henry IV*, King Henry is represented to us as the shaken, careworn outcome of reduction to a Machiavellian self (and even in his case, we see something of the psychic price he has paid for this, in the troubled if banal interiority he reveals in soliloquy and in dialogue with his son), while of course Hal is presented as in confused flight from such reductionism, seeking in Falstaff's carnival kingdom the warmth and libido so markedly absent in the emotionally cold world of Henry's Machiavellian court. And the warmth and fellow-ship of the high jinks contrast so markedly with the coldness and 'policy' of Henry IV's court that audiences consistently find Hal's preference for the tavern world one resolutely to be applauded. The tavern world is of course also the locus of sport, play, holiday, and imagining, and the intricate series of parallels and contrasts among court, rebels, and tavern works throughout, as a minority branch of traditional criticism has argued since Hazlitt, almost entirely in favour of the tavern.

But beyond Falstaff's considerable charm, it is clear that Hal values the tavern world because it affords him a kind of theatrical space in which he can try out different roles and project different kinds of identities in a way that the constrained world of the court would never countenance. As critics have long noted, he is an irrepressible thespian, constantly imagining himself as others, proposing extempore plays, and orches-trating practical jokes. This histrionic disposition can be interpreted as a Machiavellian talent, to be sure—as when Greenblatt emphasizes the Machiavellian convenience of being able to empathize with others in order the better to manipulate them. For Greenblatt, a key instance is the Prince's conversation with the tavern apprentice Francis in a kind of inter-lude at the beginning of the great tavern scene after the Gad's Hill robbery. The conversation has puzzled numerous previous critics because it puts Hal in a cruel light: he seems to be toying with this good lad of Eastcheap simply to demonstrate his ability to do so. In 'Invisible Bullets' Greenblatt

---

[59] This is the nub of my disagreement with the otherwise closely connected point of view of Kastan, 'The King Hath Many Marching in his Coats'. Kastan wrote: 'If *1 Henry IV* can be said to be "about" anything, it is about the production of power' (p. 241).

agrees with this assessment, comparing his actions to those of the Virginia colonists described by Thomas Harriot in their attempt to dominate the Algonquians:

> The prince must sound the base-string of humility if he is to play all of the chords and hence be the master of the instrument, and for his ability to conceal his motives and render opaque his language offers assurance that he himself will not be played on by another.[60]

And yet another motivation for Hal's interactions with Francis is possible, one alluded to but dismissed by Greenblatt just before the passage quoted, and one much more compatible with the analysis of the theme of subjectivity I am working with here; I mean the idea that Hal is projecting onto Francis the problem he is living out in his own royal apprenticeship, his desire to flee from his assigned role, his feeling of facing competing claims from the different lifeworlds in which he has, as it were, taken up residence. It is significant in this connection that Hal here takes up the topic of language and its efficacy as he interacts with Francis. When Poins (speaking also for the audience) asks the Prince, 'what cunning match have you made with this jest of the drawer? Come, what's the issue?' (2.5.83–5), Hal responds, curiously, by linking this figure from the bottom rung of the age's social hierarchy with another nearly at its top, contrasting them both with Sir John's and his own histrionic abilities:

> That ever this fellow should have fewer words than a parrot, and yet the son of a woman! His industry is upstairs and downstairs, his eloquence the parcel of a reckoning. I am not yet of Percy's mind, the Hotspur of the north—he that kills me some six or seven dozen of Scots at a breakfast, washes his hands, and says to his wife, 'Fie upon this quiet life! I want work.' 'O my sweet Harry,' says she, 'how many hast thou killed today?' 'Give my roan horse a drench,' says he, and answers, 'Some fourteen,' an hour after; 'a trifle, a trifle.' I prithee call in Falstaff. I'll play Percy, and that damned brawn shall play Dame Mortimer his wife. (2.5.91–101)

The answer first defines the oppressive limitations of Francis's life and language—a reaction which E. M. W. Tillyard notoriously glossed as a reference to 'the subhuman element in the population',[61] but which makes more sense here as Hal seeing in the apprentice what he sees in Hotspur: a self interpellated into an oppressively overdefining, freedom-cancelling social role. In his turn from Francis to Hotspur, Prince Hal moves from what is already a complex, double-edged assertion of his ability to communicate with and manipulate the good boys of Eastcheap: on the one

---

[60] Greenblatt, 'Invisible Bullets', 45.

[61] E. M. W. Tillyard, *Shakespeare's History Plays* (1944; repr. New York: Macmillan, 1946), 277.

hand he is asserting a proto-democratic interest in the kingdom's plebeian strata (unlike, as we are told, a 'proud Jack, like Falstaff' (2.5.10)), while also asserting his class privilege to Poins even as he boasts of his acceptance by the drawers as 'a Corinthian, a lad of mettle, a good boy, by the Lord, so they call me' (ll. 10–11). But the pay-off for Hal's submission to such humility is a highly valuable, instrumental one: 'and when I am king of England, I shall command all the good lads in Eastcheap' (ll. 11–13). And we of course think about the legendary Henry V's abilities, staged in famous scenes of *Henry V*, as a charismatic military leader in connection with all of this. In short, this scene, like so much else in these plays, lets us sense two crucial, potentially conflicting, potentially complementary themes simultaneously: on the one hand we are in contact with Prince Hal as an unfixed subjectivity of protean potentiality: 'I am now of all humours that have showed themselves humours since the old days of goodman Adam to the pupil age of this present twelve o'clock at midnight' (2.5.86–8). On the other hand, we can sense how all this experimentation and rebellion against his social role might work out as part of the formidable instrumental rationality of a future hero-warrior. And this last connection, I believe, is evoked when Hal's thoughts jump from Francis the indentured servant to Hotspur the aristocratic warrior. We are at this point almost equidistantly poised between Machiavelli and Montaigne.

Then, however, comes one of those moments of resistance that continually accompany Hal's uneven path to heroism: 'I am not yet of Percy's mind', he tells us, and demonstrates instead his ability to encompass that role imaginatively, as a potentiality, without (yet) having to instrumentalize his life to it, as Percy does. And this is emblematic of the difference between this play—which tilts toward Montaigne—and *Part 2*, which, as we will see, tilts toward Machiavelli.

Hotspur and Subjectivity

In *Part 1* even Hotspur is no one-dimensional machiavel, however, but a strongly defined stage presence powerful enough to take pride of place on the cover of one of the extant quarto versions of this play and in the Folio's title as well.[62] He is an important component of the play's developing presentation of subjectivity. Hotspur vies with Sir John (also featured on quarto covers) as a highly individuated character, and like Sir John has his

---

[62] Q1's title reads: 'The History of Henrie the Fourth; With the battel at Shrewsburie, between the King and Lord Henry Percy, surnamed Henrie Hotspur of the North. With the humorous conceits of Sir John Falstaffe'. The Folio title is: 'The First part of Henry the fourth, with the Life and Death of Henry Sirnamed Hot-Spurre'.

own distinct style, mannerisms, and qualities. And while he is considerably and comfortably 'fixed' in his social role as northern baron with a strong investment in an aristocratic code of honour, he is also involved in a conflict between two different spheres which he inhabits: the masculine rebel world and a female-dominated domestic space presided over by Lady Percy. This space, as R. A. Martin first argued, actively encroaches on Hotspur's masculine world when Lady Percy aggressively demands to know of Hotspur's political plans and complains of his neglect of her.[63] Hotspur wriggles his way out of the difficulty, but not without clearly marking this surplus in his life beyond the merely instrumental.

This 'surplus' is asserted once more in one of the most puzzling scenes in the play, Scene 3.1 at Glendŵr's castle.[64] Older critics focused on one aspect of its political implications: the rebels, like King Lear after them, discredit themselves with the original audiences by placing themselves squarely against developing English nationalism and imperial ambitions with their plan to divide the kingdom in three and by their assertions of Welsh separateness. More recently commentators have focused on the colonialist dichotomy implied by the contrast between rational, masculine England and mystical, feminine Wales, recognizing that a good deal of the first part of this long scene is taken up with the quarrel between Hotspur and Glendŵr over the latter's purported mystical powers. But the dialogue has conflicting effects, in line with the mixture of positive and negative valences working with Hotspur as a character. The interaction again illustrates his rigidity and stubbornness and need to assert dominance in the face of other considerations: he picks a quarrel over the division of the country which he does not really intend to pursue, apparently just to be combative against the rivalrous Glendŵr. We will see these traits again at the end of the play, when Hotspur chooses to fight despite a number of material difficulties. And Hotspur's irrepressible assertiveness of his commonsense world view violates a Machiavellian policy of ingratiating oneself with one's allies. The effect is small and subtle, but it is another of the play's assertions of a subjectivity beyond power.

When the dramatic mood shifts toward concord under Mortimer's

---

[63] Martin, 'Metatheater, Gender, and Subjectivity', 258. The point is further developed by Jean E. Howard and Phyllis Rackin, *Engendering a Nation: A Feminist Account of Shakespeare's English Histories* (London: Routledge, 1997), 188–92.

[64] Wikander, *The Play of Truth and State*, 14–25, is an important exception; his discussion of the scene begins with a similar observation on the tendency of critics to treat it as a mere interlude, but his reading, which emphasizes parallels between Glendŵr and Falstaff as alluring, pleasure-associated, and irrational threats to order, differs from my own.

diplomacy, however, the ambience unaccountably becomes that of an interlude, with a song, when the ladies enter. This invasion of the masculine political world by women seconds and amplifies what Lady Percy had introduced earlier. But why the sudden change of mood signalled by lines like the following translation from Lady Mortimer's Welsh proffered by Glendŵr?

> She bids you on the wanton rushes lay you down
> And rest your gentle head upon her lap,
> And she will sing the song that pleaseth you,
> And on your eyelids crown the god of sleep,
> Charming your blood with pleasing heaviness,
> Making such difference 'twixt wake and sleep
> As is the difference betwixt day and night
> The hour before the heavenly-harnessed team
> Begins his golden progress in the east. (3.1.209–17)

We are in a different world here, and, as in the banter between Hotspur and Lady Percy, we recognize it as the same erotic-domestic space from which Hotspur had been wrenched by the civil war.[65] The effect is not only to give the audience a change of pace, but also to recall to us the alternative to the masculine militarism which will take up the rest of the play.

Hotspur is thus himself quietly suspended between competing worlds, not as radically or dramatically as Hal, but in a sense that will become characteristic for an emergent modernizing society, increasingly differentiated into separable spheres and communities, the largest such divide being that constituted by a changing sexual division of labour and newly configured public and private spheres.[66] This femaleness connects as well with this scene's repeated and enigmatic invocations of 'Welshness'[67]— clearly associated with feminine otherness in the erotic language attributed to Lady Mortimer. This can be interpreted, in line with the 'conquest' of femininity enacted by Henry V's dominating courtship of Catherine in *Henry V*, as a part of the Prince Hal trilogy's instrumental project of national unification;[68] however, through the linkage of Wales

[65] Wikander, ibid. 24, argues on the contrary that these associations turn Glendŵr's castle into a 'place of incontinence' which forms part of the larger motif of disorder and chaos which must be contained.

[66] This notion is developed in Howard and Rackin, *Engendering a Nation*, 160–85.

[67] See Terence Hawkes, 'Bryn Glas', in Ania Loomba and Martin Orkin (eds.), *Post-colonial Shakespeares* (London: Routledge, 1998), 117–40, for a delineation of Welshness across the three *Henry IV–V* plays; for Hawkes Welshness is an interacting binary opposite to Englishness, associated with the mystical, the feminine and effeminate, and the Other to Saxon rationality and hegemony.

[68] Cf. Rackin, *Stages of History*, 170–5. Rackin emphasizes the crucial role in masculine

with the Prince of Wales, these associations also signify an important area of Hal's anti-instrumental project of protean subjectivity in this play.

Subjectivity and Resistance

The idea of subjectivity as a potential through which to constitute different 'selves'—radically in the case of the identity-crisis-plagued Prince Hal, less radically but significantly in Hotspur's conflict between domestic and military worlds (and of course in Sir John's world of his own imaginings, as we saw)—is a major preoccupation of *1 Henry IV*. In fact, precisely because of the play's assertion of the power of subjectivity to overflow the narrow roles of Machiavellian disguises, Hal's experimentation with such subjectivity and with pleasure should not simply be reduced to the status of instrumentalized rehearsal for a later domination—which of course *does* come (at the end of *Part 2* and in *Henry V*), but which does not and cannot cancel the complex layered thematics in this play, considered as an autonomous drama. As I argued above, Althusser's much discussed theory of subjective 'interpellation', in which a subject is formed upon internalizing a call or hail from an authoritarian ideology in social circulation, has its usefulness in the interpretation of this and several other Shakespearian plays—but only when it is wrenched out of its original Althusserian framework to describe a situation in which interpellation produces resistance at the same time as it attempts to form a self as a functionalist cog in a social machine. Hal, I believe, is a crucial case in point. In this reading, the simple answer to the question of what Hal is doing with this group of unlikely boon companions[69] is that he is resisting his social calling, exploring the myriad potentialities of his still unfixed subjectivity, and pursuing (rather plebeian) pleasures of freedom, drink, fellowship, wit, and (perhaps) sex, but without closing off the potential of

---

identity-formation of the woman as Other and notes how Wales and France, as 'foreign' nations with their own languages, are associated with the female in *1 Henry IV* and *Henry V*, thus extending the idea of male conquest to national conquest in these plays. Investigating a related subtext, Christopher Highley, *Shakespeare, Spenser, and the Crisis in Ireland* (Cambridge: Cambridge University Press, 1997), 89–97, sees the Welsh as allegorical of the Irish and the ongoing Irish rebellion under Tyrone.

[69] 'Surely one would expect to see [Hal] surrounded by daring, rather sinister, juvenile delinquents and beautiful gold-digging whores. But whom do we meet in the Boar's Head? A fat, cowardly tosspot, old enough to be his father, two down-at-heel hangers-on, a slatternly Hostess, and only one whore, who is not in her earliest youth either; all of them seedy, and, by any worldly standards, including those of the criminal classes, all of them *failures*. Surely, one thinks, an Heir Apparent, sowing his wild oats, could have picked himself a more exciting crew than that,' noted Auden, 'The Prince's Dog', 182–208; 182.

a timely 'reformation' either, as is made clear in his soliloquy, discussed briefly above in connection with the meaning of 'self' in this play. This much debated speech is the one that convinced Hazlitt, Masefield, and numerous others that Hal is a cold-hearted betrayer of his friends whom he was deceiving all along. What should we make of this opening up of interiority to the audience?

> I know you all, and will awhile uphold
> The unyoked humour of your idleness.
> Yet herein will I imitate the sun,
> Who doth permit the base contagious clouds
> To smother up his beauty from the world,
> That, when he please again to be himself,
> Being wanted, he may be more wondered at,
> By breaking through the foul and ugly mists
> Of vapours that did seem to strangle him. (1.2.173–81)

The first thing to do might be to grant Hazlitt and followers at least part of their point. Even stipulating, as I argued above, that the self referred to is a social function, not an inner essence, the soliloquy still presents precisely that Machiavellian structure (defined by Maus in her recent book[70]) of an apparent self of appearances occluding an inner reality—one exemplified earlier in Shakespeare's career by Richard III. Here, however, the two components of the Machiavellian self are presented in moral inversion to what they were in *Richard III*, inflected by the connotations of the metaphor so that the hidden self is majestical, sun-like, and eternal, the (plebeian) outer self 'foul', 'ugly', and transitory. This is the world as it is perceived and evaluated by the official ideology of the court, and it is news to the audience that Prince Hal, who up to this point has seemed a rebel to these values, shares them, at least in interiority, if not in practice. And in the much quoted peroration of the speech, the audience also learns that Prince Hal, like his father, understands the crucial importance in politics of appearances and that he understands (with breathtaking coolness) the advantages of a prodigal-son image:

> So when this loose behaviour I throw off
> And pay the debt I never promisèd,
> By how much better than my word I am,
> By so much shall I falsify men's hopes;
> And like bright metal on a sullen ground,
> My reformation, glitt'ring o'er my fault,

[70] Katharine Eisaman Maus, *Inwardness and the Theater in the English Renaissance* (Chicago: University of Chicago Press, 1995).

> Shall show more goodly and attract more eyes
> Than that which hath no foil to set it off.
> I'll so offend, to make offence a skill,
> Redeeming time when men think least I will. (ll. 186–95)

The repudiation of Falstaff at the end of *Part 2* of course does indeed make good the potentiality imagined by Hal in this soliloquy, interpellating Hal finally into the kingly role which is one of the several selves which he acts out and explores before the deathbed encounter with his father and his coronation. If we can bracket these famous moments from *Part 2*, however, and read this speech as a potentiality which goes unfulfilled in this play, a different interpretation is possible. In this case, an observation from a very conflicted Falstaff-lover, Samuel Johnson, may be of interest. He was not so sure we should take Hal here at face value:

> This speech is very artfully introduced to keep the Prince from appearing vile in the opinion of the audience; it prepares them for his future reformation, and, what is yet more valuable, exhibits a natural picture of a great mind offering excuses to itself, and palliating those follies which it can neither justify nor forsake.[71]

Johnson of course shares the court's values, but he also very happily here captures the state of mind poised between possible identities rather than one coldly plotting from a fixed point—a state of mind that is figured forth by Francis the drawer, standing dumbstruck as he is called simultaneously in different directions. Rather than being only a Machiavellian, in other words, Hal is one of Shakespeare's heroes of subjectivity (like Rosalind, Hamlet, Othello, Edgar, or Cleopatra) dislodged from (in Hal's case, not yet attached to) the stability of a fixed self and one who tries and discards numerous versions of the self in an exploration of the new possibilities for human being created by the desacralized, differentiated culture of modernity. Such a state of mind, suspended between the two lifeworlds in which he has now taken membership, is, in fact, still Hal's even in a somewhat sombre scene in *Part 2* to which I will return in the next chapter:

PRINCE HARRY. Doth it not show vilely in me to desire small beer?

POINS. Why, a prince should not be so loosely studied as to remember so weak a composition.

PRINCE HARRY. Belike, then, my appetite was not princely got; for, by my troth, I do now remember the poor creature small beer. But, indeed, these humble considerations make me out of love with my greatness. What a disgrace is it to me to remember thy name![72]

[71] Johnson, 'Notes on Shakespeare's Plays: "I Henry IV" ', vii. 458.
[72] *2 Henry IV*, 2.2.5–13.

This is the contradictory state of mind of a young man now coming to realize that his feelings for his father have somehow survived his season of rebellion, that his days with boon companions are drawing to a close, and that small beer—and Poins—will soon be in very short supply where he is going. In brief, Hal is as much the victim of the unfolding of the logic of power as soon will be his boon companions. It is reductive to assume that Hal's discomfort at attempting simultaneously to live out his friendship with Poins ('one it pleases me, for fault of a better, to call my friend') and his newly discovered sadness at his father's illness is simply Machiavellian cunning or hypocrisy.

Prince Hal is one of those legendary figures who populate Shakespeare's Roman and Greek plays particularly—Brutus in *Julius Caesar* is perhaps the best example in this context—so well known to the audience for some one particular exploit or set of them that (as Linda Charnes pointed out for a different set of characters[73]) Shakespeare is able to situate this pre-destined end within a complex model of character development that surprises by its epiphany of unexpected complications and potentialities: Brutus ends up Caesar's assassin, and Hal ends as the conqueror of France. But both of them, we come to see, were much more complex people than these roles alone suggest. In both of them Shakespeare uses the occasion to lay out and investigate all the unrealized potentialities inherent in the situations in which they functioned. In both *Julius Caesar* and *1 and 2 Henry IV*—as later in *Macbeth*—there is a peculiar fascination with the interim before grand, defining historical acts:

> Between the acting of a dreadful thing
> And the first motion, all the interim is
> Like a phantasma or a hideous dream.
> The genius and the mortal instruments
> Are then in council, and the state of man,
> Like to a little kingdom, suffers then
> The Nature of an insurrection.[74]

Brutus' images are coloured by a Stoic sensibility seeking internal harmony under the control of the reason, but the images of a self before some defining act as a divided council with multiple potentialities is an idea relevant to Hal between his own defining acts as well. Thus, Hal is shown in the play as suspended between two fathers—King Henry and

[73] Linda Charnes, *Notorious Identity: Materializing the Subject in Shakespeare* (Cambridge, Mass.: Harvard University Press, 1993). Charnes identifies such dynamics at work in *Richard III*, *Troilus and Cressida*, and *Antony and Cleopatra*.

[74] *Julius Caesar*, 2.1.63–9.

Falstaff—and between two futures—his father's nightmare of Hal as a prodigal and unsuccessful king like the Richard he replaced, and Hal (in his and his father's fantasies) as a second Hotspur, a military hero who would make good his father's ambitions by surpassing them.

The interrelated cluster of themes I have been discussing—Hal's deferral of choosing a stable identity, his divided loyalty between two father-figures, the clash of values or world views implied in the choice between the carnival and the Machiavellian, the complex and unstable interaction between the tavern and the court worlds—even reference to Hotspur's conflicting marital and martial lives—all these motifs are in play in the defining moment of *1 Henry IV's* great comic scene (surely one of the high points of Shakespeare's dramatic career), in the play extempore organized by Hal and Falstaff to celebrate the end of the Gad's Hill robbery and as a prelude to Hal's return to the court the following day to prepare for battle.

The suspension between two worlds and two fathers experienced by Hal in the earlier scenes is acted out in multiple perspectives as Hal stands in for 'himself' while Falstaff plays his king and father. The device works at one level to figure retrospectively Falstaff's status as Hal's foster-father and carnival king. But we soon realize that the play is really about the future: that is, Hal's future choice of fathers, identity, and values. In this unlikely form, Prince Hal acts out the fantasy of himself as true successor to his father that has already been shared with the audience in his earlier soliloquy and sets the course which he follows, with a few crooked byways involved, in the banishment of Falstaff at the end of *Part 2*. 'I do, I will,' he says, just before that portentous knock at the door which cuts short Falstaff's desire to speak for himself and carnival against King Harry and the court. The two performative verbs of his utterance breach the gap between the protean role-playing of Hal's experiments in identity-formation, and the ultimate, legendary choice of identity which we know he is preordained to make.

What we do not know is just how much like the father whom he impersonates Prince Hal will have to be, how many of the values of the tavern world he can retain within his new identity, and just how Machia-vellian this prince is destined to become.

What happens next, after the knock on the door has been answered, demonstrates that *1 Henry IV* gives a quite different answer to these questions from *2 Henry IV*. Here, when Hal has the opportunity to begin his reformation the night before he is to return to his father's good graces, by turning Falstaff over to the sheriff, he instead 'gilds' Falstaff's deeds with a happy lie, as he will do again after the Battle of Shrewsbury, reinforcing the values of fellowship of the tavern world and suggesting, against a harsher interpretation of what he meant by his promise of banishing Falstaff (the one we see acted out in *2 Henry IV*), that there might yet be some way to bridge the two worlds between which he is suspended. Thus this play, at two privileged dramatic points, the Act 3 turning point and the conclusion, projects the possibility that, somehow, Hal can become his father's son as hero-king without betraying the tavern world's most positive values or its Lord of Misrule.

At the conclusion of *1 Henry IV*, all of Hal's potential selves are kept in play: by defeating Hotspur, he has symbolically become him, simultaneously becoming son to Northumberland, Worcester, and Harry—as well as a prince in Machiavelli's sense as one who has astonished the world by surprise and boldness. But he manages also to satisfy Falstaff by joining in the latter's battlefield lies as if they were one more excellent jest from the tavern world. The result is that at the end of *Part 1*, Hal's protean self is very much alive over its entire network. He has in fact expanded the sense of his possible futures by establishing a heroic persona that only he seems to have dreamed of as possible before. The effect is thus affirmative of the prolixity of an unfixed subjectivity able to straddle so many contradictory worlds and roles, without ever repudiating any of them. Thus *1 Henry IV* is a play which both explores and affirms the idea of selfhood as a play of multiple roles and multiple identities.

In *Part 2*, as we will see below, Hal remains in this suspended situation—is even made to regress in his heroic development, as many critics have had it, at least up until the crown-stealing scene and coronation. But I want to discuss the specificity of *Part 2*, its continuities and differences from *Part 1*, below. Suffice it to say that the Prince Hal we leave at the end of *Part 1* survives into the first scenes of *Part 2*, but is already a sadder if not wiser man. At the end of *Part 2*, the Prince will have been fixed into his place in an early modern state, his other potential selves banished to the status of golden-age memories. His 'self' will triumph over his 'condition' and all but obliterate it in the collective memory of Shakespeare's readers.

4. AUDIENCE, IDEOLOGY, AND THE UTOPIAN IN *1 HENRY IV*

I have argued, along with a number of post-Tillyard critics of the second historical tetralogy, that in *1 Henry IV* as in *Richard II* there is a pronounced Machiavellian imprint on the presentation of power and its effects. This play like its predecessor displays the scandalous truth that political power grows, not from any objective deputation of authority from God to king and his subjects, but from the social acceptance of artfully produced illusions of legitimacy generated by the canny prince, as described by Machiavelli.[75] Shakespeare in all four plays of the tetralogy places us within that condition of modernity consequent from the destruction of religious myths justifying the political status quo. It is a kaleidoscopic world of political hegemonies, in which political power is the outcome of complex interactions among disparate and conflicting social strata and political factions, each with its own (more or less elaborate) set of justifications and beliefs for its politics. But the waning of the older mythopoeic belief systems does not necessarily mean that all supporters of monarchy are double-thinking, abject masochists irresistibly drawn to the irrational attractions of power.[76] Such a thesis ignores the logic of political ideologies and their underlying interests and social positions. The baroque tensions of Greenblatt's descriptions of a power whose fraudulent underpinnings have been exposed but which nevertheless works its way despite its exposure is much better explained, it seems to me (and several recent writers on this play), as the outcome of texts designed to appeal simultaneously to (at least) two different social interests: those of the court and those of the commons.[77] If Pistol, near the end of *2 Henry IV*, has to ask the non-comprehending Justice Shallow, 'Under which king, besonian? Speak, or die. . . . Harry the Fourth? or Harry the Fifth?' (5.3.105–6), we have to ask, 'Under which *audience*,

---

[75] See Burckhardt, *Shakespearian Meanings*, 144–205, for what I believe is the earliest articulation of this position, since adopted by a number of critics, most prominently Greenblatt, 'Invisible Bullets'.

[76] Such inclinations, I would say, indeed can be *part* of the story of authority, as Horkheimer and Adorno, following Freud, argued for the case of much of Middle Europe after the First World War and for Germany under fascism—but they are not the whole story; see Theodor Adorno et al., *The Authoritarian Personality* (New York: Harper & Row, 1950) and Max Horkheimer, 'Egoism and Freedom Movements: On the Anthropology of the Bourgeois Era' (1936), in his *Between Philosophy and Social Science: Selected Early Writings*, trans. G. Frederick Hunter, Matthew S. Kramer, and John Torpey (Cambridge, Mass.: MIT Press, 1993), 49–110.

[77] Leah Marcus, *Puzzling Shakespeare: Local Reading and its Discontents* (Berkeley and Los Angeles: University of California Press, 1988), 150–8, argued such a reading strategy for Shakespeare; see Hugh Grady, 'Containment, Subversion—and Postmodernism', *Textual Practice*, 7/1 (Spring 1993), 31–49, for a discussion of this tactic as an important solution to the blind spots of the containment-and-subversion problematic. Whitney, 'Festivity and Topicality in the Coventry Scene of *1 Henry IV*', applies the idea directly in a reading of this play, adding to the Essex faction and the commons a third possible interest addressed by the text, that of the 'middling sort'; see 417–18 *et passim*. Whitney develops this position further in general terms in Charles Whitney, 'Ante-aesthetics: Towards a Theory of Early Modern Audience Response', in Grady (ed.), *Shakespeare and Modernity*, 40–60.

besonian?' when we try to define the effects of a play which seems simultaneously to expose and celebrate political power.

In terms of Greenblatt's celebrated argument within 'Invisible Bullets',
what is most questionable in this regard is his claim that the strength of the
ideological beliefs of Shakespeare's audience would have simply blinded
'it' to those 'subversive' ideas within the play that seem to undercut the
political legitimacy of the English monarchy. Reading or watching these
plays 400 years later, 'we are free to locate and pay homage to the plays'
doubts only because they no longer threaten us. There is subversion, no
end of subversion, only not for us,' he famously concluded (p. 65).The
questions I want to ask here are: what status, then, can we attribute to
those features of the play-text which produce the doubts which we, freed
of the ideologies of absolutism, can now see? Can we be so certain that
these features remained unnoted by all Shakespeare's contemporaries?
And where did they come from in the first place?

Rather than construct for the Elizabethan audience a Foucauldian
submission to fraudulent power, it is less problematic to suppose that
we are dealing with a stratified text capable of being read for different
political messages by differing political interests. In the case of the *Henry
IV* plays we can suppose, as H. A. Kelly argued many years ago in his
important refutation of Tillyard, that many in the play's audience would
have accepted the numerous protestations within the plays' dialogue
(above all in the celebrated discussion of the crown in *Part 2*) that the
crown rightfully belongs to the Lancasters.[78] Given especially the negative
treatment of the rebels in both plays (negative, that is, with the sole exception of Hotspur, who is a personable individual tragically wasted in instrumental and bootless intrigue), there is very little vector in either play
toward organizing within the audience a desire for the overthrow of a
usurper; we should compare the clearly contrasting instances of *Richard
III*, *Hamlet*, and *Macbeth*, in which audiences typically greet the overthrow of a murdering king as a devoutly wished-for consummation of a
powerful dramatic momentum.

On the other hand, Greenblatt rightly follows the opening of Sigurd
Burckhardt in seeing that there is also ample material within all three
Prince Hal plays which undermines the monarchist ideology of primo-
geniture by presenting it as one of those socially constructed fictions
theorized as such more or less explicitly by both Machiavelli and
Montaigne and which was figured in *Richard II* in Mowbray's speech on
language previously discussed. Indeed, as I noted above and will further

---

[78] Kelly, *Divine Providence in the England of Shakespeare's Histories*, 215–32.

instantiate below, language reappears in *2 Henry IV* and in *Henry V* as a similar metaphor. But it is less clear that consciousness of the fictionality of legitimacy was in itself necessarily subversive. It did finally prove so in the case of the Essex rebellion, but it apparently coexisted with a support for the existing government, as it did for Montaigne, among the more 'Machiavellian' of the Elizabethan courtiers for years before Essex's dramatic failure.[79]

In *1 Henry IV*, in short, the audience is shown Machiavellian politics in action—and they turn out to be eminently acceptable. In the absence of some absolute, divinely sanctioned royal legitimacy, there is the social construction of legitimacy, a necessary fiction without which the kingdom is subject to all the buffets of civil conflict denounced by the wan and weary Henry IV in the play's opening speech.

The successful succession from Henry IV to Henry V is presented to us as a political necessity for the peace of the kingdom, despite the manifestly constructed nature of this claim to the throne. And this prodigal heir-apparent, by resisting his royal vocation as long as possible, is illustrating the price exacted by reified political necessity on its subjects; and Hal, while violating decorum at one level, wins the audience's approval at another—not by representing the cunning and sadism of hidden power, but by illustrating the vitality of a subject in resistance to power in the form of a role he will have to adopt. Falstaff represents in this process a 'private' subjectivity of a distinctly (and ironically) anti-Puritan sort, imbued with libido and oriented to its own pleasure and survival, itself poised between beauty and self-destruction. And at the end of *Part 1*, all these forces are still in play, so that we could say that *1 Henry IV* takes us to what turns out to be a fragile moment in which all these contradictory impulses of modernity seem not only possible but inevitable.

This brings us back to a question raised earlier: how do we understand the relationship between the tavern scenes and the 'high' political plot with which they are intertwined? I would argue that the effect is best described as a Montaignean consciousness of the realpolitik provenance of royal power proffered within the text of this play for those in the audience prepared to receive it: the Machiavellians of the Essex faction and the proto-Levellers among the plebeians of Shakespeare's public audience. It is a consciousness of the constructedness of political power, without any call for its overthrow. And thus, for any members of the

---

[79] See Kevin Sharpe, *Reading Revolutions: The Politics of Reading in Early Modern England* (New Haven: Yale University Press, 2000), for further corroboration of Machiavelli's influence among humanist ideologues of the era.

audience ideologically immunized (in the way Greenblatt imagined at the end of 'Invisble Bullets') against Machiavellianism (they have certainly been legion in the texts of the critical history of this play and were so presumably in 1596 as well), the play will seem to support orthodox monarchical ideology, exactly as with Montaigne.

Part 1, however, displays a good deal more than the Machiavellian reality of early modern politics in England. Indeed, much of its life and vitality comes from aspects which were completely absent from the court-dominated *Richard II*: *1 Henry IV* shows us that the unstable *mentalité* of modernity creates not only the possibility of amoral power struggles, but also of open-ended subjectivity operating in political, communal, and private spheres; and that this open-endedness, while potentially disorienting and dangerous, is also an arena of freedom and pleasure which can serve as a refuge from an increasingly reified world. And crucially for Shakespeare and for anyone reading this book, it creates the conditions for an autonomous aesthetic in which alternatives to reification can be imaginatively explored. Falstaff and Hal in this respect mobilize and display for us a model of the contradictory outcomes of a negative freedom which was not really yet achieved in Tudor or Stuart England, but which we live in and with, and which was imagined and enacted in a form still compelling to us heirs, benefactors, and victims of a social space open to and unprotected from the explosive outcomes of modern reification and subjectivity.

If much recent criticism of Shakespeare generally has focused on the political dimension of his plays, this reading of *1 Henry IV*, in contrast, suggests that this criticism has thus inadvertently neglected what is perhaps the most interesting and politically relevant aspect of this play: its private or domestic space, which seems so contradictory but so com-pelling.[80] This space is still not as radically sealed off from the public as that of, say, *The Duchess of Malfi*. Here the private and domestic encroach as well into the carnival-communal setting of a tavern, which itself is domestic inasmuch as it is a site of eating, sleeping, and love-making, with important female associations within the male homosocial atmosphere, as we have seen. And again through its feminine components, it encroaches as well into and humanizes the otherwise dreary world of the rebels. This space is anachronistic in two senses: since it evokes a disappearing world of the village communalism of the carnival tradition, it seems to idealize aspects of the past disappearing before early modernization; but it also

---

[80] The partial exception here is Howard and Rackin, *Engendering a Nation*, 175–85, but their emphasis is on the subordination of these spheres to patriarchy.

refunctions these qualities within an imaginary, instrumentalization-resisting realm of the aesthetic which would not become conceptualized for another hundred years or more. This space of an oxymoronic communal private thus defines the utopian dimension created for us in renewing these great texts at the beginning of a new millennium which manifestly longs for the signifieds of Falstaff and his world.

5
The Reified Worlds of
2 *Henry IV* and *Henry V*

In *1 Henry IV*, Falstaff, in one of those inverted harangues in which he is ironically reversing roles with Prince Hal, states, 'But, Hal, I prithee trouble me no more with vanity. I would to God thou and I knew where a commodity of good names were to be bought.'[1] What *Part 2* reveals to us is that Falstaff has indeed found the source of the commodities he was seeking—and, unknown to him, so has Prince Hal—although this is made known to Falstaff only when Hal turns from him at the very end. This new play in fact will demonstrate the commodification not only of names, but also of virtually everything else. 'I will turn diseases to commodity,' Falstaff states at the end of his first scene in *Part 2*, for 'A good wit will make use of any thing' (1.2.226–7). Wit here is clearly linked to the marketplace of commodity exchange (both monetary and political), and not only diseases, but friendship, love, honour, and life are among those commodities we will see exchanged for money, power, and advantage in the grim forward movement of this play.

Henry IV, Part 2 re-emphasizes a theme that was also important in the two preceding plays of the *Henriad*: the usefulness of the prolix and fungible qualities of language for Machiavellian manipulations. This play's variation on that familiar theme is indicated in its Induction. Rumour, 'painted full of tongues', is a personification clearly associated with the motif of the profligacy of words or (in terms of our own day) of the texuality of (our perceptions of) the world:

> Upon my tongues continual slanders ride,
> The which in every language I pronounce,
> Stuffing the ears of men with false reports. (Induction, 6–8)

---

[1] William Shakespeare, *1 Henry IV*, 1.2.71–4, *The Norton Shakespeare*, ed. Stephen Greenblatt et al. (New York: Norton, 1997). Unless otherwise noted, all subsequent quotations from Shakespeare are given parenthetically and are from this edn.

Here the potential of language for deception is accented, and once more, as in the motifs of counterfeiting and true and false of *Part 1*, common-sensical notions of an easily distinguished difference between truth and rumour are assumed:

> from Rumour's tongues
> They bring smooth comforts false, worse than true wrongs. (ll. 39–40)

What we learn in the opening scene, however, is not only the fact of false reports circulating about the Battle of Shrewsbury, but more pointedly the Machiavellian truth that truth itself becomes the property of the side that wins the battle. This truth seems at first to be simply a matter of a material reality principle which falsifies the early reports of a rebel victory. With the cumulative appearances of Falstaff, however (as well as by the play's devastating conclusion), we learn that what counts as truth can be constructed and enforced by the gilded lies of the victorious.

However, the celebration of the open-ended potentiality of unfixed subjectivity of *Part 1*, centred around Prince Hal, Hotspur, and Falstaff, is absent in *Part 2*—or present, as we will see, only for instrumentalization, mourning, and memory. Hal, as has been often noted, is skilfully kept in the background of this play until his big scenes at the end, and those scenes enact the irrevocable 'fixing' of self through a definitive interpellation into heroic Machiavellianism that effectively ends his experiments with alternative selves. Hotspur is dead, and Falstaff, paradoxically because of his success in the world, loses much of his own unfixed subjectivity as he has to focus on a new manufactured identity as 'man of war'.

In *2 Henry IV*, in short, the Montaignean unfixed subjectivity active in *Part 1* as a kind of 'surplus' over and above its purely Machiavellian functions for political theatricality is exhausted in Machiavellian self-serving, not only in the political but also in the private world. Subjectivity has become commodified, put to use in a political marketplace of deception and disguises as a means to power. But while subjectivity changes its function, power carries on as before. This time, however, power is no longer a laughing matter.

Part 2, while carrying forward so much that had been established in *Part 1*, shifts decisively from the earlier play in themes, atmosphere, and implied value-judgements about the Machiavellian and the Montaignean. Such differences between the two plays, while not unnoticed in the long history of Shakespeare criticism,[2] have been obscured precisely because

---

[2] For example Clifford Leech, 'The Unity of "2 Henry IV"', *Shakespeare Survey*, 6 (1953), 16–24, emphasized *Part 2*'s 'darker side', linking it thematically and atmospherically to

Part 2 is in so many of its dimensions a derivative sequel to its more popular predecessor—in plot, characters, and, most especially, in dramatic structure. Just how derivative the play is in this last sense was defined in 1954 by G. K. Hunter, who demonstrated that the alternation of court, tavern, and rebel scenes of the sequel parallels that of *1 Henry IV*.[3] Up until the unique 'rejection' scene, in fact, the duplication is nearly perfect: the dramatic rhythm established in the first play, in which we move in Act 1 from the court, to the tavern, and thence to the rebels in Scenes 1, 2, and 3, is matched by the same rhythm in *Part 2*—and similarly through Acts 2–4, with the one exception of Scene 3.1, which is a rebel scene in *Part 1* but a court scene in *Part 2*.[4] This duplication, found nowhere else in Shakespeare, suggests that *Part 2* was so closely modelled on *Part 1* that in some ways it is best seen as a virtuoso exercise in the art of variations on a theme. We feel this particularly in the recruitment scenes of the two plays, in which *Part 2* stages a closely linked variation of the scene of recruiting which Falstaff had described in soliloquy in *Part 1*. Hunter describes the resulting structure as a 'diptych, in which repetition of shape and design focuses attention on what is common to the two parts'.[5]

The close links between the two plays at this level, however, like the symmetries of Hell and Paradise in a Hieronymus Bosch diptych, also provide a context for the elaboration of enormously important differences, differences which I want to focus on here. In terms of a central thematic probing of the relation between power and subjectivity throughout the *Henriad*, *2 Henry IV* reverses the optimistic presentation of their potential compatibility in *1 Henry IV*, shifting instead toward a sobered

Troilus and Cressida and *Measure for Measure*. L. C. Knights in two related essays, 'The Public World: First Observations' and 'Time's Subjects: The Sonnets and "King Henry IV"', in his *Some Shakespearian Themes* (Stanford, Calif.: Stanford University Press, 1960), 26–44, 45–64, followed in this vein, making perhaps the strongest case for the superiority of *Part 2* (which he saw as 'one of the first plays in which we recognize the great Shakespeare'). A similar appreciation of the play as 'darker' and therefore thematically separate from *Part 1* was written by John Pettigrew, 'The Mood of *Henry IV, Part 2*', in B. A. W. Jackson (ed.), *Stratford Papers, 1965–67* (Shannon: Irish University Press, 1969), 145–67. A summary defence of *2 Henry IV*, emphasizing its 're-vision' of the materials of *Part 1* in more probing, harsher form, is David P. Young, 'Introduction', in Young (ed.), *Twentieth Century Interpretations of 'Henry IV, Part Two': A Collection of Critical Essays* (Englewood Cliffs, NJ: Prentice-Hall, 1968), 1–12.

[3] G. K. Hunter, '"Henry IV" and the Elizabethan Two-Part Play', *Review of English Studies*, 5/14 (July 1954), 236–48.

[4] The paralleling also depends on editorial judgement concerning where to break the scenes. The details need to be studied in a chart which Hunter provides in the article. Nevertheless, the overall point is clearly established, I believe.

[5] Hunter, '"Henry IV"', 247–8.

presentation of the constricting realities of power politics. Rather than simply extending the approach to subjectivity and the Machiavellian of *1 Henry IV*, Shakespeare reconceptualized them so strongly in *Part 2* that their newly refocused development threatens retroactively to transform the meaning of *1 Henry IV*, bidding the audience to extend the subordination of Falstaff and his world accomplished in the rejection scene back into the earlier play[6]—a play which, as I argued in the previous chapter, pointedly refused to make such a subordination. In short, the newer play creates a new mood and tonality to evoke a much sombrer and crueller world than we saw in *Part 1*.[7]

This new mood derives from the new theme of the incompatibility between 'surplus' unfixed subjectivity and Machiavellian power. *Part 2*

[6] This seems to be the case in Greenblatt's treatment of the two plays, Stephen Greenblatt, 'Invisible Bullets', in *Shakespearian Negotiations: The Circulation of Social Energy in Renaissance England* (Berkeley and Los Angeles: University of California Press, 1988), 47: 'When we turn, however, to the plays that continue the chronicle of Hal's career, *2 Henry IV* and *Henry V*, we find not only that the forces balanced in the earlier play have pulled apart . . . but that from this new perspective the familiar view of *1 Henry IV* as a perfectly poised play must be revised. What appeared as "balance" may on closer inspection seem like radical instability tricked out as moral or aesthetic order; what appeared as clarity may seem now like a conjurer's trick concealing confusion in order to buy time and stave off the collapse of an illusion. Not waving but drowning.' But Greenblatt's treatment of *2 Henry IV* and especially *Henry V* (pp. 47–65) is, I find, the most convincing part of this now classic essay; like him, I believe this play depicts a triumph of reified political power over potentially subversive forces. However, as I indicated, this thematic does not simply overwrite the investigation and valorization of unfixed subjectivity in *Part 1*, and I think that reading both plays as parallel to the logic of colonization in Harriot's *A Brief and True Report* tilts the interpretation of *Part 1* toward a pessimism that is far from inevitable.

[7] This focus on the new thematic departure of *Part 2* was anticipated, as I noted above, by several earlier critics and given a classic exposition after the Second World War by L. C. Knights, *Some Shakespearian Themes*. At one level, to be sure, Knights's approach is a perfect example of a familiar move of Leavisite criticism in which any distancing from the political is taken to be a 'maturing' development toward what is said to be an apolitical 'humanism' within the tragedies, and this, I would argue, amounts to an ideological assimilation of Shakespeare to an early Cold War mood of disillusionment with all politics, a mood related to that of the *Richard II* mid-century critics I discussed in Ch. 2. In the case of the *Henry IV* plays it was shared by several contemporaneous critics. See Hugh Grady, *The Modernist Shakespeare: Critical Texts in a Material World* (Oxford: Clarendon: 1991), 183, for a previous discussion of the depoliticizing assumptions in three independently written, but closely parallel arguments besides Knights's, all from the 1940s. They are Una Ellis-Fermor, *The Frontiers of Drama* (1945; repr. New York: Methuen, 1964), 34–55; Derek Traversi, ' "Henry IV—Part I" ' and ' "Henry IV—Part II" ', *Scrutiny*, 15/1 and 2 (Winter 1947 and Spring 1948), 24–35 and 117–27 (these were revised and incorporated into the 1957 *Shakespeare: From 'Richard II' to 'Henry V'*); and Cleanth Brooks and Robert Heilman, *Understanding Drama* (New York: Holt, 1945). Knights's own most explicit expression of his political assumptions was perhaps his 'Shakespeare's Politics: With Some Reflections on the Nature of Tradition', *Proceedings of the British Academy* (London: Oxford University Press, 1957), 115–32. A similar view permeates Michael Manheim's later *The Weak King Dilemma in the Shakespearian History Play* (Syracuse, NY: Syracuse University Press, 1973), 161–82.

demonstrates that power unfolds according to value-free, instrumental dynamics which are finally incompatible with the openness to community and intersubjectivity of the Montaignean unfixedness of *Richard II* and *1 Henry IV*. The last two plays of the tetralogy instead begin a new trajectory leading through *Hamlet* to the unmistakable condemnation of Machiavellian power of the central Jacobean tragedies which I discussed in *Shakespeare's Universal Wolf*. At the same time, however—and this is a point which has escaped earlier New Critics and contemporary new historicist and cultural materialist critics alike—the play backs away from an investigation of unfixed subjectivity that will become a major motif again in *Hamlet, Troilus and Cressida, Othello*, and *King Lear*.

The Withdrawal of the Counter-Societies

One important change creative of the new mood of *Part 2* is the fate of the counter-societies we had encountered in the earlier play. The female domestic space of Ladies Percy and Mortimer, the carnivalesque tavern realism of Falstaff, and even the utopian chivalry of Hotspur are missing or radically transformed in the sequel. Since in *1 Henry IV* these elements served as foils and alternatives to the Machiavellian political sphere, the effect is to diminish greatly the possibility of alternatives. Indeed, the play's opening scene among the rebels (1.1) is devoted to the memory of the dead Hotspur, and a later one (2.3) includes a brief and mournful appearance by his grieving widow Lady Percy, in marked contrast to her playful demeanour in the earlier play. The alluring Lady Mortimer and her husband the pretender Mortimer are nowhere to be found. Thus, the attractive feminine-domestic world of *Part 1* persists in *Part 2* only in the bitter accusations of Lady Northumberland and the pleas of Lady Percy ('O yet, for God's sake, go not to these wars!'; 2.3.9), which recall for us the misgivings of the wives and the existence of domestic alternatives to war of the previous play. *Part 2* is a play in which everything seems to give way before the reorganization of life by political power. The domestic sphere of *1 Henry IV*, in short, has passed out of the new realities of *Part 2*.[8]

To some extent, of course, the space in *Part 2* for alternatives to the Machiavellian world evacuated by the withdrawal of Hotspur and the rebel women is partially filled by a new pastoral-comical-domestic supplied by the two country justices Shallow and Silent. The comic world

---

[8] It landed, perhaps, in the related world of *The Merry Wives of Windsor* where, if anywhere in Shakespeare's works, domesticity reigns and triumphs at the end, even over Falstaff's (considerably subdued) carnival.

is alive, with new complexities of its own (which I will explore below), and in many ways funnier than ever. What is missing, however—and this is of the essence of the changed atmospherics of this play—is the carnival ambience of *Part 1*'s tavern scenes, with their inverted values and practices. I noted previously how in the second half of *Part 1*, as Falstaff and company removed themselves from the tavern and made their way into the world, Falstaff's self-serving habits took on new qualities in the altered social environment, transforming him from a convivial Lord of Misrule of a carnival community to a Hobbesian combatant in the war of each against all—and, as we saw, a Brechtian commentator on and definer of his own transgressions at the same time. In *Part 2*, he never re-emerges from that Hobbesian world, though he remains an ingratiating commentator thereon—and an ultimate loser in the new petty wars of competing self-interests. He continues as a plebeian speaker from Weimann's *platea*, and he continues to articulate an anti-Machiavellian vision: the great praise of sack in this play (*2 Henry IV*, 4.2.78–111) crystallizes Falstaff's inverted conviviality and anti-Machiavellian warmth better than any single speech of either play. But it is significant that this memorable articulation of a Montaignean theory of self-fashioning comes after the deceit of Gaultree Forest and before Falstaff's own rejection by the very 'son' who he believed had well learned that first of all lessons of humane education, to forswear the thin potations of narrow power politics.[9] Because of its context, the speech serves as a reminder of something already lost at the point it is articulated. And at the end of this play the tavern world is banished along with its constituent inhabitants, a victim of Prince Hal's cultivation and perfection of his father's arts of the manipulation of image to maximize political power.

The triumph of reification over Prince Hal's open-ended subjectivity is by no means represented to the audience as an unalloyed disaster, however. Prince Harry's irrevocable taking on of his father's Machiavellian role and politics is staged in the crown-stealing scenes with considerable dramatic power and strong psychoanalytic reverberations. There is even something of a 'sacralization' of Machiavellianism when King Henry imparts his deathbed advice to a son whose political astuteness he never really comes to appreciate. But Hal clearly takes as his sacred duty the (Machiavellian) naturalization and legitimization of his father's unorthodox seizure of the crown, when Hal (finally but in the other sense

---

[9] In this connection, Hal's longing for 'small beer' rather than sack in his one appearance in the tavern in this play may be another of the numerous premonitions of the rejection of Falstaff throughout *Part 2*.

prematurely) begins to 'own' his patrimony and solemnly takes on a defining sense of mission:

> Thy due from me
> Is tears and heavy sorrows of the blood,
> Which nature, love, and filial tenderness
> Shall, O dear father, pay thee plenteously.
> My due from thee is this imperial crown. (4.3.167–71)

The potent rhetoric, drawing on psychoanalytically powerful images of father–son identification and mourning, on the socially powerful discourses of feudalism, monarchism, and traditional religion, with an imagery of blood and combat played against invocations of love and tenderness—this passage and what follows, the teasing back-and-forth of betrayal and duty which recapitulates the entire previous theme of filial revolt and reconciliation and acceptance—is the pivotal moment when Hal irrevocably becomes the true son and false friend by taking the place of his father. Unlike his father's, Hal's reign is to be legitimized by a normal succession, and his language invokes all the powerful psychic and social forces reinforcing such succession. It is the end of Prince Hal and the beginning of King Harry, the moment of acceptance of and submission to the chain of meanings constituting the monarchy of which he is about to become the material signifier. We experience these scenes as Hal's triumph, which we vicariously share. But the rest of the play enacts the price that is paid for the triumph: it is precisely his success which reifies Prince Hal.

What remains is the final disposal of the resistance of Prince Hal's decentred personality to the violence of the process of insertion into the social system. And this will be ritually and politically carried out in the rejection of Hal's other—and soon banished—father, Falstaff.

Changes and Continuity in Falstaff and Hal

The role of Falstaff in *Part 2* is an almost seamless combination of continuities and innovations that is one of the great achievements of this often under-appreciated play. From his opening appearance in Scene 1.2 through the speech on sack in Scene 4.3 and his commentary to the audience on Shallow in Scene 5.2, Falstaff enacts the metadramatic *platea* role which had been his throughout the second half of *1 Henry IV*, with a direct connection to the audience and a detached, critical perspective on the world about him.[10] But as other commentators have insisted, this

---

[10] Robert Weimann, *Shakespeare and the Popular Tradition in the Theater: Studies in the*

familiar Falstaff has also changed, and the change is part of the new thematics of the second *Henry IV* play. Falstaff turns out to be one of the main beneficiaries of the power of counterfactual rumours.[11] In the wake of Shrewsbury, Falstaff cuts a new figure in the world: he has a page, he is consulting a physician, and he is ordering new clothes. Interestingly, we never do learn precisely what rumour is circulating about his battlefield prowess from Shrewsbury. The closest it comes to definition is in some words of the Lord Chief Justice:

> Well, I am loath to gall a new-healed wound. Your day's service at Shrewsbury hath a little gilded over your night's exploit on Gads Hill. You may thank th'unquiet time for your quiet o'erposting that action. (1.2.135–8)

Significantly, the Justice repeats Hal's term, 'gilded', for the lie which Sir John had created, and which Hal apparently acquiesced to in *Part 1*, that Sir John rather than Prince Hal had killed Hotspur. We see continuously in *Part 2* how Falstaff has profited from that lie and is living out a new image as a formidable swordsman and soldier. The two sergeants Fang and Snare, for example, attest to this new image of Sir John:

FANG. Snare, we must arrest Sir John Falstaff.
HOSTESS. Yes, good Master Snare; I have entered him and all.
SNARE. It may chance cost some of us our lives, for he will stab. (2.1.8–11)

A good deal of the humour of *Part 2* comes from this running gag, which depends (as so much in this sequel does) on our previous knowledge of Falstaff the proponent of the better part of valour who has unaccountably achieved a new and heroic image. But the sombrer tone of the play

Social Dimension of Dramatic Form and Function, ed. Robert Schwartz (Baltimore: Johns Hopkins University Press, 1978), does not address this issue directly, but he wrote: 'With Falstaff one has the impression that his linguistic facility increases, reaching its zenith toward the end of Part 2' (p. 145). James Calderwood, *Metadrama in Shakespeare's Henriad: 'Richard II' to 'Henry V'* (Berkeley and Los Angeles: University of California Press, 1979), 94–5, argues the contrary, that Falstaff loses much of his metadramatic role in *Part 2*, but I do not think an examination of his monologue-like speeches (including those in the presence of his page) will support this view, which is one which Calderwood is led into through his problematic thesis that 2 *Henry IV* enacts a decline of language for much of which Falstaff's speech is responsible. I agree with Calderwood, however, that Falstaff is engaged in instrumentalizing activities in *Part 2*—as he is in *Part 1* as well, I would argue, but the prolixity of his language aids rather than hinders instrumentalization.

[11] This was first pointed out by J. Dover Wilson, *The Fortunes of Falstaff* (Cambridge: Cambridge University Press, 1943), 88–9. Wilson said that the obvious changes in Falstaff's status in *Part 2* resulted from the gilded lie perpetrated by Hal that he had killed or helped kill Hotspur, and he noted that 'all the critics seem to have missed it' (p. 88). The point has not been prominent in subsequent criticism either, but see for an important exception Calderwood, *Metadrama in Shakespeare's Henriad*, 89–104.

reclaims even this joke late in the action: in the pursuit of the disorganized rebel troops at Gaultree Forest, Sir John Coleville of the Dale loses his life to the successful circulation of this new image:[12]

COLEVILLE. Are not you Sir John Falstaff?
FALSTAFF. As good a man as he, sir, whoe'er I am. Do ye yield, sir, or shall I sweat for you? If I do sweat, they are the drops of thy lovers, and they weep for thy death; therefore rouse up fear and trembling, and do observance to my mercy.
COLEVILLE. I think you are Sir John Falstaff; and in that thought yield me.
FALSTAFF. I have a whole school of tongues in this belly of mine, and not a tongue of them all speaks any other word but my name. (4.1.9–18)

The reverberations here are multiple. In his first line in the encounter, Falstaff indicates the distance between his new image ('Sir John Falstaff') and his old one of tavern parasite. The encounter parallels those of the Battle of Shrewsbury, only here it is Falstaff who employs Hotspur's and Douglas's ploy of using his name to instil fear in his opponent, but of course, with none of their battlefield prowess behind it. And the deception recalls Sir John's previous counterfeiting of death against Douglas: we are watching the effects of counterfeiting once more, but this time a counterfeit with the roles reversed and one which ultimately leads to death (Coleville's, when Prince John sends him to the block with the other rebel prisoners).

The reference to the 'school of tongues in this belly' links Falstaff with the figure of Rumour, 'full of tongues', of the Induction,[13] and this linkage ties down for us the thematic point of this little incident. Rumour rules the world of this play, not only in the form of (relatively easily correctable) falsities, but in beliefs that have passed for current for so long that they have become a kind of legal tender, cashable on demand. The political world, Machiavelli had told us, is a world of appearances, enforced by power, and, once again in this play, these are finally all that count.[14] This is

---

[12] Cf. Calderwood, *Metadrama in Shakespeare's Henriad*, 90, 92.

[13] David Bergeron, 'Shakespeare Makes History: *2 Henry IV*', *Studies in English Literature*, 31 (1991), 231–45, also notes this link between Falstaff and Rumour but goes on to argue that Falstaff's later 'rejection, expulsion, and imprisonment become the overthrow of "Rumour" or false history, so that a "correct" historical narrative can be inscribed in national life' (p. 233). I would argue on the contrary that the rejection of Falstaff, in its creation of a new kind of counterfeit in which Falstaff suffers for Hal's youthful misdemeanours, amounts to the enthronement of Rumour.

[14] And Falstaff's sly reference to his name is another (metadramatic) reminder of the power of Rumour among the audiences of this play, the continuing performance of the play an assertion of how a simple change of name from Oldcastle to Falstaff (a change addressed directly in the Epilogue of the play) can be a powerful instrument in court and theatrical politics.

perhaps most clearly articulated in Morton's Machiavellian analysis of the power of ideology in motivating the rank-and-file fighters of the rebellion. Hotspur, Morton argues, neglected this aspect of the uprising, whereas the Archbishop of York, in the famous phrase, 'turns insurrection to religion':

> He is a man
> Who with a double surety binds his followers.
> My lord, your son had only but the corpse,
> But shadows and the shows of men, to fight;
> For that same word 'rebellion' did divide
> The action of their bodies from their souls,
> And they did fight with queasiness, constrained,
> As men drink potions, that their weapons only
> Seemed on our side; but, for their spirits and souls,
> This word 'rebellion', it had froze them up,
> As fish are in a pond. But now the Bishop
> Turns insurrection to religion.
> Supposed sincere and holy in his thoughts,
> He's followed both with body and with mind,
> And doth enlarge his rising with the blood
> Of fair King Richard, scraped from Pomfret stones;
> Derives from heaven his quarrel and his cause;
> Tells them he doth bestride a bleeding land
> Gasping for life under great Bolingbroke;
> And more and less do flock to follow him. (1.1.189–208)

This reference to religion as a tool of manipulation takes its place in the long list of sombrer, 'darker' atmospherics in the play that critics have long catalogued. As L. C. Knights pointed out years ago, Falstaff in this play, unlike *Part 1*, is surrounded with the aura of disease and age.[15] When we first see him, he is informed by his new page that the physician has diagnosed him as having 'a good healthy water, but, for the party that owed it, he might have more diseases than he knew for' (1.2.2–4), and we soon have Falstaff's own testimony to the plagues of his pox and gout. Similarly, his amorous encounter with Doll Tearsheet is punctuated with references to venereal disease, age, and death. These are the lugubrious conditions which, he cheerfully informs us (in lines I quoted above), he intends to exploit for his profit.

And the new thematics even invade the genuinely funny material of this play. Falstaff's two new foils, the forgetful but unforgettable Justice Shallow, and his quiet companion Master Silent—he who has 'been merry

---

[15] Knights, *Some Shakespearian Themes*, 45–64.

twice and once ere now' (5.3.39)—bring home to us what Sir John himself has mightily laboured to obscure, his advanced years. Indeed, he does attempt one more claim of youthfulness in this play (like those of *Part 1*) in Scene 1.2, in his verbal fencing with the Chief Justice, but soon this is replaced by frank admissions of age—once to Doll (2.4.244) and again in the celebrated evocation of 'the chimes at midnight' with Shallow (3.2.197–8).

Falstaff's acquiescence to the obvious fact of his own advanced years marks another, perhaps more subtle shift of tactics employed by Sir John in the second play. Living as he is in the power-created fiction of his supposed battlefield prowess, he has more or less to abandon the self-ironizing production of obvious inversions of facts which created the old carnival fictionality we saw, for example, in the multiplying of men in buckram of *Part 1*. His self-fictionalizing has become too (potentially) profitable for him to be giving his own game away so easily. The success of the gilded lie from Shrewsbury has everyone a little awed by Sir John, including himself, and he seems as taken in as anyone by that success.

But the success has removed Falstaff from the proto-aesthetic space of imagination which he inhabited in the first half of *Part 1*; instead of being a performance-artist whose most important premiss is that his audience fully understand the inverted and fictional character of the world they are being inducted into, Falstaff has seen his fiction accepted as reality. He has, therefore, become, according to Stephen Greenblatt's definition of the term,[16] a man of power. His actions have not radically changed, however; what has most significantly changed is their effect: he is believed, he is a success. He has, in the fictional space of the stage, crossed that line between theatre and power which, as Greenblatt insisted in a different context, was a crucial one both for a political theatre and a theatrical state in the Elizabethan age.[17] Not Hal, but Hal's gilded lie, has corrupted Falstaff.

This change in Falstaff is the context for another of this play's notable innovations, the new comic character Pistol, who in this connection is a foil to Falstaff, underlining his empty reputation for bravery, much as the new consciousness of age is marked by Shallow. Like Falstaff, he is constructed from materials of the theatrical tradition, speaking a dialect which is a continual parody of Marlowe's bombastic high tragedy. He is also clearly a swaggering coward, so that Sir John is able to chase him from the tavern with a mere show of his weapon, much as he does Sir John

---

[16] Stephen Greenblatt, *Renaissance Self-Fashioning: From More to Shakespeare* (Chicago: University of Chicago Press, 1980), 13.
[17] Greenblatt, *Shakespearian Negotiations*, 12–20.

Coleville later. Pistol's undisguised theatricality and the manifest hollow-ness of his blustering exaggerate and thereby thematize similar but successfully passed off fictions of Sir John. Pistol's new comic bombast is thus also a revelation of the comic Machiavellian triumph of appearances with which this play is replete.

Falstaff's new image as battle-hero is possible in large measure because he is throughout almost all of this play without the company of his boon companion and deflator, Prince Hal. When we do briefly see Hal, in the muted reprise of the great tavern scene of *Part 1*, there is a return for the moment to *Part 1*-like wit-duels between these two. The Prince catches Falstaff in more lies, and once more Falstaff is led to new assays of wit in wriggling out of them:

No abuse, Ned, i' th'world, honest Ned, none. I dispraised him before the wicked, that the wicked might not fall in love with him; in which doing, I have done the part of a careful friend and a true subject, and thy father is to give me thanks for it. No abuse, Hal; none, Ned, none; no, faith, boys, none. (2.4.291–6)

Here we see the familiar Sir John of *Part 1* in his familiar role of inverted, self-serving, and wish-fulfilling amiability in the face of his blatant pecca-dilloes. Without his *eiron* for the rest of the play, however, Falstaff's self-serving fictions are remarkably efficacious in extending his credit and instilling fear at his prowess. The world thus gets the Falstaff it deserves— and creates.

The now-you-see-it, now-you-don't quality of Falstaff's continuity between the two plays, then, might be summarized this way. He is con-tinuous with the Falstaff of the *later* scenes of *1 Henry IV*, the Brechtian, ironic, self-exposing Falstaff who is both perpetrator and critic of a Machiavellian-Hobbesian world. He and we never really return to the carnival world of the early tavern scenes. Surely, the one reunion scene of Hal and Falstaff before the coronation (2.4) is meant to convey a sense of contrast and loss of that world: as a parallel manqué of the great tavern scene of *Part 1*, it both recalls the earlier time and marks its absence with banter between Hal and Falstaff (some of the most telling reported by third parties) that has more of an edge and a hint of great tension between the two than what we saw in *Part 1*. One of the drawers reports, for instance:

The Prince once set a dish of apple-johns before him; and told him there were five more Sir Johns; and, putting off his hat, said, 'I will now take my leave of these six dry, round, old, withered knights.' It angered him to the heart. But he hath forgot that. (2.4.3–7)

And Mistress Quickly had told Falstaff and us something similar earlier, through an allusion whose specific content is still unexplained, but whose function is unmistakable:

Thou didst swear to me upon a parcel-gilt goblet, sitting in my Dolphin chamber, at the round table, by a sea-coal fire, upon Wednesday in Wheeson week, when the Prince broke thy head for liking his father to a singing-man of Windsor. (2.1.79–83)

These recollections constitute a rewriting of the relationship between Hal and Falstaff from *Part 1*, one in which the relation between the Prince and Falstaff is more explosive and in which the Prince is more apt to express violent anger with Falstaff than was ever indicated in the earlier play. The long summer holiday of the opening acts of that play, so rudely interrupted by the knock on the door in the middle of the play extempore, never returns in either *Part 1* or *Part 2*. It is instead continually recalled in one way or another, only to be mourned.

These changes constitute, of course, not only a subtle transformation of Falstaff, but of Prince Hal as well. As I noted above, he is simply kept offstage for much of the time, until the moments of his final metamorphoses into King Henry V. But Hal's changes are as subtly shaded as are Sir John's. A Prince Hal who is recognizably continuous with the character enacted in *Part 1*, divided between two possible selves, reappears briefly early in *Part 2*, in a conversation with Poins which I partially quoted in the previous chapter and which sets up the encounter with Falstaff I have just described (2.2.1–54). As was the case in *Part 1*, the Prince at the beginning of this play is still suspended between two selves and two worlds, but with one foot already out of the tavern world, just as he seemed after his battlefield heroics at Shrewsbury, despite his acquiescence with Falstaff's battlefield lie at the end of *Part 1*. This is the only time in either play that we see Hal discuss the conflict between his two selves with any other character, and the next time we see the Prince, in Scene 4.3, he is in the process of repudiating his Falstaffian self in favour of a submission to his political role as he arrives at his father's sickbed.

Hal had told Hotspur at the beginning of their combat at Shrewsbury that two Harrys could not coexist in the same sphere, and he extended his already complex identity by 'taking in' the heroic spirit of his conquest. *Part 2* suggests another reading of Hal's challenge to Hotspur: the days of Hal's multiple identities are now ending; the two Harrys that cannot 'keep their motion in one sphere' are the Harrys of tavern and court respectively. *Part 2* enacts the death of the first at the hand of the second under the necessities of realpolitik.

Proleptic Mourning in Gloucestershire

Our last glimpses of what had been the carnival world of *Part 1* (itself an imperfect order replete with its own injustices) provide little hope for counter-community. In a brief, puzzling scene that seems primarily designed to anticipate the repression and imprisonment of Falstaff after the rejection, Doll and Hostess Quickly are haled by a beadle on uncertain charges[18]—and led to an uncertain fate. The scene signals, between two dramatizations of Falstaff's mistaken expectations of triumph through Hal's coronation, that the wheels of state repression are spinning, and we will see more of this kind shortly.

The dark, ambivalent undertone introduced by the arrest of two female denizens of the carnival world follows hard upon the bittersweet high comedy of the scenes in Gloucestershire, which oddly stage a kind of proleptic mourning—to balance, perhaps, the proleptic parody of *Part 1*—for the rejection of Falstaff which has not yet happened. The time is late August, the nights are pleasant, and the talk is full of days gone by, a time, it transpires that never really was. This is the pastoral backdrop for Falstaff's last merry prank, the fleecing of the old Justice of the elusive thousand pounds, a sum, Stephen Greenblatt wrote, which has played throughout the texts of *1 and 2 Henry IV* like some magical conjuration.[19] Falstaff rationalizes just as King Henry had in the previous scene (see below) about the putting down of rebellion; it is a necessity in the way of nature: 'If the young dace be a bait for the old pike, I see no reason in the law of nature, but I may snap at him. Let time shape, and there an end' (3.2.295–7). But here as elsewhere, Falstaff's predatory motivations are offset through a kind of exchange or implicit barter system—in this case, we learn that Shallow himself hopes to profit through Sir John's good offices under the future Henry V and that he has his own ideas about human motivation in a bad world: 'Yea, Davy. I will use him well; a friend

---

[18] At first only Doll seems to be arrested and for a minor offence. The Beadle says, 'The constables have delivered her over to me, and she shall have whipping-cheer' (5.4.4–5). The facts that the offence is under the jurisdiction of a beadle and its penalty whipping both suggest that it is relatively minor, and the line that follows, 'There hath been a man or two killed about her', is a masterpiece of indeterminacy. In another few lines, after more angry exchanges, the Beadle suddenly orders Mistress Quickly to come along as well, adding (for the first time) 'for the man is dead that you and Pistol beat amongst you'. The beating is news, but it is not completely surprising, since we had earlier witnessed the quick tempers of both Doll and Pistol. However, the Beadle never explains what crime if any Doll is being charged with in this connection, and the Hostess's involvement is a further puzzle. The scene can be as easily construed as about the arbitrariness of the Beadle's petty authority and the slipperiness of the law as that it irrevocably blackens Doll, Pistol, and Quickly.

[19] Greenblatt, 'Invisible Bullets', 41.

i' th' court is better than a penny in purse. Use his men well, Davy, for they are arrant knaves, and will backbite' (5.1.26–8).

A number of critics have suspected that something of the indefinable but indulgent aura of these scenes depends on personal associations which the depicted bucolic English countryside had with Shakespeare's own childhood memories,[20] and this may be. But if we can define the aura in question, independent of whatever authorial associations it may have had,[21] we can get one step nearer an understanding of the complex ending of *2 Henry IV*.

In these country scenes, we are in a pastoral, if one with anti-pastoral elements that might connect it to the overdetermined countryside and shepherds of *As You Like It*, or the sheep-shearing scene of *The Winter's Tale*. But the irony is more like that of Arden, simultaneously a negation of court-city artificiality *and* of (in Marx's phrase) the idiocy of rural life. Even with this ambivalence, however, the Gloucestershire scenes constitute virtually the only positively represented utopian element (one of course heavily undercut) within a play which otherwise presents one scenario after another in praise of realism and against imagination.[22]

And indeed this rural arena of a complexly balanced evocation of innocence and experience becomes the site of the haunting, mournful dialogue between Falstaff and his host which has caught the attention of so many readers and auditors. The mourning begins even before the events of Gaultree Forest, when Sir John first re-encounters his old comrade Robert Shallow after fifty-five years. In marked contrast to his claim of youthfulness with the Lord Chief Justice, Falstaff casually identifies with Shallow's age and his vice of lying: 'Lord, Lord, how subject we old men are to this vice of lying!' (3.2.276–7). Here as earlier with Doll, he is no longer pretending to be a young man, and this is a highly significant modification of Falstaff's self-presentation. And while Sir John undertakes his visit to Shallow in order to fleece him, he also, perhaps surprisingly, finds that he is well adapted to the soporific atmosphere of longing for and lying about days gone by:

[20] Phyllis Rackin, *Stages of History: Shakespeare's English Chronicles* (Ithaca, NY: Cornell University Press, 1990), 141.

[21] These scenes have been praised for their complex but genial tone at least since Hazlitt's brief but telling remarks, *Characters of Shakespeare's Plays* (1817; repr. London: Dent, 1906), 153–4; see also J. B. Priestley, *The English Comic Characters* (London: John Lane, 1925), 80–7.

[22] See, for example, the mournful discussions of Hotspur in Scene 1.3. Hotspur, who 'with great imagination | Proper to madmen, led his powers to death, | And winking leapt into destruction' (1.3.31–3), is criticized by Lord Bardolph for possessing a quality we wish we could find more of in the bleak terrain of 'necessity' of this play.

SHALLOW. Ha, cousin Silence, that thou hadst seen that that this knight and I have seen! Ha, Sir John, said I well?

FALSTAFF. We have heard the chimes at midnight, Master Shallow.

SHALLOW. That we have, that we have; in faith, Sir John, we have. Our watchword was 'Hem, boys! Come, let's to dinner; come, let's to dinner. Jesus, the days that we have seen! Come, come. (3.2.195–202)

This odd premonition that his best days are behind him is one of many details in the play pointing forward to the moment of rejection by the newly crowned King Harry V, and the atmospherics of the Gloucestershire scenes, with their simultaneous evocation of an evening afterglow and senescence, seem to represent at once the comfortable retirement Falstaff was never to know and the realization that never quite dawns on him in relation to the coming to power of Hal, that the succession marks the end of his best days rather than the beginning of them. The audience begins to understand, if Falstaff does not, that his waiting for the 'golden joy' was actually the joy itself. The mood of these scenes amounts to a proleptic mourning of Falstaff's loss of Hal and of the audience's loss of their world and its carnival values, and thus, the sudden ageing of Falstaff signifies the sudden ageing of his world. Carnival is about to become a memory—a counter-memory in Foucault's sense, carrying anti-hegemonic values into a world governed by reified power.[23] The two Gloucestershire scenes in Act 5, intercut as they are with the dramatic unfolding of King Hal's new image of pious kingliness and the repudiation of his 'wild youth', become an interlude that enacts a kind of acceptance and peace vis-à-vis the historical inevitability unfolding around them, along with the memory of a henceforth mythical time of resistance to history. The Machiavellian political world is celebrating one of the central truths of power: the king is dead—long live the king. But in Gloucestershire, the ageing survivors of carnival are ruminating over death and old age and finding solace in (counter-)memories.

Falstaff is not yet aware of it, but his Hal is no longer in possession of the possibility of choosing among his multiple selves; instead, as Greenblatt noted, there is a strong sense of impersonality and inevitability in everything that happens from here to the play's end: we are following a script

---

[23] Michel Foucault, *Language, Counter-Memory, Practice: Selected Essays and Interviews*, ed. Donald F. Bouchard, trans. Donald F. Bouchard and Sherry Simon (Ithaca, NY: Cornell University Press, 1977). 'Counter-memory' is one of those concepts within Foucault's works which 'supplement' and undermine the totalizing notion of power of which I have been critical in this book. For a discussion of these conflicting tendencies in Foucault, see Introduction above, and Hugh Grady, *Shakespeare's Universal Wolf: Studies in Early Modern Reification* (Oxford: Clarendon, 1996), 47–52.

which is beyond any individual's control. The mourning in Gloucestershire is, we could say, the play's protest against (but also a kind of acceptance of) what now is being presented to us as an inevitable outcome. The
work of mourning, Freud wrote in a famous essay, involves reclaiming
those aspects of oneself that had been invested in a dead loved one and
therefore experienced as dead with the object of mourning. Falstaff
appears to do some of that work with two unlikely companions in
Gloucestershire, only to lose it all afresh in the street in London where he
encounters Hal for the last time.

The scene set in and/or near the orchard (5.3) is particularly to the point
here. There are homely signifiers of an English bucolic, like the references
to eating pippins and a dish of caraways, and this rural counterpoint
to Falstaff's more usual urban environs provides a new invocation of
carnival spirit, but so senescent as to evoke an absence of that spirit which
had been dramatized in *Part 1*. We hear carnival talk of feasting at Shrove-
tide, and the drunken Silence is full of merry-making songs:

> Do nothing but eat, and make good cheer,
> And praise God for the merry year;
> When flesh is cheap and females dear,
> And lusty lads roam here and there
> So merrily,
> And ever among so merrily. (5.3.16–21)

Sir John manages to enter the spirit of the occasion, and we realize that we
are witnessing a geriatric carnival whose main merry-maker is soon to
pass out from the unaccustomed consumption of sack. But within a
setting of a kind of exile from the court, with Sir John on a mission to snap
at these country dace, we can detect the glow of something not unlike the
fellowship heretofore not much in evidence in *Part 2*—in fact not much in
evidence in either play since the knock at the door in the middle of the play
extempore of *Part 1*. There is even in Gloucestershire a return to talk of
loyalty and trueness to one another:

> By God's liggens, I thank thee. The knave will stick by thee, I can assure thee that;
> a will not out; 'tis true-bred.
> BARDOLPH. And I'll stick by him, sir.
> SHALLOW. Why, there spoke a king! Lack nothing, be merry! (5.3.63–6)

One last time, the carnival world asserts its values of fellowship, loyalty,
and true men, and Shallow associates these with a king. This reverie is then
broken by another knock on another door. It is Pistol, and he speaks of
Africa and golden joy: Sir John's lambkin is king. Will he, like the king

evoked by Shallow in his compliment to Bardolph's pledge of loyalty, stick by him, lack nothing, and be merry? These are the questions invoked by the aura of the end of summer, of carnival, of day, and of fellowship in these wonderfully modulated scenes that evoke the passing of a carnival— but also crucially the formation of a counter-memory to carry with us during the otherwise complete triumph of reification over fellowship in what follows.

The Rejection Scene

The dramatization of the long anticipated and long fought-over moment of Falstaff's rejection is at one level quite simple; it is all over in 100 lines or so, and the central, chilling speech of rejection—

> I know thee not, old man. Fall to thy prayers,
> How ill white hairs becomes a fool and jester!
> I have long dreamt of such a kind of man,
> So surfeit-swelled, so old, and so profane;
> But being awaked, I do despise my dream. (5.5.45–9)

—is over in twenty-five. It is of course the acting out of the successful interpellation of Prince Hal into the Machiavellian King Harry, and the new King is explicit that he has narrowed his sense of selfhood radically:

> Presume not that I am the thing I was,
> For God doth know, so shall the world perceive,
> That I have turned away my former self. (5.5.54–6)

Falstaff's first reaction, 'Master Shallow, I owe you a thousand pound'— perhaps Sir John's only unadulterated acknowledgement of monetary indebtedness of all three of the plays in which he appears—proves much more accurate than the recovery of his spirits represented by his assurances to Shallow that he will be sent for later, secretly. We are so used to Falstaff's wriggling out of tight rhetorical spots that we are momentarily suspended, with the vectors of his desire, awaiting a deliverance. But of course what comes instead is the Lord Chief Justice ordering him and his hapless party off to the Fleet. Not even John Dover Wilson's attempt to cheer us up with the learned observation that this is not the lowest dungeon in the land[24] can disguise the frigid chill in the air, nor can the light banter of those two Lenten figures, the Lord Chief Justice and John of Lancaster, change the mood, since they recall to us Henry IV's deathbed Machiavellian advice to his son:

[24] Wilson, *The Fortunes of Falstaff*, 118–20.

> Be it thy course to busy giddy minds
> With foreign quarrels, that action hence borne out,
> May waste the memory of the former days. (4.3.341–3)

These lines also call us back, however, to that other potent emotional vector in which we have been so skilfully involved, the metamorphosis of wild Prince Hal into the heroic King Henry V and the successful legitimization of Henry IV's succession to the crown. Unlike *1 Henry IV*, however, in this play there is no coexistence of carnival and power.

The audience's desire to learn something more about all this, our wish to deny what has just happened to Falstaff, is catered to by that destabilizing, metatheatrical Shakespearian device, an epilogue. And this indeed, after its preliminary matter, speaks of Falstaff:

One word more, I beseech you. If you be not too much cloyed with fat meat, our humble author will continue the story with Sir John in it, and make you merry with fair Catherine of France; where, for anything I know, Falstaff shall die of a sweat—unless already a be killed with your hard opinions. For Oldcastle died a martyr, and this is not the man. (Epilogue, 22–7)

But, as James Calderwood pointed out, this promise of more Falstaff turns out to be only one more of a number of frustrated expectations depicted in the iron-age world of *2 Henry IV*[25]—something the original audiences only discovered when Sir John failed to appear in the final play of the tetralogy, when we learn he has died of a heart 'fracted and corroborate' at his rejection. For the moment, however, at the end of *2 Henry IV*, we are inducted one final time into the resurrection of Falstaff at the moment of his banishment, a rhetorical gesture which has the effect here of a refusal to close the books irrevocably on Sir John, even as he vanishes from the world of the new Henry V. The epilogue reinforces the counter-memory of a banished carnival that was put in circulation by the last scene at Gloucestershire.

The much debated ending of the *Henry IV* plays, then, suddenly reasserts the reality of two opposing worlds or world views which had seemed in this play, as Greenblatt asserted, to have converged into a single reality of interlinked reified systems. By banishing Falstaff and his other companions, the new King reconstructs two separate domains of politics and pleasure, banishing the latter in favour of the former. Falstaff may have spent his time in *Part 2*, as so many critics have claimed, exploiting the weak rather than constructing a carnival fellowship, and in commodifying his name just as surely as Doll Tearsheet commodified her sexuality,

[25] Calderwood, *Metadrama in Shakespeare's Henriad*, 130–3.

but his banishment, following hard upon the apparent wish-fulfilling news he received from Pistol in the countryside, dashes our own vicarious carnival hopes for Falstaff and undercuts (for us) the new King's (Machiavellian) public relations triumph. In a final turn of the screw around the themes of public and private, power and subjectivity, inner substance and outer appearance, we realize that we have lost not only Sir John, but also his companion Prince Hal—and their world. The stage-worthy juggling through which at the end of *Part 1* Hal managed to keep all the aspects of his decentred self in motion has been replaced by the automaton-like, repetitive movements of a son who has become a craftier version of a Machiavellian father. England has got the ruler it wanted—and perhaps therefore deserves. It will also get, Shakespeare will not let us forget, the dark underside of heroic power, the instrumentalization of its lifeworlds.

This deflated mood, it is worth emphasizing (against a tradition which sees Falstaff's rejection as dominating both Parts 1 and 2), is very far from that at the close of *1 Henry IV*. Here the gorgeous garment of majesty completely absorbs the figure who has just put it on, and we are led to mourn the loss of a complex young man who has disappeared along with his old friends from a world he is no longer able to share, and which he is no longer able even to tolerate. The pious deceitfulness of Prince John and the humourless, single-minded, and narrow legalism of the Lord Chief Justice are now in charge, and if these two are uncharacteristically cheerful in the play's last few lines, it is less certain that the audiences which vicariously shared the ups and downs of Hal and Falstaff can or should join them.

Thus, at the very end of the play, via the complex emotional reactions of audiences to the banishment of Falstaff, we are handed a hollow victory: unexpectedly, this particular famous victory of Hal's—it was only one of public relations, but it was the *sine qua non* of many later, more substantial ones—leaves us with ashes in our mouths: those of an Ash Wednesday abruptly closing a long carnival.

This affect, I would argue, applies not only to the plebeian elements within the audience, for whom Falstaff has been an interlocutor and who are likely to have been sympathetic to his unhappy fortunes at the end, but also for the court audience and other members of the political classes, who cannot be expected to greet the news that power requires self-annihilation through surrender to reified images of the self and the impersonal rules of politics as any kind of celebration of power or its agents. The play thus concludes with an epiphany of the incompatibility of Machiavelli and Montaigne, despite earlier appearances to the contrary, an observation that power and community are incompatible and that power is limited in its ability to adopt masks to occlude its inhuman instrumentality.

Reification in 2 Henry IV

The thematic changes involved as we move from *Part 1* to *Part 2* all involve a process of reification.[26] In the first place, permeating the whole play as perhaps its major theme, are the workings of reified political power, resulting in Hal's final interpellation as a Machiavellian ruler. In addition, at a more 'local' level, there are a series of smaller reifications—the putting into social circulation of abstracted concepts and images so that the substantial or sensuous realities of, say, Falstaff's battlefield feats or of Prince Hal's youthful 'riots' become decontextualized, made equivalent to larger, desire-produced myths, and circulated within society quite independently of the concrete individuals to whom they refer.[27] We have seen how Falstaff exploits the reified image of himself as military hero. We will soon see Hal exploiting the exaggerated images of his prodigality in order to emerge as the equally reified image of the hero-king of legend. Where *1 Henry IV* focused on representing the concrete social realities which underlay these distorted, reified images, *Part 2* shows us how these images absorb, as it were, the play of specific subjectivities which at first seemed to escape or manipulate them. In the last movements of this play (and throughout *Henry V*, we will see), we are left in a reified world in which the earlier realities have no place to exist and are consequently banished in the strongly polarized, half-tragic, half-triumphant production of the great English hero-king. *Henry IV, Part 2* is thus a play about the triumph of reification over subjectivity, but this triumph is a complex affair, presented simultaneously from two opposed perspectives: one requiring the audience to mourn reification's victory over and banishment of a world we had been previously induced to celebrate and vicariously participate in; the other bidding us to share in the final falling into place of Hal's long-awaited fulfilment of filial and patriotic

[26] For fuller discussion of this term and its relevance to Shakespeare's plays, see Grady, *Shakespeare's Universal Wolf*, 26–57. This diagnosis of *Part 2* as representing a world in the grip of reified impersonal social forces was anticipated in somewhat different but related terms in passages by John F. Danby, *Shakespeare's Doctrine of Nature: A Study of 'King Lear'* (London: Faber, 1949), 84–5; Traversi, ' "Henry IV—Part II" ', 112–18; and Greenblatt, 'Invisible Bullets', 48–9.

[27] This 'local' reification is very similar to the concept of 'notorious identity' discussed by Linda Charnes, *Notorious Identity: Materializing the Subject in Shakespeare* (Cambridge, Mass.: Harvard University Press, 1993), in relation to *Richard III*, *Troilus and Cressida*, and *Antony and Cleopatra*.

duties.[28] This alignment of the new King Henry V's image with social expectations of the role of kingship which he has assumed is thus a triumph undercut almost as soon as it occurs, when we learn that, for this specific case, at any rate, the triumph entails a denial of Hal's carnival self—and of his fellows in carnival—and a courting of warfare as a specific tactic of Machiavellian politics. Hal's coronation, and the actions that follow from it, seem to be the last of a series of measures which King Henry IV had earlier characterized as 'necessities'—a word which carries much weight in this play in which the draining of the creative potential of subjectivity by Machiavellian politics is presented as both sorrowful and inevitable. *Necessity* was the term invoked by King Henry to explain his own rise to power:

> necessity so bowed the state,
> That I and greatness were compelled to kiss. (3.1.68–9)

Although it functions as a deft evasion of any admission of his own hand in the process, it also well captures that sense of impersonal autonomy which the operations of Machiavellian power display. 'Are these things then necessities?' (3.1.88), King Henry asks in reply to Warwick's Machiavellian-Montaignean insistence that with keen observation and reason, political men might

> prophesy,
> With a near aim, of the main chance of things
> As yet not come to life, who in their seeds
> And weak beginnings lie intreasurèd. (3.1.77–80)

We can take these lines as a sober, Machiavellian rejoinder to Glendŵr's pre-modern prophesying in the Welsh scenes of *Part 1*, and of course a summary of Machiavelli's famous argument in chapter 25 of *The Prince*, 'How Much Fortune Can Do in Human Affairs and How it May Be Opposed', in which fortune is granted dominion only over one-half of human destiny. In Warwick's version of the argument, it is only because of the tendency of men to repeat their previous actions—is this a version of Montaigne's 'ruling pattern'?—that prophecy is possible. Warwick's premises really do not add up to the construction which Henry gives to them—

[28] Cf. Harold C. Goddard, *The Meaning of Shakespeare* (Chicago: University of Chicago Press, 1951), 161–214; Robert Langbaum, *The Poetry of Experience: The Dramatic Monologue in Modern Literary Tradition* (New York: Random House, 1957), 160–81; A. P. Rossiter, *Angel with Horns and Other Shakespeare Lectures*, ed. Graham Storey (London: Longmans, 1961), 40–64—and numerous subsequent critics.

> Then let us meet them like necessities;
> And that same word even now cries out on us (3.1.87–9)

—since he had earlier spoken of probability, 'the main chance of things' rather than some deterministic necessity (actually, he had used the word 'necessary'). Henry has reinterpreted what was in Warwick's mouth an assertion of the force of human personality as a historical factor into a theory of impersonal necessity—a kind of secular providence, as it were, and a succinct representation of the thematic sea-change from *Part 1* to *Part 2*. The impersonal logic of political events is asserted in virtually every scene after this one—even the comic interludes *chez* Master Shallow, to the extent that they enact Falstaff's comic version of the deadly pike-and-dace power struggle that comes to an anticlimax with the capitulation and execution of the rebels. In a world where everyone is acting like Machiavelli's prince in both small and large spheres of activity, the outcome is an inevitable loss of individuality and an incorporation of human agents into the reified logic of power politics. By the end of the play, reification has completely triumphed, and the unfettered subjectivity explored and celebrated in *Part 1* has become a dead letter. The imagery of the play seems to fit reification in with a series of natural conditions of inevitable mutability and decline—death, disease, ageing, time itself—so that what happens to Falstaff, Prince Hal, even King Henry IV, seems to be inevitable, irrevocable, and part of the fallen nature of the world. What had seemed when they occurred merely local allusions to one family's disaster in the play's first scene become retrospectively an enunciation of the triumph of reification enacted in this play:

> The times are wild; contention, like a horse
> Full of high feeding, madly hath broke loose,
> And bears down all before him. (1.1.9–11)

In this world of death, ageing, mourning, and disease, the slow, steady march of Prince Hal away from the carnival-tavern, his extended self, and his boon companions seems like one more inevitability to many readers and viewers.[29] This is a play, in short, in which that slide from Machiavelli to Montaigne, apparently so easy a connection in *Part 1*, is re-presented instead as a short jump which led to a *cul-de-sac*. The strongest dramatic vector of this play is one towards the inevitability of the triumph of 'necessity'.

[29] e.g. Greenblatt, 'Invisible Bullets', 48: 'He [Hal] need no longer soliloquize his intention to "falsify men's hopes" by selling his wastrel friends: the sale will be brought about by the structure of things, a structure grasped in this play [*2 Henry IV*] under the twinned names of time and necessity.'

The reified world of 2 *Henry IV*, then, is a much more jaundiced one than that of its more popular predecessor *Part 1*. The possibilities of a complexly differentiated modernity, involving disparate worlds of resistance and values counter to those of hegemonic Machiavellian politics, had been highlighted and even celebrated in the earlier play. But in the later one they are shown collapsing before the development of Machiavellian political necessities.

How might we account for this shift? It did not of course represent some Shakespearian 'last word' on these themes. *Henry V* will take up these issues again and enact a surprising persistence of a now hidden or repressed subjectivity within the otherwise Machiavellian Henry V. *Hamlet* returns to this terrain and creates its own complex textuality around themes of the Machiavellian and the subjective. The Jacobean tragedies, as I tried to emphasize in *Shakespeare's Universal Wolf*, keep these themes in motion as we move, for example, from the frightening amorality of Iago's unfixed self to the redemptive unfixity of Edgar and Lear on the heath and thereafter. But the peculiar and sudden shift in tone I have described from *1 Henry IV* to *2 Henry IV*, subtle as it is—more a deepening of shadows than anything else—marks a decisive turning point within the *Henriad* and within the larger trajectory of Shakespeare's writing. It marks the beginning of a descent from the high point of optimism about the possible compatibility of power and subjectivity, of Machiavelli and Montaigne, that was achieved precariously in *1 Henry IV*. In the histories and tragedies that follow from this point, Machiavellian power becomes increasingly dark for Shakespeare, finally culminating in such figures from the Jacobean tragedies as Iago, Goneril, Regan, Cornwall, Edmund, and Lord and Lady Macbeth. In the serener late plays (*Antony and Cleopatra*, perhaps, marks this later turning point) power is, so to speak, less powerful, although never morally neutral. The shift in emphasis between the two *Henry IV* plays is a fundamental one in terms of the directions of Shakespeare's development as an artist and thinker.

It would be satisfying, of course, if we could say just what experiences the playwright from Stratford had that led to these changes—the world is still buying those commodities constituted by the various conspiracy theories and fictions promising to do just that or something similar. The public still thirsts for that sublime, unknowable experience even though our ignorance of it is more profound than ever. Beyond the obvious probability that the change was connected to the political currents of the day—specifically the rise and fall of the Earl of Essex—it is doubtful that we will ever be able to understand what specific personal or public subtexts underwrote this great thematic shift. Precisely for that reason, however, we should try to understand the thematic and artistic development itself—and its continuing reverberations into our own time.

2. DISSONANCE AND DISSIDENCE IN HENRY V

The last play of Shakespeare's Henriad, Henry V, is in many ways the most Machiavellian of them all, celebrating a Prince who succeeded in astonishing feats of conquest and national unification while coolly depicting how that Prince's heroic achievements were accomplished by political manipulation, image manufacture, violence, and the threat of violence. The potential tension between these two sides of King Harry's triumphs— the dark side's threat to undermine and negate the bright one—never comes clearly or unequivocally into focus, however, because so much of the play features rhetoric celebratory of Harry's successes. Neither, however, is the celebration unalloyed because the play also contains material clearly if covertly critical of the enterprises underlying Harry's famous victories. And if we thought that the young Prince Hal whom we had come to empathize with in the previous two plays of the tetralogy had been irrevocably taken from us by his coronation, Henry V disappoints us in this regard too, reviving Hal's unfixed subjectivity in the scenes before the Battle of Agincourt and revealing more clearly than ever the merely theatrical qualities of the office of the king.

Henry V has had a singular critical history, divided between admirers and deprecators of its major character and polarized into completely opposed interpretations of the play's politics. Each of these positions, I will argue, is supportable by different portions or layers of this play's text. Contrary to what might be expected, however, the play's exposure of the calculation and instrumentalization behind the heroics does not really undermine them, especially when the play is seen in performance.[30] But the play's steadily escalating sum for the price paid for the conquest of France cumulatively creates a dissonant heroics—a questioning area of resistance to the ideology of the dominant subtext of the play.

The peculiar tensions of this play have something in common with those moments in Machiavelli's The Prince when subtexts critical of cruelty and deception come briefly into view before ceding to the logic of instrumental reason (see Chapter 2), but in Henry V the tension is stronger

[30] This is a point well made by Andrew Gurr, introduction to William Shakespeare, King Henry V (Cambridge: Cambridge University Press, 1992), 1–55; 36–7.

and more dissonant. In this play more than in *Richard II*, I suspect the influence of the specific Machiavellianism of the Essex faction in the overall structure and point of view—accompanied by a growing, only partially assimilated unease with that philosophy. The tensions of this play mirror the tensions of Essex and his Machiavellian project, and this connection can help explain its dissonant, off-centred qualities. The play attempts simultaneously to heroicize King Harry and to reveal the dubious means by which his heroic image is manufactured, and this creates as much confusion for theatrical audiences as a similar problem created for Essex in his failed attempt at taking power. But what saves *Henry V* from being merely the exercise in monarchist and nationalist propaganda that its severest critics have accused it of being is the complex layering of dissident, anti-war material amidst the more overt celebrations of King Harry's conquests. The structure is something different from Shakespeare's more normal dialogism; it is more like a piece of kinetic art which takes on different meanings and self-evaluations as its different parts shift and come into new perspectives and groupings, never clearly dichotomizing or self-cancelling, but always presenting new, shifting configurations.

The resulting complexity is partially illustrated in this play's singular critical history. *Henry V* has not responded well to Romantic and Modernist assumptions of organic unity. Unifying critics have had to take one of two or three different positions—all of which now seem partial or one-sided.[31] Many Romantic and Modernist critics disparaged *Henry V* as demonstrating an apparent moment of corruption in Shakespeare's 'spiritual growth', a celebration of 'worldly' triumph which had overtaken him for a time, but which was ultimately to give way in turn to the rejection of worldly power in the great tragedies to come, beginning with *Hamlet*. George Bernard Shaw was the bluntest of this line of critics:

One can hardly forgive Shakespeare quite for the worldly phase in which he tried to thrust such a Jingo hero as his Harry V down our throats. The combination of conventional propriety and brute masterfulness in his public capacity with a low-lived blackguardism in his private tastes is not a pleasant one. No doubt he is true to nature as a picture of what is by no means uncommon in English society, an able young Philistine inheriting high position and authority, which he holds on to and goes through with by keeping a tight grip on his conventional and legal advantages,

---

[31] Cf. Gary Taylor, introduction to William Shakespeare, *Henry V*, ed. Gary Taylor (Oxford: Clarendon, 1982), 1–74, who calls the play 'a critical no man's land, acrimoniously contested and periodically disfigured by opposing barrages of intellectual artillery' (p. 1).

but who would have been quite in his place if he had been born a gamekeeper or a farmer.[32]

Mid-century 'old historicist' treatments, which situated *Henry V* within the pro-monarchical ideology of the day's official documents, agreed with Shaw as to the ideological purposes of the play but defended Shakespeare as simply reflecting the values of his time.[33] But this 'defence' left many unsatisfied, and many critics have attempted to 'save' the play by reading it ironically—an eloquent article by Gerald Gould, written in the aftermath of the carnage of the First World War, appears to be the first to argue that the play is essentially a satire against war, imperialism, and monarchy.[34] After the Second World War, recognition of ironic elements in the play became the majority position in academic Shakespeare studies, but many critics with this approach tended to read the play's ironies as subordinated to a larger celebration of monarchy and King Harry;[35] or, like E. M. W. Tillyard echoing elements of the previous generation's disparaging critics, they argued that Shakespeare-the-artist had recoiled from Shakespeare-the-ideologue and given us a half-hearted effort in which admiration and celebration had not cohered.[36]

In contrast, since the Postmodernist turn in Shakespeare studies of the 1970s and 1980s, critics have tended to start with the idea of undecidable multiple viewpoints within the text, thus subsuming both sides of the previous debate.[37] Perhaps the first of these new-wave approaches to

[32] Bernard Shaw, ' "Henry IV, Part 1" ', in *Shaw on Shakespeare: An Anthology of Bernard Shaw's Writings on the Plays and Productions of Shakespeare*, ed. Edwin Wilson (London: Dutton, 1961), 101. Similar opinions were given earlier by Hazlitt, *Characters of Shakespeare's Plays*, 156–64, and later by W. B. Yeats, 'At Stratford-on-Avon', in *Essays and Introductions* (London: Macmillan, 1961), 96–110. In the mid-20th century, Columbia University critic Mark van Doren updated this position in his *Shakespeare* (New York: Holt, 1939), 170–9.

[33] This trend was initiated by E. E. Stoll, ' "Henry V" ', in *Poets and Playwrights: Shakespeare, Jonson, Spenser, Milton* (Minneapolis: University of Minnesota Press, 1930), 31–54, and continued in such influential mid-century works as Lily Campbell, *Shakespeare's 'Histories': Mirrors of Elizabethan Policy* (San Marino, Calif., Huntington, 1947); J. Dover Wilson, introduction to William Shakespeare, *King Henry V*, ed. J. Dover Wilson (Cambridge: Cambridge University Press, 1947); and M. M. Reese, *The Cease of Majesty: A Study of Shakespeare's History Plays* (London: Arnold, 1961), 317–32.

[34] Gerald Gould, 'A New Reading of "Henry V" ', *The English Review*, 29 (July 1919), 42–55.

[35] See, for example, Traversi, *Shakespeare from ' Richard II to 'Henry V'*, 187–98; Rossiter, *Angel with Horns*, 40–64; and Ellis-Fermor, *Frontiers of Drama*, 34–55.

[36] E. M. W. Tillyard, *Shakespeare's History Plays* (1944; repr. New York: Macmillan, 1946), 304–14.

[37] As usual, elements of a previous Modernism can be found which prefigure this Postmodernist move. In the case of *Henry V*, this position can be traced back to Goddard, *The Meaning of Shakespeare*, 215–68, who argued for two disparate concepts of Henry in the play—but Goddard also thought that one of these was 'ironic' and undermined the other

Henry V was Norman Rabkin's 1977 'Rabbits, Ducks, and "Henry V"',
which makes what appears retrospectively to be a distinctly Postmodernist case for the idea that the two views of Henry promulgated in so
much previous criticism are both implied by the text, but that they are
incompatible, impossible to hold simultaneously, like the well-known
illustration from gestalt psychology that is now a duck, now a rabbit.[38] But
if Rabkin's argument incorporated (probably unconsciously) a new Postmodernist suspicion of organic unity, a new taste for aesthetic dissonance,
it did not consciously participate in any other way in the theoretical
revolutions in literary theory well under way by 1977 elsewhere in English
studies, if only fitfully within those of Shakespeare. Rabkin's agile reading
of this play's 'either-or' representations of King Harry and monarchy
takes place within a more-or-less timeless spatial textuality developed out
of New Criticism (not dissimilar to that deployed by the textualist Yale
deconstructors at about the same time). The essay lacks any sense of the
social and political contextuality which the new historicism and cultural
materialism of the next decade brought to bear in these connections, and
it lacks any larger literary theory to help conceptualize the posited textual
dissonance which is conceptualized instead in analogy with the principle
of 'complementarity' in quantum physics.[39]

  Thus, while Rabkin's article, and the several subsequent ones following
its lead,[40] rightly call attention to two incompatible images of monarchy

'lyric' and 'epic' materials, so that his case for disparateness undermines itself because it
privileges the ironic viewpoint as more inclusive.

  [38] Norman Rabkin, 'Rabbits, Ducks, and "Henry V"', *Shakespeare Quarterly*, 28/3
(Summer 1977), 279–96. A revised version appeared as ch. 2, 'Either/Or: Responding to
Henry V', in Norman Rabkin, *Shakespeare and the Problem of Meaning* (Chicago: University
of Chicago Press, 1981), 33–62, but I am citing from the original article.
  [39] Rabkin, 'Rabbits, Ducks, and "Henry V"', 296. Thus, I understand Rabkin's article to
be transitional, reflecting aesthetic but not yet theoretical change, like the four transitional
interpretations of *Timon of Athens* in the 1970s I analysed, *The Modernist Shakespeare*, 201–4.
  [40] Annabel Patterson, *Shakespeare and the Popular Voice* (Oxford: Basil Blackwell, 1989),
71–92, provides an elegant, historically contextualized variation on Rabkin's theme by seeing
the two opposed viewpoints as each governing one of the two textual versions of the play: a
1600 quarto (a 'bad' one in Pollard's terms, without the choruses, the Epilogue, and several
familiar speeches) and the 1623 Folio, the basis for modern editions. In Patterson's interesting argument, the stripped-down quarto represented an ideologically 'safe' text of the
play suited for the dangerous times in which Essex was under house arrest and in which
Sir John Hayward had just been put in the Tower for bringing out a depiction of the overthrow of Richard II—see above, Ch. 1. The Folio version, according to Patterson, was an
uncensored text in which Harry's heroism is undercut by a number of complications and
devices. Joel B. Altman, ' "Vile Participation": The Amplification of Violence in the Theater
of *Henry V*, *Shakespeare Quarterly*, 42/1 (Spring 1991), 1–32, also notes the play's unusual
dissonance and traces it to its attempts to express its audience's ambivalent attitudes about
Essex's Irish campaign, whose demands for treasure and troops made it less than universally

within the play, they tend to assume that this incompatibility is one more instance of a familiar Shakespearean practice of dramatizing competing but complementary ideologies or discourses in a dialogic relation—that is, one in which the competing discourses cannot be synthesized, nor can one be subordinated to the other. Such dialogism as a general principle seems to structure the varying viewpoints of *Richard II* and *1 and 2 Henry IV*, for example. In *Henry V*, it seems to me, however, uncharacteristically for Shakespeare, such dialogism does not apply. Instead, the play represents its principal character King Harry V—the figure around whom its political philosophy is constructed—within three incompatible 'frames' or horizons of interpretation. The most accessible of these, the one that has dominated this play's performance history and much of its critical reception, is that of the 'heroic' Henry, a strongly positive national leader displaying unalloyed honesty, piety, and courage. The second frame is much more complex, yielding a much 'greyer' King Harry, one who projects his heroic image through a keen understanding of Machiavelli's insistence on the primacy of appearance over reality in politics. This 'positive Machiavellianism' has seemed to most previous critics an unthinkable contradiction in terms, and the resulting inability to conceive of Shakespeare in these terms has been one of the principal obstacles to an understanding of this complex play. Previously in this book, I have discussed how *Richard II* and *1 and 2 Henry IV* embody a taken-for-granted, secular understanding of the provenance of power (antithetical to official ideologies of divine right, but coexisting with them among Tudor and Stuart intellectuals; see Chapter 1), but the Machiavellianism of *Henry V* is a more specified, determinate version of these principles. It is, I believe, the specific Machiavellianism of the Essex faction, and thus I am reviving the hypothesis of several previous critics that this play is closely linked to Essex and his ideology. Strikingly, the play presents that ideology (to those who can fathom it) in a distinctly positive light—so that the play seems to project an image of the monarchy designed to be 'fitted' by Essex. However, there are also moments when the apparent attempt to present such 'hard' Machiavellian doctrines as the necessity of cruelty seem to miscarry or are fatally complicated, and we are confronted—and this makes up the play's third 'frame'—with an implied anti-Machiavellianism that seems to undermine what is otherwise a quite consistent positive application of ideas that were central to much of England's sixteenth-century political discourse, but most especially to followers of the Earl

popular. Other relatively recent readings of the play will be discussed below as the argument develops.

of Essex. At these moments, then, I believe, we are in the presence of what I will call the play's 'political unconscious',[41] moments which, slyly or inadvertently—though of course we can never be certain of intentionality—register the inherent resistance to power/ideology constituted by language, experience, counter-ideologies, and the lifeworld.[42]

The problem for recent Postmodernist-influenced criticism is not, then, to recognize the play's disparateness; rather it is to conceptualize it. In 1985 Günter Walch proposed, for example, that the play's doubled messages were perhaps best understood in terms of an exploration of the workings of ideology, the gap between what the Chorus tells us to anticipate and what the scenes actually dramatize, thereby creating an exposure of choral ideology which gets refuted by a more complex, ideology-resisting reality in the scenes.[43] This welcome introduction of a concept of ideology into the discussion of this play, however, did not significantly develop it beyond earlier discussions of 'irony'. It assumes, for example, that the gap between choral enthusiasm and more realist or complex dramatizations simply negates the strong appeal of the heroic material—which inhabits not only the Chorus, but elements of the dramatization as well; and it assumes a simple opposition between 'ideology' and 'reality' which has long since seemed untenable. A more complex deployment of the concept of ideology within *Henry V* was Jonathan Dollimore and Alan Sinfield's 'History and Ideology: The Instance of *Henry V*', which conceptualized the play's representation of ideology in terms of its enactment of national unity overcoming the stresses and contradictions threatening of it, but also displaying 'an

[41] This term of course derives from Fredric Jameson's milestone *The Political Unconscious: Narrative as a Socially Symbolic Act* (Ithaca, NY: Cornell University Press, 1981), but I am adapting it for my own uses here rather than following the letter of Jameson's own development of the term (in the context of narrative theory and much else) in his book.

[42] I should clarify that a political unconscious such as I am presupposing here may have more or less conscious dimensions, as when repressions are created, for example, by the kind of wartime considerations that led to the notorious cutting of 'darker' material in the play in Olivier's film version. For the many 'pro-Henry' critics who have worked with an uncut text, this reading depends instead on an ignoring, denial, or dismissal of such material, often under the influence of conscious, professionalist assumptions that only a pro-monarchy play would have been acceptable in Shakespeare's day. In this connection I am thinking of such mid-century historicists as J. Dover Wilson, *The Fortunes of Falstaff*, and M. M. Reese, *The Cease of Majesty*, and their peculiar version of historicism can be characterized in this context as one that attempts to restore to a post-Enlightenment, more-or-less democratic audience a hegemonic Elizabethan or Jacobean ideology, thus ironically making inaccessible those resistances to official ideology of which many sectors of the original audience of the play probably *were* cognizant.

[43] Günter Walch, '*Henry V* as Working-House of Ideology', *Shakespeare Survey*, 40 (1988), 63–8.

inconsistency and indeterminacy in the representation of ideological harmony in writing'.[44] This conception gets at the susceptibility of ideologies to resistance, but, I do not think the description of *Henry V* in this provocative essay successfully captures what is startling and unusual in its treatment of the social supports of the monarchy. To my mind, of the several dissonance-recognizing treatments of the play since Rabkin, the most adequate is Stephen Greenblatt's in 'Invisible Bullets'—even though, as I have argued above, that classic essay reductively misinterprets *1 Henry IV*.[45] As I have worked with *Henry V*, however, I have been surprised to discover that for me this much discussed, much critiqued reading of the Prince Hal trilogy comes into its moment of fullest truth in its treatment of *Henry V*. Greenblatt forthrightly faced the highly unusual clash of affect implied by the play's positive Machiavellianism: the play exposes the mechanisms of deception which underlie this monarch's image, but, Greenblatt asserts, simultaneously seems to bid us to submit ourselves to them nevertheless. This reading beautifully captures the play's primarily uncritical exposure of Machiavellian manipulation— more than being simply uncritical or 'objective', the play at times seems to bid its audience to celebrate the artfulness of specific instances of Machiavellianism. But while forthrightly facing up to this unusual combination of affects, Greenblatt's milestone reading, I believe, misses the dynamics of ideological repression involved in the production of the disparate readings of the play's critical history because it fails to differentiate not only the separate plays of the trilogy, but also the socially divided components of the audience.[46]

I would argue that there are only two audiences that might have plausibly registered both of the contradictory affects posited by Greenblatt in his bravura analysis: one in our own day, the other in 1599. An interpretation like Greenblatt's was popular in the 1980s through the potent influence of early readings of Foucault on power, as I argued in the Introduction, and this play thus for a moment seemed to be a plausible

---

[44] Jonathan Dollimore and Alan Sinfield, 'History and Ideology: The Instance of *Henry V*', in John Drakakis (ed.), *Alternative Shakespeares* (London: Methuen, 1985), 206–27; 215.

[45] See above, Chs. 1 and 4; Hugh Grady, 'Containment, Subversion—and Postmodernism', *Textual Practice*, 7/1 (Spring 1993), 31–49; and Grady, *Shakespeare's Universal Wolf*, 141.

[46] Cf. Charles Whitney, 'Ante-aesthetics', in Hugh Grady (ed.), *Shakespeare and Modernity: From Early Modern to Millennium* (London: Routledge, 2000), 40–60. I made the case for resolving the paradoxes of the 'containment-and-subversion' debate by noting differences in the plays' audiences earlier, in somewhat different contexts, in Grady, 'Containment, Subversion—and Postmodernism' and in Grady, *Shakespeare's Universal Wolf*, 140–1.

example of what an early modern audience, interpellated into a monarchical ideology, might have experienced. But the popularity of Greenblatt's analysis in the 1980s now seems a function of an era when, in both the USA and the UK, aestheticized conservative politics seemed to have mass voting constituencies firmly entrapped within similar ideological straitjackets. In the meantime within Shakespeare studies, however, numerous objections to such monolithic theorizings have turned 'Invisible Bullets', as we have seen, into something of a period piece from which even Greenblatt has distanced himself,[47] and Elizabethan audiences have been in the interim reconceptualized as more heteronymous, less likely to have unified receptions of Shakespeare's (and others') multivalent plays than 'Invisible Bullets' had assumed.[48] With the multivalent audience for the play in mind, in fact, I think we can hypothesize reasons explanatory of many of the puzzling features of its critical and performance history that cohere as well with what we know about the play's original political context and audiences. I am arguing that, singularly within Shakespeare's oeuvre, this play is most coherent as it would have been constructed by the Machiavellian ideology of the Essex faction. *Henry V*'s unique structure, which discloses the strategic, instrumental formation of the image of a heroic monarch, but without thematizing or conceptualizing this production as evil or even as particularly deceptive, makes sense much less as the imputed consciousness of dutiful royal subjects than it does as the imputed consciousness of a political fraction in the process of deceiving itself about its own political viability. The contradiction for Essex and his followers, we could say, came about because, in effect, the Essex faction ignored what was classically defined by Voltaire in his *Mémoires*: the first thing a successful Machiavellian must do is denounce Machiavelli— something that Robert Cecil and Francis Bacon, as we saw in Chapter 1, consistently did in the confrontation with Essex. Essex's bold defiance of Elizabeth's explicit orders when he returned from Ireland and entered her private chambers unannounced, and even more the calculated risks of his armed march through London streets in his bid to capture the Queen with popular support, despite his lack of any plausible claim to the throne, suggest that he thought a public, calculated display of raw political power would be enough to win over the populace's support.

[47] Greenblatt, *Shakespearian Negotiations*, 2–3.
[48] Important critiques of this monolithic position were given by: Dollimore and Sinfield, 'History and Ideology'; Leah Marcus, *Puzzling Shakespeare: Local Reading and its Discontents* (Berkeley and Los Angeles: University of California Press, 1988), 137–48; and Louis Montrose, *The Purpose of Playing: Shakespeare and the Cultural Politics of the Elizabethan Theatre* (Chicago: University of Chicago Press, 1996).

Such thinking did not work for Essex in February 1601, and (if I am right in supposing that a similar belief in the attractive power of Machiavellian image-making is inherent in *Henry V*) it has not worked well dramatically for Shakespeare either, helping make this play one of the most contro-versial and puzzling in the Shakespearian canon. Most audiences, even in our own era of repeated media meta-analyses of the techniques of political manipulation, do not find this peculiar combination of claims either coherent or appealing—attitudes which explain as well much of the mixed reception of this play by the Shakespeare studies of the last half of the twentieth century. Only in our own time has the Machiavellianism of the Essex faction found an equivalent in the Foucauldian-Althusserian-'Machiavellian' moment of the 1980s. However, the play features material subversive of its strong Machiavellianism as well, at least for portions of the audience, then and now, without a strong ideological predisposition to accept unequivocally the hard political doctrines involved. The idea that the public could be so enamoured of a charismatic, conquering military hero that it not just overlooked but actually supported and encouraged a manifestly Machiavellian political policy of force over pretension to legitimacy was one certainly acted out, and possibly even consciously conceptualized, by Essex and his key advisers and followers. It of course proved a disastrous and foolhardy political philosophy (had Machiavelli lived to see this, he might have had the opportunity, like Marx speaking of his followers in the Paris Commune, to remark that he himself was no Machiavellian). And our most charitable interpretation of this strange play is to suppose that the impossible tensions and contradictions involved in this process became manifest in the play-text which attempted to square the circle of a politics of deception seeking followers by trumpeting its own deception. Viewed that way, *Henry V* falls apart as a thesis-drama embodying a coherent ideology because its ideology is not coherent; and it is not a properly Shakespearian dialogic drama because the two viewpoints it presents are not dialogically related; one (the 'insider's' view of King Harry's public pronouncements) rather is the ideological 'means of production' by which the other (the produced public image) is created: these are not opposing, disparate points of view, but simply less and more complete views of a single ideology. What makes the play most interesting for us now is the complexity created by those moments in *Henry V* when a critical distantiation from Essex's Machia-vellian ideology[49] indeed occurs for an attentive reader or viewer. The

[49] I am using this polysemous term in a sense related to but different from that of Dollimore and Sinfield's 'History and Ideology'. Rather than attempting to describe the

death of Falstaff is one such moment, and the complex, off-centred comparison between King Harry and 'Alexander the Pig' by Fluellen, after King Harry's command to kill the French prisoners, is another. To be sure, such moments are never consolidated but remain undeveloped, almost latent, while the play sweeps us ahead to its battle-climax and manipulates the audience's national pride and disdain of the French, ending with the enforced cheer and merriment of Harry's bluff-honest-Englishman's wooing of coquettishly submissive Catherine.[50] But this pro-conquest effect is based on a selective interpretation of the play-text: if it works for an audience at a performance—and performance history shows us that it has continually done so—it works because the anti-war, anti-heroic materials critical of the play's Machiavellian ideology get swept aside and so dismissed by the audience, or assimilated to patriotic themes of the cruel sacrifices required of us in patriotic wars.

Thus at one level, *Henry V* alludes to, or represents, an image of Essex. King Harry is a dramatic character with many of the qualities around which Essex's carefully cultivated 'public' image was constructed.[51] But the play contains numerous features which resist subordination to its most strongly thematized elements, constituting *Henry V*'s 'political unconscious'. Thus the play becomes coherent for us now if we are able to explain its incoherence in relation to the supercharged political atmosphere in London during Essex's Irish expedition and thereby appreciate its anti-war subtexts. Interpreted in this light, *Henry V* at the dawn of the twenty-first century is a complex and intriguing play of aesthetic dissonance and political dissidence.

---

play's representation of a basic ideology of nationalist unity and power as they did, I am exploring the play's apparent representation of the specific set of ideas and beliefs of the Essex faction. However, I believe that this Essex-faction ideology is fraught with tensions and contradictions similar to those discussed by Dollimore and Sinfield for a more general royalist ideology.

[50] In an important essay discussed in the previous chapter, Terence Hawkes, 'Bryn Glas', in Ania Loomba and Martin Orkin (eds.), *Post-colonial Shakespeares* (London: Routledge, 1998), 117–40, characterizes King Harry's implicit assumption in wooing Catherine as a matter of seeing the entire world as an '*Anglia irredenta*' in which the King is serving as a kind of national liberator (p. 131).

[51] This approach is related to those of two critics briefly discussed above: Patterson, *Shakespeare and the Popular Voice*, 71–92, and Altman, 'Vile Participation'. Altman, however, focuses less on Essex himself than on the war atmosphere in London in the spring and summer of 1599 caused by rumours of a second Spanish Armada and by Essex's campaign in Ireland, with its considerable financial and manpower needs.

Self-Revealing/Self-Destructing Machiavellianism

Two features of this play, more than any others, are responsible for the hegemony of the play's heroic elements over its other, 'darker' material: its unique choruses and Henry's powerful public rhetoric. I will return briefly below to the role of the Chorus—a topic which has been given considerable and telling scrutiny by recent critics, as we will see. But to explain how the play manages both to project a heroic image of King Harry and demonstrate the elements of Machiavellian deception behind this image—but without subverting it—we can begin with the play's opening scenes.

First, we are shown a 'behind-the-scenes' context for one of the King's official speeches, followed by its public performance—and we can note a gap between the two. The preliminary conversation in Scene 1.1 between the two archbishops is full of a worldly sense of realpolitik while the King's speech displays none of this spirit but is couched instead in a solemn, deliberative rhetoric. Everything happens as if King Harry is following two incompatible strategies, both of which produce exactly the same public utterances: on the one hand he seems to be, as he is described by the political archbishops, a scholar of statecraft with a new spirit of religious piety and reformation (1.1.24–59). On the other hand, not a word would be different if the King were simply following the dictates of Machiavellian doctrine and constructing that façade of religion and piety which *The Prince* more than once urged upon those who would be effective rulers.

Thus, the Machiavellian provenance of its protagonist's heroic politics is pointedly thematized from the play's opening scenes—although, characteristically, the implied Machiavellian point is only communicated if the audience draws certain conclusions about the interrelations between the conversation of the two archbishops in Scene 1.1 and the speech of the King in 1.2.

In the first scene we overhear the archbishops worrying about a bill in Parliament that would strip them of some possessions:

> If it pass against us,
> We lose the better half of our possession,
> For all the temporal lands which men devout
> By testament have given to the church
> Would they strip from us—being valued thus:
> As much as would maintain, to the King's honour,
> Full fifteen earls and fifteen hundred knights,
> Six thousand and two hundred good esquires;

And, to relief of lazars and weak age,
Of indigent faint souls past corporal toil,
A hundred almshouses right well supplied;
And to the coffers of the King beside
A thousand pounds by th' year. Thus runs the bill. (1.1.7–19)

The references to almshouses and aid to lepers, the aged, and the indigent seem particularly calculated, in their similarity to Gospel motifs of Jesus railing against Mammon, to turn us against the two bishops' defence of their privileges, and they also help 'sanctify' the raising of military forces and money for Henry's wars by association. This open-eyed illustration of the political operations of religious institutions within the secular world is developed in terms that must have, at least momentarily, caused the audience to see the archbishops critically.

As the scene continues, we hear Canterbury describe what seems to be a *quid pro quo* political arrangement whereby King Harry opposes the bill in favour of a counter-offer from the bishops to contribute money to the King in lieu of the loss of the properties—'a greater sum I Than ever at one time the clergy yet I Did to his predecessors part withal' (1.1.80–2). But it appears the King is not quite ready to consummate the deal. The Archbishop notes that the King seemed preoccupied instead with the details of 'causes now in hand, I Which I have opened to his grace at large: I As touching France' (1.1.78–9); and in particular

> The severals and unhidden passages
> Of his true titles to some certain dukedoms,
> And generally to the crown and seat of France,
> Derived from Edward, his great-grandfather. (1.1.87–90)

This somewhat cryptic dialogue becomes more intelligible as the next scene unfolds and we find out that King Harry is amassing the political capital he will need to undertake war with France in pursuit of his claim to the French throne. King Harry's public utterance appears to be a solemn appeal to an impartial ecclesiastical figure bringing a divine's moral perspective to a life-or-death matter:

> My learnèd lord, we pray you to proceed,
> And justly and religiously unfold
> Why the law Salic that they have in France
> Or should, or should not, bar us in our claim.
> And God forbid, my dear and faithful lord,
> That you should fashion, wrest, or bow your reading,
> Or nicely charge your understanding soul

> With opening titles miscreate, whose right
> Suits not in native colours with the truth;
> For God doth know how many, now in health
> Shall drop their blood in approbation
> Of what your reverence shall incite us to.
> Therefore take heed how you impawn our person,
> How you awake the sleeping sword of war;
> We charge you in the name of God take heed.
> For never two such kingdoms did contend
> Without much fall of blood, whose guiltless drops
> Are every one a woe, a sore complaint
> 'Gainst him whose wrongs give edge unto the swords
> That makes such waste in brief mortality.
> Under this conjuration speak, my lord;
> For we will hear, note, and believe in heart
> That what you speak is in your conscience washed
> As pure as sin with baptism. (1.2.9–32)

This is impressive and momentarily disruptive of the logic of the previous scene, which seemed to imply that the Archbishop's 'correct' answer to the question of King Harry's title to France is part of the deal in regard to the church properties. King Harry's solemn tones on the contrary convey the impression that he is himself 'above' the political deal-making which we have just heard discussed by the two archbishops. But the Archbishop's long gloss on the 'true' meaning of the Salic Law pulls us back into the thematics we have been immersed in throughout the earlier plays of the tetralogy: laws, titles, and language generally are profligate and fluid, open to multiple interpretations and subject to the pull of material and political interests. After the King's impassioned plea for truth and assurance, the Archbishop delivers a lawyer's brief which could convince only those predisposed to it. King Harry, in fact, has to ask again ('May I with right and conscience make this claim?') after the detailed explanation as to why 'There is no bar | To make against' the English claim except the French appeal to the Salic Law, which the Archbishop declares irrelevant on a number of grounds. The solemn tones of King Harry seem to brook no equivocation in their insistence on an absolute moral truth—and yet they produce a discourse which is open to questions, contestation, alternative interpretation, and legal wrangling. Here, certainly, at least for the moment, are Rabkin's duck and rabbit: King Harry is either a heroic national champion of truth and justice, or a studied portrait thereof, produced through calculation and political savoir faire.

This doubled structure, in which the King's words and deeds can be construed as following from completely disparate ideologies, is the property not just of this scene but of his public words and deeds throughout the play. King Harry manages to be simultaneously a popular, folk-hero king whose words and deeds evoke no duplicity *and* an astute Machiavellian who knows precisely how to project a feigned folk-hero image through political calculation. Unlike *Richard* III, that earlier study in the uses of political deception in which the audience is privileged throughout to see behind the Machiavellian façade of that particular prince of dark corners, this play gives us both a heroic image *and* the machinery and calculations whereby the image of heroism is created. King Harry here, for the first half of the play at any rate, is more reminiscent of Bolingbroke in *Richard II*, an 'opaque character'[52] whose interiority remained closed to us so that we could never be completely sure of what motivated his politically efficacious words and deeds. The level of piety and patriotism evoked by Harry V, however, is at a considerably higher level of idealism than the 'necessity' which his father so often evoked, and in Act 4 King Harry's interiority is in fact tellingly shared with the audience, as we will see below, as Bolingbroke's never was. Thus, in the case of King Henry V, our suspicions in regard to his possible Machiavellian strategizing must be destructive of the image which is presented to the outer world in a way that was not true for Bolingbroke as challenging duke or as king of unquiet times.

In the light of this play's unique critical history especially, it seems clear enough that the play is constructed so that King Harry's heroic rhetoric easily overwhelms the presentation of its Machiavellian provenance for ideologically predisposed auditors and readers. But it is also clear that once one becomes sensitized to it, the Machiavellian-disclosing material creates this play's peculiar and difficult affect: rather than 'exposing' King Harry as a machiavel, it bids us to accept Machiavellianism as the necessary precondition for his heroism. Henry's Machiavellianism is made to seem 'likeable', and in the great scenes before the Battle of Agincourt we begin to see how this all might be fitted together, when we finally are able to discern something of the likeable young Prince Hal—missing in action since his crown-stealing scenes in *2 Henry IV*—just before his moments of greatest triumph.

---

[52] Gurr, introduction, 12.

A Return to Multiple Selves

In the soliloquy after King Harry's fraternization with the common soldiers in Act 4, his Machiavellian image-construction—that is, his self-presentation as heroic king—is linked with his earlier experiments with shifting identities as Prince Hal, and they elicit audience sympathy and identification when he tells us in effect that the king is but a man doing a very hard job.

As noted above, the choruses play an important part in producing an interpretation of King Harry as folk-hero. And in the opening chorus, a very intriguing phrase had been introduced to capture this projected identity between the person of the King and the legend of him which has come down to Shakespeare's audience:

> O for a Muse of fire, that would ascend
> The brightest heaven of invention:
> A kingdom for a stage, princes to act,
> And monarchs to behold the swelling scene.
> *Then should the warlike Harry, like himself,*
> *Assume the port of Mars.* (Prologue, 1–6)

As I mentioned previously, Linda Charnes in *Notorious Identity* defined that peculiar structure of a number of legendary characters in Shakespeare, in which the customary identities of, say, Troilus and Cressida emerge slowly and contingently from subjectivities much more complex and fluid than the legends which give them identity for their audiences had suggested. In *Henry V* the Chorus is always the voice of that public image of King Harry as folk legend, so that in this idiom King Harry is only truly 'himself' when he 'assume[s] the port of Mars'. But as the play unfolds we learn here as elsewhere in Shakespeare that legend is partial and one-dimensional, and we are presented instead with a Shakespearian representation much more complex, layered, and nuanced than the materials of the legend were. There are in *King Henry V* many traces of the complex selves of Prince Hal we saw displayed and explored in the previous two plays in this series, and this motif comes to a head in the scenes the night before the Battle of Agincourt. We recognize in the images of King Henry at ease with the people given us by the Chorus the outcome of a strong narrative line within the two previous *Henry IV* plays—and there are similar connections within the complex scenes which follow and which contradict the Chorus's descriptions. One of the debates between Prince Hal and his father in *Part 1* had centred over the question as to whether a king should be easily accessible to his common subjects.[53] In the first father–son confrontation of *1 Henry IV*, Henry IV believes that the key to his power is a policy of extremely infrequent exposure to the public:

> By being seldom seen, I could not stir
> But, like a comet, I was wondered at,
> That men would tell their children, 'This is he.' (3.2.46–8)

Concomitantly, Henry conceives of his failed predecessor Richard's political ineptness in terms of the kind of public relations 'overexposure' with which he is charging Hal:

> The skipping King, he ambled up and down
> With shallow jesters, and . . .
> Grew a companion to the common streets,
> Enfeoffed himself to popularity,
> That, being daily swallowed by men's eyes,
> They surfeited with honey, and began
> To loathe the taste of sweetness, whereof a little
> More than a little is by much too much. (3.2.60–73)

This is the context in which the father is unable to understand (what turns out to be) the efficacy of Prince Hal's tavern phase. But in *Henry V* we hear of its success directly from two astute politicians in the opening scene, in the conversation between the two archbishops discussed above, when they agree on their surprise at the 'grace' and 'fair regard' of the young King:

> The courses of his youth promised it not.
> The breath no sooner left his father's body
> But that his wildness, mortified in him,
> Seemed to die too. Yea, at that very moment
> Consideration like an angel, came
> And whipped th'offending Adam out of him,
> Leaving his body as a paradise
> T'envelop and contain celestial spirits.
> Never was such a sudden scholar made;
> Never came reformation in a flood
> With such a heady currance scouring faults;
> Nor never Hydra-headed wilfulness
> So soon did lose his seat—and all at once—
> As in this king. (1.1.25–38)

These remarks represent a complete, retrospective vindication for the strategy first envisioned by the young Prince Hal in the 'Herein will I

[53] Altman, 'Vile Participation', 4–6, makes a similar point in somewhat different terms.

imitate the sun' soliloquy of *Part 1* and the politic interpretation of that resolution in the banishment of Falstaff and company at the end of *Part 2*, a decisive negation of the fears of his father that Hal would prove a disgrace to the hard-earned throne of England. And we might recall as well the Prince's remarks to Poins in *Part 1* after his 'language lesson' from the young, tongue-tied apprentice Francis: 'I have sounded the very base-string of humility. Sirrah, I am sworn brother to a leash of drawers ... and when I am king of England, I shall command all the good lads in Eastcheap' (2.5.5–13). Thus King Henry V's disguise as a commoner and fraternization with his troops retrospectively recode his tavern days as a necessary phase of a hero's education, an immersion in the culture of the common people that enables him to become the charismatic military leader who far surpasses his father in the popular eye. It is even something of a vindication of Falstaff, the main tutor of Hal's tavern education—and Falstaff indeed receives due homage in this play, in a form safely displaced from the Prince's discourse, in the serio-comic narrations of his death early in the play, before the invasion of France. But I will return to that scene below.

In France all the earlier material on Hal's tavern education seems to find fruition in King Harry's great battle-speech—the most famous moment in the play—in which he is able to bridge the considerable class gap between himself, the 'men of quality', and the common troops:

> We few, we happy few, we band of brothers.
> For he today that sheds his blood with me
> Shall be my brother; be he ne'er so vile,
> This day shall gentle his condition.
> And gentlemen in England now abed
> Shall think themselves accursed they were not here,
> And hold their manhoods cheap whiles any speaks
> That fought with us upon Saint Crispin's day. (4.3.60–7)

The discourse of the tavern life is revivified and refunctioned in the masculinist, utopian discourse of 'manhoods' won and lost in feats of battle and bravery. King Henry has here vindicated Falstaff's prescient claim that 'Thou art essentially made without seeming so', the true prince and no counterfeit. As we saw in the previous chapter, once we have worked through Falstaff's dizzying usage of this term, we are forced to gloss this earlier sentence in something of the following way: in a world without essences, to be essentially made is to be a highly efficacious counterfeit, one whose constructedness is never questioned. At the core of King Harry's interiority, we have discovered through his role-playing among the troops and then his belated soliloquy the night before the battle, is not so much a will-to-power as a protesting young man somewhat weary of his authority and his role of warrior-king. Just before the moment of his greatest triumph, we discover that the young prince who had charmed us in two previous plays, contrary to a much quoted dictum of Una Ellis-Fermor,[54] has not been dissolved—just firmly contained. His Machiavellianism, in other words, is presented as one more dutiful role consummately played by this gifted young man still trying to please a dead father. The emptiness noted by so many critics at the end of this play—the emptiness which the bluff comic scene with Princess Catherine attempts to cover over—is perhaps connected with the anticlimactic revelation of the manufactured qualities of King Harry's heroics. He has made himself a hero not by any self-revelation of an inner heroic essence, but by disciplined role-playing. And as with Prince Hal's heroics at the end of *Part 1*, King Harry at Agincourt ratifies his heroic credentials—and his title to the throne of France—in the only way that truly counts in the pragmatic political world of the *Henriad*, on the battlefield.

Thus *Henry V* represents a partial revival of motifs of *1 Henry IV* which had seemed to have disappeared in the more reified world of *2 Henry IV*. In this last play young King Harry is allowed to resume the role-playing which he had seemed to repudiate when he came to the crown, in part because he—and potentially the audience—begins to realize that to be king is essentially to undertake one more extended exercise in role-playing. To be sure, that role is a deadly earnest one, involving decisions leading to widespread destruction and the deaths of thousands. But it is a role nonetheless, and much of the import of the dialogue with the soldiers and the soliloquy that follows it in Act 4 is surely to signal this truth to us; thus King Harry, in his disguise, says of the King:

Therefore, when he sees reason of fears, as we do, his fears, out of doubt, be of the same relish as ours are. Yet, in reason, no man should possess him with any appearance of fear, lest he, by showing it, should dishearten his army. (4.1.104–8)

This discussion of 'the King' (with its numerous double-entendre allusions to his royal identity) is itself an assertion of the distance between the social role of monarch and the person who carries it out. And in his soliloquy King Harry drives home the point again, in the preface to that most revealing of the play's Machiavellian passages (to which I will turn in a moment):

[54] Ellis-Fermor, *Frontiers of Drama*, 45: it is futile 'to look for the personality of Henry behind the king; there is nothing else there. . . . There is no Henry, only a king.'

> O hard condition,
> Twin-born with greatness: subject to the breath
> Of every fool, whose sense no more can feel
> But his own wringing. What infinite heartsease
> Must kings neglect that private men enjoy?
> And what have kings, that privates have not too,
> Save ceremony, save general ceremony? (4.1.215–21)

Somewhat surprisingly then, near the end of the play, we are given a glimpse of that unfixed subjectivity which the young King had seemed to banish irrevocably (along with one of its principal signifiers, Falstaff) at the end of 2 *Henry IV*, and I believe that the awkward comic business after the battle and before the courtship of Catherine, in which the young King indulges in one more practical joke involving disguise and false identity with his new favourites Fluellen and the bluff, honest Michael Williams, is meant to further this recalling of the Prince Hal of 1 *Henry IV* and prepare us for his additional role as a lover and wooer to follow.

This material at the end helps explain what had seemed puzzling earlier in the play, when the King lamented the toll on what we would call his personal life of the Machiavellian intrigue of the conspirators Cambridge, Scroop, and Grey—in particular the treason of Scroop, presented unexpectedly as a close friend:

> Thou that didst bear the key of all my counsels,
> That knew'st the very bottom of my soul,
> That almost mightst ha' coined me into gold,
> Wouldst thou ha' practised on me for thy use;
> May it be possible that foreign hire
> Could out of thee extract one spark of evil
> That might annoy my finger? (2.2.93–9)

In terms of dramatic effectiveness, the lament seems isolated and unconvincing since we have witnessed no manifestation of this friendship, either in this play or in the earlier two featuring Prince Hal. Scroop here seems to stand for the private life generally, that shared gratuitous intersubjectivity contrasted here to the instrumentalized political realm which has become King Harry's element. This episode of betrayal is undoubtedly an allusion to the paranoid culture of treason surrounding the post-Armada Elizabethan court, possibly even one specifically evoking Essex's zeal in detecting—that is, constructing from the readily available cultural materials of anti-Semitism and fear of Catholic Spain—the supposed treachery of Dr Lopez towards Elizabeth. But it is also an episode whose most obvious function seems to be to register some faint resistance to the ongoing reification of subjectivity within the logic of power politics by asserting the values of the personal within a context which seems always to instrumentalize it.[55]

We hear this protest again at one of the play's most privileged moments, just before the battle, in the passage I quoted above lamenting the 'hard condition' of being monarch. There had been, of course, similar complaints from King Henry IV in both *Part 1* and *Part 2*, and King Harry will end his soliloquy with his father's favourite topic on the bad sleep of kings, the easy rest of the poor. In the mouth of his son, however, this theme takes on new meanings, recalling how this king as Prince of Wales resisted the burdens of office by cultivating a multivalent subjectivity for as long as he could. At this climactic point, after all that has happened to the young King's personal life, is an attempt to assert the role of Machiavellian prince as one more aspect of his multi-selved identity rather than, as it seemed at the end of *2 Henry IV*, the role that eats up all the others. King Harry's complaints about the loss of a private life mark for us his new acceptance and mastery of Machiavellian politics, since he sees now that a king must always be conscious of the political effects of his own subjective feelings, even though, as the disguised Harry tells this group of soldiers, the king is but a man: 'His ceremonies laid by, in his nakedness he appears but a man, and though his affections are higher mounted than ours, yet when they stoop, they stoop with the like wing' (4.1.101–4). And later comes a passage which is perhaps the closest in any Shakespearian play to an enunciation of the Machiavellian idea of the aura of monarchy as an effect of the illusory beliefs of its subjects, here figured as 'ceremony':

> And what have kings that privates have not too,
> Save ceremony, save general ceremony?
> And what art thou, thou idol ceremony?
> What kind of god art thou, that suffer'st more
> Of mortal griefs than do thy worshippers?
> What are thy rents? What are thy comings-in?
> O ceremony, show me but thy worth.
> What is thy soul of adoration?
> Art thou aught else but place, degree, and form,
> Creating awe and fear in other men? (4.1.220–9)

The form of this remarkable passage is reminiscent of Falstaff's catechism on honour from the end of *Part 1*: here King Harry identifies a reified belief carrying great weight in the world of men and poses a series of deflating

---

[55] Dollimore and Sinfield, 'History and Ideology', similarly see this soliloquy as a major instance of the play's registering of ideological faultlines.

questions which reveal the abstraction to be a phantasm of the collective social imagination—an 'idol', as King Harry puts it here, in anticipation of the use of the word in a similar deflating context in *Troilus and Cressida*.[56] The last rhetorical question in the above quote, in particular, identifies the aura of the monarchy, 'ceremony', to be entirely a function of social structure, ideology, and culture held in place, like an idolatrous god, by popular superstition. As Louis Montrose put it in a brief but telling discussion of this speech, King Harry here 'evokes both the polemical religious discourse against images, vestments, and plays, and the politic Machiavellian discourse on the utility of state spectacles'.[57] Montrose goes on to point out, quite correctly in my view, that King Harry's diagnosis of ceremony's purpose as creating 'awe and fear in other men' is more or less identical with what Greenblatt called 'Machiavellian anthropology' in 'Invisible Bullets'. This remarkable soliloquy is, as Montrose argues, a clear instance of demystification of royal power in the commercial theatre[58]—but also a moment in the play when Voltaire's dictum on Machiavellianism is most flagrantly violated, the moment when the play's Machiavellianism announces itself as such. And it is also the moment when King Harry seems more Montaignean than at any moment since his speech on small beer in *2 Henry IV*, since he is also affirming the malleability of human nature and the self.

Following this remarkably open Machiavellianism-Montaigneism, however, the passage swerves in a much more conventional direction in which the young King complains that the burden of his kingly aura keeps him from a good night's sleep, and the peasant is better off not realizing all this and so sleeping well.

Defeat is proverbially an orphan, but victory has a thousand fathers. The success of this young King's campaign in France seems to justify all his crooked steps to the crown and both of his 'fathers' in *Henry IV* and makes his Machiavellianism both the fulfilment of Falstaff's training in the finer points of fellowship, subjectivity, and counterfeiting as well as the accomplished duty of a prodigal son now reconciled with his father. Although this play does not recall it explicitly, viewers and readers of *2 Henry IV* will remember King Henry IV's deathbed advice to Prince Hal for securing a claim to the throne that would be stronger in a succeeding son than it was in a upstart father:

---

[56] ''Tis mad idolatry I To make the service greater than the god,' says Hector (2.2.56–7), diagnosing a good deal of the problem of both sides of the Trojan War in this play. The term appears two other times as well; see Grady, *Shakespeare's Universal Wolf,* 89–94, for an analysis.   [57] Montrose, *The Purpose of Playing,* 84.
[58] Ibid. 84–5.

> for what in me was purchased,
> Falls upon thee in a more fairer sort;
> So thou the garland wear'st successively.
> Yet though thou stand'st more sure than I could do,
> Thou art not firm enough, since griefs are green,
> And all my friends—which thou must make thy friends—
> Have but their stings and teeth newly ta'en out,
> By whose fell working I was first advanced,
> And by whose power I well might lodge a fear
> To be again displaced; which to avoid,
> I cut some off, and had a purpose now
> To lead out many to the Holy Land,
> Lest rest and lying still might make them look
> Too near unto my state. Therefore, my Harry,
> Be it thy course to busy giddy minds
> With foreign quarrels, that action hence borne out,
> May waste the memory of the former days. (4.3.327–43)

Thus Harry V's heroic conquest of France is the fulfilment of a son's duty and, as has long been noted, also a Machiavellian ploy to consolidate the questionable title to the throne of England by championing an equally dubious one to the throne of France. Once more the counterfeit passes for gold because everything is always already counterfeit, and what counts is its efficacy. These ideas seem to be here, as elsewhere in the tetralogy, taken for granted and unexceptional.

In short, then, the victory of Agincourt is used in this play to recall the multiple selves of Prince Hal which had been repressed in *2 Henry IV*. He emerges after the battle as warrior, dutiful son, playful jokester, and plebeian empathizer, as well as hero-king, and he is inducted into a comic ending of successful wooing and marriage to round-off his complete coming to manhood.

The problem is, of course, that it does not quite work. On the one hand, the King's weariness with power is part of his heroism and humanity, re-enforcing the ideologies of royalism and 'positive' Machiavellianism, which, as we have seen, constitute the most accessible, most strongly thematized elements of this dissonant play. But the play's strongly fore-grounded narrative line whereby Hal's previous struggles with multiple identities and affirmation of unfixed subjectivity become instrumentalized to produce a hero-king and Machiavellian master is supplemented with fainter but quite discernible counter-narrative in which we see the dark side of the heroic Hal, in the death and destruction his war with France creates. The strength of this 'dark matter' prevents the cohering of the synthesis which we can discern, but not assent to. And central to these effects is this play's treatment of a plebeian world spectators had come to know and love over three previous plays.

Henry V's *Plebeian World*

Any audience members who remembered fondly the tavern world of *1 Henry IV* would have to be made uneasy by two incidents which remind us of the costs of Harry's Machiavellian policies: the offstage death of Falstaff and the hanging of Bardolph in France. But each of these takes place within the newly reconfigured context making up the changed circumstances of this new play. In *Henry V* the trajectory from *1 Henry IV* to *2 Henry IV*, in which the plebeian world evolves from being a kind of utopian counter-culture to that of a site of worldly abuses and commodification,[59] continues and intensifies so that in this third play the plebeian world is almost completely devalued and serves as a thematic vehicle for the display of the unsavoury and inglorious side of warfare. This crucial side of *1 Henry IV* is thus never revived in *Henry V*, and this gap is one of the reasons the projected synthesis I have just discussed does not hold together. Crucial thematic differences between the plebeian world of *Henry V* and that of the two previous plays (and especially *Part 1*) become clear particularly because there are important continuities in the structural function of the plebeian world which provide a clear framework for perceiving the differences.

As in the previous two plays, the plebeian scenes here both recapitulate and preview themes of the political plot in a comic but complexly ambivalent mode. Our first glimpse of our old friends from Eastcheap (including Corporal Nim, who was in *The Merry Wives of Windsor* but neither of the two *Henry IV* plays) also introduces us to the theme of division-among-friends which will receive more serious and consequential treatment in the incident of the treachery of the three English lords which I previously discussed. In the tavern world, it is a matter of bad blood between Pistol, now married to Mistress Quickly, and Nim, who says he had been engaged to the hostess and she has been untrue to him. Along the lines we have seen before there is much blustering and threatening, with Bardolph playing the role of mediator in the name of good fellowship—this time with the

---

[59] The muted but still comic and genial atmospherics of Falstaff and company in *The Merry Wives of Windsor* to my mind are outside this trajectory. In that play the tavern world confronts an erotic-domestic domain related to the one we saw in *1 Henry IV*, but which was missing in *2 Henry IV*. But without the political-military worlds of the histories to reflect on and complexly parody, the domestic seems less significant in *The Merry Wives of Windsor*.

added incentive of action brewing in France, where the three will ultimately debark. Bardolph here enacts a comic version of his former boon
companion's Machiavellian strategy of busying giddy minds with foreign
wars. In this comic version, however, the domestic peace-making in the
cause of foreign adventure is a precarious business, as we learn after
Bardolph has brought the two to a handshake with his own threats:

NIM. I will cut thy throat, one time or other, in fair terms: that is the humour of it.
PISTOL. *Couple a gorge,*
    That is the word. I thee defy again. (2.1.62–5)

We will of course hear much more about throat-cutting before this play
ends: Pistol here, comically and proleptically, enunciates a major subject
of the play's treatment of war. And the peace between Nim and Pistol is
finally achieved only when Pistol agrees to pay the money he owed Nim
from a previous bet—shades of the tacit agreement between King Harry
and the archbishops over church property. But the exchange also recalls
the commodification of friendship that had marked Falstaff's dealings
with almost everyone in *2 Henry IV*. As we are reminded immediately,
when Falstaff's diminutive page from *2 Henry IV* and *The Merry Wives*
enters to give us news of his master's worsening health, the tone of this
tavern world without its loquacious Lord of Misrule is considerably
bleaker than it was even in the darker moments of *2 Henry IV*, and we are
simply in a different world from the tavern-pastoral of the opening of
Part 1. In this context Nim seems purposefully designed to reinforce this
bleakness. Like most of the minor characters of Falstaff's tavern world, he
is given a recurrent verbal style—in this case, as in *The Merry Wives*, it is a
trick of repeating variations of the word 'humour'. But in this play the
trick often seems tedious, more an index of his taciturnity and ill temper,
with much less wit than was evident in his previous play. Pistol, Bardolph,
and Mistress Quickly are more or less continuous with their previous
selves, but the overall effect is a dark one. It is given to Prince Hal's former
boon companions to enunciate the underside of the idealizing rhetoric of
warfare we have heard from the Chorus in terms completely devoid of
Falstaff's rationalizations and wit:

> Let us to France, like horseleeches, my boys,
> To suck, to suck, the very blood to suck! (2.4.46–7)

The plebeian is no longer a *parody* of the instrumental cruelty of dynastic
warfare, as it was (among other things) in the previous two plays. Pistol's
bilingual blustering about throat-cutting in this comic scene is not very
funny here and will seem far from comic in Act 4, after the order to kill

prisoners has been given. Thus rather than a parody, the plebeian world in many ways has *become* the cruel underside of conquest—that underside which King Harry, in his casuistic debates the night before Agincourt, will disavow as not the responsibility of the king. Machiavelli had of course pointed out the advantages of the prince's disavowing his own agents of cruelty at the right moment, when their work was done, and the play itself seems to enact such a politic separation, making it almost plausible. The gap between King Harry's intentions and his dark followers is underlined again, even more pointedly, when Nim responds to Bardolph's echoing of King Harry's celebrated 'Once more unto the breach, dear friends, once more' by urging that they stay put to avoid the risks of injury (3.2.2–4). In this play, at least after the death of Falstaff, the plebeian tavern world, which had seemed so rich in *1 Henry IV* and which provided a telling commentary on the abuses of power (while illustrating them) in *Part 2*, has become a depressing and sordid Jonsonian place with few or no redeeming qualities and with a complete separation from the new world of King Harry. This motif is climaxed when Bardolph is hanged, and the only commentary on this is King Harry's clipped, 'We would have all such offenders so cut off' (3.6.98).

Enter Fluellen

The turning point in the treatment of the old tavern world in this play occurs just after the parody of King Harry's call to the breach, with the entrance (for the first time in the play) of the Welsh captain Fluellen, who tries to enforce the King's orders rather than, Falstaff-like, wink at their subversion. His status as a kind of anti-Falstaff, on the side, say, of the Chief Justice rather than the tavern world, is affirmed when Nim objects to his beating them in an effort to arouse them to battle with the remark, 'Your honour runs bad humours' (3.2.26), an echo of his earlier comment on how King Harry's rejection of Falstaff had left the latter in poor health: 'The King hath run bad humours on the knight, that's the even of it' (2.2.110–11).

This is the moment when Falstaff's page, who had accompanied Pistol, Bardolph, and Nim to France, has an epiphany concerning these three survivors from happier times—and it is a moment which once more retrospectively recodes (even more pejoratively than before) the entire tavern world of the last three plays of the *Henriad*. In the page's newly opened eyes, these three are cowards and thieves unworthy of his service:

As young as I am, I have observed these three swashers. I am boy to them all three, but all they three, though they would serve me, could not be man to me, for, indeed, three such antics do not amount to a man. . . . I must leave them, and seek some better service. Their villainy goes against my weak stomach, and therefore I must cast it up. (3.2.27–49)

Almost ruthlessly, the survivors of the tavern world hereafter face death or humiliation. Nim joins Bardolph on the gallows (4.4.64), and the page is apparently one of the English boys slaughtered by the French in the atrocity at the camp. Only Pistol is left alive at the play's end, but he has been humiliated by Fluellen, and he reports the death of his Nell (Mistress Quickly) 'of a malady of France' (5.1.73).

The penultimate comment on the tavern world is given by Fluellen's English comrade Captain Gower in defence of both Fluellen and the leeks he wears as a symbol of Welsh national pride:

Go, go, you are a counterfeit cowardly knave. Will you mock at an ancient tradition, begun upon an honourable respect and worn as a memorable trophy of predeceased valour, and dare not avouch in your deeds any of your words? (5.1.62–5)

This reappearance of *counterfeit* near the end of the *Henriad*—the word had been used earlier in the play, also in regard to Pistol, by Captain Gower[60]—marks King Harry's Machiavellian triumph. This word, as I argued in the previous chapter, signified in *1 Henry IV* the Machiavellian condition of the political world of the *Henriad*, in which all titles to power are always already counterfeit because legitimacy is a fiction established by the most deft political practitioner. At the end of this one, after we have just witnessed one of the crowning demonstrations of this truth, with title to France now parcelled out to Harry after his military triumph, the term *counterfeit* stabilizes, in marked contrast to the profligacy it had assumed in the mouth of Falstaff at the Battle of Shrewsbury in *Part 1*. It now refers, in a quite commonsensical manner, to the peculiar combination of a blustering outside and an inner cowardice which has been Pistol's practice throughout his three plays. With the consolidation of Harry's power through the uniting of the British nationalities, the subordination or elimination of the counter-cultures, and now the conquest of France, the fiction of legitimacy has been so powerfully established that a counterfeit is now just a counterfeit again. The fictions of power are always at their zenith when they are invisible as fictions.[61]

---

[60] The earlier usage is omitted in the Oxford-based Norton text used here, even though it occurs in the Folio version of the play, but it is listed as a textual variant at 3.6.56; see *The Norton Shakespeare*, ed. Greenblatt, 1522.

[61] Cf. Calderwood, *Metadrama in Shakespeare's Henriad*, 162–81, who sees in *Henry V* the

The distance between the plebeian world of the opening of *1 Henry IV*
and that at the end of *Henry V* can be fathomed in the very last shard of the
discourse of the tavern world, the exit lines of Pistol. Falstaff's earlier
counterfactual carnival-aesthetic rhetoric, which had created alternative
utopian realities serving to expose the pretension of the ideologies of
power, is now completely absent. Instead of Falstaff's 'minions of the
moon', instead even of Pistol's usual Marlovian bombast, we hear
rhetorical but straightforward affirmations of prostitution, theft, and
lying—if also a kind of plebeian will to survive; Pistol leaves us for all the
world sounding like the very ancestor of Faulkner's Abner Snopes:

> Old I do wax, and from my weary limbs
> Honour is cudgelled. Well, bawd I'll turn,
> And something lean to cutpurse of quick hand.
> To England will I steal, and there I'll steal,
> And patches will I get unto these cudgelled scars,
> And swear I got them in the Gallia wars. (5.1.75–80)

Armies for Taverns

The tavern world, then, has now become completely discredited—as well
as virtually extinct. It has been replaced in this play by the militaristic,
multinational fellowship of Scene 3.3, the one immediately following the
page's epiphany, in which the three Celtic nations of the British Isles are
represented by Captains MacMorris (Ireland), Jamy (of Scotland), and
the aforementioned Welsh Captain Fluellen. All are presented as speaking
garbled English but as valorous representatives of their nations in service
to English hegemony—however much Fluellen may suspect Captain
MacMorris's competence or the loyalty of 'many of [MacMorris's]
nation' (3.3.60). They are all gentlemen, and Fluellen in particular henceforth serves as a kind of substitute for the discredited, extinct tavern world,
a (slightly off-centre) voice of military discipline by the book and self-
assured judge of right and wrong. Like Falstaff, he is a comic character
living in a counterfactual world, one in which the bloody business of warfare is humanized and ennobled by what he continually calls the 'laws of
war' or 'the disciplines of war'. An important part of the humour derives
from the way in which, as an imperfectly imperialized subject, he repro-
duces England's hegemonic ideology in a fractured, off-centred way, and
it is this 'off-centre' quality which allows him to be used for critical and

triumph of a pragmatic rhetoric that re-establishes rhetorically a supposedly severed relation
between signifier and signified.

ironic purposes at one of the play's crucial moments, as we will see. But Fluellen's basic positivity (from the point of view of the play's hegemonic ideology) is ratified for us by King Harry himself, who remarks:

> Though it appear a little out of fashion,
> There is much care and valour in this Welshman. (4.1.82–3)

Similarly, the soldiers encountered by the disguised King Harry are neither the subversive tavern parasites and highwaymen of *1 and 2 Henry IV* nor the 'pitiful rascals' who made up Captain Falstaff's company of foot. These soldiers speak as loyal, albeit plebeian subjects, suspicious of the class privileges of those above them (the King especially) but determined to perform their duties selflessly for all that. There is class difference, but not a hint of class conflict. Instead, these social antagonisms are firmly subordinated to King Harry's Machiavellian politics of English hegemony and French conquest.[62] Thus when King Harry begins his legendary, disguised interactions with the common soldiers before the Battle of Agincourt, he has entered into a transformed plebeian realm.

The place held by the rebels in the architecture of the previous two plays of the trilogy is here held by the French, and their treatment—for anyone critical of jingoism and the dehumanization of political enemies—is appalling. They are consistently presented as vain, falsely confident, under-appreciatory of English valour and military prowess—cardboard characters attesting to this play's uncharacteristic (for Shakespeare) representation of a set of characters constructed almost solely as foils to English valour, with almost no autonomous viewpoint of their own. Instead of a world view, the French, like the Welsh of *1 Henry IV*, are given an incomprehensible language,[63] snippets of a kind of French which make up a fair amount of their dialogue, a device guaranteeing that the great majority of the audience not knowing French will perceive them as incomprehensible Others, not, like most of the rebels of the two earlier plays, members of a common community. Thus the French are more consistently made a representative of the Other than in either version of the rebels of the *Henry IV* plays, and this substitution forms the context for the domestication of Welshness which is one of the novel features of *Henry V*. In

---

[62] Dollimore and Sinfield, 'History and Ideology', argued that this unifying effect was the main work of ideology in the play, but that it was also shown to be susceptible to the tensions which underlay it in an analysis related to my own views of the play's ideological repressions creative of a political unconscious.

[63] As opposed to the Welsh of *1 Henry IV*, this foreign language is transcribed, and the scene between Catherine and her maid requires for comprehension knowledge of French obscenities, suggesting that the players assumed the French comprehensible to at least a portion of the audience. French was studied by many in the upper classes.

1 Henry IV, as we saw, Owen Glendŵr and his followers, especially in the figure of the alluring, non-English-speaking Lady Mortimer, figured an exotic feminine Otherness which at once called into question the military rationalism of both sides of the rebellion and warned of the 'effeminacy' which awaited those who might give in to her allure. But in *Henry V* the French are placed into this space of Otherness which had previously been occupied by the Welsh, with the female embodiment of Otherness—here Catherine rather than Lady Mortimer—presented as the conquered rather than conqueror and one who becomes Anglicized as Kate while she does her best to learn English. With the French holding the place of the Other, the Welsh in this play are made honorary Englishmen, with, as I indicated, pride of place given to the sturdy Captain Fluellen, successor to Falstaff, tamer and humilator of Pistol, and spokesman for ancient military virtues reincarnated in the English army. In this role, as Terence Hawkes very cogently pointed out, Fluellen represents the outcome of the process of colonization of Wales which had been a particularly Tudor, sixteenth-century project.[64] His very name is an Anglicization of Llewellyn, the name of the last Welsh Prince of Wales, and its opening phoneme—whose 'pronunciation is a major Welsh shibboleth', according to Hawkes—has become 'brutally reduced'.[65] Thus, concludes Hawkes, 'in Fluellen's name a maimed linguistic ghost stirs, rattles its English cage, and hints darkly at things that are now literally unspeakable'.[66] Fluellen, with Captains MacMorris and Jamy symbolically behind him, unites the imagined community of Britain in triumph against England's historical enemy France. In what is perhaps the hubristic height of this play's nationalism, King Harry uses the occasion of his bilingual wooing of Catherine to project one more stage in the process of English empire-building, this time one in which the French, like the Welsh before them, are assimilated to English hegemony, with a new Other:

Shall not thou and I, between Saint Denis and Saint George, compound a boy, half French half English, that shall go to Constantinople and take the Turk by the beard? Shall we not? What sayst thou, my fair flower-de-luce? (5.2.193–7)

The merry wooing of Catherine by King Harry with which this play concludes—so oddly reminiscent of similar scenes of realist domestic comedy in *The Taming of the Shrew*, down to the heroine's pet name[67]—

[64] Hawkes, 'Bryn Glas'.
[65] Ibid. 133.
[66] Ibid. 134.
[67] The name also links her with Hotspur's wife Kate in *1 and 2 Henry IV*. Samuel Johnson

has been seen by a number of critics as a transparent attempt to conjure up a happy ending for a play which diverged oddly into untriumphant complexities as it was representing Harry's great victory at Agincourt. I want to suggest here that the echoes of the much earlier *The Taming of the Shrew* in a very different genre might have to do with the inspired, ideology-exposing moment of that much debated play, when Katherine learns the trick of managing Petruccio's overbearing 'taming' of her. She learns simply to agree with him, even though it is clear that she continues to believe that the sun is not the moon and that Petruccio understands very clearly that she continues to believe this (because, after all, so does he).[68]

King Harry's own references to the sun and moon perhaps echo this very passage. In any case, the implied audience of *Henry V* is called to a very similar act of unbelieving assent as to King Harry's legitimacy as king—now of France as well as England. Princess Catherine in this play is called to another operation of fictionalizing when she is wooed by young Harry to consent freely to take him and love him, while both she and he are perfectly aware that, in the Princess's words, 'Dat is as it shall please de *roi mon père* (5.2.229), and as Harry knows, the marriage is one of the terms of the peace treaty being drawn up. This business with the courtship, then, while it provides an upbeat conclusion to a play with much dark material, serves also as a last commentary on the Machiavellian production of statecraft which we have been privileged to watch throughout this play. Everyone is much happier, this ending tells us, when raw political power is decently veiled by the appearances of gentility and unforced accord. The mystery, of course, is why the play itself so consistently if unobtrusively violates this practice.

Henry V's Political Unconscious

The Chorus has continually presented us with a similarly upbeat, epic narration of a legendary heroism which the following scenes proceeded to complicate, qualify, or darken when they did not (as in Act 4) simply contradict it.[69] We hear the eloquent piety of England's young hero-king sandwiched between scenes which imply the manipulated, manufactured nature of the King's apparent sincerity and piety. We watch an unfolding

complained that Shakespeare had unaccountably made King Harry a replica of Hotspur in these last scenes.

[68] Shakespeare, *The Taming of the Shrew*, 4.6.

[69] A number of critics have delineated the gap between the Chorus's narration and what is narrated in the scenes introduced by the choruses. A particularly cogent analysis is given by Gurr, introduction, 6–16.

story of national unification and national conquest that at the same time entails the destruction of the holiday world and carnival community which had educated the King in the commoners' values and beliefs which he so successfully manipulates. We hear repeated references to the miseries of warfare, its destruction of the innocent, the hardships of the wounded, the widows and orphans it creates, in a play overflowing with martial enthusiasm and excitement and the near sacralization of the military triumphs of this young warrior king.[70]

We are used to this playwright's propensity to present us with dialogically organized investigations of competing viewpoints, resistant to any univocal interpretation or point of view, especially in the earlier three plays of the second historical tetralogy of which this play serves as climax and terminus. But *Henry V* presents us with interpretative problems of a different order from those we have dealt with heretofore. We are not here seeing the same events as they are simultaneously and disparately interpreted through opposing political factions and ideologies (as in *Richard II*), nor as they are interpreted from differing class, gender, ideological, and lifeworld perspectives as in *1 and 2 Henry IV*. Instead, in *Henry V* we witness a single Machiavellian political philosophy and practice, as seen simultaneously from 'inside' and 'outside'. Given the nature of Machiavellian deception, this kind of presentation should have the effect—as it does in *Richard III*—of exposing the duplicity of the prince and so subverting the entire structure of deception. However, the play has this effect, as its critical and performance history shows, only for very close readers and anti-statist, anti-war critics. And these, like Hazlitt, are more likely to complain that the play itself is a failure than to read it as a subtle exposé of the deceptions of absolutism.[71] Stephen Greenblatt, as I indicated previously, faced up to this anomaly more squarely than most with his flat assertions in 'Invisible Bullets' that the play inducts us into support for power's manipulations of ourselves. As I indicated previously, this gets at something crucial about the play. But what of the 'darker' materials that so many critics since Hazlitt have discerned and explicated? These critical, anti-war and anti-imperialist thematics are a consistent counterpoint which creates a 'political unconscious' within the play. They coexist with and contradict the play's more strongly thematized, as it were, 'conscious'

[70] Altman, 'Vile Participation', 31, shows how at moments in the ambivalent development of King Harry he seems to have a distinctly sacred aura, such as in the aftermath of the Battle of Agincourt.

[71] This comparatively rare position in the history of commentary on *Henry V* was eloquently voiced—clearly in the context of the horrors of the First World War—by Gould, 'A New Reading of "Henry V"'.

elements celebrating war and conquest. Nor are these materials the property of any organized viewpoint, in the way that similar critical materials in *1 and 2 Henry IV* were to be found in the plebeian and the female-domestic discourses. Here the critical elements are a dispersed set of local 'resistances' to an ideology which is elsewhere exemplified and celebrated throughout the piece, not really a coherent dialogical alternative to the play's Machiavellian ideology. One component is made up by the play's repeated references to violence, death, widows, orphans, and pauperism—a discourse often in the mouth of King Harry (in his speech to the Archbishop in 1.2) and before the gates of Harfleur.

However, when we hear this discourse from the mouth of one of the common soldiers the night before a historical battle, the dramatic effect is quite different:

> But if the cause be not good, the King himself hath a heavy reckoning to make, when all those legs and arms and heads chopped off in battle shall join together at the latter day, and cry all, 'We died at such a place'—some swearing; some crying for a surgeon, some upon their wives left poor behind them, some upon the debts they owe, some upon their children rawly left. I am afeard there are few die well that die in battle, for how can they charitably dispose of any thing, when blood is their argument? Now, if these men do not die well, it will be a black matter for the King that led them to it–who to disobey were against all proportion of subjection. (4.1.128–38)

Of course one of the unstated propositions of Machiavelli's reification of power (see Chapter 2) is that it functions regardless of the end to which it is theoretically subordinated; Machiavellian power is instrumental, subversive of any end which would try to contain it, and a recognition of power's instrumental character is a hallmark of all those later plays, like *Troilus and Cressida*, which mark Shakespeare's complete separation from the Machiavellian moment of the *Henriad* and the beginning of the critical treatment of power which characterizes the Jacobean tragedies and tragicomedies. When we hear King Harry's casuistic reply to Michael Williams's trenchant comments, we note that the King ignores the question of the justice of his cause in line with the hidden logic of Machiavellianism. He focuses instead on the issue of individual salvation and the king's responsibility for the souls of those fallen in battle, and the bluff soldier Michael Williams agrees readily with this proposition: ''Tis certain, every man that dies ill, the ill upon his own head. The King is not to answer it' (4.1.173–4). But Michael Williams's first argument, that the destruction of war can only be excused by a just cause, remains unanswered and uncontested. If we remember that in the beginning of the play the justification involved the dubious legalisms of the Archbishop of Canterbury's argument against the applicability of the Salic Law to Henry's claim to France—and if we remember the crooked byways through which Henry's own claim through his father was established—the effect here in Act 4 is certainly critical. In short, the conversations the night before the battle, at this particular juncture in any case, constitute one of the loci of this play's dispersed political unconscious.

An additional, and more dramatic one, is constituted by the complex matter of the English killing of the French prisoners ordered by King Harry. This action, too, at one level, is an instance of Machiavellian realpolitik, another example of necessity and the 'good' use of cruelty. But this is clearly a grisly business for any audience—especially so if, as I think, Gary Taylor's argument that the prisoners must have been killed on stage is correct.[72]

The English killings, it is true, are immediately 'balanced' by a French atrocity—the killing of the boys in the camp, presumably including Falstaff's appealing page who had just seen through the three swaggerers he had followed to the wars. Gower, of course, in a claim that violates the chronology of events just dramatized for us, justifies the slaying of the prisoners as retribution for the French attack on the boys, while Fluellen's denunciation of the French atrocity as 'expressly against the law of wars' implicitly excuses the English bloodshed and suggests that it was sanctioned by those same rules of war.[73]

But in the complex dynamics of this climactic series of actions we see not only the 'hardest' moments of the play's Machiavellian ideology illustrated (wholesale 'necessary' killing before our eyes as exemplifying cruelty used well), but this incident also serves as an occasion for the interrogation of that ideology, through indirection and emotions, creative of perhaps the most significant moment of an implied, subtextual, or politically unconscious anti-Machiavellianism.

We can of course, interpret the prisoner-killing according to Machiavellian ideology, as do Fluellen and Gower, assimilating the English killing of the French prisoners to a positive view of a heroic Henry as Fluellen does in his exclamation: 'the king most worthily hath caused every soldier

[72] Taylor, introduction, 32–4.

[73] See Andrew Gurr, '"Henry V" and the Bees' Commonwealth', *Shakespeare Survey*, 30 (1977), 61–72, for an illuminating discussion of the conflicting views of 16th-century commentators on the morality of killing prisoners, one that effectively refutes claims of several earlier critics that Fluellen's 'rules of wars' unequivocally allowed such actions. Gurr also shows that Shakespeare chose a version of the historical incident which is more unfavourable to the English action than many others would have been.

to cut his prisoner's throat. O 'tis a gallant king' (4.7.7–8). But these phrases are a prime example of how Fluellen's slightly 'off' command of English and ideology can create critical, ironic effects for the audience. We can also intuit that Fluellen quite seriously seems to think of the killings as effectively answering a French atrocity by taking timely and decisive action in the heat of battle. Knowing Machiavellians, more inclusively, should, if they are (to use a favourite New Critical expression) 'tough-minded' enough, be able to 'register' the cruelty of the order (a cruelty which Holinshed had alluded to in his narration) while admiring the King's cool-headed recognition of necessity. It is an action, of course, absolutely congruent with the play's dehumanization of the French and celebration of Machiavellianism.

However, we survivors of four centuries of Machiavellian modernity are much more likely to see each of these stances as ideological and register in our own reactions an ironic 'unconscious' within the text of the inherent brutality of the act. Fluellen's distinction between the evil child-killers and the virtuous prisoner-slayers dissolves for us into a perception of equivalent atrocities which speak for themselves in condemnation even of a 'just war', without any guiding commentary within the play.

Are these merely the reactions of later audiences, more sentimental and weak-stomached than the Elizabethans? There is, I believe, material in *Henry V*, beyond the parodic tone of Fluellen's exclamation, resistant of such an assumption; I mean the short scene showing Pistol's negotiations with his hapless prisoner Le Fer, who gives a momentary human face to the French prisoners. But we are troubled because this play, while it supplies us with material for these judgements, also inducts us into a pervasive nationalist glorification of the English and denigration of the French. Even with its moments of resistance to the cruelty of war which the play's Machiavellianism justifies, *Henry V* resists pacifist interpretation even more than it resists the purely nationalist celebrations of conquering Harry which dominate its critical history. That is, these local moments of anti-war spirit become overwhelmed by the flood of nationalism and war-enthusiasm loosed by the play's main events and rhetoric.

A reader or member of an audience who attempts to 'take in' this darker material—like Gerald Gould, the critic cited above for whom this play, after the mass carnage of the First World War, could only be read as an ironic exposure of war and its ideological justifications—can either attempt to work against the emotional grain of the drama and interpret the whole as an exposure of jingoism and political deception, thus 'saving

Shakespeare'; or conclude that the play is ideologically incoherent because it seems at several key moments to question the ideology which it everywhere else explicates and celebrates. Consciousness of this particular 'either-or' choice, I believe, is in fact the best solution to this play's contradictory materials.

All the negatives which are implicit in Fluellen's and Gower's black celebration of Henry's order, all the second thoughts concerning the play's glorification of warfare and conquest which are aroused in us by the killings of the comical Le Fer and the insightful Boy, migrate to one of the truly odd, off-centre moments of the play which comes in the immediate wake of our discovery of the killing of the boys, Fluellen's fractured comparison of King Harry with Alexander the Great—Alexander the Pig, as he has it in his stage-dialect, and the shocking association of Alexander with swine is underlined by Gower's correction of Fluellen and Fluellen's defence of his 'variations':

FLUELLEN. . . . Captain Gower, what call you the town's name where Alexander the Pig was porn?
GOWER. Alexander the Great.
FLUELLEN. Why, I pray you, is not 'pig' great? The pig or the great or the mighty or the huge or the magnanimous are all one reckonings, save the phrase is a little variations. (4.7.9–15)

Andrew Gurr has thrown important light on this serio-comic moment through his researches into the traditional discussion of the morality of wars of conquest and of the killing of prisoners. The latter practice was both defended and excused by different writers, with most agreeing that circumstances were crucial in coming to a judgement on this question. But Erasmus had specifically condemned the historical King Henry's order to slay the prisoners, and Augustine, whose just-war theories originated the archive of Christian writings on the subject, had specifically condemned the wars of Alexander the Great as unjustifiable.[74] All this gives an early modern gloss to lines which otherwise seem uncannily late modern in their shock-effect. And Fluellen goes on to press his point on the resemblance of King Harry to Alexander the Pig:[75]

If you mark Alexander's life well, Harry of Monmouth's life is come after it indifferent well. For there is figures in all things. Alexander, God knows, and you

[74] Gurr, ' "Henry V" and the Bees' Commonwealth', 68–9.
[75] Cf. David Quint, 'Alexander the Pig: Shakespeare on History and Poetry', *Boundary 2*, 10 (1982), 49–63; and Hawkes, 'Bryn Glas', 133–5, on the critical politics implied by Fluellen's remarks on Alexander.

know, in his rages and his furies and his wraths and his cholers and his moods
and his displeasures and his indignations, and also being a little intoxicates in
his prains, did in his ales and his angers, look you, kill his best friend, Cleitus—
GOWER. Our King is not like him in that. He never killed any of his friends.
FLUELLEN. It is not well done, mark you now, to take the tales out of my mouth
ere it is made and finished. I speak but in the figures and comparisons of it. As
Alexander killed his friend Cleitus, being in his ales and his cups, so also Harry
Monmouth, being in his right wits and his good judgements, turned away the fat
knight with the great-belly doublet—he was full of jests and gipes and knaveries
and mocks—I have forgot his name. (4.7.25–42)

This includes, as Gary Taylor thought, a joke about the controversy over
Falstaff's earlier name, Oldcastle, but Gower, and everyone in the
audience, knows that it is also a reference to the figure who had been
promised us at the end of 2 Henry IV but who had been killed off in the
beginnings of this play offstage in another great serio-comic moment.
And we remember that Falstaff's death, according to his boon companions, was a direct result of his rejection by the King, so that the comparison is even more apt than Fluellen is aware. And this moment of
vertiginous undermining of the play's major ideology and subtext is
reminiscent of Falstaff in one crucial way: with his inadvertent and
apparently unintended diagnosis of the horrors of wars of conquest,
Fluellen, who has up to this point been a figure much more reminiscent of
Falstaff's old nemesis the Lord Chief Justice than of the transgressive Sir
John himself, surprisingly fills Falstaff's large shoes by enunciating the
play's most pointed moment of ideological subversion.

This revelation of King Harry's unsavoury parallel to Alexander the Pig,
protected as it is by jokes and analogies, is among the most nearly explicit
of the anti-Machiavellian materials in the play which make up its political
unconscious. It is reinforced in the immediate action when King Harry
enters, full of indignation at the French killing of the boys, and threatening again to kill more prisoners. But it is lost, first in the comic byplay
around the confusions of identity involving the King, Fluellen, and
Michael Williams—these, as we saw, bring us back to remembrance of the
likeable madcap Prince Hal, with his practical jokes and shifting identities,
preparing us for the merry King Harry of the wooing of Catherine—and
then in the immediately following reports of the overwhelming English
victory in terms of the numbers killed on both sides, at which point the
interpellation of this complex figure into his own legend is culminated.
Again, instead of being pointedly thematized, such quiet, critical moments
get lost in bigger ones that follow.

The Dissidence of Dissonance

These kaleidoscopic presentations of King Harry recapitulate at the end of the play the three main ways in which he has been presented to us, which I defined above: the play by and large celebrates him as a conquering hero; it justifies the Machiavellian policies which were distributed throughout the play for those not ideologically immune from detecting them; and it registers local moments of resistance to and protest against Machiavellianism. This play, which, as we saw earlier, a number of critics have noted as structurally singular within Shakespeare's works for its choruses, is singular in the structure of its dissonance. The two images projected by this play of King Harry—and, by extension, of monarchy itself—are not, it is worth saying again, presented as dialogic alternatives. Instead the play *Henry V* gives us two competing subtexts for the motivation of its principal hero the King: he is, as the Chorus tells us and as a prominent line of critics and reviewers has dutifully repeated to us for more than two centuries, 'the mirror of all Christian kings', a sincere, law-abiding, duty-fulfilling king who also fulfils popular expectations and displays a popular touch throughout. But at the same time (as Hazlitt first hinted in print), he is a Machiavellian producer of the above image through a technology of self-production and self-representation much more calculated than the image which the public's perception of him would countenance, but which we in the audience of this play can perceive and contemplate. This second subtext is clearly the more inclusive of the two, once we notice it—although critical history demonstrates that many readers and audiences fail to notice it, or downplay it. I believe this has been possible because, like certain ideologically disturbing themes of *King Lear*, everything happens as if the Machiavellian framework of the play had been designed to be 'protected' by the strength of audience ideology from detection, so that it is possible to read the play as an uncritical ratification of popular heroics and national pride.[76] The dynamics of repression involved in such protection, however, necessarily create a 'political unconscious' within the play—thematic elements which are noticed only when the ideology which worked to suppress them from the consciousness of readers and auditors has been exposed as such, and what had been repressed becomes thematized. Necessarily any literary political unconscious is shifting and

[76] Lawrence Olivier's Second World War filmed production is of course the classic case in point, but critics from Samuel Johnson (in his 1765 edition of the plays) to J. Dover Wilson (in his 1947 Cambridge edition of the play) to M. M. Reese in his *Cease of Majesty* among many others have read the play as essentially a positive, patriotic celebration of monarchy, King Harry, and the conquest of France.

indeterminate, varying from reader to reader, audience to audience over time and social location. But I believe the critical and performance history of this play, with its widely varying suppositions as to the political vectors of the play's representations of monarchy and conquest, demands such a notion—and that the shifting discourses surrounding the Essex faction—now explicitly Machiavellian, now traditional; now aiming at the overthrow of the monarch and the ascendance of Essex as monarch, now merely seeking a redress of grievance—were peculiarly congenial to uncertain boundaries between brute facticity and unconscious-fulfilling fantasies. The difference between the conscious and the unconscious in such contexts is impossible to ascertain with any certainty, and this play replicates exactly this uncertainty in its treatment of an ideology of Machiavellianism. The result is a play which leaves those who study it with uncertainties about its moral and political judgements completely foreign to the relatively unequivocal condemnations of instrumental reason and power central to *Othello*, *King Lear*, and *Macbeth*.

In defence—if any is truly needed—of the Shakespeare of this Machiavellian moment—perhaps it is more precisely Essex's—we can say that the tensions within his project are all too visible, and that the undigested darker matter of the play is an acute replication within the drama of the tensions of the 'real-world' politics with which he was working.

Several critics have pointed out the brief window of time implied by specific reference to Essex in the Act 5 chorus, between Essex's departure for Ireland from London on 27 March 1599 and his defeated return the following 28 September (see Chapter 1). Those well informed knew by midsummer that the success imagined for the expedition in the Chorus's allusion to 'rebellion broachèd on his sword' was highly unlikely. Perhaps such knowledge influenced the somewhat guarded tone of the references to Essex, which are carefully qualified:

> As, by a lower but high-loving likelihood,
> Were now the General of our gracious Empress—
> As in good time he may—from Ireland coming,
> Bringing rebellion broachèd on his sword,
> How many would the peaceful city quit
> To welcome him! Much more, and much more cause,
> Did they this Harry. (5.0.29–35)

But there is another explanation for the tone of phrases like 'lower but high-loving likelihood' and 'As in good time he may'. The hesitations seem to me more likely to reflect, not some insider's knowledge that things in Ireland were not going well, but an authorial uneasiness with the political project whose ideal form he had just represented; and the guarded tone of these hardly ringing honorifics suggests that, as hesitations and qualifications, they should take their place, too, as fragments of this singular play's dispersed political unconscious. Only a few months after the composition and first performances of this play, the impossibilities of this version of Machiavellian politics, which inform the most accessible layers of *Henry V*, would be apparent for all with eyes to see. And it is difficult not to interpret the marked change in tone and substance in the political plays which follow *Henry V*, in the wake of Essex's house arrest, rebellion, trial, and execution, as the response of Shakespeare and company to these failed politics. *Hamlet*, *Troilus and Cressida*, and the Jacobean tragedies will re-examine Machiavellian power and find it far from the neutral, inevitable instrument which it is in these plays for Henrys IV and V. It becomes instead a dark, corrosive reification with a vast destructive potential, a 'universal wolf' as Ulysses calls it in *Troilus and Cressida*, which threatens to eat up all before it and (as was manifestly the case in the sad story of the Earl of Essex) to eat up itself as well. *Henry V* marks the limit of Shakespeare's Machiavellian moment, its maximum expression—but also the point at which the trajectory of reversal hinted at through the tones of mourning in 2 *Henry IV* become unmistakable, if not yet unequivocal. *Hamlet* marks the next stage of this reversed trajectory.

Conclusion: *Hamlet* and the Tragedy of the Subject

The End of a Machiavellian Moment

Hamlet marks a new configuration of Shakespeare's treatment of the themes of Machiavellian power and Montaignean subjectivity which I have been tracing in this book. In many ways, along with *Troilus and Cressida*,[1] it constitutes the end of the Machiavellian moment begun in *Richard II* by turning away from the *Henriad's* fractured, disparate layers of approval and disapproval of Machiavellian politics toward a clearly negative view of the Machiavellian. However, in *Hamlet* Machiavellianism remains inescapably part of the given world; so much the worse for the world, Hamlet seems to tell us, in clear distinction from the weary but triumphant Henry V.

There is no attempt in what follows to explicate in detail this great play, which takes on new meanings and dimensions in a Post-modernist age.[2] Here I want to conclude this study of works of a central five-year period in Shakespeare's career with a brief look at how *Hamlet* at once is within yet breaks decisively out of Shakespeare's Machiavellian moment of 1595–1600.

For purposes of this discussion, I am assuming a common position of recent editors, that *Hamlet* in the form(s) that we know it[3]—as opposed to

---

[1] Hugh Grady, *Shakespeare's Universal Wolf: Studies in Early Modern Reification* (Oxford: Clarendon, 1996), 58–94. Stanley Wells and Gary Taylor, *William Shakespeare: A Textual Companion* (New York: Norton, 1997), date *Troilus* as having been composed in 1602, after *Hamlet* (1600–1) and *Twelfth Night* (1601).

[2] See Linda Charnes, 'The Hamlet Formerly Known as Prince', in Hugh Grady (ed.), *Shakespeare and Modernity: From Early Modern to Millennium* (London: Routledge, 2000), 189–210, for a related reading of the play which situates it within the Postmodernist aesthetics of the present period. For Charnes, too, the play enacts its protagonist's resistance to his interpellation as prince. Charnes develops these insights further, for both *Hamlet* and the *Henriad*, in her *Hamlet's Heirs: Essays on Inheriting Shakespeare* (London: Routledge: forthcoming).

[3] Three versions of Shakespeare's *Hamlet* survive: Q1, a quarto edition first published in 1603, which many scholars believe to be a corrupted text produced from memory by a pirating actor (but believed by a minority to represent an early Shakesperian draft of the play); Q2, a second quarto edition dated 1604 and accepted by virtually all scholars as derived

an earlier, lost version mentioned in several sources and dating from the 1580s—was composed by Shakespeare in 1600 or 1601.[4] Since the period of Essex's disgrace can be dated precisely, from his defeated return from Ireland on 28 September 1599 through his failed coup attempt in February 1601, with subsequent execution on 25 February 1601, it seems highly likely that *Hamlet* was written under the shadow of Essex's disgrace, rebellion, and defeat. At the least, I will argue, everything happens as if this were the case, as if Essex's alienation from the Queen, his open use of force against her, and his failure had deepened the reaction against Machiavellianism which I have traced in one layer of *2 Henry IV* and *Henry V*.[5]

Certainly *Hamlet* was a new departure for Shakespeare in more ways than one, as numerous critics have pointed out.[6] It became the inaugural play of what has been called Shakespeare's tragic period, marking a turn away from the English histories and the comedies that had dominated his writing up to this point. Interestingly, too, *Hamlet* is not only a (non-English, non-Roman) tragedy, but it is a representative instance of a favourite Elizabethan-Jacobean subgenre, the revenge tragedy, and as such it shares conventional characteristics of this form in a marked way. Parallels with the acknowledged grandfather of this subgenre, Thomas Kyd's *The Spanish Tragedy* (published 1592, probably composed in the late 1580s or early 1590s), are much more pronounced than they were in

from an authentic Shakespearian text; and F1, the version of *Hamlet* printed in the 1623 First Folio, believed by many to be derived from the version of the play performed by Shakespeare's acting company and containing passages missing in Q2 and in turn omitting other passages found in Q2. Most modern editions of the play are conflations of Q2 and F1. Here I use the conflated text of Stephen Greenblatt et al. (eds.), *The Norton Shakespeare* (New York: Norton, 1997), which is based on Stanley Wells and Gary Taylor (eds.), *William Shakespeare: The Complete Works* (Oxford: Oxford University Press, 1988). Wells and Taylor based their version primarily on the Folio, and the Norton edition adds passages from Q2 to these, but indented and in a different typeface (not reproduced here); instead, notes will indicate when any passage quoted derives from Q2 rather than the Folio.

[4] See especially Wells and Taylor, *William Shakespeare: A Textual Companion*, 122–3 and 396–402. Internal and external evidence converges towards the dates 1600 or 1601.

[5] The earliest argument for the influence of the Essex affair on the play was Lilian Winstanley, *'Hamlet' and the Scottish Succession* (Cambridge: Cambridge University Press, 1921). More recent investigations of the connection include Eric S. Mallin, 'Emulous Factions and the Collapse of Chivalry: *Troilus and Cressida*', *Representations*, 29 (Winter 1990), 145–79 (later incorporated in revised form in Eric Mallin, *Inscribing the Time: Shakespeare and the End of Elizabethan England* (Berkeley and Los Angeles: University of California Press, 1996); and Karin S. Coddon, ' "Suche Strange Desygns": Madness, Subjectivity, and Treason in *Hamlet* and Elizabethan Culture', *Renaissance Drama: New Series*, 20 (1989), 51–75; repr. in William Shakespeare, *Hamlet*, ed. Susanne L. Wofford (Boston: Bedford, 1994), 380–402.

[6] Cf. C. L. Barber, *Creating Elizabethan Tragedy: The Theater of Marlowe and Kyd*, ed. Richard P. Wheeler (Chicago: University of Chicago Press, 1988), 50, where *Hamlet* is situated at 'the moment of most intense crisis in Shakespeare's development'.

Shakespeare's first attempt at this form, *Titus Andronicus* (composed *c.*1592). Much more than *Titus*, with its *sui generis* classical-Gothic ambience, *Hamlet* duplicates some of Kyd's most atmospheric, expressionistic effects: a ghost and multiple evocations of an afterlife, madness and near madness, prevalent Machiavellian deception within a royal court, a context of international politics, uncertainty and mystery as to how to proceed and perceive, soliloquies, treachery, a wronged heroine, suicide, a play-within-a-play (along with other metatheatrical allusions), and an ending with bodies piled on the stage.

These striking parallels suggest that there was something about the atmosphere of Kyd's work which appealed to Shakespeare at this particular juncture in Elizabethan politics and in his own artistic development. The 'Italianate' atmosphere of revenge tragedy had become a staple of the London stage with Kyd and Marlowe and would continue to serve Jacobean dramatists like Webster twenty years or more later. As such it was a shifting signifier, evoking at different periods whatever forms of corrupt political activity seemed most topical, and the court of James I became a not-so-veiled target of plays like *The Revenger's Tragedy*. In the Armada years which saw the composition of *The Spanish Tragedy*, however, corruption was publicly associated not with England's monarch but with its enemies, the Spanish empire and the Church of Rome. These two formidable institutions were not merely 'external', but constituted feared threats, real and imagined, within the court and within the nation, through, for example, an extensive Catholic intelligence operation and various Spanish intrigues. Lacey Baldwin Smith, in her *Treason in Tudor England: Politics and Paranoia* (1986), defined the culture of paranoia that often prevailed in the hypercharged atmosphere of the Cold War with Spain[7] and which manifested itself in plots and fears of plots like the infamous case of Dr Roderigo Lopez, the Portuguese Jewish convert accused in 1594 of attempting to poison Queen Elizabeth who was then zealously and successfully prosecuted by the Earl of Essex. The Essex affair itself, with its pitting of members of the Privy Council in deadly combat with each other for the highest possible political stakes, its invocations of Machiavelli and the Spanish, and its unprovable charges and counter-charges, was in many ways, as Smith argued, the culmination of this culture of paranoia. Another way of saying this is that the Essex rebellion was something of a revenge tragedy itself, and that both Essex and his court rivals and prosecutors Francis Bacon and Robert Cecil provided the

---

[7] Lacey Baldwin Smith, *Treason in Tudor England: Politics and Paranoia* (London: Jonathan Cape, 1986).

references to Machiavelli and to Spain to bring home the point. In the period from 1599 and 1601 from which *Hamlet* dates, in short, the peculiar Italianate revenge-tragedy motifs which Shakespeare had relocated to Denmark could hardly fail to suggest the intrigues and treasons of the late Elizabethan court.

Shakespeare's decision to turn to the ambience of the revenge tragedy at this juncture, then, can be explained as responding to the renewed political paranoia—the factionalism, manoeuvring, and deception— associated with Essex's failed coup and/or its prelude.[8] It was of course an era of a great number of other bitter satires. For example, Marston's brief career as a satirical dramatist began in 1599, and his best-known contribution to the revenge-tragedy subgenre, *Antonio's Revenge*, was produced in 1600–1, the year *Hamlet* appears to have been written. This parallel suggests that the moment of the Essex crisis had broad cultural reverberations (and connections to the more general cultural crisis of the transition to modernity with which *Hamlet* has so often been associated), seen in the production of so many malcontents and social critics in the drama and poetry of the time.[9] But the play's more topical connections are the ones in need of unearthing, even though its continued relevance in our own day depends on its larger connections to an unfolding modernity.[10]

The Darkening of Machiavelli in Hamlet

If the *Henriad* depicts a matter-of-fact, realpolitik Machiavellianism taken for granted by all the political actors, *Hamlet* represents a more judgemental and negative interpretation of the Machiavellian. The 'dark' aura of its revenge-tragedy ethos signals and intensifies the darkening view of Machiavellian politics in progress over the four plays of the *Henriad*, which terminates in the highly contradictory political framework of *Henry V*. *Hamlet* does not exactly dissolve the contradictions, but the dark side of power is continually on view, with little of its heroics on display. Certainly in terms of the reception history of the two plays, *Henry V*

[8] Coddon, '"Suche Strange Desygns"' argues that Hamlet's ambiguous madness was analogous to the madness many associated with Essex after his uprising, madness being seen as an equivalent of or figure for treason.

[9] The now classic work on these associations is Jonathan Dollimore, *Radical Tragedy: Religion, Ideology, and Power in the Drama of Shakespeare and his Contemporaries* (1984; 2nd edn. London: Harvester, 1989), although Dollimore unaccountably neglects *Hamlet*.

[10] For a seminal restaging of the complex interconnections of *Hamlet* and several moments of unfolding modernity (and possibly postmodernity) from Hegel, Marx, and Freud to Derrida and Lacan, see Margreta de Grazia, 'Teleology, Delay, and the "Old Mole"', *Shakespeare Quarterly*, 50/3 (Fall 1999), 251–67.

has been seen as a celebration of a heroic monarch (and, in the terms developed here, of heroic Machiavellianism), *Hamlet* as a probing anatomy of the corruptions of power and a celebration of alienated humanism. I want to suggest here that these common perceptions indeed get at the important watershed between the two plays—but that the plays are closer to each other than has often been thought, since *Hamlet*, like *Henry V*, is very much a play about late Elizabethan politics.

Hamlet's Denmark, like Elizabeth's England, is involved in a multi-power political system constituted by itself, Norway, and Poland (with displaced England a mere tributary state to Denmark). The strife between Denmark and Norway constitutes a little frame around the much more thematized power struggle in the court that makes up the political matter of most of the play, but it helps establish a parallel between this play's (formal) medieval setting and the world of late Elizabethan England, with its complex diplomatic situation within the Atlantic system. The preparations for war which are the talk of the opening scene would have all too familiar a ring for a London audience old enough to remember the Armada of twelve years before—or, more pointedly, of the extensive levying and preparations for Essex's expeditionary force to Ireland of very recent memory:

> Good now, sit down, and tell me, he that knows,
> Why this same strict and most observant watch
> So nightly toils the subject of the land,
> And why such daily cast of brazen cannon,
> And foreign mart for implements of war,
> Why such impress of shipwrights, whose sore task
> Does not divide the Sunday from the week:
> What might be toward that this sweaty haste
> Doth make the night joint-labourer with the day (1.1.69–77)

These preparations for war are seen by Bernardo and Marcello as the most obvious reason for a visit to Denmark by its previous king, Hamlet Sr., although the exact connection remains obscure to them.

But as the play reaches its first complication, the Ghost's revelation to Hamlet of the true reasons for his visit, the war preparations are in effect reconstructed as a misleading surface occluding the true nature of the 'something . . . rotten in the state of Denmark'. In these changed circumstances, we are still involved in a realm of power politics. But instead of an international arena of armies and invasions familiar to the Elizabethan audience, the focus has become much narrower, and what is in question is one of the elemental problems discussed in Machiavelli's *The Prince* and which we have seen Shakespeare depict before: how a skilled political practitioner can attain power in the absence of a legal succession. And both young Hamlet and Claudius are faced with this classic political problem. In *Hamlet*, however, King Claudius' tactics (and the aura that surrounds them) are more reminiscent of Richard III's than they are of Bolingbroke's. Claudius is slowly revealed as a fratricidal usurper different from Richard III in the lesser extent of his crimes, but not in their nature. Claudius, with an outer appearance of mild competence, is almost entirely an opaque character with whom audiences find it nearly impossible to sympathize—but also one much less hateful than Richard III or Macbeth, closer in that way to the Bolingbroke of *Richard II*.

In short, Claudius appears to be somewhere between these classes. In terms developed in *The Prince*, both Richard III and Macbeth would clearly fit into the category 'those who have attained the position of Prince by villainy',[11] to be distinguished from those, like Bolingbroke and the Roman heroes of *Julius Caesar*, *Coriolanus*, and *Antony and Cleopatra*, who achieved success through fortune and prowess. Claudius of course belongs in the first group, but it could be argued that he has committed murder 'well' by Machiavellian standards: at first it appears that a single crime will accomplish his end. But it soon becomes apparent to him that the son will have to follow the father's fate, and even more pointedly in Shakespeare's dramas of political crimes than in the mobile, self-destructing exempla of *The Prince*, the distinctions Machiavelli tries to build up come to seem unstable, even impossible, as in play after play what at first had appeared to be a crime sufficient to achieve the prince's ends is soon revealed to have been insufficient and in need of renewal. And as the example of Shakespeare's Henry V shows, even in the case of a nearly ideal Machiavellian ruler, cruelty 'used well' remains cruelty.

Thus, while there are qualifications to be made, in both of these two contexts—that of the distinctions of *The Prince* and that of the gallery of Shakespeare's Machiavellian princes in all their variety—*Hamlet*'s most Machiavellian figure, Claudius, appears to exist at an intermediary position on scales of both cruelty and efficacy.[12] And this intermediate status of the chief Machiavellian character of *Hamlet* constitutes one of the most important reasons for seeing this play as intermediate in its attitudes toward Machiavelli compared with the two most important clusters of

---

[11] Niccolò Machiavelli, *The Prince*, in *The Prince and The Discourses* (New York: Modern Library, 1950), 31; ch. 8.

[12] Cf. Peter Mercer, *'Hamlet' and the Acting of Revenge* (London: Macmillan, 1987), 137: 'Claudius, however, is so far from being so blatant a villain that what he looks like is an image of firm but benevolent authority.' .

Shakespeare's political dramas, the Machiaevelli-approving plays of 1595–1600 and the anti-Machiavellian Jacobean tragedies. *Hamlet* has neither *Richard II*'s nearly neutral, technical interest in political power struggles (continuing, as we have seen, even in the growing complexity of clashing judgements and viewpoints of the Prince Hal trilogy that follows) nor the fierce condemnations of modernizing Machiavellian amoralists of *Othello*, *King Lear*, and *Macbeth* (clearly the Roman plays present us with different dynamics and deserve separate investigation). Rather, we have to say, Hamlet—and his implied audience—can neither fully lose him/ ourselves in the political power struggle he is engaged in nor refuse to be implicated in its terms, logic, and ambiguous morality. An enquiry into the Machiavellian problematics of *Hamlet*, then, also leads us into classical critical problems of this celebrated problem play, but from a new perspective.

One of the key points in coming to terms with the 'Machiavellian' framework(s) of *Hamlet* is the recognition that the young Prince, after accepting the commission of scourge and minister delivered to him by the Ghost, himself becomes a Machiavellian agent attempting to overthrow a legally elected monarch to punish crimes he is unable to prove were committed. Like other revenge heroes, he is forced to act outside the law, within what was a culturally 'grey' area of conflicting duties and responsibilities. And the result is that he adopts the same 'Machiavellian' dissembling as has the Claudius who can 'smile and smile and be a villain'—that is, he adopts the expedient of covering over his true aims and knowledge with a false exterior of apparent virtue, friendliness—and madness. In the case of Hamlet, of course, both terms of the Machiavellian structure—both the 'exterior' semblance and the 'inner' aims and know- ledge[13]—are greatly complicated, and thereby hangs a good deal of the singularity of this play, its resistance to being understood within the terms of the ordinary Machiavellian dissemblance of an ordinary revenge tragedy.

While in some ways the 'normal' revenge tragedy's suspension of moral judgement replicates the instrumental rationality of *The Prince*—a work which has its own kind of (sometimes chilling) entertainment value, parallel to that of a violent theatre—its attitudes and implied judgements are much less sophisticated, much more ambivalent, than those of Machiavelli himself. The revenge plays are popular and non-judgemental

---

[13] As indicated at several points above, these terms constitute one of the key structures of Elizabethan interiority defined in Katherine Eisaman Maus, *Inwardness and Theater in the English Renaissance* (Chicago: University of Chicago Press, 1995).

rather than nuanced within a complex classical-humanist set of discourses and implicated in conflicting but finely defined moral distinctions, as in *The Prince* and *The Discourses*. For example, Machiavelli is well known for his dictum that 'Therefore it is necessary for a prince, who wishes to maintain himself, to learn how not to be good, and to use this knowledge and not use it, according to the necessity of the case.'[14] Doubtless there is a layer of regret and disapproval amidst the irony, realism, and aggressive plain talk, so that the rhetoric is full of complex judgements, not neutral or detached in any strict sense (see Chapters 1 and 2). However, the end result of the complex judgements, as in Kyd's *The Spanish Tragedy*, is instrumental: this is the way men and women must behave under duress, if they wish to avoid being the victims of others' malice. As with most transgression, the sense of violation of norms is part of the emotional attraction involved. Marlowe had long ago demonstrated this basic truth of the Elizabethan and all subsequent entertainment industries, and it is an effect inherent in every Shakespearian tragedy, most especially this one.

Hamlet thus represents Machiavellian politics in two interacting ways. First, the play itself depicts an international power struggle that would signify for its audience the international chess game of Atlantic-system politics[15] that had dominated English political life for twenty years or more before *Hamlet* was written, and then this becomes a context in which a more elemental political struggle over title to a throne is fought—a theme which, as critics have long noted, possibly alludes to the lack of a definite heir to Elizabeth, even possibly to Essex's shadowy candidacy for succession.

Second, *Hamlet* makes use of the conventions of the revenge tragedy to represent these political manoeuvres in a specific atmosphere evoking death, treachery, deceit, and self-conscious theatricality—an atmosphere which comes into view particularly well if we compare it with the clearer, more analytic and non-judgemental ambience of *Richard II* and the Prince Hal trilogy—even with the growing registering in those later plays of an unease with the narrowness and irreducible cruelty of power.

One of the key differences of *Hamlet* from those earlier political dramas is the relation of this particular prince to his assigned role in a structure of reified power. I tried to show in previous chapters how Prince Hal attempted through several different strategies to enlarge and enrich his own drama of the putting on of power, only to be appropriated by it as he

[14] Machiavelli, *The Prince*, 56; ch. 15.
[15] Middleton's *A Game at Chess* was of course to make a much more direct use of that metaphor in the early Jacobean era, in a play which is a clear embodiment of the potential of the London theatres to serve as political commentary on specific events.

became his own legend in plays criss-crossed with contradictory judgements and affects concerning this process. In contrast Prince Hamlet does
only one thing consistently in the play which bears his name: he never fails
to resist his assigned role as revenge-tragedy hero,[16] at least up until the
very end of the play when he stumbles onto a kind of (limited, self-
destructive) political success. Hamlet's famous alienation from his
cultural and political context in the play and his failure to achieve power
create a new, devaluing representation of a Machiavellianism in which,
however, this play and its hero still are forced to participate.

Almost as soon as he is interpellated by the Ghost as a revenge hero,
Hamlet begins a kind of unarticulated resistance to this interpellation.
Singularly, he is a revenge hero who never really formulates a plan for his
revenge. And these uncertainties are compounded because in the course
of his celebrated soliloquies we learn a good deal about Hamlet's state of
mind and emotions: his depression before the Ghost's appearance and his
anger at his mother and uncle, his idealizing love of his father and his
sorrow at his death, his contempt for his uncle, his puzzlement about the
Ghost's nature and the reliability of his message, his scepticism (at least at
moments) about the afterlife and his attraction to suicide, his puzzlement
at his own inaction. But we never learn what purpose the 'antic disposition' was to serve or what plan, if any, Hamlet had in mind in the early
period, just after the Ghost's visit, of great resolution and purpose 'to fly to
this revenge'. With Hamlet, as opposed to Hieronimo of The Spanish
Tragedy, the feigning seems to become an end in itself, as this particular
hero resists the very instrumentality he has sworn in the moments after he
talked with the Ghost. Hamlet's ambiguous feigning of madness, then,
seems to serve other purposes than Machiavellian ones, although it is first
presented as planned and politically purposeful. Hamlet's attempt at
Machiavellianism founders, and it founders for reasons which the script
of the play presents as puzzling to their subject, above all in the familiar
lines of the 'O, what a rogue and peasant slave am I!' soliloquy (2.2.527–82)
and later, in the summarizing lines beginning 'How all occasions do
inform against me' (4.4.922–56).[17]

[16] Charnes, 'The Prince Formerly Known as Hamlet', sees the protagonist as consistently
resisting the chief duties of the office of prince; and Mercer, 'Hamlet' and the Acting of
Revenge, situates Hamlet in the context formed by other Elizabethan-Jacobean revenge
tragedies and argues that Hamlet is essentially different from all of them in that in
Shakespeare's play the hero is never taken over by the revenge dynamic, which is instead
coded as merely theatrical and is resisted by a multivalent, protean Hamlet, whose 'true self'
resists theatricality. In my own view this last movement of the argument is a capitulation to
essentialism that undercuts what is otherwise a very cogent reading of the play and its
soliloquies.   [17] This last speech occurs in Q2 but not in the Folio edn.

In this way, one of the crucial implied themes of this play is a split with-in consciousness and agency, a denial of the sovereignty within the self of the speaking and feeling subject. The play thus emerges as perhaps the earliest critique of the idea of bourgeois subjectivity, if by that expression we mean belief in a sovereign, empowered self fully autonomous from a corrupt world and its ideologies. *Hamlet* indeed figured in several of the first-generation cultural materialist critiques of the bourgeois subject I discussed in general terms in the Introduction and in subsequent chapters. Three of the works alluded to above discuss *Hamlet*: writings by Francis Barker, Terry Eagleton, and Catherine Belsey extended their critiques of 'liberal humanism' (see Introduction) to a kind of emptying out or evacuation of subjectivity even as they attempted to demystify earlier Romantic and Modernist absolutizing of the subject as such. Francis Barker, for example, wrote:

The hollow pipe [which Hamlet hands Guildenstern at 3.2.322–3] is the refutation of the metaphysic of the soul which the play signals but cannot realize. For Hamlet, in a sense doubtless unknown to him, is truly this hollow reed which will 'discourse most eloquent music' but is none the less vacuous for that. At the centre of Hamlet, in the interior of his mystery, there is, in short, nothing.[18]

Barker's pioneering cultural materialist reading of the play rightly situates *Hamlet* in a narrative of emerging modernity and modern subjectivity, but it devalues that subjectivity in a problematic way.

Two years later, Terry Eagleton borrowed and developed Barker's idea:

Hamlet has no 'essence' of being whatsoever, no inner sanctum to be safeguarded: he is pure deferral and diffusion, a hollow void which offers nothing determinate to be known. His 'self' consists simply in the range of gestures with which he resists available definitions, not in a radical alternative beyond their reach.[19]

These arguments against essentialism certainly have their point, but the language of hollowness, void, and empty gesture which follows is radically insensitive to the positive potentiality of Hamlet's unfixed subjectivity. And one of the least persuasive sections of Catherine Belsey's seminal *The Subject of Tragedy* is that attempting to account for Hamlet's subjectivity as a kind of failed amalgamation of two epistemes or ideologies—medieval and emerging 'modern': 'The play, which had begun to define an interiority as the origin of meaning and action, a human subject as agent, cannot produce closure in terms of an analysis which in 1601 does

---

[18] Francis Barker, *The Tremulous Private Body: Essays in Subjection* (London: Methuen, 1984), 36–7.
[19] Terry Eagleton, *William Shakespeare* (Oxford: Basil Blackwell, 1986), 72.

not yet fully exist.'[20] As I argued in the Introduction, Shakespeare is more than a modernist manqué, and his conception of subjectivity in *Hamlet* has specificities and complexities of its own. At the very least, Shakespeare's *Hamlet* represents and probes a form of subjectivity as a structural component of this play's form. An enquiry into Hamlet as a Machiavellian agent inevitably becomes an enquiry into the state of Hamlet's subjectivity, as the repeated resolutions he takes for action and revenge always dissipate, without explanation. And certainly one of the corollaries here is that *Hamlet* demonstrates the inadequacy of the two-dimensional Machiavellian structure of the self—a façade of deceptive conformity over an interior of a will-to-power—as an explanation of the dynamics of the modern self. Instead, *Hamlet* portrays a prince with a highly complex, contradictory sense of self and one which precludes any clear Machiavellian plotting on his part. One of his speeches in particular, alluded to above in the passage quoted from Francis Barker, seems to answer generations of critics as well as it does Rosencrantz and Guildenstern:

You would play upon me, you would seem to know my stops, you would pluck out the heart of my mystery, you would sound me from my lowest note to the top of my compass; and there is much music, excellent voice in this little organ, yet cannot you make it speak. 'Sblood, do you think I am easier to be played on than a pipe? Call me what instrument you will, though you can fret me, you cannot play upon me. (3.2.335–41)

This is not to say, say, *pace* Barker, Eagleton, and Belsey, that we should reify Hamlet's subjectivity as some kind of substance or essence of absolute value. But it is to say that Hamlet's subjectivity is posited by the logic of the play as a crucial agent of resistance to instrumental reason and to univocal interpellations such as the Ghost's. It is certainly negative, in the sense of being a kind of specific opposite of the narrow interpellation which Hamlet experiences. But it is far from nugatory.

At a point like this in the argument, it would not be surprising to turn to the rich and still developing psychoanalytic literature on this play, a literature which from the very first promised to solve the mystery of motivation behind the Prince's inability to carry out his revenge—or more recently and subtly, to demonstrate how the play is a classic manifest text in which are inscribed a labyrinth of culturally significant unconscious materials relevant to the same and connected problems. I admire a great deal of this body of work and believe it has much to teach us about culture

---

[20] Catherine Belsey, *The Subject of Tragedy: Identity and Difference in Renaissance Drama* (London: Methuen, 1985), 42.

and the unconscious. However, like most of the psychoanalytic critics themselves, I do not believe that such readings exhaust the meaning(s) of the text, and I am attempting in these remarks to treat the psychoanalytic analyses of the play in much the same way as Tom Stoppard treated the text of *Hamlet* in his *Rosencrantz and Guildenstern Are Dead*: as something to be glimpsed and even highlighted from time to time, but as not forming the main content of the present business. I will be in effect pursuing the Lacanian problem of how Hamlet becomes disinterpellated from the Symbolic order, clings to his bodily ego or *moi*, and forges a series of new identities in a structure of always already inadequate desiring, but with none of Lacan's formidable apparatus. My main point in this pursuit is that such an unstable self, instead of being emptied out and objectified in the manner of Barker, Eagleton, and Belsey (critics in turn deriving from Foucault on the disciplinary self and Althusser on the interpellated subject), constitutes a Montaignean affirmation of unfixed subjectivity in a corrupt, devalued world—despite its inability to change the world or life. Hamlet is a negative hero, an assertion of the value of simple negativity vis-à-vis an impossible world. *Hamlet* is a satirical tragedy with a demonic hero in Lukács's sense in *The Theory of the Novel*—a problematic figure unable to transcend the reified world in which he is trapped, but equally unable to accept or ratify it.[21] Hamlet's subjectivity is thus always a subjectivity-in-the-world, an agency unsuccessfully seeking solutions to problems which are fundamentally insoluble because they are defined within a shifting series of mental frameworks none of which are adequate to all the intractable details playing through the story. This instability of *mentalité* is itself a Montaignean motif, but it is deployed in this play in a very non-Montaignean way—or in a way which is perhaps only a subordinated moment within the *Essais*. Hamlet's scepticism is an aspect of his larger alienation from his entire Symbolic order, a fundamental disorientation informed by depression and emotional repulsion and evocative of a cultural mood of despair and socio-political disengagement. As Coleridge and numerous others have seen, there is only a short if decisive step between Hamlet and Iago. Both employ a corrosive rationality devastating to the received ideologies of their worlds, and neither can account for his own mentality or motivation. In the case of Iago, however, all self-doubt and self-reflection have been suppressed so that he becomes a kind of automaton of his own will, a function of his own instrumental rationality, while Hamlet's divided self continually resists the logic of

---

[21] Georg Lukács, *The Theory of the Novel*, trans. Anna Bostock (Cambridge, Mass.: MIT Press, 1971), 88–93 *et passim*.

instrumental rationality and the force of his conscious will, without being able to articulate why. The Freudian diagnosis of unconscious motivations at work is an obvious answer to this quality of the play and constitutes among the most potent evidence for Joel Fineman's suggestion that Shakespeare was the first Freudian (or rather that in this regard Freud was the second Shakespearian).[22] But there is another way to get at this puzzle, and one not requiring the production of a latent unconscious subtext as a murder-mystery solution to Hamlet's riddle of the sphinx. Hamlet's inarticulate resistance to Machiavellian logic and the patterns of revenge tragedy amount in themselves to a tribute to the negative powers of unfixed subjectivity in a world of unacceptable subject positions.[23]

The Hamlet Who Would Not Be

In one of the most electrifying introductions of a character in Western drama, Hamlet first makes his presence known with a complex and punning direct address to the audience:

> A little more than kin, and less than kind. (1.2.65)

As Robert Weimann emphasized, although Hamlet is royalty, his theatrical presence is much more plebeian, in many ways like Falstaff's. He is a character who spends at least as much time on the *platea*, the intermediate zone between the play's represented reality and audience, as on the *locus*, that space normally associated with upper-class characters not engaged in direct address to the audience. Hamlet is of course the Shakespearian character with more of that direct audience interaction than any other, so that he is contradictory as a stage character as he is in so many other ways, simultaneously aristocratic and plebeian.[24] And, from the first, he seems to be simultaneously Machiavellian and anti-Machiavellian, in the elementary sense of the term as one employing subterfuge

---

[22] Joel Fineman, *Shakespeare's Perjured Eye: The Invention of Poetic Subjectivity in the Sonnets* (Berkeley and Los Angeles: University of California Press, 1986), 46.

[23] The reading of *Hamlet* in Barker, *The Tremulous Private Body*, 22–41, defines something close to this conception in its subthesis that because the play is not yet fully modern or bourgeois, it has material resistant to the subsequent ideology of bourgeois humanism which attempts to appropriate it.

[24] In addition to Robert Weimann's pioneering work *Shakespeare and the Popular Tradition in the Theater: Studies in the Social Dimension of Dramatic Form and Function*, ed. Robert Schwartz (Baltimore: Johns Hopkins University Press, 1978), see for related analyses Michael D. Bristol, '"Funeral Bak'd Meats": Carnival and the Carnivalesque in *Hamlet*', in Shakespeare, *Hamlet*, ed. Wofford, 348–67; and Robert Barrie, '*Telmahs*: Carnival Laughter in *Hamlet*', in Mark Thornton Burnett and John Manning (eds.), *New Essays on Hamlet* (New York: AMS Press, 1994), 83–100.

for political purposes. Famously, in the speech I briefly discussed above, Hamlet speaks for utter sincerity and a transparent inner self:

> Seems, madam? Nay, it *is*. I know not 'seems'.
>
> . . . .
>
> But I have that within which passeth show—
> These but the trappings and the suits of woe. (1.2.76–86)

But when Hamlet is alone on stage and speaks again directly to the audience, we learn that not all of his feelings have been put on the public display which he claims at one level in this passage. In particular the depth of his depression, his distaste for his uncle-father, and his anger with and sense of betrayal by his mother have been concealed from the court:

> It is not, nor it cannot come to good.
> But break, my heart, for I must hold my tongue. (1.2.157–8)

In short, the claim made by Francis Barker that in this speech Hamlet affirms an interiority as cause of meaning and action[25] breaks down if we examine the context in which Hamlet makes his own claim. His assertion of the transparency of his inner feelings is revealed in soliloquy to have been counterfactual, and the following sequence of events in the crucial portion of the play between the revelations of the Ghost and Hamlet's sea-journey out of Elsinore demonstrates how much of his 'self' is inaccessible even to 'himself'. Rather than affirming a bourgeois subjectivity coming to be, *Hamlet* (like so much else of Shakespeare and other classic artworks of modernity) interrogates and problematizes any idea of a fixed subject.

Being True to a Decentred Self

What makes *Hamlet* as a play strikingly different from *The Spanish Tragedy* and other revenge tragedies of the day is that the event which precipitates Hamlet's search for revenge simultaneously precipitates Hamlet's disinterpellation from an earlier identity—really an entire world—that we hear about only in his own idealizing references to his dead father and in the remarks of Ophelia:

> The courtier's, soldier's, scholar's eye, tongue, sword,
> Th'expectancy and rose of the fair state,
> The glass of fashion and the mould of form,
> The observed of all observers. (3.1.149–53)

---

[25] Barker, *The Tremulous Private Body*, 35–6. Barker, however, claims that the text falls short of delivering the interiority promised in this speech.

When we meet Hamlet in the opening scenes, he is already disinterpellated from his earlier identity and clinging like Richard II to an 'inner
substance' of emotionality and evaluation no longer anchored in a secure
sense of a social order.

Hamlet describes the radical change in his personality twice early in the
play—once in his first soliloquy and again, in similar terms, in conversation with Rosencrantz and Guildenstern shortly after their arrival, and
Gertrude and Ophelia allude to it as well more than once. What Hamlet
describes sounds very much like symptoms of depression to a twenty-
first-century audience, and scholars have discovered that it sounded
very much like the Galenic version of this, Melancholia, to those familiar
with medical discourse in 1600. But I want to bracket the objectifying
impulse to diagnose Hamlet and instead try to listen to his famous self-
descriptions. Nowhere in Shakespeare, perhaps in world literature, is the
idea of character as performance, a non-essentialist, anti-substantive view
of the human personality, carried out with such detail and in pursuit of its
paradoxes as in *Hamlet*. This conception explains a good deal of the
puzzlement that has surrounded the critical history of the play, in which
legions of critics have sought to discover precisely what this conception of
character has precluded: an essential, 'real' self underneath the mere
appearances and outward shows of performance. *Hamlet* is the climax of
the themes of performativity and theatricality opened up by the *Henriad*,
but in a new, darker context, within a devalued, corrupt world which
offers no suitable theatres worthy of the potentiality of the performers.
Hamlet is disgusted at the Machiavellianism of everyone else—real and
imagined—and he is disgusted at his own inability to engage in the part of
Machiavellian revenger with ideological single-mindedness. *Hamlet* is
indeed a tragedy of a man who cannot make up his mind, but this quality
is one that follows ethically from the nature of the world he inhabits and
from his own acute perception of that world and its possibilities. The
Prince is a puzzled hero of hesitation. Flawed as this simulacrum of subjectivity is in many ways—misogynist, given to sweeping, judgemental
generalizations, culpably hasty and rash in violence—his hesitation is
presented as the outcome of his best qualities: intelligence, creativity,
generosity, and intuition. However, the hesitation—which E. E. Stoll
claimed he could not perceive within the play—develops gradually. At
first, Hamlet virtually shouts his aptness to play this new role:

> Haste, haste me to know it, that with wings as swift
> As meditation or the thoughts of love,
> May sweep to my revenge. (1.5.28–30)

This formulation, with its oxymoronic comparison of the swiftness of revenge to the speed of meditation and love, seems already to presage problems, and of course, famously, they come. Hamlet's interpellation as revenge-tragedy hero is constantly interrupted by interference from other possible identities, which are displayed to us kaleidoscopically in the most puzzling section of the play, between the visit by the Ghost and the killing of Polonius. We see Hamlet the student and bon vivant in polished and witty conversations first with Horatio and friends, then with Rosencrantz and Guildenstern. We hear about and see Hamlet the lover of Ophelia and Hamlet the jealous rival of her dotty father. We hear Hamlet contemplating the meaning of life, doubting the received religious truths of the Christian afterlife, and contemplating a suicide which his agnosticism militates against. And we witness Hamlet the passionate connoisseur of theatre, a critic and an amateur playwright and director.

Most of this time, Hamlet never mentions revenge. He simply acts strangely, but purposefully. In these puzzling scenes Hamlet recalls the Prince Hal of the tavern, putting on and taking off social roles like clothes, trying out one identity and sense of self after another with no clearer purpose than that of putting off the inevitable day when he must surrender his subjectivity to the fixedness of a clear social—and Machiavellian—role. The emotional tonality of these scenes in *Hamlet* is, of course, very different from that of the Boar's Head and elsewhere in *1 and 2 Henry IV*. Instead of fellowship and hilarity there is a claustrophobic isolation, undercut with a manic, dark, edgy wit. Hamlet is crueller to Ophelia than Hal is to either Francis or Falstaff, but as with the earlier prince, there is a sense that events are beyond his control; they are unfolding according to a logic which he cannot escape. In the riveting scenes between the Ghost's message and the confirmation of it by Claudius's reactions to the play, Hamlet's protean subjectivity is shown to us facet by facet as Freud's 'work of mourning' becomes not just a reconfiguration of the self to compensate for those portions of identity that had been bound up with the lost loved one, but instead a series of compensatory attempted identity-formations in response to Hamlet's loss of epistemological anchoring:

> The time is out of joint. O cursèd spite
> That ever I was born to set it right! (1.5.189–90)

In all the soliloquies in these scenes, Hamlet repeatedly asks who he is, what he is supposed to be doing, and marvels over his inability to understand himself or his situation:

> Am I a coward?
> Who calls me villain, breaks my pate across,
> Plucks off my beard and blows it in my face,
> Tweaks me by th' nose, gives me the lie i'th' throat
> As deep as to the lungs? Who does me this?
>
> .   .   .   .
>
> Why, what an ass am I? Ay, sure, this is most brave,
> That I, the son of the dear murderèd,
> Prompted to my revenge by heaven and hell,
> Must, like a whore, unpack my heart with words. (2.2.548–63)

The above meditation is famously resolved of course, with Hamlet's embracing of theatricalism. The play is the thing, and he turns director, author, and vicarious actor as the solution to his dilemma. This choice in turn becomes the turning point of the play's plot structure, the moment after which its focus is no longer on whether Hamlet can convince himself of Claudius' guilt but rather on how he can or will act on his new knowledge of Claudius' crime. But Hamlet's choice of the theatre as his tool of knowledge reverberates in many other ways as well, and in this context, it clearly helps develop the positive coloration the play is suggesting of Hamlet's myriad-minded, unfixed subjectivity.

In short Hamlet's immediate strategy after his interview with the Ghost, 'To put an antic disposition on', is not so much a feigning of madness as it is an embracing of theatricalism. One of the chief meanings of 'antic' in the sixteenth century is that of a clown-like 'fantastick' associated with plays and players. The antic disposition is thus one more metatheatrical gesture in this play that is so often caught up in discussions and enactments of, and allusions to, playing itself. And in the scenes which follow, nothing is consistent about Hamlet except his histrionics, whether he is alarming Ophelia with his backward walking, jousting with Polonius, or declaiming that eloquent, memorable prose about man the quintessence of dust with Rosencrantz and Guildenstern. And the allusions to theatricality become highlighted in the Act 3 climax, and all this in turn reconfigures the unfixed subjectivity which had been a major theme of the *Henriad* by revealing not the Machiavellian histrionics with which Prince Hal dabbled and which King Harry V perfected, but a subjectivity of negativity, a subjectivity of resistance to power and power/knowledge. *Hamlet* earns its long-standing reputation as an example of emerging discourses of modernity not by attempting to stage a fixed, 'bourgeois' subjectivity, but by instead staging an unfixed subjectivity which is simultaneously a product of modernity and a potential agent of resistance to modernity's reifying effects.

Hamlet and the Tragedy of the Subject

Thus we can read *Hamlet* as a tragedy of the production of meaning and subjectivity under what was at the time of its initial production the new condition of secular modernity. While Hamlet Sr. is idealized as the embodiment of humanism, religion, manhood, meaning, and properly ordered Oedipal relations irretrievably lost by his death, Prince Hamlet is disconnected from his preordained place in his society's Symbolic order and suffers a general crisis of melancholy and meaning embodied in unprecedented theatrical language and intensity which is unmistakably represented to the audience as a condition with which to empathize and identify. We can connect this moment of alienation and disillusion with the specific mood at the end of Elizabeth's reign, when the armed rebellion of the Earl of Essex helped produce a wave of disillusioned, bitter satire. However, the subsequent career of this play as a central document of the European literature of modernity suggests, as I indicated previously, that it is connected as well to larger and more general aspects of the historical development productive of Western modernity. I want to conclude this study with a focus on those aspects as most relevant to our own readings of the play in the present.

Hamlet is famous for the characterization of its central figure, and shelves have been filled with attempts to 'pluck out the heart of his mystery' by constructing rationalized models of his motivation and actions. For the twentieth century, this tradition was both fulfilled and ended by Freud's culminating reading of the Prince as in the grip of an unresolved Oedipal crisis precipitated by his uncle's having acted out the very repressed desires which, as Freud had it, were locked within himself and were now splitting his psyche. In fact, one could show how, after the Freudian reading of the play became known, *Hamlet* diminished in cultural prestige and centrality in favour of *King Lear* and even the other Jacobean tragedies, as a recent study by F. O. Foakes demonstrates in effect.[26] Almost a century after this, our culture may have had sufficient time to digest this scandal to revive the cultural centrality of this great play,

[26] R. A. Foakes, *'Hamlet' vs. 'Lear': Cultural Politics and Shakespeare's Art* (Cambridge: Cambridge University Press, 1993).

without, I should add, necessarily diminishing *King Lear*'s hard-won status in the process.

We can do this, I believe, by returning to Prince Hamlet, not as a miraculously lifelike literary character, but as a fiction embodying his culture's and our own's puzzling attempts to act morally within a mental space now severed from any justifying, meaning-creating myths of an integrated, harmonious cosmos: 'Look you now—what is this quint-essence of dust?'

Hamlet helps inaugurate modernity by showing its namesake character thrown back into the groundless and capricious field of his era's contingent mentality and demonstrating that his own apparently self-constituted subjectivity is shaped within an epistemologically shifting, uncertain field of perception and moral values. This quality of the play is manifested throughout the soliloquies and the dialogue with Rosencrantz and Guildenstern, as we have seen, but it forms most memorably around the figure of the Ghost and the series of insoluble questions as to his nature, motivation, and relation to Hamlet.[27] And it is the subtext of the series of questions Hamlet poses to Polonius on the interpretation of clouds (3.2.345–51) between those two highly debatable and debated scenes, the play-within-the-play and the 'bedroom scene' between Hamlet and Gertrude.

In short, what makes *Hamlet* suitable for our own decentred age is its insight into the constituting fissures and fictions of the tossing life raft of subjectivity to which Hamlet clings, for Hamlet is a humanist of the Montaignean sort—one who sees into the shifting, uncertain, contradictory, and unstable qualities of the self, not a humanist of the Rousseauistic school which makes of the self a fixed, essential source of unproblematic values and perceptions. Hamlet spends much of the play attempting to 'read' himself and his contradictory beliefs and emotions and then in turn to 'read' the unclear familial, social, and political context into which he has been thrust. It is a play as much about perception as it is about mourning; in fact the two cannot be clearly separated since what is being mourned is the loss of that meaningful, unproblematic world of naive ideals and the sense of self or identity symbolized by the lost father. That is, what is being mourned is the loss of an old way of perceiving the world and defining the self. And to the extent that Hamlet has produced

[27] These associations of the Ghost in *Hamlet* were developed to great effect in Jacques Derrida, *Specters of Marx: The State of the Debt, the Work of Mourning, and the New International*, trans. Peggy Kamuf (New York: Routledge, 1994) and in a work appearing in the very final stages of work on this book, Stephen Greenblatt, *Hamlet in Purgatory* (Princeton: Princeton University Press, 2001).

alternatives to his lost *episteme* and his lost identity, they are constituted by mourning and theatricalism itself, both of which Hamlet continues to perform up until his own death.

Clearly then, one of the received ideas of poststructuralist theory which will have to be modified if we are to appreciate what it is we continue to identify with in the fictional character of Hamlet—and which audiences continue to mourn—is, as I have asserted throughout this book, the Althusserian idea of 'interpellation' and Foucault's related concept of 'subjection'. As is well known, Althusser used the somewhat humorous illustration of a self who is 'hailed' into a specific social identity from the array of ideologically possible roles like a suspect walking down the street who is 'hailed' by a police officer's 'Hey you!' but who simultaneously perceives and actualizes this identity by turning and responding to the hailing while his comrades walk innocently on. Tellingly, for this troubled Catholic-turned-Communist, the example he gives of such a process is that of a young man deciding he has a vocation to the priesthood: he has created a sense of self which he believes is the very essence of his true self-hood but which can be seen through a more critical stance to be the out-come of socialization, not the revelation of a hidden essence.[28] Similarly, Foucault described how individuals internalize an imposed identity and sense of self through the various technologies of discipline embodied in modern families, schools, and expert lore.[29]

These concepts have been powerful analytic tools and wholesome corrections to received Rousseauistic fictions of a 'natural' self corrupted by society, but, as we have seen, they create great and troubling problems of their own. The idea of the Rousseauistic self at least created a critical space from which socialization could be contemplated and resisted, whereas it has been the great weakness of both Althusser's and Foucault's theories, as numerous critics have pointed out, that they seem instead to present an inevitable process of the triumph of power and ideology over rationality and critique, with no or very little space left from which it is possible to understand how a resistance to power and received identities could be mounted.

Hamlet in fact can be read—if I may return to my main subject in this new context—as a play about the problematics of self-formation and the possibilities of resistance to interpellation. The tragedy begins in a kind of

[28] Louis Althusser, 'Ideology and Ideological State Apparatuses: Notes towards an Investigation', in Louis Althusser, *Lenin and Philosophy and Other Essays* (New York: Monthly Review Press, 1971), 127–86.

[29] Michel Foucault, *Discipline and Punish: The Birth of the Prison*, trans. Alan Sheridan (New York: Vintage, 1979).

'disinterpellation', when Prince Hamlet has been severed from the Symbolic order by the death of his father and his failure to succeed him. A fallen world, 'the unweeded garden' of the first soliloquy, has succeeded a now lost, idealized one in which Hamlet had a preconceived place and role. It is as if a new agent of (dis)interpellation had come along and said, 'Hey, you: never mind; it wasn't you after all.' And of course such a scenario is really indistinguishable from one in which some imperfectly socialized region of a layered and complex self—precisely those layers and complexities which are missing in the oversimplified treatments of Althusser and Foucault—has constituted a mental space in which the efficacy of interpellation is questioned and the separation of aspects of the self from the interpellated social role is registered.

In the case of *Hamlet* the situation is complicated and made even more uncannily psychoanalytic when it turns out that the interpreter and explainer of the world's fallen state is none other than an ambiguous, mysterious, never fully explained Ghost in the image of Hamlet's dead father, who not only evokes (embodies and disembodies) the lost world, episteme, and identity of his (presumed) son, but also defines a new role and identity for the young Hamlet that, he and we begin to realize as the play develops, simply does not 'fit'. The new straitened circumstances and proffered new identity of the Prince (as revenger) are presented as in some sense continuous with and expressive of the lost paradise. But far from restoring to the Prince a sense of purpose and meaning, they plunge him into further confusion, inactivity, and melancholy. He becomes entrapped in a Machiavellian power struggle that takes on its own dynamics independent of the will of either of its 'mighty opposites', plunging Hamlet into one uncertainty and disaster after another.

The lost world, it seems, is permanently lost, never really existed, and certainly escapes anyone who obsessively attempts to re-create it through a series of instrumental stratagems in a reified world of power. Hamlet's famous 'subjectivity' is precisely what resists such instrumentalization and searches for alternatives to Machiavellian power and the revenger's role—not, I would argue against one strain of mid- and late twentieth-century readings of the play, out of any scruple over exacting the death penalty against his usurping uncle, the execution of whom supplies one of the play's few really cathartic moments; but rather as a resistance against the narrowing of the protean possibilities of selfhood, of multiple identities and roles, which has been the outcome of the severing of the self from the Symbolic order. In other words, the Ghost's telling Hamlet the truth (if it is the truth) about his murder by the uncle enchains rather than frees

Hamlet by actualizing his bad dreams and assigning him a revenge which threatens to turn this cultured Renaissance humanist and courtier into the kind of bombastic, melodramatic revenger which Kyd and Marston had already produced on Elizabethan stages. If we must speak of an 'essence' of Shakespeare's *Hamlet*, it is certainly one that is produced in his consistent resistance to the expectations created by his stage predecessors. In this context, the play-within-the play sequence, as I previously suggested, occupying as it does the play's dramatic centre and constituting its technical turning point, also serves as an epiphany of the idea of the protean self through the Shakespearian thematics of theatricality, affirmative of the possibilities of the non-essential self.

This affirmation is necessarily and paradoxically a negative one. Hamlet's depressed description of the world as an unweeded garden is never gainsaid in this play—or hereafter in Shakespeare's works, either—and this is miles from the openness to the world's possibilities of *1 Henry IV*. The tragedy of Hamlet's subjectivity derives from the fact that the Machiavellian world in which he seeks to fulfil it has no place for it, instead continually attempting to cabin, crib, and confine it. The Machiavellianism which had seemed a morally neutral given in the unhappy world of *Richard II*, which had seemed for the space of *1 Henry IV* to be merely a component of a larger world-theatre of potential selves and fulfilments, and which seemed to engulf and contain the subjectivity which had previously resisted it in *2 Henry IV* and *Henry V*, returns again in *Hamlet* in yet a new guise and in a new, more antagonistic relation to subjectivity. Hamlet's world is bleaker, more depressed than that of any play in the *Henriad*, but the bleakness is itself a result of the great idealizations about human potentiality which Hamlet defines and which he finds missing in empirical reality. In the fierceness of Hamlet's depression burns a sense that the world need not be the way it is. The Machiavellian logic in which Hamlet-the-revenger is entrapped is very much a part of the play's unweeded garden, and while no world operating outside this logic is achieved in Hamlet's violence—let alone in Fortinbras's iron-age restoration of order—its possibility is affirmed in the perdurance of subjectivity itself as the agent of resistance to the new forms of self-reinforcing, impersonal power within modernity.

At the end of this Shakespearian Machiavellian moment, then, a Montaignean moment emerges, one which is opposed to rather than allied with the Machiavellian (as it was in much of the *Henriad*). Hamlet was the last of Shakespeare's heroes to attempt to embody both of these moments, and his play ends by asserting their incompatibility and leaving us with the critical puzzle constituted by an unfixed subjectivity that refuses to come into focus, even after death. Perhaps now, in the twenty-first century, it will be possible to read *Hamlet* as a play whose unfixedness and uncertainties are not puzzles, but, in their negative way, answers—provisional ones, to be sure—to a series of problems which preoccupied the five-year period which produced some of Shakespeare's first great contributions to a modernity which he both shares and critiques.

Bibliography

ADORNO, THEODOR, *Aesthetic Theory*, ed. Gretel Adorno and Rolf Tiedemann, trans. and ed. Robert Hullot-Kentor (Minneapolis: University of Minnesota Press, 1997).

—— *Aesthetic Theory*, ed. Gretel Adorno and Rolf Tiedemann, trans. C. Lenhardt (London: Routledge, 1984).

—— et al., *The Authoritarian Personality* (New York: Harper & Row, 1950).

—— *Negative Dialectics*, trans. E. B. Ashton (New York: Continuum, 1983).

AINGER, ALFRED, 'Sir John Falstaff', in *Lectures and Essays* (London: Macmillan, 1905), i. 119–55.

ALBRIGHT, EVELYN MAY, 'Shakespeare's *Richard II* and the Essex Conspiracy', *PMLA* 42 (1927), 686–720.

—— 'Shakespeare's *Richard II*, Hayward's *History of Henry IV*, and the Essex Conspiracy', *PMLA* 46 (1931), 694–719.

ALTHUSSER, LOUIS, 'Ideology and Ideological State Apparatuses: Notes towards an Investigation', in Louis Althusser, *Lenin and Philosophy and Other Essays* (New York: Monthly Review Press, 1971), 127–86.

—— *Machiavelli and Us*, ed. François Matheron, trans. Gregory Elliott (London: Verso, 1999).

ALTMAN, JOEL B., ' "Vile Participation": The Amplification of Violence in the Theater of *Henry V*', *Shakespeare Quarterly*, 42/1 (Spring 1991), 1–32.

ANDERSON, PERRY, *Lineages of the Absolutist State* (1974; repr. London: Verso, 1979).

ASCOLI, ALBERT RUSSELL, and KAHN, VICTORIA (eds.), *Machiavelli and the Discourse of Literature* (Ithaca, NY: Cornell University Press, 1993).

AUDEN, W. H., 'The Prince's Dog', in W. H. Auden, *The Dyer's Hand and Other Essays* (London: Random House, 1962), 182–208.

AUSTIN, J. L., *How to Do Things with Words* (Cambridge, Mass.: Harvard University Press, 1955).

BACON, FRANCIS, *Francis Bacon*, ed. Brian Vickers (Oxford: Clarendon, 1996).

BAINES, BARBARA J., 'Kingship of the Silent King: A Study of Shakespeare's Bolingbroke', *English Studies*, 61 (Feb. 1980), 24–36.

BAKHTIN, MIKHAIL, *Rabelais and his World*, trans. Helene Iswolsky (Cambridge, Mass.: MIT Press, 1968); trans. of *Tvorchestvo Fransua Rable* (Moscow: Khudozhestvennia literatura, 1965).

BARBER, C. L., *Creating Elizabethan Tragedy: The Theater of Marlowe and Kyd*, ed. Richard P. Wheeler (Chicago: University of Chicago Press, 1988).

—— *Shakespeare's Festive Comedy: A Study of Dramatic Form and its Relation to*

Social Custom (1959; repr. Cleveland: Meridian, 1963).

BARKER, FRANCIS, *The Tremulous Private Body: Essays in Subjection* (London: Methuen, 1984).

BARRIE, ROBERT, '*Telmahs*: Carnival Laughter in *Hamlet*', in Mark Thornton Burnett and John Manning (eds.), *New Essays on Hamlet* (New York: AMS Press, 1994), 83–100.

BARROLL, LEEDS, 'A New History for Shakespeare and his Time', *Shakespeare Quarterly* 39 (1988), 441–64.

BASSNETT, SUSAN, *Elizabeth I: A Feminist Perspective* (Oxford: Berg, 1988).

BAUDELAIRE, CHARLES, *Œuvres complètes de Baudelaire*, ed. Y.-G. Le Dantec and Claude Pichois (Paris: Pléiade, 1961).

BELSEY, CATHERINE, 'Feminism and Beyond', *Shakespeare Studies*, 25 (1997), 32–41.

—— *The Subject of Tragedy: Identity and Difference in Renaissance Drama* (London: Methuen, 1985).

BENJAMIN, WALTER, *Illuminations*, ed. Hannah Arendt, trans. Harry Zohn (New York: Harcourt, 1968).

—— *The Origins of German Tragic Drama* (1928), trans. John Osborne (London: New Left Books, 1977).

BERGER, Jr., HARRY, *Imaginary Audition: Shakespeare on Stage and Page* (Berkeley and Los Angeles: University of California Press, 1989).

BERGERON, DAVID, 'Shakespeare Makes History: *2 Henry IV*', *Studies in English Literature* 31 (1991), 231–45.

BERLIN, ISAIAH, 'The Originality of Machiavelli', in Isaiah Berlin (ed.), *Against the Current* (New York: Viking, 1980), 25–79.

BEST, STEVEN, and KELLNER, DOUGLAS, *Postmodern Theory: Critical Interrogations* (New York: Guilford, 1991).

BLANDPIED, JOHN W., *Time and the Artist in Shakespeare's English Histories* (Newark: University of Delaware Press, 1983).

BLOOM, HAROLD, *Shakespeare: The Invention of the Human* (New York: Riverhead, 1998).

BOGARD, TRAVIS, 'Shakespeare's Second Richard', *PMLA* 70/1 (Mar. 1955), 192–209.

BOOS, LYNDA, 'The Family in Shakespeare Studies; or—Studies in the Family of Shakespearians; or—The Politics of Politics', *Renaissance Quarterly*, 40 (Winter 1987), 707–42.

BOURDIEU, PIERRE, *Language and Symbolic Power*, ed. John B. Thompson, trans. Gino Raymond and Matthew Adamson (Cambridge, Mass.: Harvard University Press, 1991).

BOVÉ, PAUL A., 'Discourse', in Frank Lentricchia and Thomas McLaughlin (eds.), *Critical Terms for Literary Study*, 2nd edn. (Chicago: University of Chicago Press, 1995), 50–65.

BRADSHAW, GRAHAM, *Misrepresentations: Shakespeare and the Materialists*

(Ithaca, NY: Cornell University Press, 1993).

BRADSHAW, GRAHAM, *Shakespeare's Scepticism* (Ithaca, NY: Cornell University Press, 1987).

BRISTOL, MICHAEL, D., *Big-Time Shakespeare* (New York: Routledge, 1996).

—— *Carnival and Theater: Plebeian Culture and the Structure of Authority in Renaissance England* (New York: Methuen, 1985).

—— ' "Funeral Bak'd Meats": Carnival and the Carnivalesque in *Hamlet*', in Shakespeare, *Hamlet*, ed. Wofford, 348–67.

—— and MCLUSKIE, KATHLEEN (eds.), *The Performance of Modernity: Shakespeare and the Modern Theatre* (London: Routledge, 2001).

BROOKS, CLEANTH, and HEILMAN, ROBERT, *Understanding Drama* (New York: Holt, 1945).

BRUSTER, DOUGLAS, *Drama and the Market in the Age of Shakespeare* (Cambridge: Cambridge University Press, 1992).

BURCKHARDT, SIGURD, *Shakespearian Meanings* (Princeton: Princeton University Press, 1968).

CALDERWOOD, JAMES L., *Metadrama in Shakespeare's Henriad: 'Richard II' to 'Henry V'* (Berkeley and Los Angeles: University of California Press, 1979).

Calendar of State Papers, Domestic, ed. Mary Anne Everett Green (London: Stationers Office, 1869).

CAMDEN, WILLIAM, *The History of the Most Renowned and Victorious Princess Elizabeth, Late Queen of England*, 4th edn. (1866; repr. New York: AMS Press, 1970).

CAMPBELL, LILY B., *Shakespeare's 'Histories': Mirrors of Elizabethan Policy* (San Marino, Calif.: Huntington Library, 1947).

CAPELL, EDWARD, *Notes and Various Readings to Shakespeare*, 2 vols. (London: Henry Hughs, 1779–80).

CAVELL, STANLEY, *The Claim of Reason: Wittgenstein, Scepticism, Morality, and Tragedy* (Oxford: Oxford University Press, 1980).

—— *Disowning Knowledge: In Six Plays of Shakespeare* (Cambridge: Cambridge University Press, 1987).

CHAMBERS, E. K., *William Shakespeare: A Study of Facts and Problems*, 2 vols. (Oxford: Clarendon, 1930).

CHARNES, LINDA, *Hamlet's Heirs: Essays on Inheriting Shakespeare* (London: Routledge, forthcoming).

—— 'The Hamlet Formerly Known as Prince', in Grady (ed.), *Shakespeare and Modernity*, 89–210.

—— *Notorious Identity: Materializing the Subject in Shakespeare* (Cambridge, Mass.: Harvard University Press, 1993).

CODDON, KARIN S., ' "Suche Strange Desygns": Madness, Subjectivity, and Treason in *Hamlet* and Elizabethan Culture', *Renaissance Drama: New Series*, 20 (1989), 51–75; repr. in Shakespeare, *Hamlet*, ed. Wofford, 380–402.

COHEN, WALTER, 'Political Criticism of Shakespeare', in Jean E. Howard and

Marion F. O'Connor (eds.), *Shakespeare Reproduced: The Text in History and Ideology* (New York: Methuen, 1987), 18–46.

COLERIDGE, SAMUEL TAYLOR, *Shakespearian Criticism*, ed. Thomas Raysor, 2nd edn. (London: Dent, 1960).

COLLINS, CHURTON, *Studies in Shakespeare* (New York: Dutton, 1904).

DANBY, JOHN F., *Shakespeare's Doctrine of Nature: A Study of 'King Lear'* (London: Faber, 1949).

DE Grazia, MARGRETA, 'Teleology, Delay, and the "Old Mole"', *Shakespeare Quarterly*, 50/3 (Fall 1999), 251–67.

—— QUILLIGAN, MAUREEN, and STALLYBRASS, PETER (eds.), *Subject and Object in Renaissance Culture* (Cambridge: Cambridge University Press, 1996).

DERRIDA, JACQUES, *Specters of Marx: The State of the Debt, the Work of Mourning, and the New International*, trans. Peggy Kamuf (New York: Routledge, 1994).

DEWS, PETER, 'Althusser, Structuralism, and the French Epistemological Tradition', in Gregory Elliott (ed.), *Althusser: A Critical Reader* (Oxford: Blackwell, 1994), 104–41.

—— 'Adorno, Poststructuralism and the Critique of Identity', in Andrew Benjamin (ed.), *The Problems of Modernity: Adorno and Benjamin* (London: Routledge, 1989), 1–22.

DOLLIMORE, JONATHAN, *Radical Tragedy: Religion, Ideology, and Power in the Drama of Shakespeare and his Contemporaries* (1984; 2nd edn. London: Harvester, 1989).

—— and SINFIELD, ALAN, 'History and Ideology: The Instance of *Henry V*', in John Drakakis (ed.), *Alternative Shakespeares* (London: Methuen, 1985), 206–27.

DRISCOLL, JAMES P., *Identity in Shakespearian Drama* (Lewisburg, Pa.: Bucknell University Press, 1983).

EAGLETON, TERRY, *The Ideology of the Aesthetic* (Oxford: Basil Blackwell, 1990).

—— *William Shakespeare* (Oxford: Basil Blackwell, 1986).

ELLIS-FERMOR, UNA, *The Frontiers of Drama* (1945; repr. New York: Methuen, 1964).

ELLRODT, ROBERT, 'Self-Consciousness in Montaigne and Shakespeare', *Shakespeare Survey*, 28 (1975), 37–50.

EMPSON, WILLIAM, *Some Versions of Pastoral* (New York: New Directions, 1968).

ENGLE, LARS, '*Measure for Measure* and Modernity: The Problem of the Sceptic's Authority', in Grady (ed.), *Shakespeare and Modernity*, 85–104.

—— *Shakespearian Pragmatism: Market of his Time* (Chicago: University of Chicago Press, 1993).

FARNHAM, WILLARD, 'The Mediaeval Comic Spirit in the English Renaissance', in James G. McManaway, Giles E. Dawson, and Wedwin E. Willoughby (eds.), *Joseph Quincy Adams: Memorial Studies* (Washington, DC: Folger, 1948), 429–37.

FEIS, JACOB, *Shakespeare and Montaigne* (1884; repr. Geneva: Slatkine, 1970).

FELPERIN, HOWARD, *The Uses of the Canon: Elizabethan Literature and Contemporary Theory* (Oxford: Clarendon, 1990).

FERGUSON, MARGARET W., QUILLIGAN, MAUREEN, and VICKERS, NANCY J. (eds.), *Rewriting the Renaissance: The Discourses of Sexual Difference in Early Modern Europe* (Chicago: University of Chicago Press, 1986).

FINEMAN, JOEL, *Shakespeare's Perjured Eye: The Invention of Poetic Subjectivity in the Sonnets* (Berkeley and Los Angeles: University of California Press, 1986).

FOAKES, R. A., *'Hamlet' vs. 'Lear': Cultural Politics and Shakespeare's Art* (Cambridge: Cambridge University Press, 1993).

FOLLAND, HAROLD F., 'King Richard's Pallid Victory', *Shakespeare Quarterly*, 24/4 (Autumn 1973), 390–9.

FOUCAULT, MICHEL, *The Archaeology of Knowledge*, trans. A. M. Sheridan Smith (New York: Pantheon, 1982).

—— 'The Ethic of Care for the Self as a Practice of Freedom', in James Bernauer and David Rasmussen (eds.), *The Final Foucault* (Cambridge, Mass: MIT Press, 1988), 1–20.

—— *Discipline and Punish: The Birth of the Prison*, trans. Alan Sheridan (New York: Vintage, 1979).

—— 'Governmentality', in Graham Burchell, Colin Gordon, and Peter Miller (eds.), *The Foucault Effect: Studies in Governmentality* (Chicago: University of Chicago Press, 1991), 87–104.

—— *The History of Sexuality*, i: *An Introduction* (1976), trans. Robert Hurley (New York: Vintage, 1990).

—— *Language, Counter-Memory, Practice: Selected Essays and Interviews*, ed. Donald F. Bouchard, trans. Donald F. Bouchard and Sherry Simon (Ithaca, NY: Cornell University Press, 1977).

—— 'What Is an Author?' (1969), in Foucault, *Language, Counter-Memory, Practice*, 113–38.

FRAME, DONALD, *Montaigne: A Biography* (New York: Harcourt, 1965).

FREEMAN, LESLIE, 'Shakespeare's Kings and Machiavelli's Prince', in Anne Paolucci (ed.), *Shakespeare Encomium* (New York: The City College, 1964), 25–43.

FRIEDRICH, HUGO, *Montaigne* (1949, 1967), ed. Philippe Desan, trans. Dawn Eng (Berkeley and Los Angeles: University of California Press, 1991).

FRYE, SUSAN, *Elizabeth I: The Competition for Representation* (New York: Oxford University Press, 1993).

GARDINER, STEPHEN, *A Machiavellian Treatise*, ed. and trans. Peter Samuel Donaldson (Cambridge: Cambridge University Press, 1975).

GIDDENS, ANTHONY, *Modernity and Self-Identity: Self and Society in the Late Modern Age* (Stanford, Calif.: Stanford University Press, 1991).

GODDARD, HAROLD C., *The Meaning of Shakespeare* (Chicago: University of Chicago Press, 1951).

GOLDBERG, JONATHAN, 'Shakespearian Inscriptions: The Voicings of Power', in

Patricia Parker and Geoffrey Hartman (eds.), *Shakespeare and the Question of Theory* (New York: Methuen, 1985), 116–37.

—— 'The Commodity of Names: "Falstaff" and "Oldcastle" in *1 Henry IV*', in Jonathan Crewe (ed.), *Reconfiguring the Renaissance: Essays in Critical Materialism* (Cranbury, NJ: Associated University Presses, 1992), 76–88.

GOULD, GERALD, 'A New Reading of "Henry V" ', *English Review*, 29 (July 1919), 42–55.

GRADY, HUGH, 'Containment, Subversion—and Postmodernism', *Textual Practice*, 7/1 (Spring 1993), 31–49.

—— *The Modernist Shakespeare: Critical Texts in a Material World* (Oxford: Clarendon, 1991).

—— 'Modernity, Modernism, and Postmodernism in the Twentieth Century's Shakespeare', in Bristol and McLuskie (eds.), *The Performance of Modernity*, 20–35.

—— 'On the Need for a Differentiated Theory of the (Early) Modern Subject', in John J. Joughin (ed.), *Philosophical Shakespeares* (London: Routledge, 2000), 34–50.

—— 'Renewing Modernity: Changing Contexts and Contents of a Nearly Invisible Concept', *Shakespeare Quarterly*, 50/3 (Autumn 1999), 268–84.

—— (ed.), *Shakespeare and Modernity: From Early Modern to Millennium* (London: Routledge, 2000).

—— *Shakespeare's Universal Wolf: Studies in Early Modern Reification* (Oxford: Clarendon, 1996).

GREENBLATT, STEPHEN J., *Hamlet in Purgatory* (Princeton: Princeton University Press, 2001).

—— 'Invisible Bullets', in Greenblatt, *Shakespearian Negotiations*, 21–65.

—— *Learning to Curse: Essays in Early Modern Culture* (New York: Routledge, 1990).

—— *Renaissance Self-Fashioning: From More to Shakespeare* (Chicago: University of Chicago Press, 1980).

—— *Shakespearian Negotiations: The Circulation of Social Energy in Renaissance England* (Berkeley and Los Angeles: University of California Press, 1988).

GREENE, THOMAS M., 'Dangerous Parleys—*Essais* I: 5 and 6', *Yale French Studies*, 64 (1983), 3–23.

GURR, ANDREW, ' "Henry V" and the Bees' Commonwealth', *Shakespeare Survey*, 30 (1977), 61–72.

—— introduction to William Shakespeare, *King Henry V* (Cambridge: Cambridge University Press, 1992), 1–55.

HABERMAS, JÜRGEN, *The Theory of Communicative Action*, 2 vols. (Boston: Beacon, 1984, 1987).

HALPERN, RICHARD, *The Poetics of Primitive Accumulation: English Renaissance Culture and the Genealogy of Capital* (Ithaca, NY: Cornell University Press, 1991).

BIBLIOGRAPHY

HALPERN, RICHARD, *Shakespeare among the Moderns* (Ithaca, NY: Cornell University Press, 1997).

HARMON, ALICE, 'How Great was Shakespeare's Debt to Montaigne?', *PMLA* 57 (1942), 988–1008.

HARRISON, G. B., *The Elizabethan Journals: Being a Record of Those Things Most Talked of During the Years 1591–1603*, vol. iii (Ann Arbor: University of Michigan, 1955).

HAWKES, TERENCE, 'Bryn Glas', in Ania Loomba and Martin Orkin (eds.), *Post-colonial Shakespeares*, (London: Routledge, 1998), 117–40.

—— *Meaning by Shakespeare* (London: Routledge, 1992).

—— *Shakespeare in the Present* (London: Routledge, 2002).

—— *Shakespeare's Talking Animals: Language and Drama in Society* (London: Edward Arnold, 1973).

—— *That Shakespeherian Rag: Essays on a Critical Process* (New York: Methuen, 1986).

—— 'The Word against the Word: The Role of Language in "Richard II"', *Language and Style*, 2/1 (Spring 1969), 296–322.

HAYWARD, JOHN, *The First and Second Parts of John Hayward's 'The Life and Raigne of King Henrie IIII'*, ed. John J. Manning, Camden Fourth Series 42 (London: Royal Historical Society, 1991).

HAZLITT, WILLIAM, *Characters of Shakespeare's Plays* (1817; repr. London: Dent, 1906).

HEFFNER, RAY, 'Shakespeare, Hayward, and Essex', *PMLA* 45 (1930), 754–80.

HELD, DAVID, *Introduction to Critical Theory: Horkheimer to Habermas* (Berkeley and Los Angeles: University of California Press, 1980).

HELGERSON, RICHARD, *Forms of Nationhood: The Elizabethan Writing of England* (Chicago: University of Chicago Press, 1992).

HENDRICKS, MARGO, and PARKER, PATRICIA (eds.), *Women, 'Race', and Writing in the Early Modern Period* (London: Routledge, 1994).

HIGHLEY, CHRISTOPHER, *Shakespeare, Spenser, and the Crisis in Ireland* (Cambridge: Cambridge University Press, 1997).

HILTON, RODNEY (ed.), *The Transition from Feudalism to Capitalism* (London: Verso, 1976).

HODGEN, MARGARET, 'Montaigne and Shakespeare Again', *Huntington Library Quarterly*, 16 (1952), 23–42.

HOLDERNESS, GRAHAM (ed.), *The Shakespeare Myth* (Manchester: Manchester University Press, 1988).

—— *Shakespeare's History* (New York: St Martin's Press, 1985).

—— 'Shakespeare's History: "Richard II"', *Literature and History*, 7/1 (Spring 1981), 2–24.

HOMAN, SIDNEY, '"Richard II": The Aesthetics of Judgment', *Studies in the Literary Imagination*, 5/1 (Apr. 1972), 65–71.

HOOKER, ELIZABETH, 'The Relation of Shakespeare to Montaigne', *PMLA* 17

(1902), 313–66.

HORKHEIMER, MAX, *Between Philosophy and Social Science: Selected Early Writings*, trans. G. Frederick Hunter, Matthew S. Kramer, and John Torpey (Cambridge, Mass.: MIT Press, 1993).

—— and ADORNO, THEODOR W., *Dialectic of Enlightenment*, trans. John Cumming (Boston: Seabury, 1972).

HOWARD, JEAN E., *The Stage and Social Struggle in Early Modern England* (New York: Routledge, 1994).

—— and RACKIN, PHYLLIS, *Engendering a Nation: A Feminist Account of Shakespeare's English Histories* (London: Routledge, 1997).

—— and SHERSHOW, SCOTT CUTLER (eds.), *Marxist Shakespeares* (London: Routledge, 2001).

HUGO, FRIEDRICH, *Montaigne* (1949, 1967), ed. Philippe Desan, trans. Dawn Eng (Berkeley and Los Angeles: University of California Press, 1991).

HUNTER, G. K., ' "Henry IV" and the Elizabethan Two-Part Play', *The Review of English Studies*, 5/14 (July 1954), 236–48.

ISER, WOLFGANG, *Staging Politics: The Lasting Impact of Shakespeare's Histories*, trans. David Henry Wilson (New York: Columbia University Press, 1993).

JACKSON, T. A., 'Letters and Documents: Marx and Shakespeare', *International Literature*, 2 (Feb. 1936), 75–97.

JAMESON, FREDRIC, *Marxism and Form: Twentieth-Century Dialectical Theories of Literature* (Princeton: Princeton University Press, 1971).

—— *The Political Unconscious: Narrative as a Socially Symbolic Act* (Ithaca, NY: Cornell University Press, 1981).

JARDINE, LISA, and STEWART, ALAN, *Hostage to Fortune: The Troubled Life of Francis Bacon* (New York: Hill & Wang, 1999).

JAY, MARTIN, *The Dialectical Imagination: A History of the Frankfurt School and the Institute of Social Research, 1923–1950* (Boston: Little, 1973).

JOHNSON, SAMUEL, 'Notes on Shakespeare's Plays: "I Henry IV"', in *The Yale Edition of the Works of Samuel Johnson: Johnson on Shakespeare*, ed. Arthur Sherbo (New Haven: Yale University Press, 1968), vii. 453–89.

JOUGHIN, JOHN J., 'Shakespeare, Modernity and the Aesthetic: Art, Truth and Judgement in *The Winter's Tale*', in Grady (ed.), *Shakespeare and Modernity*, 61–84.

JOURDAN, SERENA, *The Sparrow and the Flea: The Sense of Providence in Shakespeare and Montaigne* (Salzburg: Institut für Anglistik und Amerikanistik Universität Salzburg, 1983).

KAHN, COPPÉLIA, *Man's Estate: Masculine Identity in Shakespeare* (Berkeley and Los Angeles: University of California Press, 1981).

KAHN, VICTORIA, *Machiavellian Rhetoric: From the Counter-Reformation to Milton* (Princeton: Princeton University Press, 1994).

—— '*Virtù* and the Example of Agathocles in Machiavelli's *Prince*', in Ascoli and Kahn (eds.), *Machiavelli and the Discourse of Literature*, 195–217.

KAISER, WALTER, *Praisers of Folly: Erasmus, Rabelais, Shakespeare* (Cambridge, Mass.: Harvard University Press, 1963).

KANTOROWICZ, E. H., *The King's Two Bodies* (Princeton: Princeton University Press, 1957).

KASTAN, DAVID SCOTT, ' "The King Hath Many Marching in his Coats", or, What Did You Do in the War, Daddy?', in Ivo Kamps (ed.), *Shakespeare Left and Right* (London: Routledge, 1991), 241–58.

—— 'Proud Majesty Made a Subject: Shakespeare and the Spectacle of Rule', *Shakespeare Quarterly*, 37/4 (Winter 1986), 459–75.

KELLNER, DOUGLAS, *Critical Theory, Marxism, and Modernity* (Baltimore: Johns Hopkins University Press, 1989).

KELLY, H. A., *Divine Providence in the England of Shakespeare's Histories* (Cambridge, Mass.: Harvard University Press, 1970).

KERNAN, ALVIN, '*The Henriad*: Shakespeare's Major History Plays', *Yale Review*, 59 (Oct. 1969), 3–32.

KNIGHT, G. WILSON, *The Imperial Theme: Further Interpretations of Shakespeare's Tragedies* (London: Oxford University Press, 1931).

KNIGHTS, L. C., 'Notes on Comedy', in F. R. Leavis (ed.), *Determinations: Critical Essays* (London: Chatto, 1934), 109–31.

—— 'Shakespeare's Politics: With Some Reflections on the Nature of Tradition', *Proceedings of the British Academy* (London: Oxford University Press, 1957), 115–32.

—— *Some Shakespearian Themes* (Stanford, Calif.: Stanford University Press, 1960).

—— *William Shakespeare: The Histories* (London: Longmans, 1962).

KNOWLES, RONALD (ed.), *Shakespeare and Carnival: After Bakhtin* (Basingstoke: Macmillan, 1998).

KOTT, JAN, *Shakespeare our Contemporary*, trans. Boleslaw Taborski (New York: Doubleday, 1966).

LACAN, JACQUES, *Écrits: A Selection*, trans. Alan Sheridan (New York: Norton, 1977).

—— *The Four Fundamental Concepts of Psycho-analysis*, ed. Jacques Allain-Miller, trans. Alan Sheridan (New York: Norton, 1981).

LANGBAUM, ROBERT, *The Poetry of Experience: The Dramatic Monologue in Modern Literary Tradition* (New York: Random House, 1957).

LAROQUE, FRANÇOIS, *Shakespeare's Festive World: Elizabethan Seasonal Entertainment and the Professional Stage*, trans. Janet Lloyd (Cambridge: Cambridge University Press, 1991).

LEE, JOHN, *Shakespeare's 'Hamlet' and the Controversies of Self* (Oxford: Clarendon, 2000).

LEE, SIDNEY, *The French Renaissance in England* (New York: Scribner, 1910).

LEECH, CLIFFORD, 'The Unity of "2 Henry IV"', *Shakespeare Survey*, 6 (1953), 16–24.

LENZ, CAROLYN, GREENE, GAYLE, and NEELY, CAROL (eds.), *The Woman's Part: Feminist Criticism of Shakespeare* (Urbana: University of Illinois Press, 1980).

LERNER, MAX, introduction to Machiavelli, *The Prince and The Discourses.*

LESCHEMELLE, PIERRE, *Montaigne: The Fool of the Farce*, trans. William J. Beck (New York: Peter Lang, 1995).

LESSING, GOTTHOLD EPHRAIM, *Hamburg Dramaturgy*, trans. Helen Zimmern (New York: Dover, 1962).

LEVINE, JOSEPH M., *Elizabeth I: Great Lives Observed* (Englewood Cliffs, NJ: Prentice-Hall, 1969).

LEWIS, WYNDHAM, *The Lion and the Fox: The Role of the Hero in the Plays of Shakespeare* (London: G. Richards, 1927).

LUKÁCS, GEORG, *The Theory of the Novel*, trans. Anna Bostock (Cambridge, Mass.: MIT Press, 1971).

MCALINDON, T., *Shakespeare and Decorum* (London: Macmillan, 1973).

MACCAFFREY, WALLACE T., *Elizabeth I: War and Politics, 1588–1603* (Princeton: Princeton University Press, 1992).

MACEY, DAVID, 'Thinking with Borrowed Concepts: Althusser and Lacan', in Gregory Elliott (ed.), *Althusser: A Critical Reader* (Oxford: Blackwell, 1994), 142–58.

MACHIAVELLI, NICCOLÒ, *Discourses on Livy*, trans. Harvey C. Mansfield and Nathan Tarcov (Chicago: University of Chicago Press, 1996).

—— *The Prince: A Norton Critical Edition*, ed. and trans. Robert M. Adams (New York: Norton, 1977).

—— *The Prince and The Discourses* (New York: Modern Library, 1950).

MCLUSKIE, KATHLEEN, 'The Patriarchal Bard: Feminist Criticism and Shakespeare: *King Lear* and *Measure for Measure*', in Jonathan Dollimore and Alan Sinfield (eds.), *Political Shakespeare: Essays in Cultural Materialism* (Ithaca, NY: Cornell University Press, 1985), 88–108.

MCMILLIN, SCOTT, and MACLEAN, SALLY-BETH, *The Queen's Men and their Plays* (Cambridge: Cambridge University Press, 1998).

MAHOOD, M. M., *Shakespeare's Wordplay* (London: Methuen, 1957).

MALLIN, Eric S., 'Emulous Factions and the Collapse of Chivalry: *Troilus and Cressida*', *Representations*, 29 (Winter 1990), 145–79.

—— *Inscribing the Time: Shakespeare and the End of Elizabethan England* (Berkeley and Los Angeles: University of California Press, 1996).

MANHEIM, MICHAEL, *The Weak King Dilemma in the Shakespearian History Play* (Syracuse, NY: Syracuse University Press, 1973).

MANNING, JOHN J., introduction to John Hayward, *The First and Second Parts of John Hayward's 'The Life and Raigne of King Henrie IIII'*, ed. John J. Manning, Camden Fourth Series 42 (London: Royal Historical Society, 1991), 1–57.

MARCUS, LEAH, *The Politics of Mirth: Jonson, Herrick, Milton, Marvell, and the Defense of Old Holiday Pastimes* (Chicago: University of Chicago Press, 1986).

—— *Puzzling Shakespeare: Local Reading and its Discontents* (Berkeley and Los

Angeles: University of California Press, 1988).

MARCUSE, HERBERT, 'The Affirmative Character of Culture', in *Negations: Essays in Critical Theory* (Boston: Beacon, 1968), 88–133.

MARTIN, R. A., 'Metatheater, Gender, and Subjectivity in *Richard II* and *Henry IV, Part I*', *Comparative Drama*, 23 (1989), 255–64.

MAUS, KATHARINE EISAMAN, *Inwardness and Theater in the English Renaissance* (Chicago: University of Chicago Press, 1995).

MERCER, PETER, *'Hamlet' and the Acting of Revenge* (London: Macmillan, 1987).

MEYER, EDWARD, *Machiavelli and the Elizabethan Drama* (Weimar: Literarhistorische Forschungen, 1897).

MONTAIGNE, MICHEL DE, *The Complete Essays of Montaigne*, trans. Donald M. Frame (Stanford, Calif.: Stanford University Press, 1965).

—— *Les Essais*, ed. Pierre Villey (Quadrige: Presses Universitaires de France, 1988).

—— *The Essayes of Montaigne*, trans. John Florio (New York: Modern Library, 1933).

MONTROSE, LOUIS, *The Purpose of Playing: Shakespeare and the Cultural Politics of the Elizabethan Theater* (Chicago: University of Chicago Press, 1996).

MUNRO, JOHN (ed.), *The Shakespeare-Allusion Book: A Collection of Allusions to Shakespeare from 1591–1700*, 2 vols. (London: Oxford University Press, 1932).

NEELY, CAROL THOMAS, 'Constructing the Subject: Feminist Practice and the New Renaissance Discourses', *English Literary Renaissance*, 18 (Winter 1988), 5–18.

NEILL, MICHAEL, introduction to William Shakespeare, *Antony and Cleopatra*, ed. Michael Neill (Oxford: Oxford University Press, 1994), 1–130.

NICHOLS, JOHN, *The Progresses and Public Processions of Queen Elizabeth*, 3 vols. (1783; repr. London: John Nichols & Son, 1823).

NUTTAL, A. D., 'Ovid's Narcissus and Shakespeare's Richard II: The Reflected Self', in Charles Martindale (ed.), *Ovid Renewed: Ovidian Influences on Literature and Art from the Middle Ages to the Twentieth Century* (Cambridge: Cambridge University Press, 1988), 137–50.

PARKER, PATRICIA, *Literary Fat Ladies* (London: Methuen, 1987).

—— *Shakespeare from the Margins: Language, Culture, Context* (Chicago: University of Chicago Press, 1996).

PATER, WALTER, 'Shakespeare's English Kings', in *Appreciations: With an Essay on Style* (1889; repr. London: Macmillan, 1910), 185–204.

PATTERSON, ANNABEL, *Censorship and Interpretation: The Conditions of Writing and Reading in Early Modern England* (Madison: University of Wisconsin Press, 1984).

—— *Shakespeare and the Popular Voice* (Oxford: Basil Blackwell, 1989).

PECHTER, EDWARD, 'The New Historicism and its Discontents', *PMLA* 102 (May 1987), 292–303.

PETTIGREW, JOHN, 'The Mood of *Henry IV, Part 2*', in B. A. W. Jackson (ed.), *Stratford Papers, 1965–67* (Shannon: Irish University Press, 1969), 145–67.

PITKIN, HANNA, *Fortune Is a Woman: Gender and Politics in the Thought of Niccolò Machiavelli* (Berkeley and Los Angeles: University of California Press, 1984).

POCOCK, J. G. A., *The Machiavellian Moment: Florentine Political Thought and the Atlantic Republican Tradition* (Princeton: Princeton University Press, 1975).

POOLE, KRISTEN, 'Facing Puritanism: Falstaff, Martin Marprelate and the Grotesque Puritan', in Knowles (ed.), *Shakespeare and Carnival*, 97–122.

—— 'Saints Alive! Falstaff, Martin Marprelate, and the Staging of Puritanism', *Shakespeare Quarterly*, 46/1 (Spring 1995), 47–75.

POPKIN, RICHARD H., *The History of Skepticism from Erasmus to Spinoza* (Berkeley and Los Angeles: University of California Press, 1979).

PRAZ, MARIO, *The Flaming Heart: Essays on Crashaw, Machiavelli, and Other Studies in the Relations between Italian and English Literature from Chaucer to T. S. Eliot* (Garden City, NY: Doubleday, 1958).

PRIESTLEY, J. B., *The English Comic Characters* (London: John Lane, 1925).

PYE, CHRISTOPHER, *The Regal Phantasm: Shakespeare and the Politics of Spectacle* (London: Routledge, 1990).

QUINN, MICHAEL, ' "The King Is Not Himself": The Personal Tragedy of *Richard II*', *Studies in Philology*, 56 (1959), 169–86.

QUINT, DAVID, 'Alexander the Pig: Shakespeare on History and Poetry', *Boundary 2*, 10 (1982), 49–63.

—— *Montaigne and the Quality of Mercy: Ethical and Political Themes in the Essais* (Princeton: Princeton University Press, 1998).

RAAB, FELIX, *The English Face of Machiavelli: A Changing Interpretation, 1500–1700* (London: Routledge, 1964).

RABKIN, NORMAN, 'Rabbits, Ducks, and "Henry V" ', *Shakespeare Quarterly*, 28/3 (Summer 1977), 279–96.

—— *Shakespeare and the Common Understanding* (New York: The Free Press, 1967).

—— *Shakespeare and the Problem of Meaning* (Chicago: University of Chicago Press, 1981).

RACKIN, PHYLLIS, *Stages of History: Shakespeare's English Chronicles* (Ithaca, NY: Cornell University Press, 1990).

RAGLAND-SULLIVAN, ELLIE, *Jacques Lacan and the Philosophy of Psychoanalysis* (Urbana: University of Illinois Press, 1987).

REBHORN, WAYNE A., *Foxes and Lions: Machiavelli's Confidence Men* (Ithaca, NY: Cornell University Press, 1988).

REESE, M. M., *The Cease of Majesty: A Study of Shakespeare's History Plays* (London: Arnold, 1961).

REGOSIN, RICHARD L., *The Matter of my Book: Montaigne's 'Essais' as the Book of the Self* (Berkeley and Los Angeles: University of California Press, 1977).

—— *Montaigne's Unruly Brood: Textual Engendering and the Challenge to Paternal Authority* (Berkeley and Los Angeles: University of California Press, 1996).

REISS, TIMOTHY J., 'Montaigne and the Subject of Polity', in P. Parker and D.

Quint (eds.), *Literary Theory/Renaissance Texts* (Baltimore: Johns Hopkins University Press, 1986), 115–49.

RIBNER, IRVING, 'Bolingbroke, a True Machiavellian', *Modern Language Quarterly*, 9/2 (June 1948), 177–84.

ROBERTSON, JOHN M., *Montaigne and Shakespeare and Other Essays on Cognate Questions*, 2nd edn.(1909; repr. New York: Burt Franklin, 1969).

ROSSITER, A. P., *Angel with Horns and Other Shakespeare Lectures*, ed. Graham Storey (New York: Theatre Arts Books, 1961).

ROTHSCHILD, JR., HERBERT B., 'Falstaff and the Picaresque Tradition', *Modern Language Review*, 68/1 (Jan. 1973), 14–21.

SCHOENBAUM, SAMUEL, *Shakespeare's Lives*, new edn. (Oxford: Oxford University Press, 1993).

SCOTT, MARK W. (ed.), *Shakespearian Criticism: Excerpts from the Criticism of William Shakespeare's Plays and Poetry, from the First Published Appraisals to Current Evaluations*, vol. vi (Detroit: Gale, 1987).

SHAKESPEARE, WILLIAM, *The Norton Shakespeare*, ed. Stephen Greenblatt et al. (New York: Norton, 1997).

—— *Hamlet*, ed. Susanne L. Wofford (Boston: Bedford, 1994).

SHARPE, KEVIN, *Reading Revolutions: The Politics of Reading in Early Modern England* (New Haven: Yale University Press, 2000).

SHAW, BERNARD, *Shaw on Shakespeare: An Anthology of Bernard Shaw's Writings on the Plays and Productions of Shakespeare*, ed. Edwin Wilson (London: Dutton, 1961).

SIMPSON, RICHARD, 'The Politics of Shakespeare's Historical Plays', *Transactions of the New Shakspere Society*, 1st ser. 2 (13 Mar. 1874), 396–441.

SLIGHTS, CAMILLE WELLS, 'Slaves and Subjects in *Othello*', *Shakespeare Quarterly*, 48/4 (Winter 1997), 377–90.

SMITH, LACEY BALDWIN, *The Elizabethan World* (1967; repr. Boston: Houghton Mifflin, 1991).

—— *Treason in Tudor England: Politics and Paranoia* (London: Jonathan Cape, 1986).

SOLOMON, MAYNARD (ed.), *Marxism and Art: Essays Classic and Contemporary* (New York: Vintage, 1974).

SOLOMON, ROBERT, *The Passions: The Myth and Nature of Human Emotion* (Garden City, NY: Doubleday, 1976).

SPARGO, JOHN W., 'An Interpretation of Falstaff', *The Washington University Studies*, 9/2 (Apr. 1922), 119–33.

STALLYBRASS, PETER, and WHITE, ALLON, *The Politics and Poetics of Transgression* (Ithaca, NY: Cornell University Press, 1986).

STARKEY, DAVID (ed.), *Rivals in Power: Lives and Letters of the Great Tudor Dynasties* (New York: Grove Weidenfeld, 1990).

STAROBINSKI, JEAN, *Montaigne in Motion* (1982), trans. Arthur Goldhammer (Chicago: University of Chicago Press, 1985).

STEDEFELD, G. F., *Hamlet: Ein Tendenzdrama Shakespeares gegen die skeptische und kosmopolitische Weltanschauung des Michel de Montaigne* (Berlin: Gebrüder Paetel, 1871).

STIRLING, BRENT, 'Bolingbroke's "Decision"', *Shakespeare Quarterly*, 2/1 (Jan. 1951), 27–34.

STOLL, E. E., 'Falstaff', *Modern Philology*, 12/4 (Oct. 1914), 65–108.

—— '"Henry V"', in E. E. Stoll, *Poets and Playwrights: Shakespeare, Jonson, Spenser, Milton* (Minneapolis: University of Minnesota Press, 1930), 31–54.

—— *Shakespeare Studies: Historical and Comparative in Method* (New York: Stechert, 1942).

STRAUSS, LEO, *Thoughts on Machiavelli* (Glencoe, Ill.: Free Press, 1958).

SWINBURNE, ALGERNON CHARLES, *A Study of Shakespeare* (London: Worthington, 1880).

TALBERT, E. W., *Elizabethan Drama and Shakespeare's Early Plays: An Essay in Historical Criticism* (Chapel Hill: University of North Carolina Press, 1963).

TATE, NAHUM, preface to *The History of King Richard the Second* (London: Richard Tonson, 1681).

TAYLOR, CHARLES, *Sources of the Self: The Making of the Modern Identity* (Cambridge, Mass.: Harvard University Press, 1989).

TAYLOR, GARY, 'The Fortunes of Oldcastle', *Shakespeare Survey*, 38 (1985), 85–100.

—— Introduction to William Shakespeare, *Henry V*, ed. Gary Taylor (Oxford: Clarendon, 1982), 1–74.

TAYLOR, GEORGE COFFIN, *Shakespeare's Debt to Montaigne* (Cambridge, Mass.: Harvard University Press, 1925).

TERRAY, EMMANUEL, 'An Encounter: Althusser and Machiavelli', trans. Antonio Callari and David F. Ruccio, in Antonio Callari and David F. Ruccio (eds.), *Postmodern Materialism and the Future of Marxist Theory: Essays in the Althusserian Tradition* (Hanover: University Press of New England, 1996), 257–77.

TILLYARD, E. M. W., *Shakespeare's History Plays* (1944; repr. New York: Macmillan, 1946).

TODOROV, TZVETAN, 'L'Être et l'autre: Montaigne', *Yale French Studies*, 64 (1983), 113–44.

TOULMIN, STEPHEN, *Cosmopolis: The Hidden Agenda of Modernity* (New York: Free Press, 1990).

TRAUB, VALERIE, 'Prince Hal's Falstaff: Positioning Psychoanalysis and the Female Reproductive Body', *Shakespeare Quarterly*, 40/4 (Winter 1989), 456–74.

TRAVERSI, DEREK, '"Henry IV—Part I"' and '"Henry IV—Part II"', *Scrutiny*, 15/1 and 2 (Winter 1947 and Spring 1948), 24–35 and 117–27.

—— *Shakespeare: From 'Richard II' to 'Henry V'* (Stanford, Calif.: Stanford University Press, 1957).

ULRICI, HERMANN, *Shakespeare's Dramatic Art: And his Relation to Calderon and Goethe*, trans. A. J. W. Morrison (London: Chapman, 1846).

UNGERER, GUSTAV, *A Spaniard in Elizabethan England: The Correspondence of*

Antonio Perez's Exile, 2 vols. (London: Tamesis Books, 1974–6).

URE, PETER, introduction to William Shakespeare, *King Richard II*, The Arden Shakespeare (London: Methuen, 1956), pp. xiii–lxxxiv.

VAN DOREN, MARK, *Shakespeare* (New York: Holt, 1939).

VICKERS, BRIAN, *Appropriating Shakespeare: Contemporary Critical Quarrels* (New Haven: Yale University Press, 1993).

—— *The Artistry of Shakespeare's Prose*, rev. edn. (London: Methuen, 1968).

VILLEY, PIERRE, *Les Sources et l'évolution des Essais de Montaigne*, 2 vols. (Paris: Hachette, 1908).

WALCH, GÜNTER, '*Henry V* as Working-House of Ideology', *Shakespeare Survey*, 40 (1988), 63–8.

WAYNE, DON E., 'Power, Politics, and the Shakespearian Text: Recent Criticism in England and the United States', in Jean E. Howard and Marion F. O'Connor (eds.), *Shakespeare Reproduced: The Text in History and Ideology* (New York: Methuen, 1987), 47–67.

WEIMANN, ROBERT, *Author's Pen and Actor's Voice: Playing and Writing in Shakespeare's Theatre*, ed. Helen Higbee and William West (Cambridge: Cambridge University Press, 2000).

—— *Shakespeare and the Popular Tradition in the Theater: Studies in the Social Dimension of Dramatic Form and Function*, ed. Robert Schwartz (Baltimore: Johns Hopkins University Press, 1978).

WELLS, STANLEY, and TAYLOR, GARY, *William Shakespeare: A Textual Companion* (New York: Norton, 1997).

—— (eds.), *William Shakespeare: The Complete Works* (Oxford: Oxford University Press, 1988).

WELLS, SUSAN, *Sweet Reason: Intersubjective Rhetoric and the Discourses of Modernity* (Chicago: University of Chicago Press, 1996).

WELSFORD, ENID, *The Fool: His Social and Literary History* (New York: Farrar & Rinehart, 1935).

WENDELL, BARRETT, *William Shakespeare: A Study in Elizabethan Literature* (New York: Scribner's, 1895).

WHITE, PAUL WHITFIELD, *Theatre and Reformation* (Cambridge: Cambridge University Press, 1993).

WHITNEY, CHARLES, 'Ante-aesthetics', in Grady (ed.), *Shakespeare and Modernity*, 40–60.

—— 'Festivity and Topicality in the Coventry Scene of *1 Henry IV*', *English Literary Renaissance*, 24/2 (Spring 1994), 410–48.

WHITTIER, GAYLE, 'Falstaff as a Welshwoman: Uncomic Androgyny', *Ball State University Forum*, 20/3 (Summer 1979), 23–35.

WIGGERSHAUS, ROLF, *The Frankfurt School* (1986), trans. Michael Robertson (Oxford: Polity, 1994).

WIKANDER, MATTHEW H., *The Play of Truth and State: Historical Drama from Shakespeare to Brecht* (Baltimore: Johns Hopkins University Press, 1985).

WILLIAMS, RAYMOND, *Culture and Society, 1780–1950* (1958; repr. New York: Columbia University Press, 1983).

WILSON, IAN, *Shakespeare: The Evidence: Unlocking the Mysteries of the Man and his Work* (New York: St Martin's Griffen, 1993).

WILSON, J. DOVER, *The Essential Shakespeare: A Bibliographical Adventure* (Cambridge: Cambridge University Press, 1932).

—— *The Fortunes of Falstaff* (Cambridge: Cambridge University Press, 1943).

—— introduction to William Shakespeare, *King Henry V*, ed. J. Dover Wilson (Cambridge: Cambridge University Press, 1947), pp. vii–xxviii.

—— 'The Political Background of Shakespeare's "Richard II" and "Henry IV" ', *Shakespeare-Jahrbuch*, 75 (1939), 36–51.

WILSON, RICHARD, *Will Power: Essays on Shakespearean Authority* (New York: Harvester, 1993).

WINNY, JAMES, *The Player King* (New York: Barnes & Noble, 1968).

WINSTANLEY, LILIAN, *'Hamlet' and the Scottish Succession* (Cambridge: Cambridge University Press, 1921).

WOMERSLEY, DAVID, 'Sir Henry Savile's Translation of Tacitus and the Political Interpretation of Elizabethan Texts', *Review of English Studies*, NS 42 (1991), 313–42.

WORDEN, BLAIR, 'Classical Republicanism and the Puritan Revolution', in Hugh Lloyd-Jones, Valerie Pearl, and Blair Worden (eds.), *History and Imagination: Essays in Honor of H. R. Trevor-Roper* (New York: Holmes & Meier, 1981), 182–200.

YATES, FRANCES A., *John Florio: The Life of an Italian in Shakespeare's England* (1934; repr. New York: Octagon, 1968).

YEATS, WILLIAM BUTLER, 'At Stratford-on-Avon' (1901), in *Essays and Introductions* (London: Macmillan, 1961), 96–110.

YOUNG, DAVID P., introduction to David P. Young (ed.), *Twentieth Century Interpretations of 'Henry IV, Part Two': A Collection of Critical Essays*, (Englewood Cliffs, NJ: Prentice-Hall, 1968), 1–12.

ZAGORIN, PEREZ, *Francis Bacon* (Princeton: Princeton University Press, 1998).

ŽIŽEK, SLAVOJ, *The Ticklish Subject: The Absent Centre of Political Ontology* (London: Verso, 2000).

Index

Mallin, Eric 37
Manning, John 35
Marcus, Leah 175 n. 77
Martin, R. A. 152 n. 43, 167
Marxism 10, 17 n., 21, 67 n. 20, 156
Maus, Katherine Elizabeth 46 n., 70, 170
Mercer, Peter 251 n. 16
metatheatre 154–61, 259
modernity 21–4, 44, 54, 60–7, 93–4, 103,
  106, 114, 175
  and *Hamlet* 246, 252, 256, 259–65
  in *1 & 2 Henry IV* 155, 157–61, 162, 171
  and *Henry V* 237–8
  in *Richard II* 67
Montaigne, Michel de 11, 13, 15, 24–5, 49,
  54, 66, 109–25, 177–8
  and *Hamlet* 254
  and *1 Henry IV* 126–7, 130, 166
  and *Henry V* 224
  and Machiavelli 109–15, 121, 199–200,
    203, 224
  and *Richard II* 98
  and Shakespeare 123–5
  and subjectivity 115–25
Montrose, Louis 41, 224
Mowbray (in *Richard II*) 68–70, 71, 94, 95

New Criticism 91, 207
Nim (in *Henry V*) 226–8, 229

Odyssey, The 158

Parker, Patricia 130 n.
Pater, Walter 85, 86
Patterson, Annabel 207 n. 40
Percy, Lady (in *1 & 2 Henry IV*) 167–8, 184
Persons, Robert 58
Pistol (in *2 Henry IV* and *Henry V*) 175–6,
  190–1, 226–7, 229, 230, 237
plebeian, the, *see* tavern world
Pocock, J. G. A. 45, 60 n. 4
political unconscious 209, 213, 233–9, 240–2
Poole, Kristen 146 n. 29
Popkin, Richard 118 n. 28, 119 n. 33
postmodernism 7–9, 122, 141–2, 206–7,
  209, 243
power 26, 29, 65–6, 99–100
  in *Hamlet* 246–51
  in *1 Henry IV* 130, 133–9, 141, 143, 144–5,
    164–6, 169–79
  in *2 Henry IV* 182–4, 197–204
  in *Henry V* 222–5, 229–33
  in *Richard II* 79–82

presentism 1–5
Prince Hal (in *1 & 2 Henry IV*) 127, 132 n.,
  142, 157, 162–6, 169–74, 192, 195–6, 258,
  259
  as King Henry V 197–200, 208–13,
    218–26, 235–42
psychoanalytic criticism 253–5
Pye, Christopher 85, 94 n., 98 n. 71

Quinn, Michael 89
Quint, David 116 n. 24, 238 n. 75

Rabkin, Norman 90, 207–8
Rackin, Phyllis 74 n.
Ragland-Sullivan, Ellie 13–14, 120 n. 38
Rebhorn, Wayne 60 n. 4, 62 n.
Regosin, Richard 114 n. 18, 115 n.24
reification 127, 185, 198, 200–4, 223–4, 235,
  242
Reiss, Tmothy J. 116 n. 24, 117–18, 119–20,
  122 nn. 42 and 44
resistance 144–5, 162–79, 209, 222–4, 235,
  251–5, 264–5
Robertson, J. M. 51
Rossiter, A. P. 89
Rousseau, Jean-Jacques 86–7, 262

scepticism 52, 116, 117, 119–20, 254
self, *see* subject, the; subjectivity
Shakespeare, William 27
  and Florio, John 50–2
  Hamlet 51–2, 56, 106, 159, 242, 243–65
  Julius Caesar 54, 172
  King Henry IV, Part 1 48, 54–5, 126–79,
    181–4
    and *2 Henry IV* 126–8, 199–200
    and *Henry V* 226–8
    and *Hamlet* 264
  King Henry IV, Part 2 48, 55–6, 126–8,
    130, 141, 171–2, 174, 180–204
    and *Hamlet* 264
    and *1 Henry IV* 181–4, 203–4
    and *Henry V* 227–8
  King Henry V 48, 55–6, 128, 130, 141, 166,
    168, 204–42, 246–7
    and *1 & 2 Henry IV* 221–2, 226–30,
      234–5
  King Lear 27, 47, 79, 81, 102, 240, 260
  King Richard II 47–8, 67–108, 126, 128,
    137, 176, 178, 219, 264
  King Richard III 48, 126, 217, 234, 248,
    249
  Macbeth 47, 65, 79, 81, 172